NOV   2005

DT
294.5
.R84
2005

WALKER

Chicago Public Library

D0166861

Modern Algeria : the origins and develop

NOV   2005

DISCARD
110/1 South Hoyne
Chicago, IL 60643

DISCARD

Modern ALGERIA

The Origins and Development
of a Nation

■

Second Edition

JOHN RUEDY

INDIANA UNIVERSITY PRESS
Bloomington ■ Indianapolis

This book is a publication of

Indiana University Press
601 North Morton Street
Bloomington, IN 47404-3797 USA

http://iupress.indiana.edu

Telephone orders	800-842-6796
Fax orders	812-855-7931
Orders by e-mail	iuporder@indiana.edu

© 1992, 2005 by John Ruedy
All rights reserved. First edition 1992
Second edition 2005

No part of this book may be reproduced or utilized in any form or by any
means, electronic or mechanical, including photocopying and recording,
or by any information storage and retrieval system, without permission
in writing from the publisher. The Association of American University
Presses' Resolution on Permissions constitutes the only exception to this
prohibition.

The paper used in this publication meets the minimum requirements of
American National Standard for Information Sciences—Permanence of
Paper for Printed Library Materials, ANSI Z39.48-1984.

Manufactured in the United States of America

The Library of Congress has cataloged the original edition as follows:

Ruedy, John (John Douglas), date
Modern Algeria : the origins and development of a nation / John Ruedy.
    p. cm.
Includes bibliographical references and index.
ISBN 0-253-34998-2 (cloth : alk. paper). — ISBN 0-253-20746-0 (pbk. : alk. paper)
1. Algeria—History.   I. Title.
DT294.5.R84   1992
965—dc20   92-4637

2nd edition ISBN 0-253-34624-X (cl.) — ISBN 0-253-21782-2 (pbk.)

1 2 3 4 5 10 09 08 07 06 05

R0405410864

In memory of John William Rees
and
Virtue Rees Ruedy
and for
Nancy Carson Ruedy

■

Walker Branch
11071 South Hoyne
Chicago, IL 60643

CONTENTS

∎

M A P S

PREFACE TO THE SECOND EDITION

When the first edition of this book went to press in January 1992, Algeria's military had just forced the resignation of the country's president, annulled parliamentary elections, and installed a collective executive under their control. Immediately afterward, the military outlawed and dismantled the Islamic Salvation Front (FIS), triggering an insurgency which attracted more international attention to Algeria than at any time since the War of Independence. That insurgency and measures taken to repress it caused as many as 150,000 deaths, inflicted great damage to infrastructures, and virtually paralyzed an already faltering economy. After the Law of Civil Concord was approved in a national referendum in 1999, the insurgency was gradually contained.

This edition, with a revised chapter 8, a new chapter 9, and an updated bibliography, explores the ideological and societal roots of Algerian Islamism, the political movement it created, and the nature of the insurgency that followed. It also inquires into counter-insurgency tactics of state security forces and chronicles the political evolution of Algeria between 1992 and 2004. Other topics considered are the impact of economic restructuring negotiated with the IMF in 1994, the re-emergence of Kabylia protests and violence in 2001, and the mixed results of programs to return the country to the political pluralism initiated in 1989.

Underlying much of the analysis in the new edition is my conviction that the search for consensus regarding national identity is as critical to Algeria's development as it has been for many other nations. From the birth of the Algerian nationalist movement in the first decades of the twentieth century, there were significantly different visions of the kind of nation Algeria should become. Mostly if not totally papered over during the War of Independence, those differences took center stage once the colonial government was expelled. The search for consensus is most poignantly illustrated in the Algiers Charter, the National Charter of 1976, and the decision of Algerians to write four different constitutions in as many decades. At the head of each of these documents, implicitly when not explicitly, is the question of who Algerians are and where they wish to proceed. The most important dimensions of that question have been religion, ethnicity, language, gender, civil rights, and the relation of Algeria to the broader western Mediterranean region, all of which I discuss to the extent possible. I also address the increasing alienation of Algeria's younger majority, which finds it difficult to identify with the heroic narrative and leadership of *moudjahidin* who won the nation's independence but whom many perceive as failing to confront its current needs.

I wish to thank the colleagues who encouraged me to write this second edition as well as the suggestions of many regarding its content. While it was not possible to include all suggestions, many have served to make this a richer study than it would otherwise have been. I also wish to acknowledge the assistance of those at Indiana University Press who contributed so positively to the development and editing of this edition, including Dee Mortensen and Miki Bird.

PREFACE TO THE
FIRST EDITION

One of the largest countries in Africa and in the Arab world, Algeria has stood in the last half of the twentieth century as a compelling model of national liberation and development. The story of its march from a segmented tribal order through five generations of colonial exploitation to an eight-year war of liberation and finally to independent nationhood is of epic dimensions. It is a story laden with lessons about challenge, response, and human resiliency. But it is one that has been unavailable, except in bits and pieces, to the English-reading public.

I have tried to write an introductory history of modern Algeria suited to the needs of the general reader and useful in university classrooms. Specialists will discover that I have not attempted a major recasting of Algerian history, although individual analyses in certain areas may provoke discussion. I hope that students and scholars will find the bibliography useful.

This book is a work of historical synthesis. While certain portions are based upon original research of my own, the bulk of the story represents my sifting and order-ing of work by hundreds of men and women over many generations. It has been an exhilarating intellectual and philosophical journey. But in my travels I have roamed through many periods and specialties that were very new to me. If in some of those places I have erred, I hope the reader wili be indulgent, perhaps finding enough places without error to compensate for his or her distress.

I consider myself an heir of the liberal school of Algerian historiography, and even though I did not study with either of them directly, I have been deeply influ-enced by the work and the spirit of the late Charles-André Julien and Charles-Robert Ageron. I am deeply indebted to Professor Jacques Berque, formerly of the Collège de France, who taught me my first course in Algerian history and who has been sup-portive of my work at many points through the years. Colleagues who shared their wisdom with me over the several years it took to write this book are legion. I want especially to thank Professor Julia Clancy-Smith of the University of Virginia, Pro-fessor Rabah Abdoun of the University of Algiers, and Professor Barbara Stowasser of Georgetown University. Without the support and confidence of my good friend Professor Thomas T. Helde and of Dean Peter Krogh of the Georgetown University School of Foreign Service, I could not have undertaken this work.

As anyone who has worked in Algerian history knows, the researcher is faced with daunting problems of transliteration. The terminology—names, places, institu-tions—comes from classical Arabic, dialectal Arabic, Ottoman Turkish, and several Berber dialects. When they came to Europe and America, most of the names and terms arrived in French transliterations, which are not in themselves consistent from one era to another or even from one writer to another. I have decided that any attempt to impose total consistency would create more confusion than it would dissipate.

With regard to the names of Algerians before the twentieth century who did not speak or write French themselves, I have generally used a standard English transliteration of Arabic or Ottoman but without diacriticals. For well-known historical figures (e.g., Hussein Dey) and for modern Algerians, I have retained the French spelling. I have also retained the French transliteration of all place names, since this is the way readers will encounter them in almost every other source. The French colonists changed the names of many places during their 132-year occupation, and they also founded many towns and villages. After independence, however, Algerians changed them back or gave them new names. In the text, I use the name prevalent at the time under consideration. The appendix carries a name conversion chart. With regard to Ottoman and Arabic institutions and legal terminology, I have usually, though not invariably, employed English transliteration.

Modern Algeria

CHAPTER

1

INTRODUCTION

Humans have lived in the land that is now Algeria since the high- or middle-paleolithic period. They experienced the neolithic revolution between the sixth and the fourth millennia B.C. and then passed successively into the ages of bronze and iron. At least by the first millennium, ancestors of modern Algerians began building cities and establishing centralized states on some parts of the territory. At the end of the third century B.C., they created a state covering most of what is today northern Algeria that lasted until the end of the second; but in the centuries afterward, they united the territory again only rarely and ephemerally. While Algeria's cultural roots go back centuries, the nation in a sociological and political sense is the product of forces that began operating only in the modern period.

It was the Ottoman Turks from the sixteenth to eighteenth centuries who established a separate political entity between Tunisia and Morocco with borders more or less where they are today; it was the French in the late nineteenth and early twentieth centuries who extended Algeria's southern frontier from the foothills of the Atlas deep into the Sahara. The Turks established an Algeria-wide political system that worked through tribal segments and urban aristocracies to assure minimum control and resource extraction. French colonialism in its determination to appropriate the major means of production dismantled the tribal and legal structures that stood between the state and society in Ottoman times and in so doing laid the bases for the integration of Algerian society and a growing consciousness of nationhood. Out of that consciousness the Algerian people themselves after five generations of French occupation realized that the only way to escape permanent dispossession and further impoverishment was to assert their nationhood forcefully. Thus a new nation-state was born.

1

NATION BUILDING

The nation-state, the state conceived as the political expression of a single or a dominant and relatively homogeneous ethnic group, is a modern phenomenon. While one can trace its roots to earlier experiences in Europe and elsewhere, it was not until the eighteenth and the nineteenth centuries that the nation-state in a mature form became the dominant model of political organization in Europe and not until the twentieth that it became so for most non-European societies. The nation-state model in Europe and in the Middle East and North Africa supplanted a universalist model that grouped very heterogeneous communities loosely under the aegis of a common religious and/or dynastic tradition. The bases of the segmentation that characterized these societies could be geographic, ethnic, religious, economic, or class/caste. But one of the oldest and most pervasive forms of segmentation is tribal. Tribes can be nomadic, sedentary, or both, but in any case they represent an organization of society on kinship principles. While certain authors emphasize the spatial, social, economic, and intellectual isolation from each other of the segments, it is clear that such absolute isolation was not the norm in premodern North Africa. Because the lineage, clan, tribe, and confederation were perceived as representing progressively larger circles of the extended family, a framework existed for wider societal interaction when such interaction was called for.[1] Furthermore, North Africans were always aware of belonging to a wider community of Muslims.

In its examination of the origins and development of the Algerian nation, this book nevertheless finds useful the notion of the contrast between segmentation and integration. Segmentation defines a social order in which most if not all of society's functions take place within and are mediated by smallish kinship segments, the differentiation of which may or may not be reinforced by geographic, economic, sectarian, or other factors. It is the tribe or village that determines the roles and statuses of individuals, controls behavior, arbitrates conflict, determines access to means of production, and projects the value system that rationalizes these arrangements. If there is a state, it has relatively little control over these functions but exists to protect against external threats and to mediate between segments when normal mechanisms of resolution break down. It extracts what taxes it can in return for these services, usually encountering significant resistance from the segments.

Integration, on the other hand, is the principal attribute of the modern nation-state. It defines a social order in which most functions except procreation and nurturing have been transferred from the kinship group to the control or mediation of the state. Such state control permits the mobilization

---

1. The theory of segmentarity originates in 1893 with Emile Durkheim, *De la division du travail social. Etude sur l'organisation des sociétés supérieures.* Monte Palmer, in *The dilemmas of Political Development: An Introduction to the Politics of Developing Areas* (Itasca, Ill.: 1973), pp. 11–12, is one of many who emphasizes the isolation of segments. My views on the North African tribe have been strongly influenced by the work of Edward Evans-Pritchard, *The Nuer* and *The Sanussi of Cyrenaica;* and by Ernest Gellner, *Saints of the Atlas.*

of human and material resources of a large territory for more effective pursuit of goals determined appropriate by the inhabitants of that large territory. Kinship groups controlling all or most aspects of an individual's life give way here to a series of functionally defined associations. The result is greater societal congruency, enhanced economic productivity, larger concentrations of wealth and power, and greater ability to control the environment. It must be emphasized, however, that integration and segmentation are relative terms used only for analytical orientation. Algeria has not in historical times known anything close to total segmentation nor has any modern nation state ever achieved ideal integration.

Building a nation–state involves political, economic, social, and cultural dimensions. Though it may also involve a territorial dimension if the territory of the state is not perceived as complete when the process of nation building gets under way, this was not the case in Algeria. The movement of a society toward national integration requires changes in political, economic, social, and cultural sectors, all of which are interrelated and interactive. It is difficult to conceive a functional modern nation without relatively balanced evolution in each of these areas. The emergence of a modern industrial economy, for instance, is not possible without a political system capable of control and mobilization, a social order flexible enough to move people into new jobs requiring new skills in new places, and a culture that interprets and justifies the passing of the old and the emergence of the new order.

Unfortunately for most of the peoples of Africa and Asia, however, balanced evolution toward modern nationhood was precluded by the very imperialist and colonialist forces that triggered the transformation from segmentarity toward national integration. The appearance of the new integrated order does not unfailingly follow the disappearance of the old segmented one. The process of nation building in fact involves twin processes of disintegration and reintegration.

At the economic level in dependent countries, the rapid disappearance of subsistence economies or self-contained local markets gives way not to modern, self-sustaining industrial economies but to economies whose function is both the provision of raw materials to the advanced economies and the consumption of finished goods from the same. Since terms of trade are by and large unfavorable to the supplier of primary goods, the result of the disappearance of the old order is progressive pauperization and growing dependency on the exterior.

Sociologically, the disappearance of segmentary tribalism in dependent countries seldom augurs immediate appearance of an integrated social order characterized by groups organized on functional rather than kinship lines. Instead, it often gives way to massive proletarianization of farmers and pastoralists and to increasing levels of unemployment and underemployment, because the industrial growth characteristic of countries blessed with balanced development is absent or insufficient in dependent economies. Proletarianization is accelerated by demographic increase brought on by falling mortality rates that generally accompany the introduction of minimal public health measures and access to wider markets for the fulfillment of food needs.

The same hiatus between disintegration and reintegration appears in the political realm. But here a distinction must be made between colonies of direct and indirect rule. In the latter, the imperialist power chooses to work through at least some existing elites. In the former, it destroys the political power of tribal elites through war, through legislation, by removing the tribe's economic base, or by a combination of the three. The political impact of such direct rule is especially apparent in countries of intensive European settlement. Here the settlers rule directly, excluding natives from any but the most peripheral and subordinate roles. To native elites who may express interest in participating in a national political process, the settlers make clear that since in their view the natives produced no national entity in the past, they need not expect participation in one in the future.

If the hiatus between the destruction of the segmentary order and the building of the national order is great, the cultural effects can be disorienting and even devastating. The native cultural system (in Algeria it was a blend of universal Islamic values and indigenous custom) becomes less relevant to the realities of life as generations of foreign influence or rule alter those realities. While the personal and family aspects of the cultural system usually remain more intact than the economic, political, and societal aspects, even these are threatened because of the objective changes in living conditions and the competition from European values. Among the narrow stratum of elites in imperialized African and Asian societies given access to European education, values and ideologies born out of European experiences begin to have currency: individualism, secularism, liberalism, capitalism, socialism, nationalism. Only bits and pieces of these values and ideologies can have meaning to illiterate and pauperized masses still clinging to what they can of a traditional cultural system, great portions of which are equally irrelevant. A considerable gap may appear between the society's natural leaders and the bulk of its members, a gap which can impede communication and hinder mobilization.

From the point of view of nation building, the main effect of colonialism's dissolution of the segmentary system, overthrow of tribal leadership, and creation of a "national" market is to clear the ground for the emergence of an authentic national community. It is the thesis of this book that in a sociological sense an Algerian nation—poor, confused, and riven with contradictions— came into existence sometime between 1871 and 1920. Between 1920 and 1962, the members of that community sorted through the contradictions as they launched a series of initiatives that ultimately drove the occupying power from the national territory. Since that time the Algerians have struggled to escape from economic dependency and to fashion an economy capable of significantly raising standards of living. They have sought to craft political institutions capable of assuring control and mobilization while at the same time accommodating the country's diversity. Finally, they have carried on a complex and confusing struggle to adjust their cultural system in such a way as to legitimize these arrangements while maintaining a sense of continuity with Algeria's historical past.

THE PHYSICAL SETTING

The area of contemporary Algeria is 2,381,741 square kilometers. Its seashore is 998 kilometers long, while the land boundaries separating it from Morocco, the Western Sahara, Mauritania, Mali, Niger, Libya, and Tunisia total 6,343 kilometers. More than seven-eighths of the country lies in the Sahara desert. Although hydrocarbon and other mineral resources combine today with major advances in transportation and communications technology to make the Sahara an indispensable part of the Algerian economy, the heart of historical Algeria is a band of valleys, mountains, and plains extending roughly three hundred kilometers inland from the Mediterranean. The northern part of this band is known as the Tell or hill country.

The most prominent feature of historic Algeria's topography is a series of mountain ranges running roughly parallel to the coast with peaks ranging in height from 500 to about 2,500 meters. These consist of a Tellian Atlas system close to the coast and a Saharan Atlas system at the edge of the desert. South of the mountains of the Tell stretches a series of plains variously known as the High Steppes, the High Plateaux, or the High Plains with an average altitude of about 1,000 meters. These end in the series of more or less contiguous ranges that collectively form the Saharan Atlas. These ranges, whose peaks rise from 1,500 to 2,500 meters, are from west to east the Ksour Mountains, the Djebel Amour, the Monts des Ouled Naïl, the virtually impenetrable block of the Aurès, and the mountains of the Nementcha on the Tunisian border. The breaks between the five ranges provide the passes through which the bulk of travel between Algeria proper and the desert takes place. The most famous of these gaps is the Hodna depression between the Aurès and the Monts des Ouled-Naïl which is prolonged by a pronounced depression in the High Steppes adjoining it to the north; this is the easiest route from the desert to the coast. In the other direction, the High Plains and the High Steppes have historically provided the most practical route for east-west travel.

Drawing an imaginary line from the Hodna depression through the town of Miliana to the sea, geographers make a major distinction between the environments of western Algeria and eastern Algeria. In western Algeria the arable lands are divided by a series of parallel chains or mini-chains. The most important of the chains are the Dahra along the coast and the Ouarsenis south of it. Between the two runs the Chélif River, whose valley and its extensions toward and beyond Oran are the most important farming regions in the Oranie (Oran Province). Because the mountains of the west are lower, because there are more rolling hills here and less flat alluvium, and because it enjoys less rainfall, western Algeria was more hospitable to pastoralists than to farmers. While peasants were certainly present, it is historically the land of the nomadic and seminomadic tribesmen.

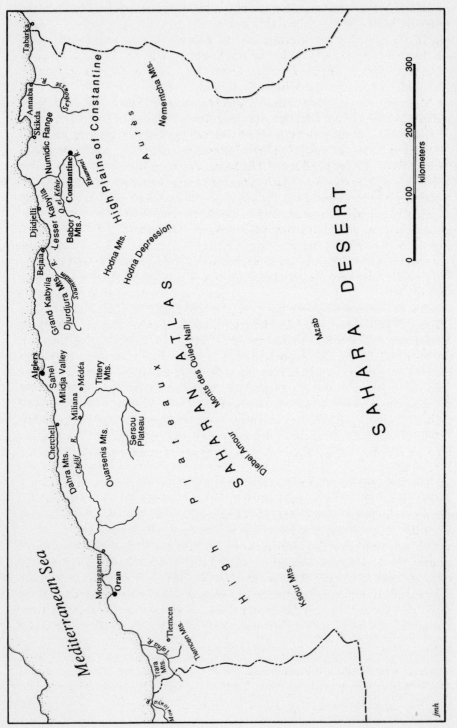

MAP 1 Northern Algeria, Physical Features

East of the imaginary line mentioned above, the Mitidjian Atlas and the Monts de Titteri continue the Dahra and the Ouarsensis respectively until they join in the Grand Kabylia range east of Algiers. The Grand Kabylia ends precipitously in the deep valley of the Soummam River, beyond which is a series of systems known as the Lesser and Eastern Kabylia. North of the Mitidjian Atlas lies the Mitidja Plain, which, separated from the coast and the Mediterranean by a low range of hills known as the Sahel d'Alger, was the agricultural jewel of both Ottoman and French Algeria. East of Algiers, mountains rise dramatically out of the sea, leaving room for agriculture along the coast at Bejaïa (Bougie), Djidjelli, Skikda (Philippeville), and especially in the lush Plain of Annaba (Bône).[2] The heart of eastern Algeria, however, is the large Plain of Constantine, which, separated from the sea by a single chain of mountains and protected from the desert by the massive Aurès, is historically the most productive single region in Algeria. In spite of its higher mountains, eastern Algeria, which in many parts receives double the rainfall of western Algeria, has favored sedentary farming over pastoralism not only in fertile valleys and basins but even on steep, terraced hillsides. Throughout most of history, it has supported a population density double that of the western half of the country.

The availability of water has been the most important physical variable shaping Algerian history. Like the rest of the Maghrib, Algeria's climate is Mediterranean subtropical with the great bulk of the rain falling between October and April. The major function of the Atlas ranges is to provide a barrier that traps the moisture blowing in from the Atlantic and the Mediterranean during those months, moisture that would otherwise be dissipated over the vast expanses of the Sahara. Unfortunately, the Algerian ranges are not high enough to generate the extensive snow packs whose gradual melting could enhance water supplies during the dry season; there are no navigable rivers in Algeria, and, except in the Kabylia, most streams diminish to a trickle by late summer.

The dry culture of cereals, which are the staple of the Algerian diet, is estimated to require an annual rainfall of 400 millimeters. As shown by map 2, the 400 millimeter isohyet extends between 100 and 200 kilometers inward from the Mediterranean, narrower in the west and widening in the east. It is within this band that the great majority of Algerian populations have traditionally lived, while the areas to the south have been given over progressively to pastoralists. Unfortunately for the stability of the economic system, however, rainfall averages in Mediterranean climates are poor indicators of the moisture that can actually be expected in any given year. Because of wide swings in rainfall from one growing season to the next, the agricultural

2. During their occupation the French changed the names of many Algerian towns and cities and gave names to several hundred towns they founded. After independence Algerians reverted to the original names of the older towns and gave new Arabic names to most of the rest. I have chosen in my text to employ the name current during the period on which I am writing, because this is the way the reader who wishes to explore farther will usually find them. A list of some of the more important places whose names have changed is included as an appendix.

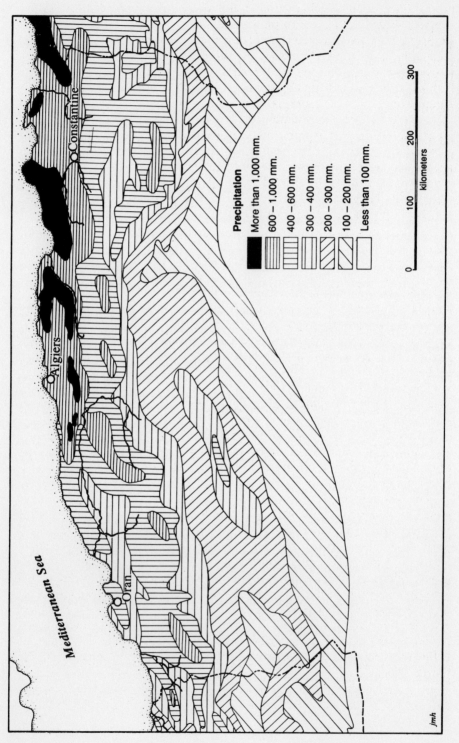

MAP 2 Precipitation

Precipitation

More than 1,000 mm.
600 – 1,000 mm.
400 – 600 mm.
300 – 400 mm.
200 – 300 mm.
100 – 200 mm.
Less than 100 mm.

0   100   200   300
kilometers

Mediterranean Sea

Oran

Algiers

Constantine

jmh

productivity upon which economic and fiscal stability depend has varied enormously from one year to the next.

Another problem related to rainfall is that of deforestation. It is clear that the Maghrib, like most of the lands around the Mediterranean, was generously forested in antiquity but that these forests receded as human population grew. Nature was unable in these climatic conditions to replace the flora as rapidly as humans and their beasts consumed it. Colonial authorities, well aware of the corrosive effects of deforestation, took major steps to preserve and replant forests and to prevent overgrazing. Unfortunately, the progressive European appropriation of the best lowlands drove Algerian peasants and pastoralists to put greater and greater pressure on forest and range lands, which vitiated most conservation attempts. By the end of the colonial period only 11 percent of the Algerian Tell region was forested, a condition hastening soil erosion and inhibiting the soil retention of water.

PEOPLE AND LANGUAGE

Today the majority of Algerians are Arab and 20 to 25 percent are Berber. Since it is evident that the great majority of Arab as well as Berber Algerians are descended from Berber ancestors, the criteria for the distinction are linguistic rather than racial. Algerians whose native language is Arabic are called Arabs in this book, and those whose native language is Berber are called Berbers.[3]

The word Berber goes back to the Greeks, who called the people they found living in the Maghrib at the dawn of history barbarians, a terminology subsequently adopted in various forms by Romans, Arabs, Europeans, and others. But the term is not used by Berbers themselves when speaking their own languages. The Kabyles, the largest and most politically active community of Algerian Berbers, call themselves *Imazighen* (singular *Amazigh*), which means free or noble men.

The literature on the origin of the Berbers is full of problems and ambiguities. The balance of opinion at present holds that the Berbers of history were the descendants of a paleolithic stock to whom had been added a variety of other racial inputs—minor ones from Western Europe and from sub-Saharan Africa, and two major ones from the northeast and the southeast. The language, which over the centuries splintered into scores of dialects distributed among three main families, may be Hamitic in origin. If so it is a relative of Galla, Somali, and Pharaonic Egyptian, a cousin rather than a sister to Arabic and the other Semitic languages. The language may have been brought to the region by migration from the Horn of Africa that would have taken place before the most recent desiccation of the Sahara, which began at the start of the fourth millennium.

3. It is difficult to settle on a figure for the number of Berbers because since 1966 the Algerian census no longer distinguishes between Berberophones and Arabophones.

The de-Berberization of the Maghrib began with Punic settlement and accelerated under Roman, Vandal, Byzantine, and Arab rule as the cities, their environs, and the most productive crop lands came to be dominated by the newcomers. The Arab invasion of the seventh century brought about the Arabization of many cities and several coastal areas, but it is clear that most Algerians in the countryside continued to speak Berber until well into the twelfth century. The factor that accelerated linguistic transformation from the late eleventh century was the invasion of the Banu Hilal and Banu Sulaym, nomadic Arabs from Egypt who progressively overwhelmed the countryside, absorbing as they did many Berber-speaking peasants and nomads who eventually forgot their ancestors had once been Berbers. The Arabic speech most widespread in Algeria today is a dialect descended from these nomadic invaders. The sedentary Arabic dialects presumed to be pre-Hilalian are limited to the Arabic-speaking parts of the Lesser Kabylia, the hinterland of Bejaïa, and a small coastal band in the extreme west at the foot of the Traras mountains.

By the eighteenth century, Berberophony had been relegated to the least accessible parts of the country—high mountains, distant oases, and isolated desert plateau and mountain areas. Small groups of Berbers remained in the Dahra, Ouarsenis, and Mitidjian mountains. The Mzab oasis was home to a thriving culture of Ibadi Muslim Berbers, and a vast quadrant of what was to become the southern and southeastern Algerian Sahara was dominated by a nomadic group known as the Touareg. The Aurès and most of the Nementcha mountains were home to the Chaouia; but by far, the largest group—at least three-fourths of all Algerian Berbers—lived in the Grand Kabylia and the western part of the Lesser Kabylia. The economic, military, and political significance of the Kabyles grew from the sixteenth century onward when Algiers became home for the first time to the rulers of the country. The Grand Kabylia was a stone's throw from the capital, and its inhabitants were available to fill jobs, provide military services, and frequently to mobilize resistance against unpopular regimes.

PREMODERN HISTORY

Archeological and anthropological evidence indicates that by the fifth century B.C., Berbers in what is now Algeria had established economies based on a mix of farming and pastoralism, had mastered a variety of manufacturing skills, were commercializing many of their products, and had established a number of states. By the third century B.C., classical authors took notice of Berber kingdoms for the first time, noting in particular the existence of two: the kingdom of the Masaesyles that stretched from the Moulouya River in eastern Morocco to the Rhummel in eastern Algeria and the kingdom of the Massyles in extreme eastern Algeria and western Tunisia. By 203 B.C., Massinissa of the Massyles defeated his western rivals who had sided with Carthage in the Second Punic War and created what classical authors called the Kingdom of Numidia, stretching from Tabarka in Tunisia to the Moulouya. This kingdom, with its capital at Cirta (later Constantine), which may have had as many as 100,000 residents, represented a high point in the evolution of Berber civilization not matched for more than a thousand years until the rise of the great medieval Berber kingdoms and empires.

In spite of the dogged resistance of Massinissa's descendant Jurgurtha (109–106 B.C.), the Romans, who feared the power of the unified Berber kingdom, defeated Numidia and divided its territory amongst three of his successors. In the first century B.C., they turned the Berber kingdoms into protectorates, and in the first century A.D., they abolished them altogether and imposed their own direct rule.

Entranced by the magnificent remains of Roman buildings and engineering works, many European scholars have thought the Roman era to be a high period in North African history. But the net impact on North African civilization of Roman rule, which lasted over coastal regions and limited portions of the interior until the fifth century, appears to have been negative. As Roman landlords assisted by Latinized Berbers turned the agricultural lowlands and plains into vast latifundia worked by poorly paid *coloni* and day laborers for the production of grains for export to Europe, the rest of Berber society was driven back into the hinterland where, rapidly retribalized, it mounted a generations-long opposition to Roman hegemony. By the time the Vandals ended Roman rule in A.D. 429, the entire hinterland and most of the western Algerian coast had reverted to Berber tribal rule. Little trace remained of the sophisticated civilization of the pre-Roman era.

While Christianity in the third and fourth centuries spread extensively through eastern and coastal Algeria, its implantation was hindered after the time of Constantine by its association with the Roman establishment. The Donatist heresy, which racked Roman Africa in the fourth and early fifth centuries, is thought to have reflected the disillusionment of Berber Christians with the domination of a Latin hierarchy tied to the exploitative Roman system. When Donatism was finally extirpated under the leadership of Augustine, Bishop of Hippo (Annaba), in the early fifth century, Christianity disappeared very quickly in most Berber communities.

With the exception of a few coastal ports where the Byzantines hung on, the Berber society the Arab conquerors encountered in the seventh century had been free from Roman control for more than two and a half centuries. The social order which had begun the process of integration under the early kingdoms had been widely resegmented. It is thought that the highest form of political organization in this period was the tribal confederation. While sedentary agriculture persisted in the most favored environments and in places like the Grand Kabylia, the majority of Berbers by the seventh century were probably herders. By this time, too, the Sahara, which had posed since the fourth millennium an impenetrable barrier to the expansion of civilization, had been opened up by a new breed of grand nomads and traders. With the importation from western Asia of a saddle technology that for the first time made reliable the use of camels for riding and as beasts of burden, the desert that for Carthaginians, Romans, and earlier Berbers had been the end of the world now became a highway inviting to distant lands, new sources of wealth, and great power.

The Berbers of the central Maghrib, which was to become Algeria, mounted the fiercest and longest lived opposition the Arab conquerors of the seventh century met anywhere in the world. While most of Tunisia and Morocco succumbed to Arab rule after a few years of resistance, the Muslim hold over the area that became Algeria was not assured for thirty-five years. Early Arab histories of the conquest preserve in particular the name Kusayla, head of a powerful confederation based in the Ouarsenis and, intriguingly, that of a female warrior in the Aurès whom they named the Kahina or priestess[4] who ultimately laid down her life in a vain attempt to preserve her people's freedom. Explanations for the tenacity of the resistance in this part of the Maghrib cite either the cohesiveness and military culture of tribal communities or the determination of people with blood memory of centuries of foreign domination not to submit to it again.

While their resistance to Arab military and political control was fierce, the Berbers once conquered seem to have converted quickly to the Islamic faith the Arabs bore with them.[5] With the exception of small Christian communities on the coast that survived for about three centuries, it appears that a large majority of Berbers converted to Islam during the eighth century, which is a very different pattern from that followed in the Near East, where Islamization required centuries and was in fact never total. Because of the effect Islam had on the subsequent evolution of nearly every aspect of life in the Maghrib, this conversion is undoubtedly the greatest and most enduring fact in North African history.

But Berber embrace of Islam did not include embrace of the Arabs. In 740, Berbers in Morocco and western Algeria, smarting under the oppressive taxation and discriminatory practices of Arab governors, raised a revolt in the name of Khariji Islam, the most egalitarian and democratic of the medieval Islamic sects. For a brief period, the Arabs were driven completely out of the Maghrib. Later they reconquered Tunisia, which they called Ifriqya, and a small slice of what had been Numidia; but everything to the west, including all of Morocco and three-fourths of Algeria had shaken off Arab rule for good. The success of the Khariji rebellion opened a period that many call the golden age of North African history, which witnessed the rise, flourishing, and decline of a succession of remarkable Berber kingdoms and empires. Three of

4. One school of thought holds that al Kahina was Jewish, another that she was Christian. In either case she would be one of the few Berber resistance leaders who did not follow the indigenous animist cults.

5. The claim by Ibn Khaldun centuries later that the Berbers apostatized up to twelve times in seventy years is not borne out by historians closer to the period. His assertion may well reflect the memory of the long period of seesaw conflict in which Arab commanders would require acceptance of Islam as a corollary of military surrender. When tribes took the next opportunity to revolt, superficial and forced conversion would be shrugged off.

these, the kingdoms of the Rustamids (759–910), the Hammadids (1011–1151), and the ᶜAbd al Wadids (1235–1545), were centered in territory that became Algeria.

The first of these states was the Kingdom of the Rustamids, which established its capital at Tahert on the southern slope of the Ouarsenis mountains facing the High Steppes. This remarkable Khariji state, collaborating with that of Sijilmassa at the base of the Anti-Atlas to the west, survived for more than a century and a half. Its prosperity was based upon the regularizing of trade routes across the Sahara, over which passed cargos of gold, ivory, and—unfortunately—slaves in return for products manufactured in the Maghrib and beyond the Mediterranean. From this point on for centuries, much of Maghribi prosperity depended upon control of these trade routes and upon the region's intermediate position between black Africa and the Mediterranean.

To the northeast, the Berbers of what had been the Roman Province of Numidia had lived in very uneasy relationships with Ifriqya to the east, which was ruled by the Arab Aghlabid dynasty on behalf of the ᶜAbbasid caliphs of Baghdad. When Ismaᶜili Shiᶜis, who also claimed the caliphate, came looking for allies to help them evince the Aghlabids, they were able to enlist the powerful Kitama Berber confederation centered in the Lesser Kabylia, the Plain of Constantine, and the coastal ports. With a largely Kabyle army, the Ismaᶜilis drove the Aghlabids out and, by the early tenth century, established the Fatimid caliphate in Tunisia. There ensued two generations of struggle in the Muslim west which transformed the Maghrib into a battleground pitting the Fatimids and their allies against the Umayyad caliphate of Cordoba and its allies.[6] Much of the struggle was for control of the gold trade, and an early casualty of that struggle was the Rustamid Kingdom of Tahert, destroyed by the Fatimids with their Kitama army in 910. Kharijism survived eventually only in a few oases of the Sahara, the most important of which was the Mzab.

In 969, when the Fatimids, whose main objectives had always lain in the Muslim east, conquered Cairo and relocated their capital there, they left their Maghrib possessions in the hands of a Kabyle leader from the Titteri mountains named Ziri. The Zirids had earlier founded the towns of Miliana, Médéa, and Algiers, making central Algeria politically consequential for the first time in history. On behalf of the Fatimids, the Zirids now governed the eastern two-thirds of Algeria and all of Tunisia. By the early eleventh century, with their hands full in Ifriqya, the Zirids entrusted the governorship of their western lands to a branch of the family named Banu Hammad. These constructed a remarkable capital at the Qaᶜala Bani Hammad that dominated the heavily traveled Hodna depression and its access to the caravan routes. Later they founded Bejaïa, which, during the mid-eleventh century and thanks to the Saharan trade it brokered, was the most important port in the Maghrib. Very soon after their rise to power, the Hammadids broke with their Zirid

6. By 929, when the Umayyad amirs of Cordoba declared themselves caliphs, there were three contenders for Islam's highest office: the Umayyads, the Fatimids in Ifriqya, and the ᶜAbbasids at Baghdad.

cousins, signalling this by renouncing loyalty to the Fatimids. Shiᶜism, as it turned out, had never taken root in Algeria and survived only temporarily in Tunisia. By breaking with the Zirids, however, the Hammadids had created the second major Muslim state on what was to become Algerian territory, one whose location was precisely in the heartlands of Massinissa's ancient kingdom.

A combination of factors in the last half of the eleventh century helped to drain the vitality of the Hammadid system, dependent as it was on both maritime and desert trade routes. The rise of the Almoravids in Morocco diverted much of the caravan trade to Sijilmassa and to their newly founded capital of Marrakech, while at the same time the arrival of Norman marauders in the western Mediterranean seriously dislocated the sea trade. The gradual spread of the Hilalian Arab nomads may also have impeded commerce through the Hammadid cities. The regime held on in weakened state, however, until the middle of the twelfth century when the Almohads, founders of the most successful of all the medieval empires emanating from Morocco, extended their rule over the entire Maghrib. But Almohad ability to police such a vast empire was limited, and during the late twelfth and early thirteenth centuries, the central Maghrib was periodically exposed to the depredations of roving bedouins or of Almoravids hold outs in the Balearic islands seeking vengeance on these now Almohad shores. As opposed to the western Maghrib, where the Almohad century was one of great creativity, the period for the middle Maghrib marked a considerable regression.

As the Almohads in their turn declined in the thirteenth century, the central Maghrib fell into a bipolar political arrangement whose main features survived until the arrival of the Ottomans in the sixteenth century. In its western region, a tribe of Zanata Berbers known as the Banu ᶜAbd al Wad had allied themselves with the Almohads and, as their mentors weakened, were able to carve out for themselves a new kingdom centered on Tlemcen. Tlemcen in its heyday was also a hub of the Saharan trade and soon became the most important cultural centre in what was to be western Algeria. In succeeding centuries, the ᶜAbd al Wadids found themselves in intermittent conflict with the sultans of Morocco who normally considered Tlemcen their own territory.

In the eastern Maghrib, the Almohad governors of Tunis, the Hafsids, survived the fall of that sultanate to create a separate dynasty that survived until it succumbed to the Ottomans in the sixteenth century. Hafsid sovereignty extended over eastern Algeria up to the base of the Grand Kabylia. Although Bougie, Constantine, and other Hafsid towns were subject to periodic attacks by the ᶜAbd al Wadids from the west, the Hafsids managed to hold on to them.

The thirteenth and the fourteenth centuries marked a period of accelerating economic decline for the entire Maghrib, which in turn weakened its political structures. The decline is clearly associated with the region's loss of control of both the desert and maritime frontiers through which flowed the wealth upon which urban life, armies, and states had depended since the eighth century.

Reasons for the loss of control are multiple and not completely understood. The penetration of Egyptian Mamluks deep into the Sudan appears to have diverted much of the Sahara trade eastward, while the increasing control of the western Sahara by Arab nomads unconnected with the Berber cities to the north served further to limit the trade into the Maghrib. At the same time, the rise of Christian powers in the western Mediterranean, under way since the eleventh century but sealed by the fall of Cordoba and Seville to the Castilians in the mid-thirteenth century, made it increasingly difficult for Maghribi merchants to profit from maritime commerce. Faced with declining revenues from commerce, governments attempted to increase extraction from sedentary farmers, which met with much resistance but whose net effect was to drive peasants off the land and back to pastoralism where they were less vulnerable to the tax collectors but also less productive. By the fifteenth century, the central Maghrib was in a period of deep economic, political, and moral crisis. It was at this difficult time that the Spanish *Reconquista* exploded across the Mediterranean to bring further destabilization.

CHAPTER 2

OTTOMAN ALGERIA AND ITS LEGACY

As the forces of Castile and Aragon overran one North African port city after another in the early sixteenth century, the residents of those cities sent out anguished calls for help. When Aruj and Khayr al-Din, the brothers Barbarossa from the Aegean island of Mytilene, arrived in the central Maghrib in response to those cries, they entered upon a seriously disorganized and dispirited land. The eastern portions, from Constantine to the sea and southward to the caravan portal of Biskra, were under the sovereignty of the declining Tunisian sultanate of the Hafsids. The western portion was under the shaky control of the ⁀Abd al Wadid dynasty of Tlemcen, which was engaged in a struggle for survival with dynamic new forces in Morocco. Within but especially between these two remnants of the medieval political order, power was disputed by a bewildering array of tribal power centers; along the coast a series of city-states, often led by merchant aristocracies only recently escaped from a collapsing Andalusia, struggled to maintain their autonomy in the face of pressures from the competing sultanates, the tribal confederations, and the expansionist exuberance of the *Reconconquista*.

Three centuries later, when the commander of a French expeditionary force deported to Turkey the last successors of the Barbarossas, the state of Algeria had come into existence. While the Regency of Algiers of 1830 was theoretically a dependency of the Ottoman sultanate, the state that had come into being possessed all the classical attributes of sovereign independence: a defined territory, a human community, organized political authority, effective independence, and recognition by other states. After generations of contest, the borders between Algeria on the one hand and its Tunisian and Moroccan neighbors on the other had been almost completely defined. This chapter describes to the extent permitted by uneven documentation the structures and

16

institutions of that new state, the society over which it presided, and the relations between the two.

THE REGENCY OF ALGIERS

It was not mainly out of altruism that the privateers Aruj and Khayr al-Din first came to the eastern Maghrib in 1504 and subsequently responded to pleas from the notables of Algiers in 1516. But while pursuing their own interests, they soon became major participants in the historic struggle between Ottomans and the Spaniards and Hapsburgs for control of the western Mediterranean. To be effective in that struggle, they needed to consolidate their land base by assuring a minimum of unity amongst the competing power centers of the middle Maghrib. This effort elicited as much opposition from native populations as had earlier attempts by dynasties of Marinids, Hafsids, ᶜAbd al Wadids, and others. Aruj was to die in battle against a coalition of Spanish and Muslim enemies near Tlemcen in 1518. But Khayr al-Din went on doggedly to drive the Hafsids from Constantine and its coastal regions (1521–25); to evict the Spaniards in 1529 from the Peñon, which dominated the harbor of Algiers; to defeat Charles V before Algiers in 1541; and by 1545, to expel the ᶜAbd al Wadids permanently from western Algeria.

In order to secure those victories, Khayr al-Din had in 1519 sought moral and material reinforcement of his position by offering his submission to the Sublime Porte. Accepting that submission, the Sultan granted Khayr al-Din the prestigious title of Beylerbey (Governor General) of North Africa and put at his disposal the services of Janissary contingents of infantry and artillery. Armed with its new legitimacy, small but efficient land forces, and an aggressive fleet, the beylerbeylik grew rich, powerful, and increasingly independent.

A half century later, presumably in order to secure tighter control of this most distant of the Ottoman provinces, Constantinople began assigning pashas to Algiers for fixed terms of three years and shortly afterward eliminated the office of beylerbey completely. But the new arrangement did not produce the expected results. Far from assuring central oversight of Algerian affairs, the replacement of a strong and independent governorship by a dependent rotating one caused power to devolve progressively upon the ojaq[1] of the Janissaries, now the most cohesive and permanent Ottoman institution in the province.

While the foundation of the Algerian state was laid by seafaring men whose talents and interests were primarily maritime, it was the Janissary officers who became the principal architects of the state's political institutions and arbiters of power. Renewed through the generations by continuous recruitment of Anatolian Turks, the ojaq reached a maximum enrollment of 15,000 in its

---

1. Ojaq (wujâq) is an Arabic and Ottoman term for hearth or fireplace. It originally designated a platoon-sized unit of men who ate, lived, and maneuvered together. It was subsequently applied to the whole body of Janissaries.

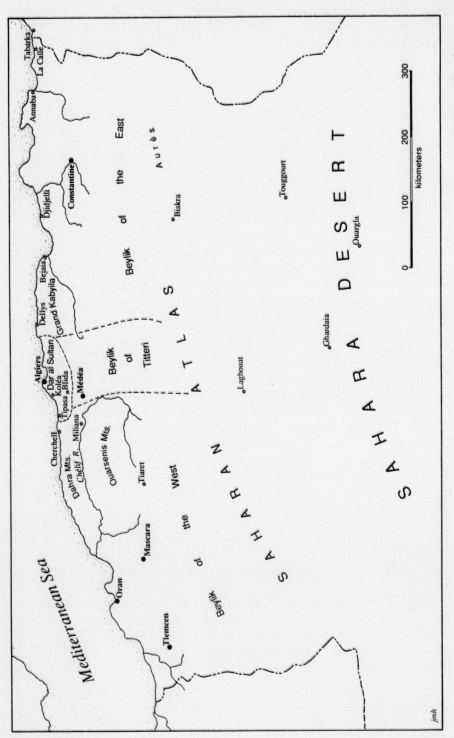

MAP 3 Ottoman Algeria

heyday and declined to about 3,700 by 1830. But following a pattern that had proved effective in many parts of the Islamic east, a small, ethnically distinct and jealously exclusive military caste, or the elites it supported, were able to rule, control, or neutralize for the better part of three centuries a native population of millions.

Unlike the equally durable Mamluks of Egypt, who could fund themselves through extraction from easily accessible rural estates as well as from the profits of trade, the Turks of Algeria found their fiscal options narrowly limited. Because Algerian agricultural surplus was smaller, less accessible geographically, and tapped by many levels of intermediate extraction, the primary sources of funds to pay the Janissaries and run the government were overseas trade and especially corsair operations. These operations were managed by the ship captains, whose organization, the *taifa al rais,* controlled by far the largest share of liquid wealth that flowed into Algiers.

While the ojaq was the force that made possible continuing Ottoman hegemony over the lands and peoples of Algeria, the taifa sat upon the only source of income capable of assuring regular remuneration of that force. The mid-seventeenth century inaugurated a tumultuous period which saw the ojaq repeatedly revolting against pashas chronically unable to pay their bimonthly stipends. Eventually the *agha* or commander of the Janissaries assumed de facto rulership, but the aghas were no more successful than the pashas at guaranteeing regular payment. Finally the military turned to the taifa. In 1671, they transferred supreme power for the first time to a *rais,* conferring upon him the new title of dey,[2] with the understanding that he would in turn assure the remuneration of the troops. By institutionalizing the relationship between the holders of military and financial power, the Algerian elite had hit upon a formula which eventually permitted both stabilization of the political process and de facto independence of the Ottoman central government. From 1683 to 1700, there were eight deys; from 1700 to 1750, ten; and from 1750 to 1800, four. The office of pasha became increasingly symbolic until 1710 when the dey added that title to his own. The memory of this root of the dey's authority was perpetuated afterward by the practice of sending a triennial gift to the Sultan.

Selection of the dey was the responsibility of a council of some sixty dignitaries known as the *divan.* During the seventeenth century, this divan was primarily an extension of the ojaq, in that while it contained a number of religious and non-Turkish dignitaries, its majority were always Janissary officers. As the institution evolved during the eighteenth century, however, the composition of the divan changed as did the relative importance of its key members. Gradually, the paramount roles in the council were taken over by a group of officials who were clearly the creatures of the dey rather than of the ojaq and who collectively comprised an oligarchy related to but largely in-

2. The title dey was used earlier in Tunisia where it originally denoted a Turkish officer commanding a unit of about 100 troops. The title acquired political significance after 1591 when deys supplanted the Ottoman appointed pashas at Tunis.

dependent of the ojaq. These officials included (in descending order of influence): the *khasnaji*, or treasurer; the agha of the Arabs, who commanded the indigenous cavalry and auxiliary forces; the *khujat al khil*, or master of cavalry, who controlled taxes raised in kind and became a kind of minister of supply; the *vakil khariji*, who was a combination naval and foreign minister; and the *atji-bashi*, or head of the horses, who managed the dey's household. During much of the eighteenth century, the khasnaji was the unofficial heir presumptive to the deycat; the remaining ministers each moved up one position in the divan when he succeeded to the highest office.[3]

The changing composition of the divan reflects a shift toward a quasi-monarchical institution, but it also reflects changing economic realities. As the eighteenth century progressed and the Christian powers' domination of the Mediterranean grew, the amount and profitability of Algerian privateering declined. This decline undermined the fiscal bases of the regime and called into question the institutional arrangements of the late seventeenth century. After the early eighteenth century, the office of dey was not so frequently offered to a rais. One new source of income that helped for a long time to compensate for the decline in corsair profits was the revenue extracted from Tunisia in the aftermath of Algerian victories over the Husaynids. This income took the form of several large hauls of booty and, after 1728, of concessionary advantages and tribute payments. But internal rather than external revenues were nevertheless increasingly critical to the solvency of the central government, a reality which is reflected by the new precedence awarded to the officials entrusted with bringing in those revenues.

THE POPULATION

Because the Ottomans never took a general census of Algeria that we are aware of, judging the size of Algeria's population on the eve of the French conquest presents serious methodological problems. These problems are complicated by the fact that, as nationalist leaders have claimed, colonial officials and scholars may have deliberately underestimated the 1830 population in order to obscure the devastating demographic impact of French conquest and colonization.

Because of the absence of hard data from the period itself, attempts to estimate the 1830 population have depended either on extrapolation from contemporary estimates or performing regressions from colonial counts. Estimates from a dozen contemporary or near contemporary observers range disconcertingly between a low of 400,000 and a high of 14,500,000. Since they are all based to a great extent on hearsay or other informal evidence, most are unacceptably anecdotal and conjectural in nature.

3. The proliferation of titles drawn from equestrian traditions reflects the importance of cavalry in early Ottoman history. Connoting mobility and power, such titles by the seventeenth and eighteenth centuries often reveal little or nothing about the duties of a particular office.

The first more or less systematic counting was undertaken by the occupation army in 1844 and 1845, fourteen years after the beginning of the invasion. The first official census was not completed until 1856. These counts in their turn pose serious problems because much of the country, including the densely populated Grand Kabylia, had not yet been brought under colonial control and data for those regions is based on estimates. It is difficult to count peoples against whom one is in a state of open warfare or who, recently defeated, remain still deeply suspicious of the intentions of the victors. Even without this climate of hostility, assuring accurate counts of mobile populations is very difficult, especially without sophisticated techniques of enumeration unknown in the nineteenth century.

In spite of these caveats, the bulk of modern scholarship has preferred to estimate the 1830 population by counting back from the 1845 or 1856 figures rather than depending upon the speculative contemporary numbers. This procedure has in turn posed the question of the appropriateness of various assumptions in establishing the regression curve. The most careful of these regressions, which tests a number of curves and which has won acceptance in many quarters, is that of Xavier Yacono, who concluded that the population of Algeria in 1830 stood at about 3,000,000, with the most plausible variation extending about 200,000 in either direction.[4] The eastern Province of Constantine may have contained nearly half of that population; the Province of Algiers would have had about 1,000,000 inhabitants, and that of Oran about 500,000.

URBAN SOCIETY

While only 5 or 6 percent of the population lived in the cities in the early nineteenth century, those cities exerted disproportionate influence over the country because of the moral, economic, and military power concentrated there. In the cities were clustered the principal institutions of the official faith, including the great congregational mosques, the *Shariʿa* courts, and the *madrasas* or institutions of higher learning. Algiers boasted thirteen congregational mosques including those of the Hanafi rite, which served mostly Turks, those of the Maliki rite, which served most native Algerians, and those of the Ibadi Kharijites from the Mzabi oases in the Sahara. All important cities had *qadis* or judges of each rite, and Algiers was the seat also of Hanafi and Maliki *muftis* who interpreted the law. A traditional center of learning such as Tlemcen possessed fifty *kuttabs* or Koranic schools and two madrasas.

Near the central mosque or mosques stood the *hammam,* baths required by Islamic laws of purification and Muslim standards of personal hygiene. Also near the mosque lay the *suq,* or bazaar, which marketed goods brought to the city by sea or caravan, farmers' produce, and the product of the city's artisans.

4. Xavier Yacono, "Peut-on évaluer la population de l'Algérie vers 1830?" *Revue africaine* 98, nos. 438–39 (1st and 2d trimesters, 1954).

The most important cities also possessed a citadel *(qasba, qasr)* housing the local military force. The garrison's function was to defend the city and to control the surrounding countryside, but the location of the qasbas—apart from and usually above the main town—makes it clear that another of its functions was the control, if need arose, of the cities themselves.

The population of many cities, especially those on the coast, was ethnically diverse and predominantly non-Algerian in origin. Turks dominated the political life of Algiers and along the way had obtained significant economic interests in many sectors. Kouloughlis, men of mixed Turkish and Algerian blood, played key roles in Algiers, Tlemcen, Miliana, Médéa, Constantine, and other cities. Descendants of Andalusian refugees, whom the French called *Maures* (Moors) and whose culture and dialect clearly distinguished them from the populations of the countryside, constituted a large majority of the population of Algiers and other cities. Proud, urbane, and reputedly relaxed in moral sensibility, Moors dominated the commercial and cultural life of Algiers, Tlemcen, and some other towns. Continuing inputs of Christian converts or "renegades" from around southern Europe adapted over time to Moorish culture, but in so doing they enriched Moorish culture, contributing to its widespread reputation for cosmopolitanism.

During the early Ottoman centuries, Christian slaves were an important component of the population in the coastal towns, numbering as many as 35,000 in Algiers during the seventeenth century, where they labored mainly in quarries, shipyards, or on the docks. A minority were employed in domestic and other service jobs including, interestingly enough, the management of government-owned taverns, where quantities of Spanish red wine were consumed. The logic behind this arrangement appears to be that while the authorities could overlook consumption of alcohol by Muslims, they found it harder to overlook their dispensing it. With the decline of privateering during the eighteenth century, the number of white slaves declined, reportedly to 2,000 in the late eighteenth century and to around 200 by 1830.

Black slaves, of whom there were about 1,000 at Algiers in the early nineteenth century and uncounted concentrations in other towns, worked as laborers and domestics. A cultural dynamic that favored manumission had created a substantial free black community whose vocations included music, masonry, and dock work.

Small Jewish communities, composed primarily of descendants of the Andalusian or Balearic communities, had planted roots in several towns. Reports of travellers to Algeria indicate that the social standing of these Jews was low and that the economic situation of most was marginal. As the eighteenth century progressed, Italian and French Jews assumed important middleman positions in the Regency's European trade. Communities of these wealthy and influential *"juifs francs"* remained distinct from native Jewry and grew rapidly in Constantine, Bône, and Algiers.

Many cities of the Tell also hosted self-contained communities of hinterland Algerians known as *barraniyun* (strangers). Among such communities were the industrious and close-knit Mzabis of the Ibadi faith, who operated baths and owned butcher and grocery shops; Biskris, who were water carriers and porters; Kabyles, who hired out for a variety of unskilled and semiskilled jobs. While they performed different functions and enjoyed very different social and economic standing, the barraniyun communities seemed to share a common sense of distance from the rest of the urban population. Reminiscent of twentieth-century Algerian émigré communities in Europe, most barraniyun identified more with their towns and villages of origin than the host city and most returned significant portions of their earnings to the families at home.

Sociologically, the main divisions of the Algerian city were quarters, ethnic communities, and guilds. The quarter was geographically self-contained, offering only one or two openings to the rest of the city which for security reasons were closed and guarded at night and during emergencies. Each quarter was capable of providing most services and most goods required on a daily basis by the residents, so the necessity to travel outside the familiar surroundings was limited. Its notables tried to manage the quarter's internal affairs in such a way as to minimize the opportunity or necessity for outside interference. Guilds regulated the techniques and economics of the major trades and also organized the practitioners of those trades. Under the patronage of its own saint, whose feast day served as an annual expression of group solidarity, the typical guild was for its members the principal focus of loyalties, arena of social life, and hedge against emergencies. For city dwellers the guild filled in many ways the needs that the clan or tribe filled for country populations. Because ethnic groups were often associated with specific trades and because individuals engaged in the same trade often inhabited the same neighborhood, the structures of quarter, guild, and ethnicity often reenforced each other. The degree to which the state was able to use the *amins* (heads) of Algerian guilds to assure control over urban populations, as it did in eighteenth-century Egypt and other parts of the Arab world, remains unclear.

With a few exceptions, urban population was declining during the latter eighteenth and early nineteenth centuries. This regression was due in the first instance to increasing European domination of the Mediterranean that led to the decline and then to the virtual termination of privateering. More immediately it was due to the massive disruptions in European trade brought on by the Napoleonic wars and their aftermath. It is estimated that the population of Algiers, which stood at 100,000 in the early eighteenth century, had contracted to 30,000 by the time the French army occupied that city. An early French count in the west put the population of Oran at 9,000, while that of Bône, the main eastern port, probably did not reach 5,000. The population of Tlemcen, traditional commercial hub and cultural center of western Algeria, had contracted to around 10,000. The only large city to resist the negative trend appears to have been Constantine, which with its income from Saharan and Tunisian trade and from agricultural production of vast estates in the surrounding plain, rivaled Algiers in population in 1830.

RURAL SOCIETY

The most significant and universal characteristic of Ottoman Algeria's rural society is its segmentary tribal form of organization, which encompasses the great majority of populations whether sedentary, nomadic or seminomadic. Beginning with the extended family, which is usually three generational, relationships extend outward in concentric circles to reach first a lineage, next a clan, sometimes a tribe, and less frequently a confederation of tribes. In the Grand Kabylia, the largest sedentary area in Algeria, the *adhrum,* or clan, was the liveliest and most socially interactive unit, while the fourth circle, that of the village, assumed greater economic and political significance because of its relationship to the basic territorial unit and the mediating role it played in land and other disputes. Among nomadic and seminomadic Arab populations, the poverty of vegetation and meteorological and geographic vicissitudes seem to cause the tribe to subdivide more readily so that the third circle, that of the clan *(firq),* assumes political as well as social importance. In both sedentary and nomadic zones, the tribal confederation, so powerful in the days of Khayr al-Din, appears by the nineteenth century to have declined measurably in importance, a possible reflection of the effectiveness of Turkish policies.

Within each circle of the system, the main organizational principle is consanguinity, which means that the relationships of individuals to community are defined and legitimized by reference to blood relationships whether these are actual or, as frequently occurs with regard to the outer circles, fictitious. No matter how far out one progresses through the concentric circles, the model of social organization is still the extended family. Since the family is patriarchal, patrilineal, and patrilocal, the ideal larger community is a projection of notions of fraternity and solidarity and also of patriarchy derived from the primary circle.

It has been suggested that because the Algerian vision of social and political relationships was based upon intuitive, largely unquestioned assumptions felt and experienced in intimate familial and communal settings rather than upon abstract, transferable principles, that vision decreased in practicality when one arrived at circles where names were unfamiliar and lineages mere abstractions. Thus, the farther out in the circle one traveled, the more fragile social and political organization became and the greater the likelihood of fragmentation into preexisting or newly formed subdivisions. Others have suggested that tribal society, inherently anarchical and self-regulating, more or less consciously subdivided periodically in order to assure groupings small and homogeneous enough to permit internal management of their affairs and to avoid attracting outside attention or intervention. Writing of Berber tribes in the Moroccan High Atlas, the British anthropologist Ernest Gellner suggested that they followed the maxim "Divide that ye be not ruled."[5]

The segmentary tribal system sought to manage tension by institutionalizing it. Adjacent segments within any circle tended to view competition as a

5. Ernest Gellner, *Saints of the Atlas,* p. 41.

normal state of affairs but to make common cause against threats from outside. Larger unities were always potential but characteristically did not materialize until danger common to the smaller units was perceived. In Algeria segmentary tribalism proved an excellent system for allowing enough conflict to resolve differences that arose over land, water, and other resources without putting society itself into mortal danger.

French anthropology of the nineteenth and early twentieth centuries, in conscious or unconscious attempts to deny the existence of an Algerian nation and to justify French occupation, emphasized the discreteness of the tribal segments and the destructiveness and sterility of their conflicts. Later scholarship (French, English, and Maghribi) has stressed the futility of analyzing the segments outside the framework of the larger whole. This scholarship insists that while political bifurcation is a profound empirical reality, this bifurcation can be accurately perceived only within the framework of a broader social unity. That unity is in the first instance conceptual and normative, formed and conditioned by a deeply internalized Islamic world view and value system. This conceptual and normative framework is reflected by widespread adhesion to religious brotherhoods, many of whose branches spread throughout the country, and by participation in local and international pilgrimage. Second, the unity is economic, related to the absolute need of the constituent units to exchange products of theirs and others' labor. Third, it is argued that inherent in the system of consanguineous groupings was the underlying premise of the interrelatedness and therefore the unity of society, and that even when they were fighting each other, the participants were conscious of struggling within a common framework whose rules governed even the conflict.

About 45 percent of Algeria's population in 1830 were nomads or seminomads, while 50 percent are estimated to have been sedentary cultivators. From a juridical point of view, the three main categories of sedentaries were landless peasants, *qsouriens,* and freeholders. The great majority of landless peasants were located in the farmlands adjacent to major cities (e.g., the Mitidja Valley, the Sahel of Algiers, and the Plain of Constantine). While some of these lands were held by their landlords as *mulk,* or freehold, most belonged directly or indirectly to the dey or the beys and could be managed either directly for their accounts or assigned to civil or military officials as compensation for services. Most labor on such lands was performed by *khamamisa,* or sharecroppers, whose traditional contract accorded them one-fifth of the harvest on the theory that of the five elements of production—labor, land, seed, tools, animals—the peasants supplied one. Many were constantly indebted and lived almost as serfs on latifundia bearing resemblance to classical feudal estates. During harvest or during other peak periods when more hands were needed, additional labor was supplied by nearby seminomads or by Kabyles descended from their mountains in search of supplemental income.

Fewer in number were the qsouriens, inhabitants of desert oases who grew vegetables under irrigation on intensively cultivated plots and frequently tended the date palms or other fruit trees. While there are many examples of freeholding qsouriens, most were under the protection, amounting to a kind of vassalage, of powerful nomadic tribes who extracted from them a large share of their produce and returned cereals, hides, wool, and manufactured products.

By far the greatest number of sedentaries were the predominantly Berber peasantry who farmed the steep slopes and narrow valleys of the mountain regions. Besides the Grand Kabylia, significant peasant populations were located in parts of the Aurès, in the Atlas of Blida, the Dahra and Ouarsenis massifs on both sides of the Chélif River Valley, and in the mountains of extreme western Algeria. Unlike cultivators of the valleys and oases, the majority of mountain peasants held their land as mulk. Each extended family owned its own land but properties were in fact held in indivision, since the clan or village could exercise a preemptive right of acquisition known as *shuf^ca*, should an individual family wish to sell its share. The nearly total limitation of small freeholding to mountainous zones is explained by the difficulty free peasantries encountered competing for access to richer lowlands either with the powerful urban elites or with the militarily superior nomads and semi-nomads. Compared to the sparsely populated plains, the mountains of the Grand Kabylia were thickly settled and intensively cultivated even in the nineteenth century. Because of the inelasticity of the land base, mountain folk frequently descended to the plain in search of supplementary income. While sometimes able to avail themselves temporarily of unoccupied land, they invariably succumbed to various kinds of dependent relationships and ended up either as sharecroppers, subject tribes, or casual laborers. But in the mountain heartlands, nothing close to feudalism emerged because peasants held on tenaciously not only to their lands but also to their guns.

In the Grand Kabylia, whose culture has been the most thoroughly studied of the sedentary regions, the typical village was built at or near the top of the mountain with the cultivated land laid out in stages below. Self-contained and inwardly oriented, the village turned blank walls toward the outside and doors toward the inside. At the approaches to the settlement, a detour path pointed the way around the agglomeration for those not having business there. The village itself was divided into quarters inhabited by the clans or larger lineages within which the closest relationships were knit and most day-to-day transactions took place.

Nearest the houses were located the vegetable gardens, cared for by the women. Down the slopes were the narrow, often terraced fields where hard wheat, barley, and other crops were grown. At the bottom grew the carefully cultivated fig and olive orchards that were the mainstay of the Kabyle economy. Most Kabyles also maintained a few animals for local consumption, which grazed on brush and grasses of rocky slopes unsuitable for cultivation.

At the heart of the settlement stood the building where the *tajma^cath*, or village assembly, met. This institution, composed of *tamans*, or heads of the lineages, created and administered a code of village laws known as *qanuns*, acted as arbiter of village disputes, and determined punishments for infractions of the code. Each village was affiliated with a circle of villages or tribe (*^carsh*), in whose assembly it was represented by an *amin*. While a number of scholars have seen in these Kabyle "village republics" traditions that might under appropriate circumstances have propelled Algerian political development toward representative government, others hold that the patriarchal structure of these institutions represents instead a prolongation of the authoritarian and patriarchal structure of the family, which is very different from democracy.

The lowland valleys and hills of the Tell, the semiarid high plains, and the Sahara were the domain of nomads and seminomads. These tribes lived essentially by herding sheep, goats, or camels around the countryside in search of suitable pasture. Grand nomads generally wintered in the Sahara, traveling northward in late spring to find forage on the higher ground of the Tell's southern edges. Seminomads tended to winter in the lowland valleys and summer on the high plains. Both types of nomads raised animals and grew grains, the difference between them being the relative importance of the two activities. Seminomads planted seed in the fall and generally stayed in the vicinity until after the harvest in late spring, spending the summer in cooler elevations where fodder for flocks matured later in the season.

Grand nomads would plant grains and return to them only at harvest time. Tribes from around Laghouat and Ouargla would summer in the western Tell in the Sersou or near Tiaret. Tribes from Touggourt and Biskra would travel to the high plains of Constantine. Their livelihood depended upon the milk, wool and wool products, hides, and meats supplied by their flocks and herds, in addition to the dates and vegetables from oases they frequented or controlled. While the exchanges and interaction among nomadic tribes often took place on a complementary and amicable basis, there were numerous occasions of conflict over access to pasture, water, crops, and animals, and the surplus of subject groupings.

The lands occupied by nomads and seminomads accounted for about one-third of the area of the Algerian Tell. While certain of those lands were considered *beylik* or government domain, the majority fell under the juridical category known as ᶜarsh in the east and center and as *sabiqa* in the west. Under Islamic law as interpreted in Algeria, the ultimate ownership of such lands rested in the Muslim community as personified by the state, but more important than the theoretical right of ownership were the right of occupation and cultivation, the right of usufruct, and the right to transmit to male heirs, all of which were guaranteed to the tribesmen. Among seminomads, individual families enjoyed the right of usufruct and succession over lands they cultivated, while the grazing lands were considered the common property of the tribe or clan. Even the grazing lands, however, were identified with specific tribal fractions.

MARABOUTISM AND THE BROTHERHOODS

Reference has already been made to the important function of religion in providing a conceptual and normative framework for Algerian society. Underpinning that framework institutionally, helping to bridge the gaps between different life styles and among competing clan and tribal units, were the *tariqas* and the *marabouts*. One of the most representative features of Maghribi Islam was the cult of saints, or maraboutism. These cults celebrated the lives, deeds, and powers of holy men and occasionally women, some of whose followings were narrowly localized while others were famous throughout the country. Saints of whatever category were believed to be conduits and repositories of *baraka,* divine grace, which they in turn could share with their followers. Their sanctuaries, *qubbas*, dotted the hilltops and road junctions of Ottoman Algeria, and became objects of pilgrimage where believers tried through prayer, offering, and ritual to appropriate a part of the baraka with which the site was suffused. The term marabout (English transliteration *murabit*) originally signified a holy man resident in a fortified mountain or desert hermitage; but over time in popular idiom its meaning expanded to include a living saint, a saint's remains, the qubba that sheltered his tomb, the successor of the saint, and sometimes even objects, trees, or animals associated with the holy site. The status of marabout could be achieved by personal merit, by lineal descent, or by nomination of a predecessor, so that maraboutism was in a state of perpetual renewal and proliferation. Anthropologists have suggested that maraboutism, with its geographic and genealogical specificity and its mediatory functions, was the religious counterpart of the ordered anarchy of segmentary tribal society.[6]

Related to maraboutism, but more systematic theologically and more widely spread geographically, were the tariqas, or brotherhoods, mystical sufi orders which had attracted increasing numbers of adherents from the high Middle Ages onward. Sufism offered Muslims an alternative or supplementary path to salvation which emphasized the intuitive, the affective, and the mystical as contrasted with the ritualism and legalism of Sunni orthodoxy. Each order prescribed a separate road to salvation composed of its own initiation requirements, mysteries, and physical and devotional requirements. While the tariqas were not generally considered heretical, the tension between their *shaykhs* and followers on the one hand and the orthodox *'ulama'* on the other was endemic. This tension reflects not only a competition for the loyalties and resources of believers but also some basic differences between urban and rural culture as well as the political and economic interests of each. While the interpenetration of the urban and the rural was such that both styles of Islam could be found in both places, the Islam of the great city mosques, the scholars, and the jurists was essentially a reflection of literate culture physically, economically, and politically dependent upon the urban milieu. The Islam of the marabouts and the shaykhs, relying upon signs and symbols—holy and marvelous men, places, things, deeds, events—clearly reflected a rural, less literate, dispersed and often mobile culture.

Early Middle Eastern sufism had represented an intensely personal search for the Divine Reality and may have survived the hostility of official Islam

6. Written Arabic of the period does not use the term murabit, but either *wali* (plural, *awliya*) or *salih* (plural *salihun*).

precisely because its followers withdrew from the world more than they tried to change it. Maghribi sufism, however, while continuing to provide mystical answers to the personal quest, was almost always activist to some degree, involving itself intimately in major social and political issues. The tariqas established chains of *zawiya*s which served as monasteries, schools, hostelries, shrines, and sometimes as centres for revolt. Marabouts, shaykhs, and the representatives of shaykhs often stood above the ordered anarchy of seg- mented tribalism, acting as arbiters, mediators, mentors, and guarantors of access to resources shared by different groups. They mediated between com- munities and the holders of political power, and when such mediation proved unavailing, the tariqas in particular became the vehicles through which pop- ular resistance to that political power was channelled. At the same time, the existence of more than one order in a region or community could serve to create societal divisions or, more frequently, to give expression to divisions already existing.

Among the most important brotherhoods in the late eighteenth and the nineteenth centuries were the Qadiriyya, named after ᶜAbd al Qadir al Jilani, one of the most revered of Islamic saints, who died in Baghdad in 1166. It centered mainly in Oran Province but established some branches in the other *beylik*s (provinces) as well. Especially influential during this era were three newer orders, whose founding was inspired by the neo-Sufi movement that progressed westward from Islamic South Asia during the eighteenth century and was transmitted to the far West through the mediation of Maghribi pilgrims and scholars in the Haramayn and Cairo. These orders included: the Darqawa, founded by Sidi Mawlay al ᶜArabi al Darqawi of Fez, whose Algerian strongholds were in the Ouarsenis mountains and the southern regions of central Algeria; the Tijaniyya, founded by Ahmad al Tijani from southwestern Algeria, which spread internally as far as southeastern Algeria and widely into Morocco and West Africa as well; the Rahmaniyya, founded by Muhammad ibn ᶜAbd al-Rahman al-Azhari al Qubrayn, a Kabyle from the Djurdjura mountains who had devoted years of study at al-Azhar in Cairo and whose movement spread throughout eastern and southeastern Algeria and into the Jarid of Tunisia.

THE ECONOMY

Some wealth in Ottoman Algeria was generated by manufacturing; more was generated by international trade and privateering; but the most came from agriculture. The twin bases of Algerian agriculture were grains and stock raising. Wheat and barley were grown mostly through dry farming techniques in the valleys and on the hillsides of the northern Tell within the 400 millimeter isohyet. Stock raising, whose major products were sheep, goats, and camels, took place in many of these same regions but extended also to the High Plains, the Pre-Sahara, and the Sahara.

Tools and techniques of grain cultivation appear not to have been improved for centuries, some implements seeming strikingly similar to those employed in Roman times. Seed was planted whenever in October, November, or December rainfall had softened the soil sufficiently for plowing; harvest took place between late April and early June. Plowing was very shallow, fields were planted only in alternate years, and average yields were very low. But average had little meaning in a land where unpredictability of rainfall, insect attacks, and political and intertribal turmoil caused yields to fluctuate enormously from one year to the next. One overview of the grain sector suggests that in a typical six-year period cultivators could count on one good harvest, two fair ones, one or two poor ones, and one or two total failures. When European markets for Algerian grain were disrupted as a result of the Napoleonic wars and their aftermath, prices of grain fell so dramatically that considerable grain growing land—near ports like Bône, Arzew, Miliana—was turned back to pasture.

Although sedentaries grew vegetables and variable quantities of grain and also raised some sheep and goats, their principal contribution to the market was fruit. The urban-oriented farms and latifundia produced a variety of them, the oasis farmers supplied dates, and the Kabyles and other mountaineers sold figs and olives. Along with grains and meat, olives were staples of the Algerian diet, not only as fruit but more importantly as the chief source of cooking oil. They were also a major component of lubricants, cosmetics, lamp fuel, and related products.

Crafts were well developed and sufficiently diversified in the major cities to provide most of the manufactured products required by the urban populations. They do not seem to have been marketed in significant quantity in Morocco, Tunisia, or overseas, however. Nor was there much internal market beyond the towns. Demand in the countryside was limited by the high level of rents and taxes extracted from the rural surplus by the city elites and by a predisposition of rural populations to minimize contact with the towns, whose ways they had come over the generations to know and to fear.

A more important role of the Algerian cities was in intraregional and international exchanges, which, at least since the Middle Ages, had provided the key to their economic prosperity and the viability of their political systems. Important trading networks linked Mascara and Oran via Tlemcen with Fez. Much of Constantine's economy depended upon trade with Tunisia. Across the northern Sahara, oasis and Pre-Saharan tribes throve on the commerce and travel connecting Fez, Marrakech, and Meknes with southern Tunisia, Tripoli, and the Arab East.

Of considerably greater economic importance were the north-south linkages—across the Sahara by various routes to the Sudan and across the Mediterranean to Southern Europe. In the sixteenth century, Ottoman forces had penetrated the Sahara as far as the oases of Touggourt and Ouargla in an apparent effort to capture a share of the trade in slaves, gold, ivory, and ostrich feathers, which had enriched such centers since the early Middle Ages. This initiative and others like it enjoyed only temporary success, and the Turks withdrew northward without establishing a permanent presence astride the caravan trails. The regime continued to profit, however, from duties when such goods arrived at the portal cities of the Pre-Sahara and the Tell. From the seventeenth century onward, Saharan trade through Algerian territory declined steadily in reaction to European success in attracting this trade to the Atlantic, from whence cargoes could be transported by ship more cheaply to world markets. By the early nineteenth century, no cargoes from the Sudan passed through Constantine and only a trickle flowed along the more westerly trails.

During the sixteenth and seventeenth centuries, pashas and deys paid far more attention to privateering with its spectacular returns than they did to routine maritime commerce. Within the context of the Franco-Ottoman alliance against the Hapsburgs, a Marseille merchant had in 1520 been granted a coral-fishing and trading concession on the coast of the Constantinois. This concession, added to and expanded over the years, gave French merchants a dominant share of the overseas trade of eastern Algeria. As time went on, Dutch, British and eventually Swedish and Spanish merchants also won concessions. While the deys received periodic payments for these concessions and surer access to tariff revenues, overseas trade was being progressively monopolized by foreigners. When privateering declined by the eighteenth century, the Regency found itself in a dangerously vulnerable position with regard to the international exchanges upon which important sectors of the economy as well as the solvency of the regime depended.

From a macroeconomic standpoint it is clear that a largely fragmented market was the counterpart of a segmented social order. The 95 percent of Algerians who lived in the countryside consumed most of what they produced and produced most of what they consumed. Yet, few segments enjoyed total economic independence, and for most some exchanges were not only beneficial but necessary. For this reason, an economic system that was largely communal and compartmentalized displayed unmistakable aspects of a genuine market. Grand nomads from the deserts brought northward with them in late spring animals, skins, and wool, as well as dates and other oasis products. On their southward return they carried grains produced by semi-nomads; olives, oil, and figs supplied by sedentaries; and metal products—tools, pots and pans, weapons—manufactured in or imported by the cities. Peasants, for their part, needed the same metal products and usually were deficient in grains, leather, and wool. The city consumed all of these products and more.

If a "national" market clearly existed, however, that market was partial, fragile, and beset by difficulties. Problems included the primitive condition of roads and trails. There were no carriage roads beyond the suburbs and fields directly controlled by the cities; it took eight or nine days by pack train to travel from Algiers to either Constantine or Oran. Other hindrances to trade arose from the endemic hostility which made it difficult for some groups to interact economically or socially with others. Finally, the government itself, realizing that access to markets was absolutely essential to the livelihoods of many of its subjects, used the market towns and other points of exchange as locations at which to extract taxes and political concessions. Such intervention by government naturally had a depressing effect upon whatever tendencies existed for further expansion of the economy.

GOVERNMENT AND SOCIETY

If the Regency of Algiers was sovereign in a formal sense over a large territory, the kind of rule it exercised differed markedly from one part of the country to another and from one population to the next. By the seventeenth century, the Regency had created the three territorial subdivisions known as beyliks, which met with varying degrees of success in projecting the authority of the dey and the divan over the interior of the country. These subdivisions were the Beylik of the East, with its capital at Constantine; the Beylik of the West, whose capital was Mascara until the Spanish evacuation of Oran in 1792; and the Beylik of Titteri in the center, whose capital was Médéa. While the common translation of the term beylik is "province," there are grounds for considering "protectorate" a more appropriate rendering because of the divergent patterns of institutional development and the degree of autonomy they frequently enjoyed. In every case, the highest official was the bey, increasingly chosen from one of the region's leading families, who frequently attempted and occasionally succeeded in keeping the office in their families for considerable periods. A truly hereditary succession never emerged in any beylik, however.

Each of the beyliks was subdivided into smaller units called *watan*s, a term which here could be translated either as district or as canton depending upon the degree of internal autonomy exercised there. Watans could be defined solely by territory, could be composed of several tribes or other nonrelated populations, or could be the territory of a single tribe. The head of the watan was a *qa'id*, who was almost invariably a local tribal shaykh in the case of a canton occupied by a single tribe, the head of a competing clan or tribe if the bey or dey found himself needing to bargain to maintain his authority, or an official external to the district when heterogeneous populations needed no special consideration.

The largest and richest of the beyliks was the Beylik of the East. Its greater wealth seems related to the fact that a higher percentage of its territory was devoted to intensive agriculture, and it was able to exploit to its advantage both a brisk Saharan trade and profitable exchanges with nearby Tunisia. Considerable Mediterranean commerce passed through ports such as La Calle, Bône, and Djidjelli in sometimes successful attempts to avoid the customs exactions of the central government.

With its wide expanses of plains and valleys, the Beylik of the West was primarily a land of nomads and seminomads. The prevalence of nomadism was conditioned not only by geography but also by political and military considerations. Because of the ongoing hostility of Sharifian Morocco to its Ottoman neighbors and the existence at Oran through most of the period of a Spanish presence capable of inciting tribes against Turkish rule, conflict was endemic and many tribes made the military their primary vocation.

The Beylik of Titteri, smallest of the provinces, was the most consistently subordinate to the dey and the divan and therefore corresponded more to authentic provincial status than its two larger neighbors. This dependency related not only to Titteri's geographic proximity to Algiers but also to the fact that a number of its tribes and lands fell under direct authority of the khujat al khil or other officials of the central government. Its geographical position precluded unmonitored access to the Mediterranean, while a powerful family who were both tribal aristocrats and marabouts dominated the whole south independently of Médéa.

A small territory close to Algiers was not assigned to any beylik but as Dar al-Sultan was administered directly by the central government. Dar al-Sultan included the four cities of Algiers, Blida, Koléa, and Tipasa, as well as the Sahel of Algiers and a large portion of the Mitidja Valley, the agricultural jewel of the Regency. Government officials and wealthy families from Algiers drew income from many of the Mitidja's and Sahel's estates or had country residences there.

The fact that formal administrative arrangements existed for the governance of the whole of Algeria should not obscure the fact, suggested earlier, that the actual power of the dey over the Regency's diverse lands and peoples varied enormously. For a sizeable minority of Algeria's population, the dey was ruler in a direct sense. For others he was suzerain; for others, he was ally; and for still others, he was irrelevant. For any of these four categories of peoples, the dey under certain circumstances could also become an adversary.

One model of political organization suggests that the Algerian state can be analyzed in terms of three concentric circles. The heart of the first circle consists of the city from which political and military power traditionally emanate and toward which flows the surplus extracted from the countryside. The periphery of the first circle is composed of tax-exempt *makhzan* tribes who help to protect the urban core, who collect taxes from other populations, and who exercise military control either alone or as auxiliaries of the central armies. Surrounding this inner circle of privileged urban and rural peoples— *ahl al makhzan* (government people)—is a second circle inhabited by taxpaying tribes and nontribal sedentaries. These are called the *rayat,* or subjects. Finally, at the outer circle reside the dissident or usually dissident tribes who refuse to submit and refuse to pay taxes. While there is no exact type within each circle to which all elements unerringly correspond, the model approximately renders the power relationships that characterized eighteenth- and early nineteenth-century society. The system was composed, according to Elbaki Hermassi, of "people who raise taxes, those who submit to exploitation, and those who refuse it."[7] Louis Rinn, the nineteenth-century French Arabist, recorded that Algerians remembered the society of the Turkish period as consisting of *mangeurs* and *mangés*.[8]

As certified by the etymology of many languages, cities, with their ability to concentrate surplus and provide for a high degree of division of labor, have always lain at the heart of civilized cultures. Nowhere is the political preeminence of the urban more clearly manifested than in North Africa. The names of ancient and medieval North African states were taken from peoples, families, or movements: Mauritania, Ifriqya, Rustamids, Hafsids, Murabitun. By contrast, the names of all the modern North African states, with the exception of Morocco, were identical to the names of their capital cities: *Tarabulus, Tunis, al-Jaza'ir*. Equivalents of Tripolitania, Tunisia, and Algeria do not exist in Arabic.[9]

Algiers began to achieve naval and economic significance in the eleventh century when it was realized that four rocky islets immediately off the coast offered protection from dangerous north winds, a situation which while far from ideal was superior to that afforded by other harbors of the central Maghrib coast. After Khayr al-Din built a jetty 200 yards long and 80 feet wide linking the four islets to the mainland, the harbor acquired much greater protection from those winds. Some time later, when a mole to the southeast was completed, Algiers became the undisputed queen of Algerian maritime cities. With their superior wealth, political power, and elaborate life styles, the capital's Moorish, renegade, and Turkish elites considered themselves socially and culturally superior to the Arab and Berber folk of the hinterland. Ironically, however, for all of its military, naval, and commercial preeminence, Algiers never achieved the cultural status of neighboring capitals such as Tunis or Fez or even of the Algerian provincial centers of Tlemcen and Constantine. Its functions were largely military and material, and there is little evidence that the Algerines ever exerted serious effort to transform their town into a major cultural center.

The majority of the Regency's Turkish troops were stationed either in Algiers or surrounding Dar al-Sultan. Unless war or internal peacekeeping problems dictated otherwise, their main military duties were spring and fall campaigns called *mahalla*s through the countryside for the purpose of "showing the flag" of the dey and extracting taxes from rayat. The Janissaries maintained a small number of garrisons (*nuba*s) at widely scattered strategic forts and crossroads. The southernmost nouba in the Regency, located at Biskra on the edge of the Pre-Sahara, held only sixty troops in the early

---

7. Elbaki Hermassi, *Leadership and National Development in North Africa*, p. 9.
8. Louis Rinn, "Le royaume d'Alger sous le dernier dey," *Revue Africaine* (1897): 124. Rinn, of course, had every interest in emphasizing societal divisions.
9. Morocco, whose official Arabic name is *mamlakatu 'l maghrib*, Kingdom of the West, is the exception, presumably because of the competition of Marrakech, Fez, and Meknès for dominion. It is at least arguable that the fact that Fez was never dominated by foreign military elites had something to do with the distinction.

nineteenth century, while the total Turkish military presence in the Province of Constantine during the same period was about 400. In order to rule or maintain minimum control with so few troops, the Turks depended upon auxiliaries. The auxiliaries were the Kouloughlis, the Makhzan tribes, and occasionally Kabyle mercenaries.

As sons of Turkish fathers, Kouloughlis naturally shared the paternal sense of superiority and desired to continue in the privilege to which they had been born and bequeath it to their own children. Early in the seventeenth century, the Kouloughlis were playing increasingly important roles in political and military affairs, but they found their way blocked by new generations of recruits from Turkey. By 1629, in alliance with their maternal relatives, they launched a fierce revolt against the system. But after four years of bloody struggle, the pure Turks defeated them and managed ever afterward to keep Kouloughlis in subordinate auxiliary roles between themselves and the Arab and Berber majority. Speculation about the failure of the Kouloughlis to win full membership in the ruling establishment centers both around the internal dynamics of the constantly renewed ojaq, whose members resented competing for limited promotion possibilities with "inferior" half castes, and, alternatively, upon the reluctance of the ojaq to share scarce financial resources with the sons of their elders.

Proud and distinctive appearing, Kouloughlis often pretended to speak only Turkish and insisted on worshipping in Hanafi mosques with men of their own ethnic background. In times of emergency they were called upon to supplement the forces of the ojaq. In normal times they garrisoned a number of provincial towns and fortresses, assuring the principal defense of Tlemcen, Mostaganem, Chendah, Mazouna, and other towns of the Beylik of the West. They were the majority of the garrison at Médéa in Titteri as well as of those at Blida and Koléa in Dar al-Sultan. While the military contribution of Kouloughlis in the Beylik of Constantine is more difficult to document, it is well known that the intermarriage there of Turks with families of local notables and tribal aristocrats, *jawad,* served to create mixed blood families of privilege and great power, who, except for the last years of the Regency, generally served as agents of the status quo.

Though the Kouloughlis constitute one important pillar of Turkish power, their limited numbers and their distance from the internal dynamics of much of Algerian society compelled the central government to rely even more upon the cooperation of makhzan tribes. In most of the literature, makhzan tribes are described as those who either are relieved of tax liabilities or enjoy use of beylical lands, or both, in exchange for policing and extracting taxes from rayat and for serving when needed as auxiliaries in the Turkish armies. While this description fits the average tribe, it is clear that makhzan tribes functioned under a great variety of arrangements, some more favorable then others. Certain tribes had only to collect taxes and rents, others had to fight, and still others did both. Some supplied their own arms and equipment; others received them from the state. Some received free use of lands without remittances of any kind; others received lesser benefits.

Makhzan tribes were constituted in two ways. The Douaïrs and Zmalas in the Beylik of the West composed the so-called *makhzan al-kabir,* a highly integrated body of forces created out of diverse tribal elements and based upon rich beylik lands near Mascara. Other makhzan populations, however, were preexisting tribes selected by the beylik or the divan for their privileged role. There were many such individual makhzan tribes in Titteri but fewer in Dar al-Sultan, where direct Turkish rule was more direct. In the Beylik of Constantine, the system had been widespread early in the eighteenth century, but it became rare as the authority of the beys was consolidated and as the beylical government was able to let out vast tracts of the public domain to Arab or Kabyle families in return for individual commitments to military service. For the whole of Algeria, nineteenth-century French studies identify 126 tribes as makhzan, controlling directly 3,400,000 hectares or nearly one-fourth of the land surface of the Tell.

Upon the rayat fell the burden of funding most of the institutions that assured provincial governance and control as well as a growing share of the revenues of the central government itself. There were several categories of rayat. First were the khamamisa and the minority of sedentary freeholders who could not avoid taxes. More numerous were the inhabitants of ᶜazl lands, which were state properties let to tribes in return for payment of a special tax known as *hukr*. Most ᶜazl lands, particularly prevalent around Constantine, had apparently been confiscated in the past as punishment for revolt and subsequently farmed out to tribal or non tribal populations under the new and onerous arrangements. Finally there were the rayat tribes who occupied their own lands, ᶜarsh, but were liable to a range of payments to the beylik, to surrounding makhzan tribes, or to both. The 104 rayat tribes identified by French officers occupied about 5,000,000 hectares or 35 percent of the Tell. The status of rayat tribes, like that of their makhzan cousins, varied widely. Most, but not all, were seminomads. Some were well treated, either because of their traditionally helpful roles, or because of connections with influential tribes, or because of geographic isolation. Most, however, were subjected to levels of exploitation which left them in perennial economic jeopardy.

Of the 2,381,741 square kilometers of territory that comprise contemporary Algeria, only about 140,000 lie in the Tell. All of the Sahara and most of the Pre-Sahara lay outside the Algeria of the Ottomans. Around 1800, the Turks could claim direct or indirect rule over about 80,000 square kilometers of the Tell. The rest of the Tell, and the Pre-Sahara were the homelands of the third circle of populations who usually managed to stay beyond the fiscal and military reach of the Regency system but who could never totally ignore its presence either. These peoples included between eighty and ninety tribes or confederations in the Tell and the nearer Sahara who could be classified either as vassals or as allies of the Ottoman regime. Amongst such groups were the Awlad Sidi Shaykh, powerful in southwestern Oran, the hereditary shaykhs of the Djebel Amour, the influential Awlad Mukhtar of Titteri, the Muqranis of Medjana, the Benhabylès of Djidjelli, and powerful sedentary federations in the Grand Kabylia. Each allied or vassal group was tied by its own historically derived arrangements to the central power in patterns susceptible of as many nuances as existed in Europe in the Middle Ages.

As observed earlier, the farthest south Turkish garrison in the nineteenth century was in Biskra at the base of the Aurès. The makhzan system, too, was confined to the Tell. Beyond the Saharan Atlas resided a few allied tribes, but this region was primarily the domain of the independents, over whom the Regency maneuvered to maintain as much influence as possible and to prevent the emergence of anti-Turkish combinations. The most powerful card in the Turkish deck was their control of access to Tellian market towns, which provided the locus for the levying of duties and a lever for the extraction of political concessions. By such controls Turks were able to maintain influence over developments in nearer oases such as Touggourt, Laghouat, and Ghardaia. When economic pressures were insufficient, diplomatic maneuver and play upon internal or regional divisions could be effective. Recourse to military coercion or its threat could also produce results. The farther one travelled southward, the more episodic Turkish military penetrations became, but they were sufficiently effective over a wide enough zone to engender a degree of respect for the power of the north, and at the very least to prevent for generations combinations of tribes capable of seriously threatening the Regency system. While Turkish influence in the east extended several hundred kilometers into the desert, its penetration in the west was far more limited. In neither region did Turkish power in the eighteenth or nineteenth centuries reach as far as the major caravan crossroads of ʿAyn Salah or Ghadamès or any of the territories beyond, so that what remained of the once lucrative Saharan trade was beyond their grasp.[10]

THE MODE AND RELATIONS OF PRODUCTION

Attempts to identify the dominant mode of production in Ottoman Algeria are complicated by the inadequacy of research into precapitalist formations in general and into non-European precapitalist formations in particular. They are also made more difficult by the scarcity of reliable data on Ottoman Algeria, by the extraordinary geographical and communal diversity of the country, and by the question of the transferability from one setting to the next of the fragmentary hard data that does exist.

It is clear that the level of economic productivity in early nineteenth-century Algeria was extremely low, a situation which in turn was related to lag in technological development, inadequacy of market arrangements, and coun-

10. In the 1890s, Louis Rinn, assuming that the 480,000 square kilometers then claimed by France corresponded to the land surface of the Regency of Algiers, concluded that the Regency had contained some 200 independent tribes; but since the Regency system even in its most diffuse manifestations never extended beyond a fourth of that territory, it is clear that at least half of these independent tribes cannot be viewed as Algerian at the time.

terproductive fiscal policies. Most communities tended toward autarchy even though few if any actually achieved it.

One school of thought holds that below a certain level of productivity, extraction of significant surplus from the peasantry becomes virtually impossible and, therefore, that significant social stratification fails to appear within most Algerian communities. While economic domination of individuals by other individuals exists, it is far from a universal or even majority pattern. Most genuine exploitation is the exploitation of one group by another rather than that of a village community by a lord. Nor is the central government, which also attempts to extract surplus, representative of class interests, because its agents, not being hereditary, do not constitute a true social class. This being the case, the dominant mode must be considered profoundly archaic and not clearly identifiable with any of the five "classic" modes of production.[11]

Another school, observing the same data, concludes that Algeria presents a clear pattern of movement away from communal toward feudal relationships. This school sees the progressive emergence of an intricately layered extractive system pressing upon the basic communal framework, which is becoming more hereditary and more independent of the central government and whose progressive entrenchment makes it increasingly difficult for the central government to command the resources it needs to function effectively.[12] Elements of the same school, coming from a different direction, hold that observers have been blinded by the apparent egalitarianism of nomadic and village tribalism to the emergence of real distinctions in wealth and property within the consanguineous units themselves, which in turn establishes the pattern of class relationships at the wider levels as well. While the social relationships of earlier models of feudal society were defined by the ability to appropriate ground rents, the Algerian model of relationships emphasizes fiscal extraction, and the reenforcement of the privileged positions of certain aristocracies gained through moderate economic advantage by their assumption of public military and fiscal roles. This variant of feudalism, which can also be seen in the Byzantine, Turkish, and Mashriqi Arab experiences, has been qualified as "command feudalism."[13]

A third mode of production is the commercial tributary mode identified by Samir Amin. While the communal systems in place did not absolutely prevent social differentiation, the available surplus was limited to the extent that lasting and obvious class distinctions were difficult to obtain without access to outside surplus. This outside surplus was supplied by the profit of regional and international trade, from which the majority of the aristocracies benefited. A variant of the commercial tributary mode is the military democracy, also

11. For a summary of this school of thought, see Lucette Valensi, *On the Eve of Colonialism: North Africa Before the French Conquest,* pp. 13–34; also in *Sur le féodalisme* (Paris: Editions sociales, 1971), pp. 223–32.
12. See, for instance, André Prenant, in Yves Lacoste, André Nouschi, and André Prenant, *L'Algérie. Passé et présent,* pp. 146–50.
13. See, for instance, René Gallissot, *L'Algérie précoloniale. Classes sociales en système précapitaliste. Mise en question du mode de production féodal* (Paris: 1968), passim.

dependent upon profits of long-distance trade, which is the "hinge between the last classless society and the first class society."[14]

Finally, a minority of scholars would continue to hold, as did Marx, that the dominant Algerian mode of production was Asiatic and that direct extraction of agricultural surplus by government had prevented the emergence of authentic Algerian classes. While under other circumstances, the agents of government, who extracted these resources over centuries, might have been expected to make that privilege hereditary and become a true social class, the structure of the ojaq and its appendages prevented such evolution amongst the Turks and tended to discourage it amongst their Algerian auxiliaries. A variant interpretation ascribes an increasing role in that extraction to the overseas impact of the activities of European bourgeoisies.[15]

It is evident that no consensus has yet emerged regarding the mode of production in late Ottoman Algeria. It is perhaps wise to avoid attaching a single label to the extremely complex Algerian socioeconomic formation. In fact, it was characterized by no clearly dominant mode of production but, rather, by a multiplicity of military democracies and primitive communities. These were undergoing varying pressures from a quasi-Asiatic state and long-term influences from European commercial capitalism, which combined were in the process of modifying in varying ways and to varying degrees some of their original structures. The mode and relations of production were in full evolution, with different communities at different points in that evolution.

THE CRISIS OF THE EARLY NINETEENTH CENTURY

During the last decades of the eighteenth century, the deys of Algiers, working through a series of increasingly effective beys in both the East and the West, succeeded in extending their government's authority to the greatest limits it would reach. The beys of Constantine, who issued from marital unions between Turks and Algerian jawad, utilized a judicious combination of family politics and strong military presence to extend the direct authority of the state over wider and wider areas. While the Kabylia was never brought under permanent submission, the independent mountaineers' ability to spread sedition to the surrounding valleys was limited by the energetic activity of the Dey Muhammad ibn ʿUthman (1766–91) who established a series of forts in the valley of the Sebaou and skillfully played upon the internal rivalries of tribal segments. In the Beylik of the West, subjugation of some of the most powerful tribes was begun at mid-century under ʿUthman Bey and continued under Muhammad al-Kabir Bey between 1780 and 1797.

14. Yves Lacoste, as quoted in Abdelhamid Merad Boudia, *La formation sociale algérienne précoloniale,* p. 289. This work contains a lucid overview and analysis of the debate over the precolonial mode of production in Algeria.
15. Abdelkader Djeghloul, "La formation sociale algérienne à la veille de la colonisation," *La Pensée* 185 (February 1976): 61–81.

With startling suddenness, however, the Regency, in the first years of the nineteenth century, plunged into a prolonged period of violent crisis, which dragged the political order to the brink of collapse. The multifaceted crisis shook the institutions of central government, called into question the prerogatives and stability of the beyliks, and saw massive ongoing revolt in the countryside spearheaded by key tribal elites and especially by the religious brotherhoods.

While specific institutional inadequacies and personality clashes can be adduced for many of the conflicts, the leitmotif of the whole period of disorder is a profound economic and fiscal crisis caused mostly by the commercial dislocations produced by the Napoleonic wars. France had always been Ottoman Algeria's principal European trading partner, but this trade was disrupted by the break in relations upon Bonaparte's 1798 invasion of Ottoman Egypt. Following this the extension of the continental blockade and Britain's counterblockade cut off the regency from its traditional customers in Livorno, Marseille, and Spain. The English, who after Trafalgar reaffirmed their mastery of the seas, acquired in 1806 the concessions long held by the French Compagnie d'Afrique, but this monopoly, which the English held until 1816, in no wise compensated for the loss of trade and customs revenues flowing from the earlier arrangements. In the meantime, Napoleonic Europe was discovering substitute suppliers—particularly Russia for grains—which proved so commercially attractive that even after the Congress of Vienna in 1815, Algeria was unable to win back more than a fraction of its European markets. In the meantime, European navies, particularly the British and the Dutch, were taking such a toll of the remnants of the Algerian fleet that a return to broad-scale privateering was clearly impractical even though dreamers in Algiers continued to talk as though it were.

Since the financial margin that kept the Algerian political system viable was supplied by international trade, its precipitous decline had repercussions throughout the country. Elite elements dependent upon fiscal extraction found themselves increasingly competing with each other rather than cooperating in maintaining the system. The dey and the divan, who had been able to tolerate and even benefit from the enhanced power and effectiveness of the beys in Constantine and Oran, began to question their growing autonomy as the beyliks' share of revenues grew relative to their own. Between 1790 and 1825, eight beys were removed from office and sixteen were executed. So great was the tumult in the Constantinois that seventeen beys succeeded each other in the thirty years between 1796 and 1826.

The fiscal crisis weighed most heavily, of course, upon the tribal populations. But it was the leaders of the tariqas, arbiters of morality with access to vast networks of followers amongst those populations, who controlled the most effective instrument for mobilizing collective action against the mounting burden. In the western regions the harsh measures employed to subjugate tribes and the heavy indemnities imposed to punish them had led to widespread alienation for which the shaykhs of the Darqawa order became the principal spokesmen. Resentment and revolt simmered for years. Finally, in 1805, ʿAbd al-Qadir al Sharif, head of the order in western Algeria, succeeded in mobilizing the whole of Oran Province and parts of the Titteri against Turkish rule. In time most of the countryside fell to them, they won over the key town of Mascara, penned up the Kouloughli garrison in the citadel of Tlemcen, and laid siege to Oran. Between 1810 and 1815, with the west still out of control, Darqawa leaders in eastern and central Algeria succeeded in raising massive Kabyle revolts in the Babors behind Djidjelli, in the Djurdjura, and in the Wadi Djer. When the Darqawa-inspired revolts began to flag, the banner was picked up in the 1820s by Muhammad al-Kabir, leader of the newly founded Tijaniyya tariqa. The heart of the Tijani coalition was an alliance between tribal followers of the order and the tribe of the Banu Hashim, which was affiliated with the Qadiriyya order and to which the Amir ʿAbd al Qadir, future leader of resistance to the French, belonged.

The harm which fiscal oppression caused to the deys' standing was exacerbated by their increasing reliance upon the Livorno Jewish families Bushnaq and Bakri to assure commercial relationships with Europe. In 1805, Nephtali Bushnaq, a wealthy merchant who had great influence on Mustafa Dey (1798–1805) was murdered by a Janissary. After some ʿulama' signalled approval of the act, Turks and other elements of the Algerine population went on a rampage that took the lives of about 200 Jews and led directly to a revolt of the ojaq which murdered Mustafa and his Treasurer and acclaimed a former Master of Cavalry, Ahmad, as dey. The ensuing decade witnessed a return to the kind of political turmoil reminiscent of the seventeenth century. The ojaq competed with elements of the divan in propelling a succession of candidates to the highest office in search of one who could please all of the factions and assure fiscal stability. Including Mustafa, seven deys occupied the Janina palace on the Algiers waterfront in eleven years and all but the last met violent ends. Ali Khodja Dey, an obscure but literate Janissary nominated in 1816, drew appropriate conclusions from the fates of his immediate predecessors and determined to break the hold of the ojaq upon the government. Supported by contingents of Kouloughlis and Kabyles, the new dey deserted the Janina Palace for the protection of the Qasba fortress, after having secretly transferred there the contents of the state treasury. Alarmed at what was happening and refusing ʿAli Khodja's summons to allegiance, the garrison rose in revolt, supported by the mahalla of Constantine and an urban mob. Thanks to effective use of artillery from the forts, 1,700 rebels died in ʿAli's successful repression; a significant number of the survivors were repatriated to Turkey. While ʿAli Khodja died soon afterward, it was the plague rather than the sword that carried him away. Before he succumbed, he personally nominated as his successor Hussein Dey, who ruled until the arrival of the French and who, in the twelve years allotted him, made marked progress toward restoring the authority of the central government in several parts of the country.

ALGERIA AND THE ALGERIANS

It was observed early in this chapter that a primary achievement of the Ottomans in North Africa was the creation of an Algerian political entity possessing all the classical attributes of statehood. But was there an Algerian nation? This question assumed major importance during the early days of the nationalist struggle against French rule, when colonialist apologetics argued that Algerian nationalism was illegitimate because no nation had existed in 1830. Before France, it was argued, a materially impoverished Algerian society had been prey to countless debilitating internal divisions and a destructive Turkish tyranny that played upon and nurtured those divisions for its own selfish ends. Whatever material progress, sense of unity, and identity had been achieved by the twentieth century were clearly the result of the progressive policies of the colonial regime. Writing in 1936, Shaykh ʿAbd al Hamid Ben Badis, leader of the Islamic Reform movement in Algeria, protested passionately that an Algerian nation existed then and had existed historically. Other Algerian writers since have pointed to two generations and more of tenacious resistance to French aggression as an expression of Algerian unity and one proof among many of collective Algerian identity.

Given what has been observed in this chapter about the segmentary nature of Algerian society, the fragility of the markets, and the systemic tension that existed among competing segments and between the segments and the central government, it is clear that the term "nation" in the modern sense hardly applies to the Algerian society of 1830. It is worth observing, nevertheless, that in the three hundred years since the Barbarossas arrived in the country, the Turkish policy of manipulating, and balancing tribal segments had resulted in the neutralization of tribal power to the extent that even during the catastrophic period 1800–25 they were unsuccessful in changing the form of government. Such neutralization of the political potential of segments is clearly a major step toward genuine centralization of power which is a prerequisite of nationhood. It is also clear that a process of "deturkification" had begun early in the eighteenth century and accelerated as the state became increasingly dependent upon internal resources and hence upon the support of indigenous elites. This process had resulted in a *prise de conscience* among certain layers of Algerian society whose exact strength and dimensions can probably never be known from this distance. Given these political, ethnic, and psychological transformations, three kinds of Algerian institutions at different levels might have given concrete political expression to the emerging sense of identity. These are the institution of dey, that of the beyliks, and purely indigenous tribal or religious elements.[16]

When ʿAli Khodja Dey forsook the Janina Palace for the security of the Qasba of Algiers, he removed his person and the treasury from the covetous

---

16. I am indebted in this analysis to the work of Charles-André Julien and Pierre Boyer; and especially to Jean-Claude Vatin, *L'Algérie politique,* pp. 96–104.

grasp of the traditional arbiters of power. At the same time, by relying upon indigenous troops rather than the Turkish garrison which had supported the office for centuries, he also took a giant step toward the Algerianization of the state. It is possible that between 1817 and 1830 the office of dey was being converted into a genuine monarchy, which could have become the focal point for the rallying of national forces and aspirations. Whether this is true or not cannot be known, because the French invasion cut short whatever process might have been underway.

It is possible as well that the office and institution of bey, more distant geographically and ethnically from the Turkish power structure, could have served as foci for the crystallization of national consciousness. During most periods competition for this office was significantly less than for that of dey, and in general the tenure of beys was longer than that of deys. The beys transmitted power more easily, legitimized themselves through alliance with important tribal and religious elites, and through the Kouloughli element built an ethnic and cultural bridge between native and outlander aristocracies. The beys of Oran during much of the nineteenth century showed increasing inclination to ally with indigenous elements against Algiers. In the Beylik of the East, Ahmad Bey, a Kouloughli, related on the maternal side to the powerful Ben Ghana of the southern Constantinois, was able through his influence on local elites and his identification with local populations to create something like a national consciousness within the confines of his own province. Both in Oran and in Constantine, then, it is possible to hypothesize a national rallying of peoples under the leadership of provincial aristocracies.

It is among the tribal elites and the religious elites of the countryside that contemporary Algerians most frequently search for the roots of their nationhood. As time had gone on, certain important families like the Ben Ghana or the Muqranis of the Medjana, had transformed once elective leaderships into quasi-hereditary positions of power and wealth from which they presided over vast collectivities capable of mobilizing sizeable numbers of clients, vassals, relatives, and allies. The tariqas, for their part, as custodians of the religious values of the countryside and arbiters of what did or did not constitute appropriate behavior on the part of leaderships, controlled by far the most powerful instruments of mass mobilization. As was demonstrated in the first three decades of the nineteenth century and again in the case of ʿAbd al Qadir's resistance to the French, the combination of lineage and baraka could generate passionate loyalties and impressive force. The union of a few powerful families, particularly if it could have included alliance with one or another of the great religious brotherhoods, might have provided the vehicle for Algerians to undercut Turkish rule and substitute a more truly national polity. Yet in the long run, neither jawad nor shuyukh were ever able to mobilize more than a part of the country at once and both were undone by rivalries with competing tribes or orders which prevented ultimate victory.

It is clear that by any acceptable definition of the term, no Algerian nation existed in 1830. Yet sociopolitical evolution was clearly such that, given time, that nation might have emerged from one of several possible formations or combinations of formations. That evolution was brought up short and pointed in different directions by the long years of conquest, colonial implantation, and resistance that followed the French invasion of 1830.

INVASION, RESISTANCE, AND COLONIZATION, 1830–1871

Considering the enthusiasm with which the merchants of Marseille greeted the preparations for the French expedition against Algiers, the invasion of Algeria appears to confirm the thesis that imperialism is the creature of capitalism. But if one looks at the actual mix of historical, class, and conjunctural factors preceding the expedition, the question of causation—at least initial causation—becomes less clear.

Historically, France enjoyed more satisfactory relations with the Regency of Algiers than did the other European powers. As recently as 1816, France had refused to join the squadron of Lord Exmouth of Great Britain that administered a devastating nine-hour bombardment to Algiers in retaliation for Barbary slaveholding. France's resistance to British pressures in this instance had netted her in the very next year the return of the trading concessions at La Calle and Bône that she had forfeited to the English during the war. Subsequently, France's voice was the one voice in the concert of Europe that most consistently counselled moderation when sanctions against the Barbary state were proposed.

With regard to the influence of the capitalists, it should be remembered that it was precisely during these last years of the Restoration that the power of the ultras was peaking and that of the bankers and merchants was the lowest. The wishes of the middle classes—Marseillais or other—simply did not enter into the calculations of the aristocratic ministry that determined upon the expedition.

But a financial problem had nagged for years at Franco-Algerian relations. During the period 1793 to 1798 the Jewish houses of Bushnaq and Bakri had arranged shipments of Algerian grain to the southern French provinces and to Bonaparte's armies in Italy and Egypt. When Franco-Algerian relations were subsequently broken, a debt of 7,000,000 to 8,000,000 francs had not yet been settled. By the time relations were restored at the end of the Napoleonic wars, Bacri, who owed money to the Algerian state, had convinced the Dey he could not make good his debt until the French made good theirs; so a private business disagreement was transformed into an affair of state. Negotiations dragged on for years, partly because of the exaggerated interest claims made by the Algerians and partly because of the reluctance of Restoration ministers to make good on obligations of their republican predecessors, especially when the ethical standards behind some of the original dealings were open to some question.

The persistent difference degenerated into a major crisis on April 29, 1827, when the long-time French consul at Algiers, Pierre Deval, went to pay his respects to Hussein Dey on the occasion of ʿId al Fitr.[1] When the Dey asked why the King of France had not responded to his personal inquiries about the outstanding balance, Deval allegedly responded in words to the effect that His Most Christian Majesty could not lower himself to correspond with the Dey. Losing his customary self-control, Hussein struck the consul three times on the arm with the handle of a peacock-feather fly whisk and ordered him to get out.[2] In the following weeks as news of the surprising confrontation spread among the foreign community and then around the ports of the Mediterranean, the Dey repeatedly explained that his actions were aimed only at the inadmissable conduct of an individual and in no way diminished the high esteem in which he held the King and the nation of France. Nevertheless, a French squadron appeared at Algiers during the second week of June demanding apologies and requiring that the Fleur-de-Lys be flown above the Qasba and honored with a hundred-gun Algerian salute. When the Dey refused these demands, the consul and his staff boarded the ships and the commander of the squadron declared a blockade of Algiers. In retaliation, Hussein ordered the destruction of the French trading posts at Bône and La Calle. These dramatic opening blows were followed by a drawn out stalemate. Since the blockade was only marginally effective, the Dey saw no particular reason to capitulate to the humiliating terms France held out. The costs to France in the meantime were mounting. The size of the squadron was increased from four, to seven, to twelve, and eventually to eighteen ships without for all that its being able totally to guarantee French merchantmen from Algerian retaliation. Shipping was obliged to travel in convoys, insurance rates soared, and the port of Marseille, which was at the moment trying to adjust to the dislocations of the Greek war, found itself plunged into an economic depression.

As the standoff continued through 1827 and into 1828, Charles X's domes-

1. The joyous Muslim feast of Breaking of the Fast, Bairam in Ottoman, which marks the end of the month long fast of Ramadan.
2. The versions of the exchange communicated by Hussein to the Sultan Mahmud II and by Deval to his government differ markedly. Both agree, however, that the conversation ended with the famous "coup d'éventail."

tic power base began to erode. When the elections of November 1827 returned an opposition majority to the Chamber of Deputies, the King agreed to appoint as Prime Minister the moderate vicomte de Martignac. The latter decided in summer 1829 to send a plenipotentiary to Algiers in pursuit of a negotiated settlement. But after the plenipotentiary had delivered an armistice proposal to the Dey and was starting to sail out of Algiers port, batteries opened fire on his flagship. Charles X, who had never trusted moderates anyhow, now fired Martignac and, trampling on the principle of ministerial responsibility, replaced him with the archconservative Prince Jules de Polignac. The outraged parliamentary opposition and the liberal press condemned this exercise in royal absolutism and, in increasingly strident terms, most of the government's other actions, including the futile and expensive Algerian policy.

Polignac shared with others of the generation that had watched Great Britain's grasp on transoceanic empire tighten, the conviction that France's overseas destiny now lay primarily beside the Mediterranean, upon whose shores she was the only great power. While the vision of a French base at Algiers was perfectly consistent with that conviction, he tempered realization of that vision with a caution composed of equal parts financial restraint and respect for British naval superiority. Polignac first pursued a face-saving compromise by trying to convince the Porte to extract concessions from its vassal. When the Sultan pleaded lack of means, he turned to Muhammad ʿAli of Egypt, whose aspirations France increasingly encouraged as a counter to Britain's support of the sultanate. Egyptian forces, aided by a French subsidy and supported by French artillery and naval power, would march across the North African littoral overturning autonomous Ottoman regimes as they went and replacing them with Egyptian rule, which would make various unspecified concessions to its French sponsor. But Muhammad ʿAli ultimately declined the invitation, fearing public reaction to open collusion with the infidels and also the reaction of Britain.

Only when indirect approaches had failed did Polignac begin to heed voices that had for more than a year been counselling direct French assault upon "the nest of pirates." His conversion was hastened by the argument that the alienation of the French public from the monarchy could be overcome by a striking foreign victory such as the conquest of Algiers. To prepare the ground diplomatically, French emissaries, invoking the solidarity of Christian Europe against the latter-day Turkish menace, took steps to assure themselves of the benevolent attitude of all of the major and many of the minor continental powers on the correct assumption that, although the Tory government of the Duke of Wellington might grumble, it would not in such an international climate militarily obstruct a French expedition. In the meantime, the War and Navy Ministries retrieved a contingency plan for the occupation of Algiers devised by Major Boutin during the summer of 1808 and began the preparations for the expedition. Charles X chose the March 2, 1830, inaugural session of Parliament to make the decision official, announcing that "In the midst of the grave events that have preoccupied Europe, I was obliged to suspend the effect of my just resentment against a Barbary power; but I can no longer allow to go unpunished the grave insult to my flag; the resounding redress that I hope to obtain in satisfying the honor of France will with the Almighty's help turn to the profit of Christendom."[3]

When new elections that spring returned a Chamber more solidly anti-royalist than its predecessor, a glorious victory to retrieve the fortunes of the monarchy became all the more urgent. An air of the absurd characterized the polemics that filled the newspaper columns. As open preparations for the expedition progressed in the south of France, the ministry kept repeating that a victory would win over the opposition to the policy of the King, while the same opposition consistently repeated that no matter what the magnitude of the victory they would never be reconciled to such an authoritarian regime. Only Marseille, on this issue oblivious to partisan distinctions, was unanimously and unreservedly supportive of the Algiers expedition.

THE FALL OF ALGIERS

Toward Marseille, Aix, and Toulon converged armies of suppliers and purveyors, specializing in every manner of goods and services the expeditionary force could require. On the docks and in the warehouses accumulated the mountains of stores required to equip and maintain a force that was to include 34,184 fighting men and 3,389 noncombatants in addition to the sailors who were to convey them to Africa. Under the command of the ultraconservative War Minister, Count Louis de Bourmont, the army was composed of three infantry divisions plus field artillery, siege artillery, and cavalry.

As a cheering crowd of onlookers covered the hillsides around the roadstead of Toulon, the fleet of 635 assorted ships hoisted sail on May 25 and heeled off toward Africa. It was the largest naval force assembled by France since the Napoleonic wars. The fleet raised the Algerian coast on May 31, but threatening weather convinced the admiral to retreat to the shelter of Palma de Mallorca, a day's run downwind to the north. It returned on June 12, anchoring the next day twenty-seven kilometers west of Algiers in the shallow harbors created by the promontory of Sidi Ferruch. The spot had been selected by Major Boutin twenty-two years earlier because of the gently rolling land adjacent to the beach and the absence of significant fortifications. At first light on the morning of June 14, the landing began. In the next five days, against limited Algerian fire, the French were able to secure a perimeter, offload their mountains of supplies and equipment, and establish a bustling encampment the size of a city.

Under the command of the Dey's son-in-law, the Agha Ibrahim, the defenders had assembled a heterogeneous force of about 7,000 Turks, 19,000 troops from the Beys of Constantine and Oran, and about 17,000 Kabyles. The Algerian artillery was vastly inferior to that of the French but their rifles

3. As quoted by Charles-André Julien, in vol. 1 of *Histoire de l'Algérie contemporaine*, p. 38.

were of longer range and most Algerians were better marksmen than the French. While testimony on both sides certifies the Algerians' individual valor as fighters, they appear to have been badly supplied and inadequately led. Probably bespeaking poor organization and inadequate logistics rather than the arrogant overconfidence some French writers ascribed to him, Ibrahim's forces directed only moderate fire at the French for six days, allowing Bourmont to consolidate a bridgehead that they could not subsequently reasonably hope to dislodge. By the time the Agha launched a major attack on June 19, the invaders were too well entrenched. They turned back the Muslim charge, went on the attack themselves, and eventually overwhelmed Ibrahim's camp on the plateau of Staouëli, sending the defenders back toward Algiers in disorder.

After considerable delay and confusion, including one commander's mistaking the fog of the Mitidja Valley for the sea, which resulted in troops marching west rather than east, the French began their advance on Algiers. On June 29, they reached the plateau of El-Biar overlooking the Sultan Kalassi (Fort l'Empereur), the principal work guarding the western approach to the city. On July 4, after five hours of artillery bombardment, the defending Turks evacuated that crumbling fort and blew up what remained of it.

The expeditionary force had come to Africa with a large supply of proclamations in Arabic reassuring the inhabitants that the French were come to liberate the people of Algeria from the tyranny of the Turks. But numerous reports, mostly true, of French cruelty and destructiveness made the population of the city skeptical. When the defenses collapsed, panic filled the streets as thousands of citizens fled the city by boat or by land to the south and east. When a delegation of Moors went to learn the victors' terms, Bourmont personally dictated the convention of capitulation which was signed the next morning by the last Ottoman Pasha:

> The fort of the Casauba [*sic*], all the other forts belonging to Algiers, and the port of that city will be delivered to the French troops at 10:00 this morning French time.
>
> The General in Chief of the French Army pledges to His Highness the Dey to allow him the freedom and possession of all his personal property.
>
> The Dey will be at liberty to retire with his family and his personal property to whatever place he determines; and as long as he remains in Algiers he and his family shall remain under the protection of the General in Chief of the French Army. A guard will guarantee his security and that of his family.
>
> The General in Chief guarantees to all the soldiers of the militia the same advantage and the same protection.
>
> The exercise of the Muslim religion shall be free. The liberty of the inhabitants of all classes, their religion, their property, their business and their industry shall remain inviolable. Their women shall be respected.
>
> The General in Chief makes this engagement on his honor.[4]

4. France, Ministère de la Guerre, *Collection des actes du gouvernement depuis l'occupation d'Alger jusqu'au 1er octobre 1834* (Paris: 1843), pp. 1–2.

The convention actually went into effect at noon on July 5, 1830, when the white flag of the House of Bourbon was raised above the Qasba. But its guarantees were meaningless. Before the day was over, rampaging French soldiers, including numerous officers, had violated persons, property, and holy places many times over and had left much of the city in a shambles. On July 10, the Dey and his family departed for Naples with only 30,000 gold sequins out of their enormous personal wealth. Unmarried Janissary soldiers were repatriated to Turkey during the same week. On August 16, the rest of the Turkish establishment was summarily deported with little opportunity to liquify and export their assets. The fact that the deportations were encouraged by Moorish elements hopeful of replacing their erstwhile superiors does not make the Count de Bourmont's casual attitude toward his commitments look better.

The issue of French treatment of the natives at the beginning of their occupation is worth dwelling upon, because it foreshadows a pattern of relations between victors and vanquished that was to make discourse between the two peoples difficult at best. The physical violence and usurpation of property with which the era began continued for many years, gradually giving way to institutionalized forms of violence and usurpation which even in the later years could be reinforced by the former means when the colonials felt threatened. A parliamentary commission of inquiry sent to Algeria in the fall of 1833 to gather facts and make recommendations concerning the future of the territories wrote:

> We have sent to their deaths on simple suspicion and without trial people whose guilt was always doubtful and then despoiled their heirs. We massacred people carrying [our] safe conducts, slaughtered on suspicion entire populations subsequently found to be innocent; we have put on trial men considered saints by the country, men revered because they had enough courage to expose themselves to our fury so that they could intervene on behalf of their unfortunate compatriots; judges were found to condemn them and civilized men to execute them. We have thrown into prison chiefs of tribes for offering hospitality to our deserters; we have rewarded treason in the name of negotiation, and termed diplomatic action odious acts of entrapment.[5]

The report vigorously condemned the transformation of mosques into barracks, the occupation of buildings without indemnity, the seizure of *habous* (*waqf*, or religious endowment property), and the destruction of cemeteries "in contempt of a solemn capitulation and the most fundamental and natural of the rights of people. In a word, we have outdone in barbarity the barbarians we

5. *Procès verbaux et rapports de la Commission nommée par le Roi, le 7 juillet 1833, pour aller recueillir en Afrique tous les faits propres à éclairer le Gouvernement sur l'état du pays et sur les mesures que réclame son avenir* (Paris: 1834), vol. 1, pp. 333–34.

have come to civilize and complain about our lack of success with them."[6] Concurrently, colonial apologetics was justifying *l'oeuvre française* on the grounds that it was liberating the natives from the hold of an obscurantist worldview and offering them the advantages of a superior civilization. Few Algerians comprehended the argument.

EXTENSION OF THE CONQUEST

By the 1870s, Algeria had been transformed into what is still considered the archetype of a settler colonial regime, an outcome that resulted not from preplanning by the constituted political leadership of France but, rather, from a painful forty-year process of interaction among metropolitan France, European *colons,* and the native population. While in retrospect the victory of the settlers appears the most logical outcome to this dialectical process, their victory was attained only after years of tenacious Algerian resistance, efforts by the army and the home government to limit them, and wide swings in national policy.

The greatest policy uncertainty characterized the first four years of the French occupation. News of Bourmont's victory at Algiers reached Paris just after parliamentary elections had returned another large antigovernment majority to the Chamber. On July 25, Polignac invalidated the vote and called for new elections under restrictive new rules designed to reverse the outcome. This interference in the constitutional process sparked the three-day revolution that ended the Restoration and propelled the liberal Louis-Philippe to the throne. Consistent with the calculation of the Prince de Polignac and his advisors, the majority of the French public had been delighted by news of the conquest of Algiers, but contrary to their calculations, their approval was insufficient to save the regime.

By August 1, power devolved upon a ministry most of whose members had been loudly condemning Polignac's North African project for months. Shorn overnight of its partisan political connotations, the real issues connected to the Algerian adventure now stood out with greater clarity. There were many negatives. Besides its worries about the expense of continuing occupation, the July Monarchy was uneasy both about leaving so many troops overseas during a time of rising European tensions and about the occupation's negative impact on Great Britain, whose goodwill it needed during the mounting Belgian crisis. Moreover, liberal economists, well represented in the new government, believed mercantilist colonial arrangements to be economically counterproductive. For these reasons astute observers during the fall of 1830 considered evacuation of Algiers to be imminent. They were wrong. To save money, the ministry did order the withdrawal of a portion of the expeditionary force. But to many ministers it seemed poor domestic politics to

6. Ibid.

jettison the fruits of a widely popular victory; it also seemed risky foreign policy, now that the Turks had been expelled, to leave a political vacuum south of the Mediterranean. For the next four years, an uncomfortable and divided government temporized.

In the absence of an official Algeria policy, facts were created on the ground; ad hoc policies established by commanding generals or their subordinates, or imposed by the logic of events, limited more narrowly every year France's real options. An even more important limiting factor that emerged during the four years of temporizing was a burgeoning Algeria constituency. In that time the original Marseille interest was significantly reinforced by an on-site constituency composed of new property owners, speculators, would-be settlers, merchants, military officers and civil administrators, all of whose interests in different ways depended upon retention of the conquest.

French troops looted the Qasba on the afternoon Algiers fell, diverting more than half of its 100,000,000 francs of public treasure to private hands. This rampage and the uncontrolled pillaging of private properties in and around Algiers were early signs of the great importance the pursuit of personal gain would have in the calculus of France's Algeria policy. But more tangibly it was the transfer of real property to Europeans that contributed the most to creation of an Algeria constituency. As the Regency collapsed, and thousands of Algerines fled or were driven into exile, their unprotected houses, shops, and country estates were summarily occupied by others or sold off at ridiculously low prices, often changing hands many times in a short period. Within days, word of the bargains available across the water spread north of the Mediterranean, and a horde of fortune hunters joined the military and civil cadres and the suppliers already in place. The first colonial decree of sequestration targeted at properties of absentee owners was promulgated in September 1830. Theoretically, this and subsequent sequestration measures aimed at extending government protection to properties until ultimate resolution of claims could be made. In 1834, the War Minister ordered the drafting of procedures to return properties irregularly or unfairly seized by the state, but attempts to draft those procedures floundered time and again, because the majority of sequestered properties had in fact fallen into the hands of individual Europeans little inclined to give them up and whose influence at Algiers had already become enormous.

Early impetus to acquisition of rural land was provided by Count Bertrand Clauzel, the second Commanding General, who replaced the legitimist Bourmont on September 2, 1830. In many ways a man of the eighteenth century, Clauzel saw Algeria replacing France's lost new-world empire as a source of exotic commodities, and he became a vigorous proponent of active settlement in Algeria. He established a *Ferme Modèle* a few miles southeast of Algiers on which he encouraged soldiers to settle. While this project was ultimately unsuccessful, Clauzel acquired for his own account three rural properties in the region, thereby helping to trigger a land rush that saw Europeans buying and selling agricultural lands at a feverish pace. Many of these lands were not mulk and therefore not legally alienable under existing law; many lay beyond the perimeters of French occupation. But these technicalities did not halt the land rush.

After four years the French zone of occupation was confined in the center to Algiers and a very small hinterland, in the east to Bône and Bougie, and in the west to Oran, Arzew, and Mostaganem. At Algiers and Bône during the early years, the occupiers associated the local merchant classes with the city administration. In Oran they worked for a time through Turks who remained, while in Mostaganem they depended principally upon the Kouloughli aristocracy. Over more than 90 percent of the country, however, the French did not rule at all. Their economic and security interests required the creation of mechanisms for relating this vast interior to their enclaves. The most logical solution was to persuade the beys to accept French sovereignty in replacement of the Turkish.

Soon after the collapse of Ibrahim's army, Moustapha Bou Mezrag, Bey of Titteri, agreed to become the vassal of France, but when he realized Bourmont was not respecting the guarantees of the Capitulation, he renounced the agreement. Subsequent French efforts to install surrogates in this Beylik and the former Dar al-Sultan, which had traditionally been most closely controlled by the deys, met with some temporary but no permanent success. In the other Beyliks as well, efforts to locate Algerians of stature willing to accept a tributary relationship to the infidel proved extraordinarily difficult, and those agreements actually cut were characteristically unstable. The aged Hasan Bey of Oran did accept French suzerainty, but many powerful tribes around him rejected his leadership in the matter. Ahmad Bey of Constantine, who along with Bou Mezrag had fought the French at Staouëli, categorically rejected inclusion in the emerging new order.

In a search for alternative leaderships, Count Clauzel concluded agreements with Hussein Bey of Tunis under which the latter would supply beys from the Tunisian ruling family to govern both Constantine and Oran. The arrangements collapsed partly because the Bey of Tunis came to understand that his representatives would be more dependent on France than on himself and partly because the government at Paris ultimately vetoed their Commanding General's initiative.

In the fall of 1833, the parliamentary commission conducted its exhaustive on-site investigation into the Algerian problem. In its report the commission observed that the first three years of French occupation had been marked mostly by failure—administratively, economically, and in both native policy and settler policy. It decided with singular lack of enthusiasm, however, that because of public opinion and for reasons of national prestige, France should stay on in its newly acquired territory. Behind the prestige question, of course, was the specter of Great Britain, which from Malta and Gibraltar was offering moral and some material support to elements of the Algerian resistance. The commission believed, however, that any permanent French establishment in

Algeria should be accompanied by a complete overhaul and rationalization of the colony's administration and by measures to make it economically self-sufficient. The Chamber of Deputies, after six tumultuous sessions of debate on the report that pitted colonialists against anticolonialists, found itself unable either to accept or reject the recommendations.[7] Ultimately it was the War Minister, Soult, Duc de Dalmatie, who resolved the deadlock by drafting for Louis-Philippe's signature the Royal Ordinance of 22 July 1834, recognized as the "birth certificate" of French Algeria. This decree created a military colony named "les possessions françaises dans le Nord de l'Afrique," placed under the authority of the Ministry of War. A Royal Ordinance of 1838 changed the official name to the newly coined "Algérie." The War Minister was represented in the colony by a Governor General invested with both civil and military authority. While the Governor General was assisted by civil intendants and an Administrative Council, an enabling decree of 1 September 1834 provided that legislation until further order was to be by Royal Ordinance, drafted by the War Minister upon recommendation of the Governor General. This measure conferred upon Algeria a regime of legislation by executive decree totally at odds with French public law, which recognizes the principle of separation of powers but which in attenuated form survived until 1946.

The question of the precise boundaries of the French Possessions was not resolved in 1834. Instead the politically expedient notion of "limited occupation," generally confining direct rule to areas on or near the coast of greatest commercial and strategic interest to France, became official policy down until 1840. Concurrently, however, the state for the first time officially encouraged colonial settlement—as a means of making the colony more secure and especially of making it pay its own way. Since many Europeans had already acquired interest in lands beyond the French enclaves and would continue to do so, such a policy unfailingly favored expansion of the zones of occupation, inviting continuing native resistance and French countermeasures. Such dynamics clearly doomed from its inception the concept of limited occupation.

Major Boutin, during his clandestine reconnaissance of 1808, came to the conclusion that Arab and Berber distaste for the Turkish regime was such that if the French scrupulously respected the Algerians' religion, their women, and their property, they would be able to occupy the coast with little effort and penetrate the interior peacefully. Emerging French colonial theory of the late 1830s and the 1840s invoked in vague terms the need to "assimilate" the natives by demonstrating to them the advantages of France's superior form of civilization. Both scenarios beg many questions, including whether Algerians would have tolerated non-Muslim rule under any conditions and whether the resource extraction implicit in any kind of colonial presence would not unfailingly generate serious opposition. In the event, the conduct of the Army of

7. There were actually two *Commissions d'Afrique*. The travelling commission's report was delivered to a broader commission in Paris, which included peers and others. It was this second commission that took up the bulk of the report and transmitted it to the Parliament.

Africa and the accelerating *colon* drive to appropriate lands left the underlying conditions of the Boutin scenario unfulfilled.

THE EARLY RESISTANCE AND AHMAD BEY

When the Dey of Algiers capitulated, organization of Algeria's defense devolved upon the Algerians themselves. As early as July 23, 1830, a council of tribal leaders and marabouts met at Tementfous near Cape Matifou to concert resistance in the Algiers area. While French forces in the central zone succeeded more than once in penetrating to key cities like Blida and Médéa, the resistance was such that they were never able to stay or even to maintain their native surrogates in the early years for more than brief periods. Resistance from the tribesmen around Bône kept the occupation so constrained that the place was twice evacuated before its permanent occupation in March 1832. The ferocity and persistence of resistance were such that no region of the country failed to generate a rich store of heroic and sacrificial acts with which to inspire the collective memory for generations to come. During the era of conquest, 1830 to 1871, only the year 1861 passed without major armed resistance in one part of the country or another. Given the geographic dispersion of the population, the segmentation of Algerian society, the hierarchical ordering of many tribal systems, and the centuries long Ottoman policy of pitting tribes against each other, construction of common and durable fronts was difficult, however. Not all traditional tribal conflicts could be muted. Many makhzan tribes, like the powerful Douira and Zmala of the Oranie who were reluctant to forego their traditional privileges, agreed to serve the French as they had the Turks before them. Organized religion, which provided the most potent and universal rallying point for opposition, was rendered less effective than it could have been by the competition amongst powerful brotherhoods and their leaderships.

During the early years, two movements made significant progress in overcoming such divisions and uniting disparate social elements in their resistance. That of ᶜAbd al Qadir, who became the greatest Algerian national hero, commanded the loyalty of most of the populations of western and central Algeria by the late 1830s. Even before ᶜAbd al Qadir entered the scene, Ahmad Bey had extended his authority over much of the Beylik of Constantine and blocked French expansion there until 1837.

Ahmad ibn Muhammad of Constantine was born about 1784 of the union of an Ottoman father and a mother from the powerful Ben Ghana tribe of the Pre-Sahara. As a young man he made the pilgrimage to Mecca and lived for a period in Egypt observing the reforms Muhammad ᶜAli was implementing there. Born to privilege, he apprenticed in several important beylical offices before rising in 1826 to the office of bey. In 1830, he led Constantinian contingents at the battle of Saouëli, but when the Dey was defeated, he

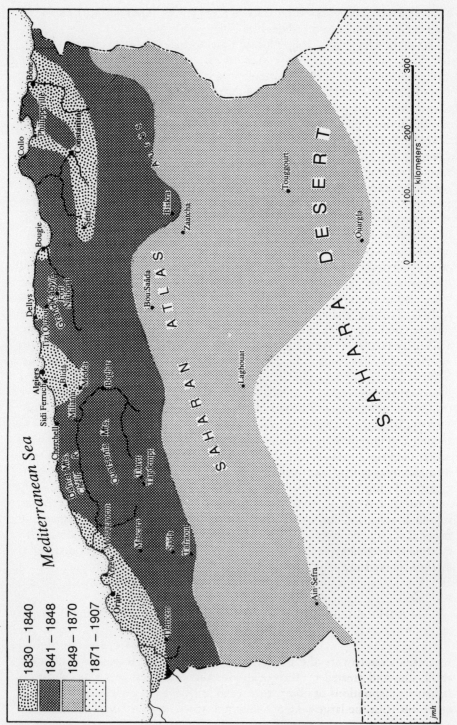

MAP 4 The Stages of French Conquest

1830 – 1840
1841 – 1848
1849 – 1870
1871 – 1907

Mediterranean Sea

Bone
Collo
Philippeville
Bougie
Dellys
Algiers
Sidi Ferruch
Cherchell
Tizi Ouzou
Grand Kabylie
Fort National
Miliana
Blida
Médéa
Boghar
Orléansville
Mascara
Ténès
Mostaganem
Tiaret
Tiaret
Tagdempt
Dhra Mts
Ouarsenis Mts
Oran
Saïda
Tlemcen
Tafraoui

Sétif

ATLAS

Biskra
Zaaicha
Bou Saäda
Laghouat
Aïn Sefra

SAHARAN ATLAS

SAHARA DESERT

Touggourt
Ouargla

kilometers
0   100   200   300

jmh

returned to mobilize his home province, which he was determined to keep from suffering the fate of Algiers.

With the Dey gone, Hajj Ahmad now considered his authority to flow directly from Ottoman Sultan Mahmud II, with whom he was in steady communication. If the Constantinois was still part of the Ottoman Empire, however, it was an Arab province of that Empire and thus entitled to its own administrative and institutional structures. He made Arabic the first language of his administration, abolished the Ottoman system of government, and created a council of provincial notables invested with legislative and executive authority. Considering himself but one Muslim among others, he appears to have given considerable authority to the council and frequently to have followed its preferences. His reaching out to local elites, his substitution of local zouaves for the tyrannical Janissaries, and his attempts to implement a more equitable and Islamically based fiscal order, clearly mark this aristocratic ruler as a reformer if not a revolutionary. With all of the changes, however, Hajj Ahmad's power was based fundamentally upon his connections with a number of great families of the province: the Ben Ghana, the Muqranis, the Awlad Achour, and the Awlad Azzedin, for example. The very successes of a system based on the interconnections of the leading jawad alienated competing tribes, particularly those lower in the power structure. Some members of these tribes took refuge with the French at Algiers, while others in the coastal regions and the Pre-Sahara kept whole regions perennially beyond the effective control of the Bey.

The French invaders, determined to occupy Bône at a minimum and showing increasing interest in other coastal points as well, made several attempts to negotiate a settlement with the Bey. Because Ahmad Bey considered the lands he administered Ottoman territory held in trust, however, he was unwilling to enter any agreement ceding territory to France or recognizing its suzerainty in any form. This uncompromising stand made him the most formidable early opponent the French had to deal with. Exasperated, Count Clauzel, during his second North African tour in 1836, sent a force of 8,700 men to take Ahmad's capital and break the resistance in the east. Badly supplied, weakened by illness, pelted by November rains, and harassed by tribes along the route, the French forces failed to dent the defenses of Constantine and retreated in ignominy, suffering the loss of a thousand men. This victory marked the high point of the Ahmad Bey's career.

ᶜABD AL QADIR AND THE INDEPENDENT ALGERIAN STATE

In the western part of the country there was no comparable elite network to fill the void created by the collapse of the Turkish system. Lacking such structures, aspirations of competing tribal leaderships would only cancel each other out. But the large religious brotherhoods had demonstrated repeatedly in recent years their capacity to mobilize the dispersed energies of this predominantly pastoralist region.

ᶜAbd al Qadir of the Hashim Gharaba tribe was born on September 26, 1807, near Mascara in the village of Guetna Oued el-Hammam, which was the headquarters of the Qadiriyya tariqa. His father Muhi al-Din, was the venerated *muqaddam* of the Maghribi branch of that order and claimed an illustrious lineage through Idriss, the eighth-century founder of Fez, to Hasan, the elder grandson of the Prophet. Known even as a child for his strong physique and excellent horsemanship, ᶜAbd al Qadir received an education the quality and breadth of which were unusual in Oran Province in the early nineteenth century. Studying Qur'an, Arabic grammar, Islamic jurisprudence, and theology at the Qadiriyya zawiya with its 800-volume library, the young marabout was also tutored in the essentials of mathematics, astronomy, and geography. Later he attended for almost a year an elite school in Oran, and still later, after he and his father had made the canonical pilgrimage to Mecca, ᶜAbd al-Qadir attended lectures at Damascus, Cairo, and Baghdad.

While the Qadiriyya leadership do not appear to have played prominent roles in the brotherhood-led revolts of the first part of the century, the Banu Hashim during the 1820s became associated with an anti-Turkish coalition inspired by Muhammad al-Kabir, the Moroccan-based head of the Tijaniyya. This relationship, plus the fact that the zawiya at Guetna was a sanctuary which sheltered large numbers of fugitives from Turkish justice, made the provincial leadership more than a little suspicious of Muhi al-Din and his son. Hasan Bey actually kept the two under house arrest at Oran for two years. Then, in 1826, he permitted them to depart for Mecca, which kept them out of his way for an additional two years. The return of the two marabouts to Guetna in 1828, shortly after a failed Tijaniyya attack on the Turkish garrison at Mascara, was the occasion of such spontaneous joy and widespread celebration that they made a conscious decision to lower their profiles by devoting themselves almost exclusively for the next years to the studious and contemplative life. Even though the careful maneuvering of the Bey neutralized the direct impact Muhi al-Din could have on the political situation, it is clear that both father and son during the 1820s personified the anti-Turkish sentiment of significant elements in the society of far-western Algeria. In fact, their influence only increased with their growing reputation for sanctity—enhanced even by their seclusion—and as apocryphal stories came to be circulated about the younger man.

With the defeat of the Dey, Mawlay ᶜAbd al-Rahman, the Sultan of Morocco, initiated measures to recover Tlemcen and other portions of western Algeria to which his dynasty still laid claims going back to the Middle Ages. When active French diplomacy at Meknès convinced him that direct pursuit of these goals was at the moment imprudent, the Sultan appointed the soundly anti-Ottoman Muhi al-Din to serve as his khalifa at Tlemcen. With the mandate of the Sultan of the West in hand, Muhi al-Din launched a campaign to liquidate the still considerable remains of the Ottoman power structure in the Beylik. These vestiges included a substantial Kouloughli military presence at Tlemcen, which he blockaded in the citadel of that city, and the powerful Douaïr and Zmala makhzan tribes now serving the French at Oran. It appears to have been only gradually that the leaderships in the interior of Oran province became aware of the serious threat posed by the French on the coast. This lag in perception is probably related to the fact that Muslims, who had accustomed themselves for centuries to living with Oran or Melilia in nearby Morocco in Spanish hands,[8] could not initially make the distinction between the weakened, status quo imperialism of Spain and the aggressive, capital-rich imperialism of France. But concern did grow. In April 1832, Muhi al-Din accepted from an assembly of notables at Mascara the position of leader of the jihad, and from this point on the struggle against the elements still clinging to their Ottoman era privileges merged with the struggle against the French.

From April to November 1832, Muhi al-Din's forces launched attacks on the French garrison at Oran and upon their makhzan allies. Although these operations succeeded in dislodging neither, they did provide numerous opportunities for ʿAbd al Qadir to demonstrate his leadership abilities and his personal valor. By November, when Muhi al-Din, pleading advancing age and infirmity, asked to be relieved of his responsibilities, an assembly of tribal notables chose the twenty-five-year-old sharif to replace his father as leader of the jihad, conferring upon him the historic religious title of Amir al-Mu'minin (Commander of the Faithful) and the ancillary title of Khalifa of the Sultan.

Raised to his position by the election of a few tribes around Mascara, the Amir had in seven years extended his authority over more than two-thirds of Algeria. By launching a movement which blended defense against the infidel with opposition to the privileged remnants of the Ottoman system, some of which now served the French, ʿAbd al-Qadir was able during 1833 to win the loyalty of the majority of towns and tribes of the Chélif Valley. In so doing he denied the French garrisons at Oran, Mostaganem, and Arzew access to auxiliaries and reliable sources of supply, rendering their position increasingly untenable. This dangerous situation convinced the Oran Commanding General, Baron Louis-Alexis Desmichels, to seek an accommodation with this new enemy. The result was the Desmichels Treaty of February 1834, in which the Amir, in return for freeing French prisoners and recognizing French rule over their three enclaves and their right to trade in his domain, won recognition of his own sovereignty over the rest of the province from the Moroccan frontier to at least Miliana and the headwaters of the Chélif.[9] The French government thought the Baron had conceded far too much on the issue of sovereignty, but they were not in 1834 in position to question the fait accompli. On the issue of territory, a French construction of the agreement assumed any lands conceded

8. Oran was under Spanish rule from 1509 to 1792. Spaniards occupied Melilia in northeastern Morocco in 1497 and still do at this writing.

9. Neither the Governor General nor the government at Paris knew about this treaty before it was signed, and they wanted all such agreements to include Algerian recognition of French suzerainty by requiring payment of tribute. This treaty contained no such provisions. On the other hand, by recognizing ʿAbd al Qadir's title, his right to issue visas to Frenchmen travelling his territory, and his right to appoint what the Arabic version called consuls *(qunasil)* to the French-held towns, the document clearly recognized the Amir's sovereignty. A secret addendum whose text became available only in 1964 makes this fact even clearer.

lay in Oran Province, over which Desmichels had command; but such a reading was not evident to the Amir, who before long was projecting his authority into Titteri, the western portions of Dar al-Sultan, and to the edges of the Constantinois.

Between late 1832 and late 1839, when the uneasy peace between the two parties was broken for good, ᶜAbd al Qadir laid foundations of a truly Algerian state. Determined as this deeply religious leader was to build an independent state on Islamic principles, he was sufficiently pragmatic to understand the necessity of accepting French presence in the coastal enclaves and even of defending those interests against threats from more militant compatriots if this were the price for constructing his state on the bulk of Algerian territory. Such pragmatism may have flowed naturally out of his region's experience of accommodating Spanish presidios. It was a disposition mostly absent, at any rate, in a Constantinian such as Ahmad Bey.

Given the textual ambiguities of the Desmichels Treaty and its essential inconsistency with the emerging imperial vision of the French, it is not surprising that peace between them and the Arabs was fragile. The French were gratified at the Amir's crushing of the Darqawi brethren who were calling for renewed jihad, at his reining in of potentially hostile tribes, and at his facilitation of supply to the French enclaves. They were disturbed, however, by his installation of a khalifa at Médéa, by his support of the resistance of the Hadjoute tribe of the western Mitidja, and especially by his insistence, pursuant to the secret addendum of the Desmichels Treaty, on a trading monopoly in western Algeria. In 1835, when a new commander of the Oranie sent a 2,000-man column to punish him, ᶜAbd al Qadir defeated it resoundingly at the swamps of the Macta. Count Clauzel returned to the attack that winter, sending columns throughout Oran Province which seized and burnt several key cities, including the Amir's capital at Mascara. Because the Algerian continued to hold the countryside and could ambush the Europeans almost at will, however, the main effect of these campaigns was to leave French forces isolated amidst populations made more hostile than ever by the destructiveness of their punitive measures.

Clauzel's stunning defeat before Constantine, in November 1836, not only ended his career as Governor General but also convinced the War Minister of the folly of trying to fight all the Algerians at once. Lieutenant General Thomas Robert Bugeaud, whose name would one day crown the hagiography of colonial Algeria, was authorized to enter new negotiations with the Amir, which eventuated in the Treaty of the Tafna concluded on May 20, 1837. In addition to the bulk of the Oranie, the new agreement explicitly conceded to the Amir for the first time most of central Algeria, leaving to France in this region only Algiers and the Sahel and part of the Mitidja Valley to its south and west. The border of the French zone southeast of Algiers was less clearly drawn.

At peace with the French once again, the Amir moved rapidly to consolidate his hold over the area allotted to him. After defeating dissidents on the

Plain of Angad near the Moroccan frontier, he confronted and won over a powerful tribal coalition in southern Titteri, moved southeastward into the desert as far as Bou Saada, and then began establishing his authority northward in the Sebaou region of eastern Titteri and in the western Constantinois. By 1838, even Biskra had accepted his rule. The most steadfast Algerian opposition to ʿAbd al-Qadir's unification drive came from the populations of the Grand Kabylia and from the leaderships of the competing religious brotherhoods. After defeating Hajj Musa, of the Darqawa, he laid siege to the Tijaniyya headquarters at ʿAyn Madhi, which he captured after a six-month siege. The stubbornly independent Kabyle mountaineers were never won over in significant numbers, however. The embittered Tijani leadership subsequently called upon Algerians to rally to French rule.

In the meantime, with ʿAbd al Qadir neutralized, the French army could move forward with confidence to avenge the previous fall's humiliation before Constantine. After Ahmad Bey rejected another request to recognize French sovereignty, Clauzel's successor, Charles-Marie comte de Damrémont, mounted the second campaign against Constantine. After an eight-day siege that included four days of artillery bombardment followed by bitter house to house fighting, the city fell to the Europeans. Even after their victory, the French continued attempts to co-opt Ahmad, proposing to restore his beylicate, his capital city, and his army in return for a tribute of 100,000 francs per year. The former Bey rejected the compromise, and he spent the next eleven years as a fugitive and guerrilla harassing the invaders from the southern reaches of the province and the Sahara. He finally surrendered in 1848 and died two years later at Algiers. Unable to find an Algerian of stature willing to govern the whole of the Constantinois on their behalf, the French entered into quasi-feudal arrangements with a series of powerful tribal leaders, who, left on their own with little monitoring from above, frequently imposed such regressive and exploitative conditions upon the local peasantries that the province entered a period of progressive impoverishment.

The willingness of Amir ʿAbd al Qadir to make peace with the French at the very moment they were openly preparing the renewed campaign against Constantine represents the single most troubling aspect of his heroic career. It is the most outstanding example of the difficulties Algerians encountered in building unity after three centuries in which government stability had depended precisely upon the exploitation of society's divisions. It is clear that the personal political ambitions of Ahmad Bey and ʿAbd al Qadir stood in direct conflict with each other. In 1833, Ahmad and the notables of Constantine had petitioned Mahmud II to name him pasha of all Algeria in replacement of Hussein Dey. In 1835, a year after the Amir concluded his treaty with Baron Desmichels and terminated the jihad, Ahmad signed letters urging the marabout Musa ibn ʿAli ibn al-Husayn to lead a new jihad in ʿAbd al-Qadir's territory. It is evident from the language of the Tafna treaty and other documents, however, that ʿAbd al Qadir believed all Algerians outside the French enclaves were to be subject to his rule alone. But if personal ambition counted, it is probably less important than background and ideology in explaining the conflict. The two men represented radically different views of how post-Ottoman Algeria should be structured. While Ahmad Bey stood for the persistence in reformed style of a hierarchical system dominated by the old aristocracies of blood, ᶜAbd al Qadir stood for a more egalitarian system rooted uniquely in Algerian society and based more explicitly upon Islamic principles of justice and equity.[10]

In the seven years between his rise and the outbreak of the final war with France, ᶜAbd al Qadir laid the bases of what might have become, given sufficient resources and time, a thoroughly reformed Algerian state. By abolishing the fiscal and command privileges of the makhzan tribes as well as the kharaj tax paid mainly by subject tribes, he made himself the hero of the rayat majority and established the foundation for a far greater unity of the body politic than was conceivable under the Ottoman system. While he continued to appoint socially or politically prominent individuals to key positions, showing a marked preference for religious elites, he nevertheless selected his officials from a far wider range of tribal, urban, and religious elites than under the previous regime.

Using the traditional but more or less representative format of a council of notables as a starting point, the Amir set about creating a more centralized and responsive system of government to parallel his more unified view of society. This system included a paid central bureaucracy and a subdivision of the country into eight khalifaliks of roughly comparable size, all of which were subject to the same law and were expected to follow the same administrative procedures. The territorially based khalifaliks were subdivided into mostly tribally based aghaliks. Because his authority was religious as well as civil, ᶜAbd al Qadir directly appointed the qadis and could achieve a more uniform and responsive judicial system than the Turks had enjoyed.

Given the twin imperatives of defense against the French and repression of internal opposition, the main focus of the Amir's governmental as well as economic initiatives was the creation and maintenance of a reliable military force. The heart of his army was a paid professional corps of about 9,500 men, composed mostly of infantry along with some artillery. Khalifas maintained local professional contingents that the Amir could call to his own service when needed and were also required to raise self-armed militias, often *mujahidin,* in time of emergency. While it is almost impossible to know how big ᶜAbd al-Qadir's army ultimately became, a knowledgeable French observer estimated it at 50,000 in the late thirties.

Like Muhammad ᶜAli of Egypt, whose accomplishments may have provided a model, the Amir attempted to stimulate economic development with the primary aim of strengthening his military capacity. Although his accom-

10. Most Algerian historians do not discuss at length the impact of the Tafna Treaty on the fate of Constantine and the unity of Algerian resistance. One of the more interesting discussions is contained in the work of the Tunisian historian Abdeljelil Temimi, *Le Beylik de Constantine et Hadj 'Ahmad Bey (1830–1837),* pp. 184–90.

plishments were modest, they were not inconsiderable given the short amount of time allotted to him. In the agricultural sector, suppression of the kharaj, a policy of increasing the grain reserves, and active cultivation of foreign grain markets all stimulated grain production, which by the 1840s was considerably greater than in the recent past. Industrially, he founded sawmills, tanneries, and especially industries related to arms manufacture. The latter included foundries, forges, a cannon factory, and a small arms industry, all on a modest scale. After Clauzel sacked and burned Mascara and other towns in 1836, ʿAbd al Qadir determined to transfer his industrial development to a series of fortified new towns in the south between the Tell and the High Plains. These towns included Boghar, Taza, Saïda, Qalʿaa, Tafraout, and Tagdempt. The most important city was the last, founded southwest of historic Tahert, which, after the burning of Mascara, became the new capital. In an excellent location astride important trade routes, it contained by 1840 a still rather primitively housed population of 2,000, a mint, an arms factory, and a large supply depot storing powder, iron, lead, silver, and ammunition in addition to major food reserves.

It is clear that the capture of Constantine marked the beginning of the French shift away from the policy of restricted occupation. One element of that shift was abandonment of the attempt to rule the province through a single autonomous prince and appointment instead of a series of tribal shaykhs. The other was the necessity of assuring unimpeded land communication between Algiers and the newly occupied city of Constantine. The Tafna Treaty had left the eastern boundary of France's Algiers enclave unclear, however, and ʿAbd al Qadir had extended his authority into regions occupation troops would have to cross in order to travel to Constantine.[11] After attempting and failing to get a modified convention, the French forced the issue in October and November 1839 by sending a force headed by the Crown Prince on a fateful march from Constantine through the disputed territory to Algiers. ʿAbd al Qadir and his advisors, who had seen the break coming, had been collecting arms and making other preparations for months. Now the Amir issued a formal declaration of jihad and on November 20 Arab irregulars descended on French farms in the Mitidja Valley, destroying in a few days the settlement efforts of several years and sending those colons fortunate enough to survive fleeing back to Algiers in panic. It was now clear that the policy of restricted occupation—never, as we have contended, a realistic option—had reached the end of its road. France must evacuate the country or subjugate it completely.

While the politicians in Paris grappled with this hard and expensive reality, ʿAbd al Qadir, with his people more solidly behind him than ever before, was

11. Article 2 of the Treaty of the Tafna placed the eastern border of French holdings in Algiers Province at the "Wadi Khadra and beyond," a confusing and ungrammatical construction which took away the boundary with one word that it had created two words previously. The French text reads "bornée à l'est jusqu'à l'Oued-Kaddara, et au delà." The Arabic text, which ʿAbd al-Qadir signed, reads "min jihat al sharq lihadd wad khadra ila qaddam."

everywhere on the offensive and, by March 1840, had reached the apogée of his power. Governor General Sylvain Charles comte Valée, receiving much needed reinforcements, succeeded subsequently in establishing garrisons in towns like Cherchel, Miliana, and Médéa, as well as at several other key points; but as the individual garrisons were small and mostly isolated from a countryside firmly under the Amir's control, 1840 ended with the two sides in a stalemate.

At this point General, later Marshal, Bugeaud reentered the scene. While Paris was not particularly pleased with his abrasive personality or reactionary politics, he submitted the only plan that appeared likely to break the stalemate, and he was appointed Governor General in November 1840. His tactics included placing at a few key strong points six contingents of 7,000 men, whose mission it was to sweep through ᶜAbd al Qadir's realm, destroying his own strong points first and then laying waste the countryside. Crops were to be burned or hauled away, stock slaughtered or driven off, and Arabs forbidden to sow or to herd. It was total war, which depended for its effectiveness more upon destituting and starving noncombatant populations than on battlefield results per se. In at least three cases, populations that fled this scourge to the refuge of caves were burned or asphyxiated there with the permission or acquiescence of Bugeaud. It was an all-out effort which by 1846 saw French effectives in Algeria rise to 108,000, a third of their entire army.

After Tagdempt, Mascara, and most of ᶜAbd al Qadir's towns were occupied during 1841, the Amir created a mobile capital called in Arabic a *zmala*[12] of about 30,000 people, which included his family, administrators, loyal tribesmen, his 5,000 man central army, the treasury, and all his goods and herds. In May 1843, when a small force headed by the duc d'Aumale surprised and defeated the zmala, the populations, already shaken by the systematic devastation to which they were subjected, began to defect en masse, and ᶜAbd al Qadir's painfully built political order disintegrated rapidly. During the second half of 1843, the war deteriorated into a manhunt for ᶜAbd al Qadir, who with his greatly reduced entourage finally crossed the border into Morocco, where ᶜAbd al Rahman granted him asylum.

Using Moroccan soil as a base, the Amir now proceeded to launch raids against French units near the border and consciously to try to internationalize the conflict. Dragged along reluctantly because of ᶜAbd al Qadir's enormous popularity amongst his own subjects, the Sultan permitted more and more Moroccan troops to become involved. This led to a brief Franco-Moroccan war in 1844, which culminated in Bugeaud's crossing the border and annihilating a Moroccan force on the Wadi Isly.[13] Most French observers thought the war was over at this point, but it was actually moving into a new and more violent phase. As organized resistance collapsed and the populations—already bewildered, hungry, and displaced—were faced with both the often ex-

12. Literally family, household.
13. Bugeaud was subsequently raised to the peerage as duc d'Isly; the principal commercial and ceremonial avenue of Algiers was called the rue d'Isly until Algeria regained its independence.

tortionist demands of their military rulers and the mass confiscation of lands for the benefit of colons, the west and center of the country erupted, seemingly spontaneously, into scores of uncoordinated resistance movements. The most notable of these was that of Bou Ma°za, the "Goat Man", who claimed to be the mahdi, or Islamic messiah, come to drive out the infidels. In September 1845, °Abd al-Qadir was able to return to Algeria, score a number of impressive victories against the French, penetrate into Titteri and the Sebaou region, and even briefly to threaten Algiers from the east. Gradually, the French regained control of the situation, however, and by July 1846, the Amir, having suffered serious casualties and being everywhere pursued, returned to his Moroccan refuge. By international agreement after Isly, the Sultan had already declared him outlawed. It was not until 1847, however, that °Abd al Rahman, under pressure from the British (who feared the Amir's presence might give France the pretext to invade and annex Morocco) and fearing the Amir was plotting insurrection in the north of his country, decided to send his troops against him in his border refuge. Caught on the Moulouya River between the Moroccan and the French forces, °Abd al Qadir chose the French. On December 21, 1847, he surrendered to General Louis de Lamoricière, Commander of Oran Province, in return for a safe-conduct permitting him to retire to Alexandria or Acre. The government refused to honor Lamoricière's commitment, however, and transported the Amir instead to France, where he was held prisoner until after the accession of Louis-Napoleon Bonaparte. In October 1852, the Prince-President permitted him to leave for Brusa and settled on him a French pension of 100,000 francs per annum; three years later he settled in Damascus, where he maintained his home for the rest of his life. During the bloody disturbances there in 1860, °Abd al Qadir made an enormously favorable impact on French public opinion by intervening to save the lives of thousands of Syrian Christians. The Emperor demonstrated the nation's gratitude by increasing his pension to 150,000 francs and awarding him the *grand cordon* of the Legion of Honor. Invited to visit Paris in 1865, the former prisoner was received with the greatest official and public respect. °Abd al Qadir died in Damascus at the age of seventy-five on May 26, 1883. His remains were returned to his native land in 1968 after Algeria won its independence.

Throughout the colonial period, the French were at considerable pains to manipulate the legacy of °Abd al Qadir in such a way as to limit its value for Algerian reformers or nationalists. One line of this manipulation focused on what appear to have been the Amir's rather good relations with the French after he left for the Near East: his friendship with Napoleon III, the contention that the resistance leader in his later years believed the French occupation to be beneficial for Algeria, and in particular the claim that he condemned the massive Kabylie insurrection of 1871. Algerian nationalist historiography argues vigorously that the latter contention is either a distortion or complete fraud. Colonial authorities also took steps to assure the loyalty of the Amir's descendants, who from 1892 onward were permitted on a selective basis to return to Algeria. These steps were usually, but not invariably, effective, as will shown in chapter 5.

Struggle over the Amir's legacy was also conducted at the scholarly level. Some of the earliest colonialist writers condemned him as a brutal religious fanatic playing upon the worst instincts of semicivilized populations. A later and broader strain of colonialist treatment saw him as a decent, even heroic, leader who, after failing in his efforts to maintain the independence of a hopelessly backward and "oriental" society, eventually saw the light and rallied to the cause of a "superior" civilization. In the twentieth century, as nationalist historiography began to claim that ʿAbd al Qadir's career and accomplishments were proof either that an Algerian nation existed even before the French invasion or that his state was in fact a nation-state, the ground of the debate shifted. Certain European historians argued that since his authority and appeal were clearly religious and the entity he constructed was based on an Islamic model, he could not possibly be considered a nationalist. Others looked at the single-minded fierceness with which he suppressed internal opposition as proof that the Amir was motivated mainly by a taste for personal power or that he was not much more than a traditional tribal shaykh fighting much as his ancestors had for generations for the advantage of his own group.

It is clear that western political theory that insists on the secularism of the nationalist model is of little value in understanding the integrative dynamic in a historically fragmented social order where religious identity supplies the most important unifying element. Even though the basis of ʿAbd al Qadir's authority was religious, his uses of that authority were far from traditional. While the conceptual and legal bases of the state he tried to build were clearly Islamic, the territorial and human bases were national: it was an Arab state, a state built on historically defined Algerian territory, a state organized and governed in accordance with principles of Islamic law. If the Amir used military force to suppress internal opposition to his centralization, so have countless builders of states and nations the world over. While the unfinished edifice he was able to erect during the unsettled decade before the full weight of imperialism descended on him was not yet a nation-state, it was a major departure from the state-building efforts of North Africa's past and a sign that important segments of Algerian society were ready for a new, more unified social and political order.

RESISTANCE IN THE MOUNTAINS AND THE OASES

With the defeat of ʿAbd al Qadir and the surrender the next year of the fugitive Ahmad Bey, the struggle for Algeria entered a new phase. It is possible to view the French conquest of Algeria as taking place in three phases defined by the spatial objectives most central to each. Within each of these spatially defined phases of French penetration, a dominant resistance leadership and a characteristic ideology can be identified. The first phase focuses on the major cities and encounters initially defenders from the deylical establishment and later elites associated with it, both determined to preserve what they can of the old order. The second focuses on the open plains and the smaller interior towns and confronts defenders drawn from the predominantly pastoralist Arab tribal leadership which, inspired by neo-Sufi visions of renewal, is bent upon establishing a more egalitarian and authentically Islamic order. The third targets the mountains, the desert rim, and the oases and encounters scores of more popular resistances, which when they do become organized frequently do so under the leadership of a mahdi, belief in whose advent was an integral part of popular culture and piety of the era. The mahdi proclaims the apocalypse, the direct intervention of God in the historical process, and thus the imminence of His reign. It is precisely at those moments when recognized elites are perceived as letting history get out of hand that masses are ready to see the action of the Divine Hand.

One of the first such popular upheavals was the spontaneous and multi-centered explosion of 1845 mentioned earlier. It began in the Dahra mountains north of the Chélif Valley, spread to the Ouarsensis to the south and ultimately into the Titteri, the Kabylia, and parts of the Saharan rim. It was in the context not only of Bugeaud's oppression but also of the bewilderment caused by the collapse of ʿAbd al Qadir's leadership in the lowlands that the twenty-year-old Bou Maʿza proclaimed the apocalypse and for nearly two years confounded Bugeaud's attempts to bring him under control.

A second important millenarian movement appeared almost immediately afterward in the southeast. During the early months of 1849, not long after the capitulations first of ʿAbd al Qadir and then of Ahmad Bey, one Bu Ziyan of the fortified oasis of Zaʿatsha in the Ziban southwest of Biskra learned from the Prophet in visions that he was the mahdi. Alarmed colonial officials tried twice to arrest him, but when both attempts failed, apparently miraculously, his reputation and credibility soared. Then when a small French contingent sent in mid-July to punish him retreated with heavy losses, the whole of the Ziban, the Hodna, and much of the Aurès rose to support him. In the fall of 1849, the commanding general of the Constantinois arrived with massive force. After a fifty-two day siege, the longest in the history of the conquest up to that time, the oasis fell. All 800 inhabitants of Zaʿatsha were methodically slaughtered, including Bu Ziyan, whose severed head was displayed on the wall of the town. In further punishment the town was leveled and more than 10,000 date palms in the Ziban oases were systematically cut down. But Bu Ziyan became a legend. His ideals and exploits were celebrated for generations in poetry and popular ballads, and there were many successor movements. One of the most significant of these was that of the Sharif Muhammad ibn ʿAbdullah of Ouargla, who inspired resistance in the oases of the southeast until 1855, after which he took refuge across the border in Tunisia. Millenarianism maintained its mobilizing power for years as larger or smaller mahdist movements, many in the names of his family members, reappeared until late in the century.

By the 1850s, the only major unoccupied regions left north of the desert were the Grand and Eastern Kabylias. The doggedly independent spirit of the peasant mountaineers combined with the difficulty of terrain for more than twenty years to frustrate French efforts to bring these regions to submission. For years resistance was inspired by leaders of the Rahmaniyya brotherhood and by a reputed sharif known by as Bu Baghla, or "mule man." After Bu Baghla died in battle in 1854, the female marabout Lalla Fatima became the principal symbol of the resistance. The tactics of General Armand Leroy St.-Arnaud and his successor, Marshal Jacques Louis Randon, amounted to a mountain variant of the total war policy of Bugeaud. They cut down or uprooted tens of thousands of olive and fig trees, which were the lifeblood of the economy, and at the same time, they torched hundreds of villages. By 1857, Randon was able to establish French control on the dominant, 1,700-meter ridge line of the Grand Kabylia, establishing Fort-National and other bases at strategic positions.

With the establishment of permanent military and administrative presence in the mountain heartland, the French had established formal control over all of the Tell, the Pre-Sahara, and the northern desert. As the colony extended its dominion, Algerian resistance retreated into more and more inaccessible places, from the fertile plains to the rocky hillsides, from the grassy plateaux to the mountaintops, from the lush and productive oases to the emptiness of the desert. In Eastern Kabylia, attempts by the authorities to limit the powers previously granted to the Awlad Achour and the Ben Azzedin, provoked a general rebellion by 1858 under the leadership of Bou Renan, a qa'id who had previously served as French representative. After his defeat and exile in 1860, the populace turned to the leadership of the Rahmaniyya; they were not subdued until 1865. During the same period, the occupiers also had to cope with a massive uprising in the southwest of the country, that of the Awlad Sidi Cheikh, which spread from the Djebel Amour to Titteri and even into the Dahra mountains. It was not until the last decades of the century that French Algeria felt secure enough to become other than an armed camp.

COLONIZATION

If the motives behind the early French advances were complex and fraught with contradictions, the Algeria constituency was becoming an irresistible force by 1840. By the time Thomas Robert Bugeaud outlined his master plan for destroying the state of ʿAbd al Qadir, colonization had become both the engine of conquest and the guarantor of its permanence. During the bloody decade of the 1840s, which witnessed the subjection of most of the fertile plains of the Tell, the European population of Algeria more than quadrupled from 26,987 to 125,963 while 115,000 hectares of agricultural land were distributed to colons. By the mid-twentieth century, the colon population would grow to nearly one million and had long since acquired a total monopoly of political and economic power, including ownership of more than 2,700,000 hectares of the richest cultivable land in the country (see table 3.1).

Table 3.1   European Population and Land Ownership

Year	Land in Hectares	Population
1841	20,000	37,374
1851	115,000	131,283
1861	340,000	192,746
1872	765,000	279,691
1881	1,245,000	412,435
1891	1,635,000	530,924
1901	1,912,000	633,850
1921	2,581,000	791,370
1954	2,818,000	984,031

Sources: Adapted from Gallissot, *L'Economie de l'Afrique du Nord* (1969), p. 28, and selected censuses of the Service de Statistique générale.[14]

The colonial constituency was made up of two major components, of which one was demographic and the other financial. During the nineteenth century, as population in southern Europe grew more rapidly than the economy, population pressures generated continuous overseas emigration, a portion of which went to the southern shores of the Mediterranean. The overwhelming majority of the settlers who came to Algeria in the nineteenth century were from Spain, Italy, or southern France, some so poor, according to colonial mythology, that they arrived barefoot and were popularly called *pieds noirs*. Nearly half were not French, though their children later received French citizenship. In France itself, the population pressures sent waves of displaced peasants searching for jobs in the northern cities, particularly Paris, where, underpaid or underemployed, they contributed to the chronic social unrest of the French capital from 1830 until the 1870s. The government deported for labor in Algeria many of the proletarian revolutionaries of 1848, encouraged other Parisian workers to emigrate voluntarily, and deported still others rounded up after the Napoleonic coup d'état of December 1851.

Even more important was the influence of French capital. The infrastructural needs of the expanding colony, in port facilities, roads, railways, telegraphs, housing, and public buildings provided multiple opportunities for profitable investment. Capital was also attracted to the agricultural sector. With the right connections, enormous acreages could be had free or virtually so and could be exploited with native labor for a fraction of going European rates. At a period when slow growth kept French interest rates in the neigh-

14. Population figures for Europeans from 1872 onward include Algerian Jews who were naturalized by decree of the Government of National Defense in 1870. In that year the census counted 34,574 native Jews.

borhood of 2 or 3 percent, the returns on investment in Algeria provided irresistible alternatives.

While a large majority of the colons settled in the cities and towns rather than the countryside, it was rural colonization which had the greatest impact upon Algerian society because of its overwhelmingly peasant and nomadic composition. By systematically expropriating both pastoralists and farmers, rural colonization was the most important single factor in the destructuring of the traditional society. Until 1871, the state, master of an ever-expanding public domain in rural properties, was the principal intermediary in transferring Algerian land to Europeans; from the 1870s onward, changes in land legislation facilitated direct acquisition from Algerians and made this as important a vehicle as the domain for transfer.

While some attractive properties, mostly around Algiers, passed into European hands directly in the early years, the fact that most desirable rural properties were not mulk and not legally transferable from individual to individual, made most of these acquisitions irregular and manifestly risky. Until a series of ordinances between 1840 and 1873 succeeded in eliminating the rights of collectivities in land, the surest way to acquire landed property was to apply to the state. Holdings of the public domain, already considerable in the 1830s, continued to increase as the conquest advanced in the 1840s and 1850s and as the government enacted successive measures to limit the spaces available to the tribes.

The heart of the rural public domain was the state lands of the Turkish regime known as beylik, to which the Government General fell heir by right of conquest. Some 158,000 hectares of beylik had been identified and recuperated by 1851. Very little of this land was vacant, however. The majority was assigned to tribes or individuals in return for services or under various hereditary usufructuary tenures. When it was turned over to settlers, the consequences for the natives differed little from any other form of dispossession.

The second largest source of domain lands was confiscation, meted out either directly, as punishment for insurrection or support of the enemy, or indirectly, because of vacancy pursuant to the common-law principle that "les biens sans maître sont à l'état." Most vacant lands became so through the flight of populations fleeing before the advance of the French army. Still others reverted to the state when, pursuant to the Land Ordinance of 1846, all claimants to vacant land had to submit their titles for verification to a Council of Claims. The procedure resulted in state appropriation of thousands of hectares of "empty" land, much of which had in fact been communal grazing land of the nomadic or village communities. Hubus[15] lands were taken under control of the Domain Administration in 1839, which assumed responsibility for the funding of the religious institutions to which their revenues had been dedicated but which proceeded to alienate the properties as it saw fit. Finally, the government also resorted to the procedure of judicial condemnation in the public interest, the public interest being defined in this case as the need to settle Europeans on the affected lands.

15. Waqf in the Middle East.

During the 1850s, as European demand for lands grew and the supply of good agricultural lands available to the domain decreased, the Second Empire adopted the procedure of *cantonnement* to replenish the supply. Under the assumption that most nomads controlled more territory than they really needed, the government concentrated them onto the area of land it thought suitable and took the rest for the purposes of colonization. The questionable legal rationale behind cantonnement was that the tribes did not have hereditary right to the ⁱarsh and sabiqa lands they occupied; instead, by virtue of the original Islamic conquest, the state was the owner and could grant or withhold usufructuary rights at will. Cantonnement inflicted immense material hardship on many tribes, who usually were left with the poorest of their lands, while the best went to the Europeans. It also created a debilitating sense of vulnerability among peoples who feared the erosion of the whole basis of their way of life.

During the 1840s and early 1850s, it was official colonial policy to populate Algeria as rapidly as possible with a class of small European freeholders. The first colonization decree, that of April 1841, provided for the state to make provisional grants of four to twelve hectares to immigrants possessing a minimum capital of 1,200 to 1,800 francs and who agreed to effect minimum improvements within a specified period. When these improvements were completed, the colon could apply for clear title to the property. Other versions of basic colonization law followed, but France never succeeded in creating the society of smallholders at which it aimed. Part of the problem was bureaucratic delays, part was an absence of credit to would-be farmers who could not use the land as collateral, and part was the fact that authorities in the métropole used the program as a safety valve for ridding themselves of surplus urban workers rather than recruiting experienced peasants. Of a European population of 109,000 by 1848, only about 15,000 were rural settlers, and of these only 9,000 were French.

With the Second Empire even more supportive of private enterprise than the July Monarchy, the role of big capital and large corporations expanded rapidly in the 1850s and 1860s. In 1853, a corporation known as the *Compagnie genevoise* contracted to settle 500 families on some 12,000 hectares of domain land near Sétif in the Constantinois. As compensation for its efforts, the corporation received for itself the right to exploit another 8,000 hectares. The company found a multitude of reasons for delivering on only a fraction of its obligations, and the state did not press. Ultimately, it became by far the largest enterprise in the region, exploiting the entirety of the 20,000-hectare estate for its own account by employing thousands of underpaid Arab farm laborers, many of whose fathers had once farmed or herded on the land in their own right. After the Compagnie genevoise had shown the way, other investors hastened to follow. In the early sixties, 160,000 hectares of prime forest were turned over to thirty entrepreneurs. The *Société générale algérienne,* controlled by two large banks and headed by the Governor of the *Crédit Foncier de France* and the Director General of the *Compagnie des Chemins de Fer de Paris à la Méditerranée et de l'Algérie,* received a huge land grant in the Constantinois of

100,000 hectares; the *Société anonyme de l'Habra et de la Macta* in the Oranie was granted 24,100 hectares for a cotton plantation.

While colonialist mythology would for generations extol the legend of the intrepid, hardworking pioneer taming a harsh land by sheer willpower and brawn, the agricultural development of the Algerian countryside was in fact overwhelmingly the achievement of large individual and corporate landholders. If there were a few individual pioneers on the land, the typical European colon did not become a farmer but became instead a small businessman, a tradesman, or a government employee, or he involved himself in the construction or other support industries. A typical European who came to Algeria expecting to become a farmer might well end up opening a bar to serve wine and absinthe to French soldiers. The hard labor in both the rural and urban economies was supplied by the dispossessed Arabs and Berbers.

COLONIAL GOVERNMENT AND ADMINISTRATION

While Bugeaud briefly considered maintaining ᶜAbd al Qadir's administration based upon large khalifaliks, he ultimately abandoned that concept in favor of smaller aghaliks and qa'idates more amenable to direct French control. In the Oranie, the Amir's original six khalifaliks became thirteen subdivisions; the khalifalik of Tlemcen became three qa'idates. Invested by the divisional commanders or their subordinates, most of the appointees were tribal shaykhs rather than religious figures, often those who had opposed the Amir. Responsible for the maintenance of order and the payment of their own salaries through collection of taxes and fines, many of these shaykhs became notorious for their heavy-handed exploitation of fellow tribesmen. In much of Algeria, French administration was taking on some the worst characteristics of the Turkish that had preceded it.

The principal intermediary between colonial authority and native society during the mid-nineteenth century was an Arab affairs establishment popularly known as the *bureaux arabes,* a separate service within the army composed of Arab specialists. While the model of such a service was established in the 1830s, its final form only appeared after Bugeaud's destruction of the state of ᶜAbd al Qadir made more direct administration of the Arabs inevitable. A ministerial decree of February 1, 1844, formalized the existence of an Office of Arab Affairs at Algiers and of subsidiary offices attached to each army division. The fieldwork of these divisional offices was carried out by whatever number of bureaux arabes was needed for effective performance of functions. The officers of the bureaux arabes were assigned the dual tasks of gathering intelligence on native affairs and providing for native administration. While they reported formally to the divisional commanders, the latter, burdened with command and logistical problems, were largely dependent upon their Arabists for the information and analyses upon which their decisions in this sphere were based. Thus the bureaux arabes, down to the time of their elimination in the 1870s, were the de facto formulators of most native policy as well as its executors.

While it appears that in the early years some Arab affairs officers hoped to assimilate the Arabs to European civilization by associating them with colonization and turning them into French style peasants, by the middle forties most were convinced that colonization's main effect was to despoil Algerians of their land and thus vastly to complicate military efforts at pacification and their own task of governing. Increasingly, they became spokesmen for Arab rights, which caused them to be viewed by the colon lobby as the principal obstacle to realization of their own ambitions in the Algerian countryside. Unfortunately, however, the Arab affairs officers were not all idealistic defenders of the Arab patrimony. Left to themselves with little supervision from higher military command and none from the political level, many turned into overbearing tyrants guilty of arbitrary government, summary and often brutal justice, and scandalous venality. The result was that long before the end of the Second Empire, the bureaux arabes had earned the unanimous enmity of the colons and the nearly unanimous enmity of the Algerians.

The Royal Ordinance of 15 April 1845 recognized the de facto division of the colony into three provinces, dissolving the Titteri and Dar al-Sultan into Algiers Province. It also created three separate types of local administration to accommodate the different populations of which the colony was composed. These were the civil territories, known later as *communes de plein exercice,* where concentrations of European population were considerable and in which French common law was applicable. Next were the mixed territories ruled by the military with limited internal self-government for the small communities of European residents. Finally, there were the Arab territories, subject to completely military administration. One scholar has suggested that this tripartite regime amounted to the division of the country into territories that were occupied, those in the process of being occupied, and those still to be occupied.[16] By design, the distinctions among them were flexible and expected to change as the conquest advanced. The three forms of administration, with periodic modifications, lasted until well into the twentieth century.

As the settler population swelled during the 1840s and the victories of French arms became more impressive, the European population became more certain that the military and their bureaux arabes were putting unnecessary impediments in the path of their enjoying the fruits of those victories. Popular opinion accused the military of coddling the natives and of exaggerating security concerns or of encouraging insurrection in order to justify their own control and make themselves indispensable. Civilian leaders began to call for an end to the "*régime du sabre*" and the assimilation of the colony to France so that colons could enjoy their full rights as Frenchmen. Opposition to military rule and the monarchy it represented made the majority of settlers welcome the republican coup that overthrew the monarchy in February 1848. But the

16. Jean-Claude Vatin, *L'Algérie politique,* p. 114.

settlers were far from being republicans in the liberal mold of the 1848 revolutionaries. Their republicanism was a means to end arbitrary military rule so that they would be free to impose their own rule unhampered upon the colony and to exploit the colony for their own advantage. Because of their predominantly lower-class origins, their antipathy for the army, their support of the republican idea, and their opposition to the Monarchy and the Empire, the European population of Algeria before 1870 had a reputation for radicalism that needed careful monitoring. In fact, because both capitalist and lower-class colons shared a common goal in dominating the Muslim majority, the class distinctions which provided the political dynamic of métropole politics had little political significance in Algeria. While many colons insisted down until the 1870s and 1880s that "assimilation" was designed to improve the lot of natives, they had no intention of extending to the Algerian majority the civil or political rights of Frenchmen, and they would be hard pressed to explain what specific aspects of the assimilation they proposed would benefit them.

It was the Second Republic that, for the first time, declared Algeria to be French territory and transformed the provinces created in 1848 into *départements* as in the métropole. The process of assimilation went only part way, however, because the Republic went only part way in attaching governmental functions in Algiers to the appropriate ministries in Paris. Really critical functions stayed in the War Ministry. The Republic did, however, permit the French inhabitants of the civil territories to begin, for the first time, electing municipal councils and choosing their own mayors and some other officials. The principle was established that citizens would be assured a two-thirds majority on the councils, while appointed Algerians would hold the other third and could not serve either as mayors or assistant mayors. The principle of assuring by law that the majority community would constitute a minority in representative bodies would survive until the last years of the colonial period.

After Louis-Napoleon had succeeded in reestablishing the Empire, most of the steps taken toward civilianizing the government of Algeria were rescinded. The Emperor considered military rule all the more appropriate after two trips to Algeria convinced him that without such controls the greed of the settlers would run rampant. Advised by a number of Arabists, it was the personal involvement of the Emperor that led to two watershed pieces of legislation that projected their shadow down through much of the rest of the colonial period, often in ways Louis-Napoleon would never have anticipated. These were the *sénatus-consultes* of 22 April 1863 and of 14 July 1865.

The first of these represented the coming together of two ideas: the need to protect native property from the colons, and the desirability of introducing the Muslims to the benefits of a nineteenth century liberal order. The policy of cantonnement had terrified the natives, depriving them of hundreds of thousands of hectares of land, and had cast an aura of desperation and hopelessness over many communities. The first article of the sénatus consulte of 1863 declared the tribes of Algeria owners of all lands they traditionally and permanently occupied under any title whatsoever, thus effectively terminating the state's claim to ultimate ownership. The legislation then went on to prescribe three operations of implementation: the first was to identify the lands belonging traditionally to each tribe; the second was to divide these lands among the constituent duwars of each tribe, each of which would be governed by a jama°a or council, in whose name the title would reside; the third was that, wherever and whenever possible or appropriate, the lands of the duwar could be further subdivided into individual private property of the members. Only then would the tribal lands become legally transferable. But given the complexities of clan and family structure, it was assumed that the final stage would take decades or generations to reach.

The colons were unanimous in viewing the sénatus consulte of 1863 as another imperial maneuver to deny them their rightful access to Algerian land. Happily for them, the civil authorities responsible for the law's implementation were largely sympathetic to the colon point of view, and they managed in their proceedings to transfer to the public domain a significant portion of the land inventoried. By 1870, the lands of 372 tribes with a total population of 1,037,066 had been surveyed and divided among 667 constituent duwars. Of the 6,883,811 hectares processed, 1,186,175 reverted to the domain, 1,336,492 were declared communal property and 2,840, 591 were declared mulk. The constitution of individual property on tribal land had been completed for only 7,355 hectares in one duwar.

The creation of duwars at the expense of historically constituted tribes and the assignment of authority to tribal councils was explicitly aimed at detaching the Algerians from the control of traditional tribal leaderships. None of the authors of this legislation doubted for a moment that this process, combined with the ultimate constitution of individual private property, was the best formula for achieving the emancipation of the natives from "feudal" constraints and for assuring their moral and material progress. While such faith seems today naive, the question of whether such outcomes would have been achieved remains forever open. With the collapse of the Second Empire, the colons won overnight their long battle for control of Algeria, its people, and its resources. The sénatus consulte of 1863 provided an ideal platform for the final destructuring of Algerian society, sociologically and economically.

The companion legislation of 1865 represents another example of good, if naive intentions, gone awry. The Emperor, after his second visit to the colony in 1865 had given him greater familiarity with the contradictions of its different constituencies, concluded that there were really three Algerias. These were a military base, a French colony, and an Arab kingdom. Each had different needs, each was called upon to perform different functions, and each required a separate status. Legislation was needed to define those functions and statuses. The sénatus-consulte of 1865 formally recognized and attempted to codify for the first time the difference in personal status required by the different cultural heritages of Frenchmen and Muslims. Its first article declared that Algerians were French but specified that they were to be ruled under Muslim law. They could serve in the military, become civil servants, and perform other functions in the French establishment, but they were not citizens of France. In order to

become citizens, they would have to renounce their Muslim civil status and
agree to live under French law. Since the latter would be tantamount to
apostasy within a society where civil status was determined by religious law,
only about two thousand Muslims ever requested naturalization during the
eighty years the law remained in force. The sénatus consulte of 1865 became
the cornerstone of a legal edifice that consigned Algerians to a status of
permanent civil and political inferiority.

THE VICTORY OF THE COLONS AND
THE KABYLIA INSURRECTION

The defeat of the imperial armies by Prussia and the proclamation of the
Third Republic in September 1870 paved the way for the colons at long last to
assume full power in the colony and also provoked the last massive armed
revolt of the Algerians. Across Algeria the colon communities responded
energetically to the call of republican War Minister Léon Gambetta for the
formation of local committees of national defense. With fervent patriotism,
these committees welcomed the coming of republican freedom, promoted the
most expeditious "democratization" of colonial institutions, and encouraged
the departure of troops for the front in Europe. Verbal and even physical abuse
was heaped upon troops that remained. European opinion had long argued
that the possibility of major insurrection was a threat conjured by the military,
who, they argued, even went so far as encourage native unrest in order to
prove themselves indispensable.

The position of Bonapartist Governor General Durrieu, a symbol of the
régime du sabre, became so difficult that he requested and was granted recall in
October 1870. The Government of National Defense at Tours, which was
already considering legislation to establish a civilian regime in Algiers, made
the tactical error of designating another general, Walsin Esterhazy, commander of Oran Province to assure the interim. On October 28, a massive riot
in the city of Algiers forced him to resign as well, and the government fell into
the hands of the Municipal Council of Algiers and the local Committee of
National Defense. At Tours, where the Government of National Defense sat
while Paris was under siege, the new republic proceeded in the fall and winter
of 1870–71 to issue a series of thirty decrees designed to break the power of the
army and its bureaux arabes and to implement the colon program of assimilating the colony to France. The most significant of these decrees were those of
24 October 1870, which instituted trial by jury, and of 24 December 1870,
which aimed at vastly expanding the civil territory. The one extended colon
judicial power over hundreds of thousands of Algerians, and the other extended their legislative and executive authority.[17]

17. The logistical, and financial problems of extending the authority of the mayors overnight into
overwhelmingly tribal areas were so great that this decree as such was never actually implemented.
But the psychological effect upon native populations was as great as if it had been. More measured
legislation in the next decade secured to the civil communes part, but not all of the territory
targeted by the 24 December decree.

Algerian society was in such a fragile and vulnerable state in 1870 that it was unusually ill prepared to cope with the new pressures applied to it. The country was just beginning to recover from four successive years of natural disasters, which had included drought, insect infestation, earthquake, and epidemics that had taken a frightening toll of native lives and seriously affected economic stability and morale in many regions. During the same years, the military administration had been gnawing perceptibly at the prerogatives of the tribal jawad, through whose offices most of the country was still ruled. Behind the military, the colon press regularly demanded the deposition of the tribal "aristocracy", whose alliance with the bureaux arabes it saw as the principal mechanism blocking the march of civilization into the hinterland.

It is clear that the news of the defeat of the Emperor and his armies in Europe had a profound effect upon Algerian consciousness. The subsequent revolt of the civilians against the military and the scorn they endlessly heaped upon the institution whose word had heretofore been law to most Algerians compounded the effect. At the same time, the prospect of rule by the colons, who had made no secret of their program for Algerian society, filled the country with fear. More tangibly, the new civil administration signalled its contempt for native leaderships by refusing to honor the previous regime's commitment to reimburse wealthy shaykhs for emergency loans government urged them to make to the needy during the economic crisis of the sixties. Many tribal aristocrats felt financially as well as politically threatened.

During extensive investigations conducted after the insurrection, a number of European observers contended that outrage over the so-called Crémieux decree,[18] which naturalized the Algerian Jewish community, had helped spawn the insurrection. It seems clear, however, that the colons were more distressed than the Algerians about this measure, because it admitted to citizenship a sizeable community of natives whose culture they considered abhorrent and backward and whose numbers could dilute their own authority. While at the height of the revolt some native rhetoric did condemn the Crémieux decree, the great majority of Arabs and Berbers in the regions that revolted met few if any Jews in the conduct of their daily affairs and were little concerned with the question. It is worth noting that the département of Oran, where the greatest concentrations of Jews were located, remained the quietest area of the country. It seems clear, moreover, that the overwhelming majority of Algerian Muslims would not have considered acquisition of French citizenship an honor but, rather, a sign of disloyalty to one's own religion and community.

The first shots of the revolt were fired in late January 1871 at Moudjebeur and Ain Guettar when units of the native police refused orders to be transferred to France. The spirit of rebellion spread during February from tribe to tribe; there were attacks on individuals, trouble in the market towns, and cutting of telegraph lines. But it was the leadership of Muhammad al-Hajj al-Muqrani, the most important tribal leader of the Constantinois, that

18. Named after the minister in the Government of National Defense who promulgated this and more than two dozen other measures relating to Algeria during the period.

brought scattered unrest to the level of general insurrection. Given all that had happened in recent months, Muqrani became convinced the time was ripe to attempt to return to the kind of autonomous khalifalik his father had enjoyed in the early days of the occupation and to keep the French at a greater distance. Local colonial authorities, of course, would not entertain such a proposal. As the situation grew more tense, word spread that the government considered him responsible for some of the violence and might seek his detention. On February 27, he wrote to the local commanders submitting his resignation as bachagha and asking permission to withdraw with his family to Tunisia. When the commanding general replied in the peremptory manner of a superior to a subordinate, Muqrani called a council of war on March 14 and went on the attack two days later with the not inconsiderable but nevertheless limited aim of forcing the occupiers to reestablish the khalifalik.

While many of the jawad joined him, some stood on the side or were positively hostile. This insurrection of tribal leaders, many of whom had long since become associated with the exploitative regime of the occupiers, would never have become as widespread if it had not been able to tap into the mobilizing power of religion. To accomplish this, Al-Muqrani solicited the support of the Rahmaniyya. The aged muqaddam of that brotherhood, Sidi Muhammad al Haddad, after urging from his son, proclaimed the jihad in the marketplace of Seddouq on April 8, 1871. Al-Muqrani now assumed the title of *amir al mujahidin,* commander of the holy warriors. Within a week, 150,000 Kabyles and others, impoverished and fearful after years of natural disaster and colonial spoliation, joined the revolt. Tariqa support had turned an aristocratic action with limited objectives into an authentically popular war. The war spread quickly from the outskirts of Algiers in the west to Collo in the east and from the desert in the south to the Mediterranean, including the Grand Kabylia, the Eastern Kabylia, and most of the valleys and plains round about. The insurgents burned farms, destroyed villages, sacked Bordj Menaïe and Palestro, and attacked towns as far apart as Dellys, Sétif and Ouargla. When al-Muqrani was killed by a shot to the head on May 5, his brother Bu Mazraq picked up the standard of leadership. The resistance continued to hold under siege ten major strong points, including Bougie, Fort-National, Tizi-Ouzou, Dellys, and Sétif. In the west it spread as far as Cherchel, well beyond Algiers. But already by the time of Muhammad al Hajj al-Muqrani's death enormous French reinforcements were arriving from Europe. As the weeks went by, the tide began slowly to turn. As the French managed to relieve one of their towns and forts after another, the resistance was driven back into the mountains—the Djurdjura, the Babor, the Hodna. The last major battles were fought in early October 1871; on June 20, 1872, a French patrol apprehended Bu Mazraq when they discovered him passed out from exhaustion by a pool of water near the oasis of Ouargla. The rebellion was officially over. Including deaths from illness, it had claimed the lives of 2,686 Europeans, and although the exact toll of Algerian lives will never be known, it was clearly many times greater.

Even the most thoroughly colonialist historians of the insurrection, who

never questioned France's inherent right to occupy and rule Algeria, agree that
the repression the colony meted out to the defeated rebels was out of all
proportion to the alleged misdeeds. The colonial mind is chillingly reflected in
the newspaper rhetoric of the times. One editor asserted that "with such wild
beasts the only law is that of the noose." Another demanded "a holocaust of
marabouts offered for the memory of our dead colons." Such outrage soon
blended, however, with the optimistic realization that "the insurrection fur-
nished a providential occasion to retake possession of this soil that the tribes do
not know how to profit from and which is essential for the firm seating of
European rule."[19] The colon reaction to the insurrection was therefore an orgy
of vengeance compounded with a pell-mell rush for economic gain.

The inhabitants of the eastern half of Algeria were punished as defeated
belligerents, as native subjects, and as Frenchmen. As defeated belligerents, the
inhabitants were saddled with a reparations bill of 36,500,000 francs even if
they belonged to tribes who had taken no part whatsoever in the insurrection.
As native Algerian subjects, they were struck with collective punishment in
the form of land confiscations which, by 1875, had reached the awesome total
of 574,000 hectares. Those lands which the Europeans did not want or could
not use could be bought back, and eventually Algerians paid 63,000,000 francs
to regain possession of some of their poorer properties. Finally, as Frenchmen,
thousands of rebels were haphazardly dragged before colon juries clearly bent
more on vengeance than on justice.

It took two generations for many of the affected regions to recover from
the direct effects of repression. From the social dislocation and the economic
dependency most regions never recovered. Kabyle poets preserved for the
generations the pain and the bitter memory:

> Your heart, oh France, is implacable;
> Since we faltered, your blows never cease.[20]
> . . . .
> They have sowed hatred in the villages.
> We store it under the ground where it remains,
> The abundant yield of a harvested field.[21]

19. As quoted by Charles-Robert Ageron, in vol. 1 of *Les Algériens musulmans et la France
(1871–1919)*, p. 24.
20. Smaïl Assikiou, as translated from a French version in Ageron, *Les Algériens*, I, p. 35.
21. Anonymous, as translated from the French in vol. 1 of Ageron, *Les Algériens*, ibid.

CHAPTER 4

THE COLONIAL SYSTEM AND THE TRANSFORMATION OF ALGERIAN SOCIETY, 1871–1919

Under the Second Empire, the army had not actually slowed the European drive to monopolize Algeria's landed resources, but because it said it wanted to, the colons were frightened and angry. They were relieved to encounter in the Third Republic, however, the most supportive political environment since 1830 in which to pursue their goals. One reason for this was political uncertainty in France. From 1870 until well into the 1880s, it was by no means clear to the republican leadership there that it could withstand the forces pressing for restoration of the monarchy. The colons, militantly republican since the 1840s, were awarded three seats in the Senate and three in the Chamber of Deputies. There, in return for much needed support, the parliamentarians enacted with little dissent the bulk of the program presented to them by their trans-Mediterranean colleagues. Republican gratitude went so far by 1881 that Parliament doubled the colon representation in the Chamber to a grossly disproportionate six seats. Beyond the obvious political trade off, however, there is evident in the thinking of many metropolitan politicians of the era a desire to compensate south of the Mediterranean for the demoralizing losses France had sustained on her eastern frontier. The allocation of 100,000 hectares of Kabyle land for the purpose of settling some 1,200 refugee families from Alsace and Lorraine is the best remembered initiative born of an instinctive drive to offset the humiliation of defeat by a program of vigorous expansion and national rejuvenation at Arab and Berber expense.[1]

1. Of the 125,000 Alsatians and Lorrainers who chose to leave their home provinces after German annexation, no more than 5,000 settled in Algeria. Of the 1,183 families recipient of land grants in the 1870s, only 387 remained on those grants by the turn of the century, and 277 had left Algeria for good. Nevertheless, as late as the 1950s, French voices could be heard citing the Republic's commitment to the descendants of the refugees from the lost provinces as reason to retain the Algerian colony.

As the colon program for expropriating Algerian lands moved into high gear, it accelerated the disarticulation of the native economy and the progressive impoverishment of Algerian society. Economic disarticulation in turn was the most important of several factors precipitating, by the last years of the century, the first clear signs of destructuration of the society which up to then, in spite of multiple trauma and dislocation, had largely maintained its traditional forms and relationships. By the 1890s, many observers in France, including a number of influential politicians like Jules Ferry and Jules Cambon, were becoming alarmed at the destructive effects unbridled colonialism was having upon a people who against their will had been forced into French tutelage. By the turn of the century, new Algerian elites beginning to emerge out of the sinking traditional society were in a better position than their predecessors to analyze the Algerian situation and enter into dialogue with the metropolitan leadership. The resulting series of reform proposals, effectively countered by massive colon opposition, were so diluted in final form that most Algerians found that little about their situation had improved by 1919. These issues provide the main subjects of the present chapter.

THE HIGH TIDE OF RURAL COLONIZATION

In spite of the enormous quantities of land made available to the public domain through the operations of the sénatus-consulte of 1863, the colons continued to see that law as the principal hindrance to colonization. The sénatus-consulte therefore became one of the first targets of the settler parliamentary delegation at Paris, which was headed by Dr. Auguste Warnier, the most articulate and effective colonialist spokesman of the era. When it became clear that legal and administrative complexities made outright repeal inadvisable and that repeal was opposed by the first nonmilitary Governor General, Warnier adopted the new goal of reorienting the existing statute so as to make it a vehicle for dismantling native property. The so-called Warnier Law of 26 July 1873, along with the Law of 22 April 1887 became the principal instruments through which the colons between 1877 and 1920 came into possession of some 1,750,000 hectares of native property in addition to those acquired under the previous regimes and through the Kabylia sequestration. The Warnier Law began a process of gallicization of property by subjecting all transactions between Europeans and Muslims to French law, as well as transactions between natives when these took place on lands previously subjected to cantonnement or to inventory of the sénatus-consulte. It also abrogated the instructions for implementation of the 1863 law, so that the goal of the statute was now explicitly the dismemberment of native properties rather than their protection. Finally, it narrowly limited the right of *shuf*a, by which owners of jointly held mulk could preempt prospective outside purchasers. The complementary law of 1887, sometimes known as the lesser sénatus-consulte, mandated the resumption of land delimitations among populations not

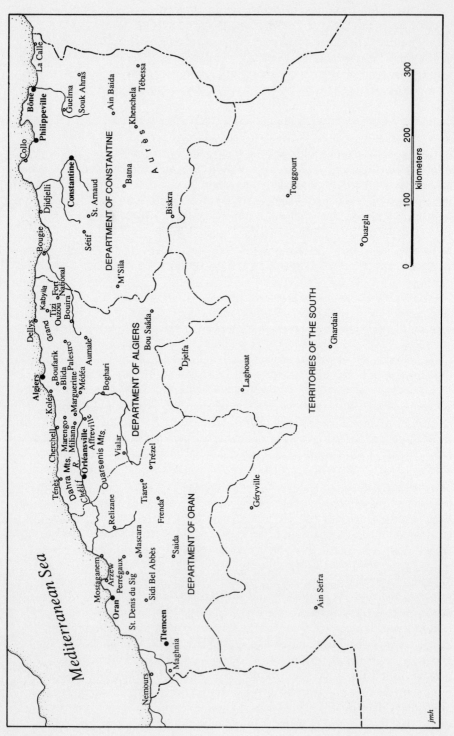

MAP 5 Colonial Algeria

Mediterranean Sea

DEPARTMENT OF CONSTANTINE

DEPARTMENT OF ALGIERS

DEPARTMENT OF ORAN

TERRITORIES OF THE SOUTH

La Calle
Bône
Philippeville
Collo
Guelma
Souk Ahras
Ain Baida
Tébessa
Khenchela
Constantine
St. Arnaud
Djidjelli
Bougie
Sétif
Batna
A u r è s
Biskra
M'Sila
Dellys
Grand Kabylia
Tizi Ouzou
Fort National
Bouira
Palestro
Aumale
Bou Saâda
Touggourt
Ouargla
Ghardaia
Algiers
Boufarik
Blida
Marengo
Marguerite
Miliana
Médéa
Koléa
Boghari
Cherchell
Ténès
Dahra Mts.
Chélif R.
Affreville
Orléansville
Ouarsenis Mts.
Vialar
Trézel
Djelfa
Laghouat
Géryville
Relizane
Tiaret
Frenda
Mascara
Saïda
Mostaganem
Arzew
Perrégaux
Oran
St. Denis du Sig
Sidi Bel Abbès
Nemours
Tlemcen
Maghnia
Ain Sefra

0   100   200   300
kilometers

jmh

affected by the 1863 statute and hence the progressive gallicization of the rest of the native patrimony. By 1900, 4,000,000 hectares had been inventoried, and by 1934, 9,000,000. This legislation also directed the administration to proceed wherever possible to inventory jointly held mulk and, wherever feasible, to issue deeds of property for the individual shares.

After the Second Empire, which had looked increasingly to large-scale capitalist initiative to develop the colony, the Third Republic returned to the vision of populating Algeria with a class of small European freeholders. The principal instrumentality for realizing that vision was a reinvigorated program of official colonization, which in turn required mechanisms for steady replenishment of the public domain. Between 1873 and 1892, the state "recovered" 309,891 hectares of public land in the 2,239,000 hectares gallicized. As the state attempted to deal with what became a perennial problem of diminishing colonizable reserves, the percentage of lands assigned to the domain through operation of the lesser sénatus-consulte rose. Some 26 percent of ᶜarsh lands were declared to be state forest or vacant during the inventories of the 1890s and 1900s. In northern Algeria, the procedure left the tribes an average of only 10 percent of their communal lands.

At the same time, individual initiative was taking advantage of the new laws to move hundreds of thousands of hectares of ᶜarsh and jointly held mulk into the European sector. Wherever a European, by buying out a single joint owner or by being able to claim a loan default on any joint owner, could demonstrate the smallest interest, the French courts could proceed to the dissolution of the entire property. Some real-estate agents became specialists in programming such scenarios. Because hundreds of native owners could be involved in such litigation and because each had to pay court costs to defend his interests, the legal fees were often more than the individual co-owners could raise and frequently totaled more than the value of the property; many extended families and even whole villages were expropriated by default.

Since settlement was such a highly charged political issue in the European community, figures concerning its progress were subject to manipulation for political purposes, particularly those related to official colonization. Official recapitulations never accord with annual figures of which they are ostensibly composed and hardly ever with the data in parliamentary reports or those of the local representative body. Table 4.1 represents an attempt to show the relative importance of official colonization and private colonization during the period.

In the long run, the effort of the Third Republic to recreate on Algerian soil a replica of rural French democracy was a failure. Of 32,976 people settled in the countryside between 1871 and 1885 at a cost of 66,000,000 francs, roughly 17,000 were new French immigrants, the rest were foreigners or settlers already in the colony. One study showed that of 13,301 properties created through official colonization after 1870, only 9,558 remained in 1902. Of these, 202 were in the hands of foreigners, and 616 were held by Muslims. At the same time, powerful forces throughout the entire period favored the

Table 4.1 Rural Colonization, 1871–1910

Period	Official Centers Created	Hectares Distributed by State	Net Private Purchases (ha)
1871–80	264	401,000	60,000
1881–90	107	176,000	227,000
1891–1900	46	126,000	159,000
1901–10	112	175,000	352,000
TOTALS	529	878,000	798,000

Sources: Benachenhou, *Formation du sous-développement en Algérie* (1978), p. 217; and Ageron, *Histoire de l'Algérie contemporaine,* vol. 2 (1979), pp. 76–97.

increasing concentration of property. While the operative colonization statutes called for grants of not fewer than twenty nor more than fifty hectares, depending upon quality of soil and accessibility of water, it is clear that such plots were, in most districts, incompatible with topographical and climatological realities. Since the North African agricultural base was grain grown through the winter on rain-watered tracts requiring alternation of planting and fallow years, twenty- to fifty-hectare farms were inherently too small. The scale and demands of the expanding market economy, which made most small farms non competitive, bolstered the natural forces. As the plains were transformed from the nomadic or seminomadic mode of exploitation to the intensive agricultural, estates reminiscent of the latifundia of antiquity were reemerging. Table 4.2 demonstrates how little impact official settlement policy had in the short and middle term upon rural European settlement. In spite of enormous effort and expenditure, the percentage of rural settlers in the total European population at the turn of the century was nearly what it had been in 1871. This percentage was much lower than in France, where rural inhabitants were two-thirds of the population in 1870 and remained in a majority until the census of 1931. In the longer term, official policy proved even less effective. The data, seldom totally reliable, show the number of European rural settlers peaking in the 1890s, declining, and then stabilizing in the next decade. But as a percentage of total European population, agricultural population declined steadily in the twentieth century until it reached 21.7 percent in 1948. It seems clear from the figures in table 4.1 that had the lesser sénatus-consulte of 1887 not spurred the dismemberment of jointly owned and ᶜarsh properties by individual entrepreneurs, the percentages of rural settlers would have been far smaller.

After experimenting in the first decades of the occupation with a variety of exotic crops (e.g., hemp, cotton, indigo, tobacco), European farmers fell back mostly on hard and soft wheat by 1870. By the 1880s, however, two factors converged to produce a marked shift toward viticulture. One was the devastating spread of phylloxera in France, which made the métropole for several years dependent on wine imports. The other was a twenty-year slump

Table 4.2   European Rural Population

Year	European Rural Population	% of Total European Population
1872	100,549	41
1881	146,647	38
1893	201,541	41
1900	189,164	39
1911	153,441	35
1926	236,672	28
1936	230,311	25
1948	201,009	22

Source: Ageron, *Histoire de l'Algérie contemporaine*, vol. 2 (1979), p. 97, *Les Algériens musulmans et la France*, vol. 1 (1968), p. 551; and selected censuses from the Service de Statistique générale.

in world wheat prices brought on by the arrival on the market of large new overseas supplies. Vineyards, which covered fewer than 10,000 hectares under the Second Empire and had expanded to 18,000 hectares by 1878, grew explosively to 71,000 hectares in 1885 and 103,000 three years later. While viticulture was both labor and capital intensive, it required less extensive plots of land than cereals, so that its spread tended to mask to some extent the overall acceleration in concentration of agricultural property. By 1914, vineyards accounted for 44 percent by value of European real property, while wine contributed one-third by value of the colony's exports. But as time went on and metropolitan wine production recovered, it was the political influence of the trans-Mediterranean deputies that kept France importing very large quantities of Algerian wine. Thus, the extraordinary growth of the Algerian wine industry rested less on genuine market forces than on political factors, a situation which would later present independent Algeria with serious problems of agricultural readjustment.

THE INSTRUMENTS OF COLONIAL CONTROL

The last militarily significant resistance to the French occupation occurred during the decade after the Kabylia insurrection in the form of three small disturbances in regions still on the margins of effective occupation. The first of these took place in the Biskra area in April 1876, when the nomadic tribe of the Bu Azid, eventually joined by other elements of the Ziban, occupied the oasis of El ʿAmri and kept a French garrison surrounded until reinforcements arrived two weeks later. The second took place among Chaouia Berbers of the western Aurès in May and June of 1879 and was directed initially at the French appointed qaʾid, whose fiscal and other exactions appear to have exacerbated an already difficult economic situation in the area. The last and largest revolt, from spring 1881 until the end of 1882, was characterized by a series of raids led by the marabout Bu ʿAmama against native silos and new settler facilities in the northern Sahara and southern Oranie.

It had taken the Europeans a half century to overcome the Algerians' determined but perennially disunited military resistance. They assured maintenance of the occupation for another seventy years by institutionalizing a system of legal discrimination that kept the native majority in a position of permanent inferiority. The major elements of that legal edifice were civil, political, juridical, and fiscal inequality.

As was noted in chapter 3, the de facto inequality of the two peoples was institutionalized by the sénatus-consulte of 1865, which declared Algerians French without according them citizenship. In order to become citizens, Algerians were required to renounce their Muslim civil status and live under the *code civil,* a step taken by only 1,557 of them between 1865 and 1913. Very few Muslims would commit what amounted to apostasy by renouncing the religious law that defined their individual status, but even those who chose to make the great leap were not assured of a warm welcome on the other side. In the decade between 1899 and 1909, 551 Algerians applied for citizenship, and 337 received it. Many of the 214 rejected were turned down on the vague grounds of "unworthiness."

The heart of the colon program coming into the republican era was the drive for "assimilation" of Algeria to France. But as Auguste Warnier made clear, immediate assimilation was appropriate only for the Europeans. Since Muslim society was still in a "relatively barbarous state," it should be assimilated only "gradually and sensibly."[2] Through legislation enacted from 1870 into the early 1880s, this minority colonial community was assimilated organically to the French Republic by limiting the powers of the Governor General, by attaching most functions to the relevant ministries in the métropole, and by giving the colons a high level of parliamentary representation. Thus, by 1881, the colony was effectively theirs to do with as they pleased. A decade later, however, many metropolitan observers were becoming alarmed at the destructive effects colon freedom was having upon a native society that was sinking into greater and greater poverty and disorganization. When a parliamentary commission began to propose serious reforms, the colons concluded that the policy of assimilation and "rattachements" cut two ways. While it had certainly accorded them freedom to design and implement programs favoring their goals in the country, it had also permitted an alarming degree of metropolitan meddling in their affairs. During the 1890s, therefore, settler opinion backed away from assimilation toward something called "association." Most of the colonial offices went through a process of "dé-rattachement" in order to diminish Parisian control over them; the governor generalship was reconfigured so as to make it as much as possible a conduit for colon opinion and interests; by decrees of 1898 and 1900, the colons were given budgetary autonomy through the creation of a new body called the

2. As quoted by Charles-Robert Ageron, in vol. 2 of *Histoire de l'Algérie contemporaine,* p. 11.

Délégations financières. The latter remained for half a century the most important representative body in the country, the closest institution Algeria had to a colony-wide assembly. While Délégations financières budgetary decisions were legally subject to approval by parliament, the Prime Minister and ultimately the President of the Republic, these authorities seldom involved themselves in such internal matters. The assembly was made up of sixty-nine members, of whom forty-eight were elected Europeans. The twenty-one Muslim members were partly elected by a small electorate of about 5,000 men and partly appointed. Except for occasional plenary sessions, the Muslims met and debated separately and had little if any actual impact upon the allocation of resources.

The patterns of local and provincial governance of the colony had already been established during the preceding periods, but now there was a substantial increase of the amount of territory assigned to the communes de plein exercice, a dramatic expansion of the mixed communes, and an equally dramatic shrinking of the military territories. Effectively, the latter were confined after 1881 to the *Territoires du Sud* in the Pre-Sahara and beyond, in which by 1918 about one-ninth, or 500,000, of the native Algerian population lived.

The total of 12,000 kilometers under the jurisdiction of ninety-six civil communes in 1869 was increased by 1881 to more than 17,000 square kilometers under the control of 196 communes, many of which had been very hastily constituted. Europeans, of course, dominated the municipal councils. By a law of 1884, a limited Muslim electorate was granted, for the first time, the right of choosing the Muslim members of the municipal councils, but at the same time their representation was cut from one-third to one-fourth and they lost the right to participate in the election of mayors. In order to qualify as a municipal elector, a Muslim needed to be a male at least twenty-five years of age and a resident in the commune for a minimum of two years. Additionally, he had to be either a landowner, a leaseholder of land, an active or retired civil servant, or a recipient of a French decoration. In the 1880s, about 38,000 Algerians out of 3,300,000 met these criteria, a number which grew only to about 50,000 by 1920. While in the larger towns and in the cities the Europeans who dominated the councils were fairly numerous and sometimes actual majorities, in many regions the commune de plein exercice represented a caricature of French democracy. In 1914 the commune of Randon contained 561 Europeans and 4,978 Muslims, that of Charon 197 Europeans and 5,105 Muslims, and that of Mekla 140 Europeans and 9,098 Muslims. Whole duwars were attached to communes with as few as fifty or sixty European voters, who through their statutory control of the councils collected and disposed of tax revenues extracted overwhelmingly from the native majorities. Travelers from the motherland remarked on the affluence and amenities of the rural colonial towns they visited, which they found generally in far better material condition than comparable communities in France. Besides the supply of cheap labor they enjoyed, the principal reason for this was the taxing authority the towns exercised over the Algerian population and their total control of budgetary allocations. They were subject to little or no higher control in such matters. The European town might boast statuary, fountains, and tree lined and beautifully paved streets while the Algerians of the surrounding countryside did without the most rudimentary dirt road upon which to bring their produce to market. The 1911 census showed that 1,078,365 Muslims, or 25.3 percent of the native population, lived in the communes de plein exercice.

The other major instrumentality for bringing the Algerians under civilian control was the extension and restructuring of the mixed communes. Under the Second Empire, these were transitional regions into which a few colonists had moved but which, because their populations were still overwhelmingly Muslim, continued to be governed by the local military commander. The commander was advised and assisted by an appointed council of settlers and natives. Most of his representatives within the various tribal jurisdictions were politically prominent qa'ids, bachaghas, or shaykhs. Under the Third Republic, the military commanders were replaced by civilian officials drawn mostly from the colonial bureaucracy and advised by joint European-Muslim municipal commissions. The Europeans on these commissions were elected, but the Muslims were appointed by the Governor General upon nomination of the prefect of the département, and they were removable at will. During this period, as the integrity of the tribal system eroded and the great families declined, the appointment of natives of stature to the commissions and the qa'idates gave way progressively to the appointment of "dependable" and dependent individuals to whom both Algerians and French applied the derisive label of "Beni oui-oui." The successful civil administrator listened carefully to the advice of his colon commissioners and sought out native *adjoints* who would be satisfied with the material profits to be won from their positions without interfering with the "civilizing" programs of the Europeans. In the meantime, the jamaᶜas of the duwars, which through operation of the sénatus-consulte of 1863 were supposed to become the centerpiece of a program of democratization and "de-feudalization" of tribal society, had been abolished in 1874. By 1881, the greatest part of the territory of the Algerian Tell, more than 87,000 square kilometers, had been organized into seventy-seven *communes mixtes*. They varied greatly in size, but were characterized ethnically by the existence of extremely small, politically powerful European communities surrounded by immense Muslim majorities. The average mixed commune covered 1136 square kilometers and contained a population of 294 Europeans and 20,348 Algerians. It was central to the Algerian experience because, while economic opportunities were drawing Algerians slowly toward the communes de plein exercice, some 3,000,000 of Algeria's 4,500,000 Muslims still lived in the mixed communes by 1920.

Midway between the communal councils and commissions and the Délégations financières stood the general councils of the départements. Beginning in the 1870s, the Algerians were represented in each of these assemblies by six *assesseurs musulmans,* who were appointed by the Governor General. Most of these assesseurs were members of the municipal councils or commissions or were chosen from the ranks of native civil servants. The latter in particular showed little disposition to question the system or its priorities. From the start, the colons resented participation of Muslims, even as a minority, in the work of the General Councils, while from the 1890s onward, a recurrent issue in Algerian reform petitions was the demand that the delegates should be elected rather than appointed.

It was noted in the last chapter that an October 1870 decree of the Government of National Defense extended trial by jury to the civil communes, which meant that as these jurisdictions spread more deeply into the country more and more natives were subject to settler justice. Such inherently biased justice was at best paternalistic. When it dealt with alleged crimes by Algerians against Europeans, however, it could be savage and vindictive; when it dealt with alleged crimes by Europeans against Muslims, it could be scandalously indulgent. In cases affecting only Muslims, on the other hand, the juries were often singularly detached and even careless. In the mixed communes, justice was dispensed either by a French justice of the peace without assistance from a jury or by the civil administrator himself.

Beginning in the 1870s the colon delegation in Paris induced parliament to enact a series of exceptive laws outside of French common law designed to ensure peace and order among the natives. Passed in the decade after the Kabylia uprising, this legislation was supposed to deal with a temporary security emergency. Yet, it in fact imposed on Algerian Muslims a humiliating regime of exception, known as the *code de l'indigénat,* the basic elements of which survived until World War II. The heart of the code was a list of thirty-three infractions which were not illegal under the common law of France but which were illegal and punishable in Algeria when committed by Muslims. These included such offenses as speaking disrespectfully to or about a French official, defaming the French Republic, or failing to answer questions put by an official. They also included travelling without a permit, begging outside of one's home commune, and shooting weapons in the air at a celebration. Avoiding corvée, refusing to fight forest fires or grasshoppers, and forgetting to declare a family birth or death were equally punishable. Failure to pay taxes and some other infractions were punishable both under the common law and the code de l'indigénat. In the communes de plein exercice, the code was enforced by the justice of the peace, and in the mixed communes by the administrator. The rare appeals from this summary justice were seldom successful. While the maximum penalties under the indigénat were five days imprisonment and fifteen francs fine, the frequency of their application, particularly in the early days, provided a constant humiliating reminder of the power relationship between the two communities.

In 1902, in the aftermath of a small disturbance known as the Margueritte Affair, Parliament voted a new court system to deal with more serious cases of flagrant delict. These courts, the *tribunaux répressifs,* were designed to afford quicker disposition of cases than was provided by the jury system and to try cases more serious than those listed in the code de l'indigénat. In dispensing justice, the presiding judge or administrator was assisted by a European and a Muslim *adjoint,* neither of whom was necessarily trained in the law. From prison sentences shorter than six months or fines less than 500 francs there was no appeal. In the same year, Parliament created special criminal courts to hear cases involving only Muslims. These, too, were presided over by justices of the peace or administrators aided by European and Muslim assistants. Because the native criminal courts removed many cases from the jurisdiction of the colon juries, some Algerians thought them an improvement. Critics of the criminal courts observed, however, that the training of the presiding officers was frequently deficient and that the sentences handed down were characteristically harsher than those of the juries.

As a kind of safety device, the Governor General during the entire period exercised a power of administrative detention. It was applicable in a variety of cases whose definition the government kept deliberately vague, until spelled out by reform legislation in 1914. In principle, administrative detention was aimed at threats to colonial authority, at seditious speech, or at religious incitement. But it was also used to administer punishment in cases where insufficiency of evidence or other procedural difficulties in the courts had resulted in the exoneration of individuals the regime wanted out of the way. The Governor General, usually upon application of a département prefect, could intern the accused at Calvi in Corsica, send him to one of the three Algerian penitentiaries, or place him under "town arrest" in an isolated duwar. Terms could extend as long as three years. Between 1901 and 1909, 415 sentences of administrative detention and 540 town arrests were handed down.

At least as effective as the regime of judicial inequality in assuring subordination of the Algerians was that of fiscal inequality. This inequality began in the earliest days of the occupation when the French had claimed the right to continue collecting taxes levied by the preceding regime, which they called *impôts arabes.* But at the same time they gradually subjected the Algerians to a range of French taxes as well. Algerians were responsible for both. The colons, on their side, were naturally exempt from the impôts arabes, and, as a matter of public policy aimed at encouraging European immigration, they were also exempted from the era's most burdensome direct tax, which was that on land. They began to pay taxes on developed real estate only in 1891 and remained exempt from taxes on undeveloped real estate until 1918.

The Arab taxes included the ʿushr,[3] or tithe, collected on the annual cultivated acreage of six categories of crop. They also included the zakat, classically a canonical alms but in Algeria a very heavy tax on camels, horses, cattle, sheep, and goats that yielded as much as the ʿushr. Kabyles paid significantly lighter taxes known as *lazima.* Both Kabyles and Arabs were subject to compulsory labor obligations (corvée), which included fire duty in forests, grasshopper and locust drives, and official transport. Both also paid a tax, originally in kind but increasingly in specie, which the French called

3. The ʿushr, or tithe, was collected in the Algiers and Oran départements. In the Constantinois the comparable tax was the hukr.

prestations, theoretically collected for the maintenance of roads and other public services and facilities. As the period went on, receipts from ⁿushr and zakat tended to fall, reflecting declining productivity of the native economy, while the burden of the prestatîons became heavier.

In addition to the impôts arabes, European-style direct taxes the Algerians were liable for included the property tax on developed land, trade and professional licence fees, rent taxes, market usage fees, and additional herd taxes. Indirect taxes included customs duties, tariffs on tobacco and other goods, and various registration fees. As the expansion of colonization effected the gradual impoverishment of the Algerians, the receipts from the Arab taxes declined, but the European taxes were boosted so that total taxes remitted by Muslims increased. From 1901 to 1919, their tax contribution increased by 26 percent, while population grew by only 16 percent, this at a time when economic productivity of the native sector was slipping. By 1909, Muslims were paying nearly half of all taxes in the colony, contributing about one-third of the central budget, two-thirds of the département budgets, and half of the communal budgets. An Algerian jurist concluded in 1912 that while Algerians owned 38 percent of the land and capital goods of the colony, they paid 71.19 percent of its direct taxes. While certain European analyses yielded somewhat lower figures, it is clear that the prosperity of the settler community rested in large measure upon their ability to extract a strikingly disproportionate tax contribution from the Muslims.

A control policy that was ultimately less effective than those outlined above was that of dividing the Arab and the Berber communities. As early as the 1830s, French observers, taking note of cultural differences between Kabyle mountaineers and predominantly lowland Arabs, came to the conclusion that Algeria was inhabited by two distinct "races." In time a Kabyle myth grew up that in one form or another survived down to the end of the colonial era. The Kabyle, attached to his ancestral soil, was industrious, practical, curious, democratic, expansive, and far less religious than the Arab, who was soft, lazy, slow-witted, introspective, and given to dreaming and fanaticism. Depending upon whom one read, the Berbers were Celts, the descendants of Roman settlers, or former Christians only reluctantly and superficially Islamized. As the myth developed, along with theories of assimilation, important strains of colonialist thought concluded that the Kabyle culture was destined to be fused with the French and that this fusion would become the principal vehicle for the projection of European civilization over the barbarous Arab majority.

Prelates developed elaborate programs of evangelization. Beginning under the Second Empire, priority in locating French schools was given to the Kabylia; a vocational school was established at Fort-National. Taxes were lowered, village jamaⁿas were encouraged, and many Kabyle towns were assigned new French names. Efforts were made to codify customary law with a view to having it supplant shariⁿa more than it already did in that region; Kabyle qadis were urged to draft and deliver verdicts and opinions in French.

Berber linguistic studies were officially encouraged: effort was expended to subject the different dialects to systematic grammatical analysis, and, at the Faculty of Letters at Algiers in 1885, a chair of Berber studies was established.

Behind all of the pseudoscientific cultural, racial, and historical analysis hid, of course, the self-serving policy of *divide ut impera,* which France and other colonial powers followed extensively in the nineteenth and twentieth centuries. In the long run, efforts to implement a policy of assimilating Berbers to colonial society were wrecked because they rested on two basic fallacies.

The first was that the cultural distinctions that obviously existed between some of these mountain people and the Arabs were so fundamental that the former could be weaned from loyalty to the common Algerian heritage. While Berbers during the colonial period did learn French in greater numbers than Arabs, those numbers were not greater than might be expected given the larger number of French schools in the Kabylia and the traditional mobility of the mountaineer labor force. Attempts at evangelization were a total failure except in cases where orphans or the children of the very poor came under the care of the clergy. Colonial analysts were shocked during the last part of the century to observe that in spite of all of their efforts to define and strengthen the Berber community, the number of berberophones was actually declining and that knowledge of Algerian Arabic was spreading rapidly. This phenomenon was the unexpected outcome of political and economic integration forced by colonialism. Wherever French railways and highways went, there also went dialectal Arabic as the principal language of commercial and intercommunal discourse.

The second fallacy underlying the Berber policy was the assumption that settler ambitions were reconcilable with a policy of favoring this or any sizeable native group. Through the 1870s and the 1880s, when the guiding ideology was assimilation, colons could be induced by metropolitan planners to sanction programs aimed at accelerating integration of the Kabyles. But in the 1890s, as the dogma of assimilation gave way to that of association, colonial leaders put more and more impediments in the way of initiatives favoring Kabyles. Ultimately, government stepped back from its more ambitious assimilation programs while quietly continuing to privilege this region educationally, to encourage emigration, and to promote where it could pride in the Berber heritage. At the same time, however, by its insistence on the maintenance of traditional Kabyle communal structures and customs, some observers believed that the government was deliberately trying to slow modernizing transformation of the region.

DEMOGRAPHIC IMPACT OF COLONIZATION AND THE DETERIORATION OF THE ALGERIAN ECONOMY

Four decades of warfare combined with the shock of massive land expropriations, forced relocations, and disruption of traditional markets, to

Table 4.3
Algerian Population, 1830 – 1886
(In Millions)

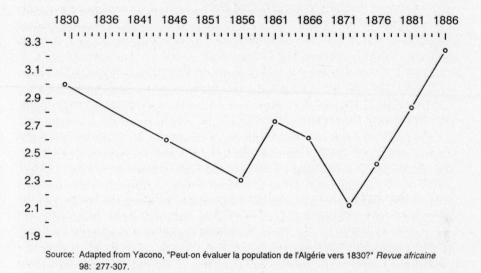

Source: Adapted from Yacono, "Peut-on évaluer la population de l'Algérie vers 1830?" *Revue africaine* 98: 277-307.

make Algerian society more vulnerable than usual to the ravages of drought, insect infestation, and epidemic. The result was a devastating decline in population, the main outlines of which are demonstrated in table 4.3.

Between 1830 and the first official census in 1856, population fell from about 3,000,000 to an official 2,307,000, or an average of 0.8 percent annually. Since that portion of the curve represents a backward projection, with the only fixed point a military count in 1845, the actual decline for the period is probably less regular than it appears. While it seems unlikely that the surge of population in the decade after 1856 could have been as marked as this graph shows, there is much evidence to indicate that the famine and epidemics of the period 1866–70 in fact took an enormous toll of Algerian lives. Liberal and anticolonialist opinion in the métropole was shocked at the results of the 1872 census and the evidence they bore of the appalling impact of the occupation on the native population. But colon opinion, fresh with social darwinian insight, saw in the apparent disappearance of some 600,000 natives between 1861 and 1872 corroboration of their conviction that the barbaric culture of Algeria must unfailingly vanish before the superior civilization of Europe.

With the winding down of armed resistance in the 1870s and the end of the era of most violent turmoil, population began to increase again, a trend that has continued at varying rates until the present (see table 4.4). The steady growth of population, even under oppressive colonialist circumstances, is imputable partly to the decline in mortality related to improved control of diseases like small pox, cholera, and typhus. It may also have been stimulated by the rapid increase in demand for labor that accompanied the concentration of the factors of production in colon hands, a progression discussed in greater detail later in this chapter.

But if the era of violent assault upon Algerian lives and livelihood was ending, the Algerian economy was entering into an irreversible deterioration which entailed inexorable pauperization of the society. Economic deterioration was due to the increase in tax burden discussed earlier, to steady and catastrophic loss of land, and to insertion of native agriculture into a market economy dominated by the Europeans.

Land was, of course, the principal factor of production in a society that was 95 percent agricultural. As indicated in table 4.1, nearly 878,000 hectares of that land had been granted to colons by the state between 1871 and 1910 under the colonization laws. Of equal or greater importance as a cause of economic deterioration was the commercialization of land brought about by the land laws of 1873 and 1887. Commercialization reduced the viability of native agriculture both by breaking up jointly held and communal holdings and by progressively fragmenting them at a time when population was growing. Many of the remaining farms became so small as to be economically nonviable, particularly during the recurring bad agricultural years. Eventually, as many plots were sold to Europeans because of economic hardship as were lost to them through legal maneuvers. Natives could buy back such commercialized property, of course, and they frequently did. But the final out-

Table 4.4 Growth of Algerian Population[4]

Year	Muslim	Non-Muslim	Total
1830	3,000,000	—	3,000,000
1845	2,600,000	96,000	2,696,000
1856	2,307,000	159,000	2,466,000
1861	2,737,000	193,000	2,930,000
1872	2,134,000	280,000	2,414,000
1881	2,842,000	412,000	3,254,000
1891	3,577,000	531,000	4,108,000
1901	4,089,000	634,000	4,723,000
1911	4,741,000	722,000	5,463,000
1921	4,923,000	791,000	5,714,000
1931	5,588,000	833,000	6,421,000
1936	6,201,000	946,000	7,147,000
1948	7,460,000	922,000	8,382,000
1954	8,546,000	984,000	9,530,000

Source: Selected censuses from the Service de la Statistique générale.

4. Native Algerian Jews are included with the Muslims through 1861, and with the non-Muslims beginning in 1872 after they had been naturalized. By deleting the Jews from the non-Muslim column in 1872, the actual European population was about 245,000, representing what colons considered a dangerously slow growth rate since 1861.

come, as seen from the table, was a net transfer to the settlers of around 800,000 hectares—almost always of the better lands. Equally significant is the fact that commercial exchanges over time favored the capital-rich Europeans, who bought cheaply in times of native distress and resold to them at higher prices when the cycle put more Algerians back in the market. Land records show that from 1878 to 1914, Europeans purchased from Algerians 1,224,000 hectares of land at an average price of 119 francs per hectare. During the same period, Algerians bought from Europeans 337,000 hectares of distinctly poorer land at an average price of 223 francs per hectare.

It was not only to individual Europeans that native property was transferred, however. The state long before 1919 had become by far the largest land holder in the colony. While figures for the public domain like most figures for the period present problems, it appears that in the late 1880s, the public domain held about 3,000,000 hectares of forest and other land. By operation of the lesser sénatus-consulte, the government appropriated an additional 1,900,000 hectares of farm and pasture land, only a part of which it turned over to individuals, and about 1,200,000 hectares of forests. By 1919, in spite of the more than 900,000 hectares it had granted to colons since 1870, the public domain still held between 5,000,000 and 6,000,000 hectares.

The constitution of the national and communal forests was for the native economy one of the most damaging facets of colonial policy. The *Service des Eaux et Forêts,* inspired by the forestry experiences of France, was determined to preserve, to replant, and to make, as the Service saw it, more rational economic use of Algeria's limited wood resources. These priorities ran directly into the new pressures placed on these resources by Algerian peasantries driven by colonization from the lowlands to the hillsides and also into traditional usage by nomadic and seminomadic populations, whose flocks and herds historically fed upon different kinds of forest vegetation. One pattern that particularly appalled the Forest Service was the native practice of burning off the dry brush in late summer or early autumn so that the first rains would cause more grass to grow. The difference in perceptions and priorities that existed between the Forest Service and the Algerian pastoralists constituted one of the most fundamental and painful cultural confrontations of the entire colonial period. Algerians saw forest-burning as a routine procedure necessitated by their pastoral life style; many Europeans saw it as an act of open insurrection. To counter it, they levied huge fines, imposed criminal penalties, and confiscated lands of entire tribes.

On the morning of April 26, 1901, about a hundred men from the Adelia duwar in Algiers département killed their French-appointed qa'id and a forest ranger and then seized the colon settlement of Margueritte, where they executed five of the inhabitants for refusing to pronounce the *shahada,* the Muslim profession of faith. A company of sharpshooters from nearby Miliana soon arrived, and by five o'clock that afternoon, they retook the town, killing sixteen of the rebels against the loss of one of their own. Small as it was, the so-called rebellion of Margueritte shook the colony and strengthened the hand of antireform forces. It also produced a careful investigation of conditions and causes which is an instructive case study of the impact of colonial land policy upon one native group. The operation of the sénatus-consulte of 1863 had taken 1,463 hectares from the duwar so that in 1868, the Adelia, who numbered 2,194 people, held 9,286 hectares of mulk and about 3,000 of communal grazing and forest land. Between 1868 and 1900, the colony condemned a total of 3,285 hectares for the creation of Margueritte and the neighboring centre of Changarnier; individual colons managed through bilateral transactions or legal intervention to acquire 3,329 hectares, almost the entire proceeds of which went for payment of legal fees; and the Forest Service had virtually closed off the brush lands where their animals grazed. In 1900, however, the duwar was able to rent nearly 1,400 hectares of European land. The result was that the Adelia, whose population had grown since 1868 to 3,206, now had access to only 4,068 hectares of land. This meant that by the turn of the century this particular native group was living off of 1.2 hectares per capita compared to 5.6 hectares per capita thirty-two years previously. They were farming only 2,343 hectares; their cattle herd had shrunk to 1,122 from 2,000 in 1868 and their flock of sheep from 10,934 to 1,537.

It was observed in chapter 2 that, although elements of a "national" market existed in Algeria before the French invasion, the dominant characteristic of the Algerian market was its fragmentation. But if agricultural productivity was low, it was peculiarly adapted to the cyclical conditions imposed by climate. In general, peasants and seminomads relinquished only the portion of their harvests required to satisfy tax liabilities and acquire the few necessities they could not produce locally. In good crop years, the balance of the harvest was stored in silos as insurance against poor harvests that could be expected in the future. The penetration of the national and global market induced peasants to sell off the surplus of the good years (usually at depressed prices caused by the overproduction of those years), which left them without reserves to see them though the bad years. In such years, they would have to buy food and seed grain for the next year's planting. Most had to borrow to survive, at annual rates normally ranging between 25 percent and 50 percent but which frequently went as high as 100 percent. But the cost of loans to peasants was not expressed as an annual rate. For small sums, it was expressed as seven or eight douros due for each five lent. For larger sums, the debtor who received a loan of 100 francs for three months might sign a note for 150 francs. It was ordinarily assumed that loans were automatically renewable (with interest compounded) until the lender judged the risk too great, which led to many families being tied to the same lenders for years or for lifetimes. Foreclosures became, of course, a principal instrumentality for transferring Algerian farms to Europeans and small peasant holdings to wealthy Algerians. The debt burden in time became as onerous for many Algerians as the fiscal burden, and in many cases it was an even more important mechanism than taxation for draining the resources of the native economy.

Table 4.5

Native Wheat and Barley Production, 1875 – 1915

(In Millions of Quintals)

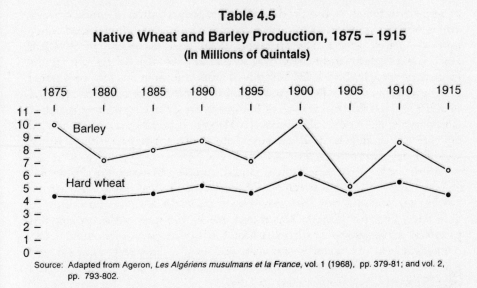

Source: Adapted from Ageron, *Les Algériens musulmans et la France*, vol. 1 (1968), pp. 379-81; and vol. 2, pp. 793-802.

Agriculture continued, as in the past, to be based primarily on grains and livestock. But as population increased, the amount of land cultivated by the Algerians was falling, from 2,571,892 hectares in 1876 to an average of 1,967,955 in 1916–1920. The contraction of the land surfaces available to the Muslims, the expropriation of the better lands, and the absence of significant improvement in agricultural technique, meant that production after 1870 leveled off and then, in all the important sectors, began an unspectacular but marked decline. Since this decline occurred at a time when population was growing steadily, per capita agricultural production was falling sharply during the period. See Table 4.5 for the grain sector.

Given the dispersion of nomadic populations, systematic and continuous data for livestock production were considerably more difficult to collect than those for crops before the late 1880s. The total cattle herd in the 1870s appears to have averaged somewhat more than 1,000,000 head. The number of sheep in 1876 was put at 9,699,000. Because animal population is affected by longer-range variables than crop production, the livestock figures in Table 4.6 are expressed in five-year averages.

As with the grain sector, the absolute decline in number of livestock is less troubling than the sharp per capita decline. The number of sheep fell from 285 head per 100 population to 165. Goats went from seven for each five people to four for each five. Cattle were down from one for each three people to one for each five people. Reduction of the herds reflected a significant change in life styles brought about by the irresistible contraction over eighty-five years of the open spaces available for grazing. By 1914, only 1,000,000 Algerians, less than 20 percent of the population, were still predominantly pastoralists. It will be recalled that 45 percent had been nomads or seminomads in 1830.

Table 4.6
Native Livestock, 1885 – 1914
(In Millions of Heads)

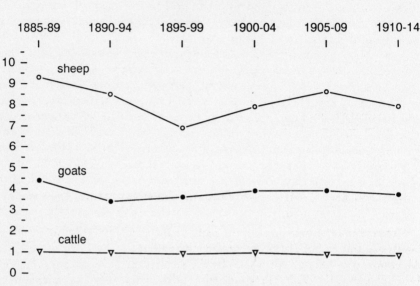

Source: Adapted from Ageron, *Les Algériens musulmans et la France*, vol.2 (1968), pp. 806-11.

THE BEGINNINGS OF THE DESTRUCTURATION
OF ALGERIAN SOCIETY AND THE EMERGENCE
OF NEW SOCIAL CLASSES

Pauperization of Algerian society was clearly documented by changing modes and relations of production. In 1914, the percentage of khammis, or sharecroppers, in the peasant population had grown to about 32 percent. In the last years of the Second Empire, settlers had been surprised, for the first time, to see large numbers of natives searching for work in the colonization centers. By 1914, wage labor had become one of the most characteristic features of colonial agricultural production, and there had come into existence a rural proletariat of some 600,000 Algerian men, women, and children, more than 16 percent of the rural population. It is true that by 1914, 48.6 percent of the rural population still farmed land they owned, but the majority of the landed peasants lived on plots of insufficient quality or size to provide for their total support. The colonial government calculated that ten hectares on the average was the minimum space necessary to support a native peasant family. But in 1914, fully 60 percent had farms smaller than that, while only 1 percent boasted holdings larger than 100 hectares. Thus many freeholders sup-plemented income by working during peak times on colon or larger Algerian farms or by encouraging family members to enter the full- or part-time labor force. Daily wages ranged from 50 centimes or 1 franc for women and children to 2.25 francs for male ploughmen. Permanent full-time labor earned annual salaries of from 360 to 500 francs.

The turn of the century also witnessed a still small but accelerating migration of workers to the cities. This urban proletariat—in small factories, workshops and businesses, on the docks, in semiskilled or unskilled public sector jobs—numbered some 50,000 in 1905. By the start of the First World War, about 10,000 Algerians had already found jobs in France itself, the pioneers in a movement that would become enormous as the century went on, with important demographic, economic, cultural, and political consequences.

Sociologically, the most important effect of colonization was clearly the proletarianization of the most vulnerable layers of rural society, a process that would accelerate after the Great War. But colonization also jolted the other end of the social order by bringing about the rapid disappearance in the last third of the century of the great tribal jawad. With French law undermining the legal bases of their authority, with French army and police relieving them of their military functions, with French administration and tax authority removing the sources of much of their income, the jawad became historically redundant. The son of Shaykh al Aziz, a grandson of al-Haddad, was a lowly *khuwaja,* or secretary, in a commune mixte; one branch of the Muqranis became shopkeepers; the great grandson of Shaykh Benchérif who had besieged the Turkish garrison in Oran was a day laborer in the same city. By 1938, of the 721 qa'ids who were France's principal officials in the communes mixtes, around 100 only were of jawad descent. Those aristocratic families that survived did so by managing to adapt to the new order, either by entering into the spirit of the new economic system, by making themselves administratively or politically useful to the French, or by encouraging their sons to attend French schools as preparation for entering the liberal professions or the colonial bureaucracy.[5]

If the traditional tribal nobilities were rapidly disappearing, there still remained before the First World War in the larger cities—Algiers, Tlemcen, Constantine—a few descendants of the great "Moorish" families who made up the urban bourgeoisies of the Ottoman period. As time went by, these families, proud of the ancient heritage, became principal repositories of the old values. This small but tenacious class formed the core of the group the French came to call the *vieux turbans.* Deeply religious, they were noteworthy for their opposition to innovation and for their insistence upon faithful application of the letter of Islamic law. Because of the narrowness of the native electorate constituted by the French, they enjoyed more influence in the early twentieth century than many larger constituencies.

During the 1890s, there also appeared a newer Muslim bourgeoisie, which before the war, at least, mixed very little with the traditional families. In the lesser colonial towns and villages, small businessmen, town-dwelling landlords, and government officials began to constitute a small more or less

5. For a thoughtful discussion of the disintegration of the jawad, see Augustin Berque, "Esquisse d'une histoire de la seigneurie algérienne," in *Ecrits sur l'Algérie,* pp. 55–68.

gallicized middle class that had learned how to work and more or less thrive within the new system. In the larger cities, the middle class was made up partly of businessmen (e.g., small shopkeepers, agricultural wholesalers, building owners, operators of oil presses and flour mills). To these were added the small French-educated elites who staffed the religious institutions and the native schools, or who were members of the liberal professions or the bureaucracy.

Finally, in the countryside there was emerging a new landowning class that had managed to take advantage of the commercialization of collective and jointly held lands. If, at the poorer levels of native society, the tendency was toward such subdivision of land that plots were becoming economically non viable, the other end of the spectrum saw increasing concentration, through purchase from Europeans or from other natives, or through foreclosure. While data on the distribution of native property for the entire colony are not yet available, such data do exist for the Constantinois.[6] These data conclude that, just before 1914, there were in that département 1626 Muslim owners of farms larger than 100 hectares and 7,650 of farms between 41 and 100 hectares. While large personal estates had existed in Ottoman times in the suburbs of the major cities, these new estates were being created principally out of the wreck of the tribal system with the progressive privatization of collective lands.

RELIGIOUS AND
EDUCATIONAL CONFRONTATIONS

The most poignant and permanent cultural confrontation during the colonial era took place in the area of religion. Frenchmen, who throughout the nineteenth and early twentieth centuries were struggling to institutionalize the secular and liberal society they had first envisaged in 1789, were largely incapable of comprehending or respecting a society which insisted on the centrality of religion to its identity and behavioral norms. Most Muslims pitied the minority of Frenchmen who were observant Christians and held in secret contempt those who were not. For many Muslims, the conqueror's aversion for their religion and his assaults on its institutions must have been a greater cause of bitterness than economic and political oppression. They did not forgive the closing of mosques and zawiyas, the confiscation of hubus, the desecration of cemeteries, the harassment of Islamic education, or the periodic interference with the canonical duty of pilgrimage. Most of all, perhaps, they resented the colonial government's takeover of the principal religious institutions. After confiscating the hubus, the government assumed management of the official religious establishment, including appointment and supervision of the ʿulama as well as their remuneration. It also controlled the three madrasas, the only institutions in the country licensed to train men for

6. See the thesis of André Nouschi, *Enquête sur le niveau de vie des populations rurales constantinoises de la conquête jusqu'en 1919*, p. 591.

clerical positions. These schools, staffed by Arab and French professors, dispensed a bilingual and bicultural education, whose quality at both levels was mediocre at best.

Not only did French cooptation of the official religious establishment erode its credibility in the eyes of the faithful, but the parsimony of France's funding arrangements assured its stagnation and even regression. By decree of 23 March 1843 the government had absorbed into the general public domain the hubus properties previously only sequestered. Therewith it ceased to keep a separate accounting of hubus revenues but undertook to fund from the general budget the institutions and organizations those funds traditionally underwrote. The total of these funds in 1843–44 was put by the Ministry of the Interior at about 100,000 francs, and this figure became effectively a ceiling on state expenditures for Islamic religious institutions for many years. When population growth and plant deterioration made increased funding of religion inevitable, colon councilmen and delegates who controlled the appropriations process assured that such increases were never adequate. In 1875, there were in the whole country only 100 official imams and qadis,[7] assisted by 390 subordinate employees, to minister to 2,600,000 faithful. Even though population continued to grow over the next decades, there was no increase in the total number of paid religious positions before World War I. More imamates were created, but at the expense of the lower positions. Because physical facilities after half a century of neglect were in advanced stages of disrepair, a modest program of mosque construction was authorized in the 1890s, but many older buildings continued to deteriorate. Total enrollment in the three madrasas, in the meantime, fluctuated from fewer than 100 to a maximum of about 250. The Muslim consensus was that imams trained in Morocco or Tunisia, however, were far superior to those produced at home.

Reluctance of colons to spend tax revenues on religious institutions they considered incubators of fanaticism came to a head in 1904 with the enactment of the Law of Separation terminating the Napoleonic Concordat with the Roman Catholic Church. If the links between the Church and the Republic were severed, why, they asked, should France continue to support the mosques? Natives were quick to respond that France should, because it had undertaken to do so when it nationalized the hubus. Eventually, more pragmatic colonial voices convinced the majority that it was more in their interest to maintain control of the Islamic institution, even if at some financial cost, than to allow it to develop freely.

The second half of the nineteenth century saw, in the meantime, a considerable increase in the membership of the tariqas.[8] One reason for this growth seems to have been popular alienation from the official orthodox establishment, too tightly controlled by the infidel. Indeed, the greater authenticity and freedom of the orders are attested by the virtual paranoia with

7. In colonial bureaucratic usage an imam was a qadi, a mufti, a muezzin, a *hazzab*, or a *mudarris*.
8. Augustin Berque, in "Décadence des chefs héréditaires" (*Ecrits*, pp. 42–48), argues for a very pronounced increase in membership; Ageron, in vol. 2 of *Histoire*, pp. 172–75, believes growth was more moderate and probably ended about 1880.

which colonial officials beheld them and by their frequent closing of zawiyas, arrests of shaykhs, and continuing policy of playing the leaders off against each other. It has been suggested that another reason for the growth of the brother-hoods was the decline of the secular aristocracy, which had long served as a check on the ambitions of the sharifs and important marabouts. One effect of their demise was clearing the field for religious aristocracies who were in a sense the last traditional leaders still in place. There is general agreement, however, that the rush of faithful to the zawiyas caused a rapid erosion in the neo-sufi orthodoxy that had characterized the most renowned of them, a decline in the search for authentic mystical experience, and an increase in eclecticism, superstition, and charlatanism. By the twentieth century, the quality of the leaderships declined to such an extent that they became more and more susceptible to colonial cooptation. Historical process combined with colonial policy to produce the irony that, in the twentieth century, the colony depended for much of its religious support upon the movement that had been the principal mobilizer of resistance to its implantation in the nineteenth.

In 1903, when the renowned Islamic reformer Muhammad ᶜAbduh visited Algeria from the far livelier intellectual climate of the Arab East, he was appalled by the backwardness of most aspects of Algerian Islam. His visit galvanized a number of Algerians to launch a campaign for the rejuvenation of the faith in their country. Prominent reformers included a noted legal scholar, Abdel Halim ben Smaïa, and also the Imam of the Safir Mosque in Algiers, Kamal Mohammed ben Mostefa. The latter, to give an idea of reformist concerns, was author of a book called *La tolérance religieuse dans l'Islamisme* and of another called *Les droits de la femme*. For these two and kindred jurists and writers, the true spirit of the Koran was one of liberalism, scientific enlighten-ment, and tolerance. Almost all readers of ᶜAbduh's famous journal *al-Manar,* these reformers launched in Algiers, Constantine, and Tlemcen an attack upon the "superstition" and "decadence" of the marabouts, which was the begin-ning of a movement of Islamic renewal that would gather momentum as the century moved forward.

For a certain number of Muslims neither holding on to the past nor dreaming of Islamic reform could compensate for the sense of powerlessness and hopelessness generated by the colonial situation. Faced in 1907–08 with the probability that they would be compelled to serve in the Christian army, even perhaps to fight against the Commander of the Faithful in Morocco, some 140 young men of Tlemcen simply left the country. Others followed them in 1910 and 1911, heading mostly for Syria. By 1912, in spite of government attempts to retain them, some 4,000 individuals from Tlemcen and other districts had succeeded in emigrating, choosing exile to submission.

Almost as central as religion in the struggle for cultural dominion was the conflict over education. Education is never culturally neutral but exists to transmit to the young the values of the culture within which it is established. In most societies until very recently education was one of the essential func-tions of religion. Ironically, it was precisely during the period when France was fighting to impose itself upon Algeria that the major battle between church and state for control of education was being fought in the métropole. It was only with the watershed public education law of 1881 that France itself finally made up its mind that education should no longer be the province of religion and laid the groundwork for the final triumph of the *école laique*. It is natural that Algerians should have seen in the French school an institution appropriate to the education of Christians but not to that of Muslims. Since education by definition existed primarily to transmit a religious heritage to the young, attendance by a Muslim boy at a French school, even a secular school, could only be viewed as a step toward apostasy and toward secession from the community of his fathers.

It has been argued by Algerian historians that because of traditional Muslim emphasis upon scriptural literacy and the wide attendance at Koranic schools, *kuttabs*, the Algerian literacy rate in 1830 was greater than the French. While hard data to prove the point have not been produced, such a contention seems reasonable. It is clear, however, that one result of colonial implantation was the rapid dismantling of the existing educational system, and this caused the spread of illiteracy, which worsened as the forced illiteracy of one generation disabled the next. The dismantling of kuttabs and madrasas was the result of hubus confiscation, destruction of buildings and displacement of peoples. For a time, zawiya schools filled some of the void, but because they were politically suspect, they were subject to arbitrary closure for security reasons.

At the same time, the conquerors were establishing their own schools. For Europeans, they created public or church primary schools, replicating those in the métropole, along with a secondary system of *collèges* and *lycées* and a group of faculties that eventually became the prestigious University of Algiers. A very small number of Algerian pupils, usually the sons of notables, attended elementary and occasionally secondary schools from the beginning. Some sons of notables, held as virtual hostages, were educated in France.

There was a parallel school development. The original doctrine of assimilation, co-opted after 1870 by the colons, reflected the Enlightenment view of the brotherhood of man. In that tradition, a few early colonialist idealists dreamed of a fusion of the races through a network of schools where French, Muslim, and Jewish pupils would all be immersed in an identical bilingual curriculum. Besides French schools, the colony therefore established in 1833 the first experiment in what later became a system of bicultural schools called *écoles arabes-françaises*. But the results were disappointing. European parents early made clear their objections to associating their children with semicivilized natives, while Muslim parents of all classes were equally horrified at delivering their sons up to infidel teachers. In the 1830s and 1840s, the écoles arabes-françaises were frequented principally by Jews (then considered the lowest stratum of Algerian society), by foundling Muslim children the authorities collected in the streets, and by children of poor families to whom the authorities paid bounties or scholarships in return for attendance. As the écoles arabes-françaises spread under the Second Empire, a few native functionaries began to see the advantages for their own careers and their children's future in sending their sons to the schools. Attendance grew a little, but the overwhelming majority continued to boycott them. By 1870, some 1,300 Muslims were enrolled in thirty-six Arab-French primary schools in addition to a few who attended the all French schools, and some 200 older students who attended two *collèges arabes-français*. There was also a small normal school for training teachers as well as a vocational school in the Kabylia. Given the impact of the invasion on traditional education, attendance at Koranic schools had fallen at the same time to an estimated 27,000. If the numbers are at all correct, less than 5 percent of Algerian children were attending any kind of school in 1870. After forty years of association with the French, Algerian society was in the throes of a cultural disaster. Aléxis de Toqueville had written a little earlier that "Around us the lights are going out. . . . We have made Muslim society much poorer, more disorganized, more ignorant and barbarous than it was before it knew us."[9]

Colons, who had always been critical of the attempt to create a special school system for natives who did not want it, were quick, after 1870, to dismantle the Arab-French system. They claimed that Muslims were now free to attend the French schools, most of which at the time were still operated by the clergy. Few accepted the invitation. A major crisis developed in 1883 when the Paris government attempted to apply to Algeria the compulsory education laws of 1881 and 1882 and required the construction in each commune of at least one school for native Algerians. The colons, who now controlled municipal expenditures, managed largely to avoid implementing this law, pleading, among other things, lack of funds. All through the years before World War I, they worked at limiting both the quality and content of education available to the natives. They insisted that whatever education was offered should be vocationally oriented, focus on the needs of the agricultural labor market, and avoid academic subjects that might tend to politicize the natives. While there were several versions of the native school curriculum from the 1880s, all courses of study shared an emphasis on the practical rather than the theoretical, and all were taught almost exclusively in French. A graduation test in written Arabic was required only until 1898. After 1900, the choice to administer an oral Arabic examination was left to the local academic commissions. As the years went by, in fact, few Algerian and even fewer French schoolmasters had sufficient command of literary Arabic to teach in or about it.

The geographical distribution of schools followed a political logic that bore little relationship to educational needs. Even though the central government agreed to pay between 60 percent and 75 percent of the costs of native schools in the communes de plein exercise, most municipal councilmen were reluctant on philosophical or financial grounds to appropriate their budgetary shares. Most schools in the Kabylia and in the communes mixtes, however, could be established without approval of colon councils. Thus, the majority of the schools were built in backward, rural areas, where education, particularly in

9. Aléxis de Toqueville, part 1 of vol. 3, *Oeuvres complètes*, p. 323.

French, was the least needed, whereas in many urban areas, where it was more appropriate, Algerians found access to schooling difficult or impossible.

For about two generations, a combination of massive Muslim boycott and colon hostility limited the expansion of European-style education in Algeria. Around 1890, however, the climate began to change. Some Algerian families were realizing that France was in Algeria to stay and that, if their children were to maintain or improve their standard of living, they would have to learn to function in the world France had created. The new mood spread slowly but unmistakably in the last decades before World War I. In 1882, there were 3,172 Muslim children in French primary schools; but by 1914, there were 47,163, an increase from less than 2 percent of school-age population to almost 5 percent. In the same year, in deference to Muslim sensibilities, there were only sixteen schools for girls, however, whose total enrollment was 3,992. Secondary school enrollment rose from 86 in 1899 to 180 in 1910, and it then spurted to nearly 400 by 1914. Without exception secondary scholarships were awarded to sons of qa'ids or aghas, an indication of the extent to which access to education was being used as a reward for correct political behavior. Between 1877 and 1911, only 226 Muslims had received either the baccalaureate, awarded after secondary school, or a higher degree. There were, in 1914, eight or ten Muslim physicians, twenty to twenty-five lawyers, a doctor of pharmacy, and about fifty holders of predegree certificates in letters or science.

THE VIEUX TURBANS AND THE YOUNG ALGERIANS

The crushing of Algerian armed resistance and the systematic impoverishment of the country had, for practical purposes, eliminated the society's elites—Turks, Koughlouglis, jawad, sharifs, even the bulk of its traditional intelligentsia. For a long time after 1870, Algeria was eerily silent. Then in the late 1890s and particularly in the first years of the new century, Algerian voices were once again heard contesting in different ways what the French were doing to the country. Conventional history has retained most vividly the memory of the Young Algerians, the first generation of what were called the "*évolués*," men educated in the French manner and functioning primarily within the intellectual, professional or economic world created by the victors. This narrow elite of 1,000 or 1,200 men of the twentieth century are one of the major sources of Algerian nationalism. But before discussing the Young Algerians, it is necessary to indicate that there were other voices, less clearly heard because they were speaking a different language, literally and figuratively. These voices reflect a more profound cultural reality than those of the modernists and belong to a group of traditional, largely religious leaders the French and the évolués called *vieux turbans*.

Economic, administrative, and legal strictures had constrained the ᶜulama materially and intellectually and had relegated them politically to marginal positions far from the Christian-dominated centers of power. The typical vieux turban was moderately to well educated in Arabic and in traditional Islamic disciplines. But some were ignorant by any standard, and others, such as the jurist Mohamed ben Rahal, had extensive exposure to French education and were perfectly bilingual. But here on the margins of the official world, they stood their ground and defended traditional religion, its teachings, and its prerogatives. They condemned the moral laxness of the young, their wearing of European clothes, their growing fondness for wine, and their neglect of religious obligations. They defended the institutions of Islam: the shari^ca, whose sphere the French were systematically narrowing, as well as French attempts to codify and update it; the prerogatives of the qadis, increasingly usurped by the civil courts; and the threat to disestablish Islam by applying the Law of Separation to Algeria. They excoriated the French-speaking elites who applied for French citizenship, and they condemned the proposal to conscript Muslims into the French army.

Some of the things traditionalist leaders condemned could have proved or ultimately did prove beneficial to the cause of Algerian liberation. Service in the French army, for example, became the surest ladder of upward mobility for impoverished young peasants. While improving their economic standing, such service afforded an environment of relative egalitarianism that rewarded personal achievement and equipped many Algerians with personal self-confidence and a social vision they had not had before. In the case of disestablishment, on the other hand, which did not occur, and which the traditionalists opposed, such a measure by freeing the Islamic institution from government control could have made it to be more responsive to the needs and interests of the Muslim faithful. But the point is that, for the great majority of the population, Islam had become consciously or unconsciously the principal repository of the collective personality and the ultimate psychological bulwark against total domination by the Christians. Thus, any attempt to tamper with Islam was an attempt on the moral survival of the people. While it was not the vieux turbans or their descendants who eventually led the great movement of liberation against colonialism, it is clear that had they not helped the masses guard the ideological and psychological fortress of national identity, the modernist nationalists later in the century would have found few followers.

The first signs of a secular political opposition to colonial policies appeared during the hearings of the 1892 Senatorial Commission of Eighteen, where a few Algerian officials convincingly articulated their objections to a range of colonial policies. But these petitioners were individuals. The Young Algerians who appeared in the next decade were the first to form a recognizable opposition movement. They included a new class of young Muslims who had found their way to and through the French educational system and were beginning to constitute a small professional and intellectual elite. They also included a few Muslim businessmen who had integrated successfully into the European world of commerce and finance. The majority of the Young Algerians were frankly and openly assimilationist, demanding rights in the name of the values and principles they had learned from France in France's schools. While a minority stressed the need to preserve the Muslim and Arab heritage, most spoke only of a desire for acceptance into the French community and body politic. They were looking to France to emancipate them not only because of the degree of their understanding of and commitment to French civilization but also because they could become a bridge to the millions of their compatriots who in their view had been consigned by centuries of ignorance and barbarism to their present state of poverty and degradation. The Young Algeria movement was not monolithic, however. Even more diverse than the vieux turbans, they covered a considerable spectrum of évolués from a tiny handful of Christianized Kabyles and self-proclaimed agnostics to a larger group of French citizens who continued to consider themselves Muslims, to a still larger group who refused to take the step of seeking individual naturalization. The question of whether it was more appropriate either to accept citizenship individually, as a few had, or to work for collective naturalization was the largest single issue separating wings of the Young Algeria movement.

After the model of the Young Tunisians who had created influential societies such as the Khalduniyya and the Sadiqiyya, the Young Algerians founded a number of fraternal and cultural clubs within which to discuss the important ideas and promote the vital causes of the day. The Rachidiyya was the most durable and visible society in Algiers; it spawned branches in the surrounding département as well as in the Oranie. The most serious of the societies intellectually was the Circle of Salah Bey organized in 1907 at Constantine. Societies were also active in Tlemcen, Mostaganem, Mascara, Bône, and other towns.

Unlike the vieux turbans, who were never able to launch a periodical publication that lasted, the Young Algerians founded and sustained a half dozen or more successful periodicals and newspapers in the years before World War I. Some of these were bilingual, but the majority were written exclusively in French. The most influential was the French language *L'Islam* which styled itself "the democratic organ of the Algerian Muslims." A weekly published in Algiers, *L'Islam* was the best written of the Young Algerian journals; it enjoyed good contacts with the Parisian press and attracted many French contributors. While it may not in all instances have been the most representative native publication, its visibility and good connections won it recognition as the more or less official voice of the évolués. Quite different in tone was *El-Hack*,[10] subtitled *Le Jeune Egyptien*, which began publication at Oran in the fall of 1911. On many questions, its editorial views were similar to those of *L'Islam*. But the paper's choice of a masthead invoking the Egyptian reformers, its launching of a fund drive to aid Muslim victims of the 1911–12 Italo-Ottoman war, and its opposition to Franco-Algerian marriage were all indicators of a concern for cultural solidarity clearly at odds with the assimilationist views of *L'Islam*. Neither the editors of *El-Hack* nor other Algerian activists of the period spoke of Arab or Algerian nationalism or seemed

10. Al Haqq in standard English transliteration, the truth.

explicitly attracted pan-Islamic ideologies. Yet, behind *El-Hack*'s thinking lay a sense of identity and cultural pride that are elemental ingredients of authentic nationalism.

Of the several score évolués whose names became prominent in the prewar period, four will illustrate the range of Young Algerian types. Omar Bouderba and Dr. Benthami ould Hamida were both French citizens, both municipal councilmen, and both extremely ambitious politically. Bouderba, scion of an old Algiers family that had long ago made its peace with France, was a successful businessman. Benthami, of more modest family, a practitioner and professor of ophthalmology educated at Montpellier, France, was granted citizenship after a considerable struggle in 1906. He was elected to the Algiers Municipal Council in 1908, headed the most important Young Algeria delegation to Paris in 1912, and was generally considered the leader of the Young Algeria movement. Both he and Bouderba were Freemasons and members of the *Ligue des Droits de l'Homme,* and both were scornfully labeled by vieux turbans' opponents as "ashab al bulitik" or "political types." Of somewhat different stripe was Fekar Ben Ali, of an old scholarly family of Tlemcen, who earned a doctorate in law, taught for a time in Lyon, and became an editor of a bilingual paper in Oran, which he described as the link between the French and Muslim communities. The most intellectually powerful of the four was the qadi Chérif Benhabylès, who had also earned a French doctorate of law and was one of the guiding lights of the Salah Bey Society. His book *L'Algérie française vue par un indigène* is a thoughtful and, in places, poignant exposition of the cultural and psychological contradictions faced by Algeria's évolués.

The first collective political action taken by the Young Algerians was the sending of a delegation to Paris in October 1908 to discuss with Prime Minister Georges Clemenceau the then pending proposal to conscript Algerians into the French army. While their petition expressed opposition to conscription under current circumstances, it agreed in principal to the idea if Arabs and Berbers were awarded the totality of civil rights. When Clemenceau signalled that he was ready to consider reasonable quid pro quos, the Young Algerians began to orient their demands toward the compensations they hoped to extract in return for supporting compulsory military service.

Examination of the position papers, petitions, and debates of the movement reveals two very different themes in their program, parts of which were potentially contradictory. At one level is a group of demands aimed at benefitting the Young Algerians as a group. This first level included easier access to citizenship, preferential exemption from the code de l'indigénat, extended voting rights, and alteration of qualifications for public office in such a way as to shift the balance for elective or appointive office away from traditional classes—alternatively very conservative or very compliant—toward people like themselves. At the second level, they promoted initiatives aimed at improving the status of the Algerian masses. Perhaps the closest to an "official" program the Young Algerians ever produced was the list of demands that appeared in *L'Islam* in April 1911. The list called for the unification and equalizing of the tax codes, elimination of the indigénat and tribunaux répressifs, broadening of the municipal voting rolls, and reform of Muslim representation in elective bodies in such a way as to "reserve a preponderant place for the intellectual elements of the country able to collaborate effectively."[11] In addition to this last self-interested demand, the Young Algerians asked for the end to the practice of filling appointive offices with members of traditionally cooperative families and the establishment instead of a process of competitive examinations. More disinterested parts of the program included extension of schooling, opening forests to native livestock, protection of native property from usurers, and more careful monitoring of governmental abuse and corruption. A separate element of their program requested either parliamentary representation or membership in a special council in Paris which would give them the regular access to the central government enjoyed by the colons.

The Young Algerians attracted enormous European attention at the time, eliciting enthusiastic encouragement from many metropolitan politicians. Charles Gide, an eminent economist, warned in a 1913 lecture at the *Ecole des Hautes Etudes Sociales* that the program of the *Jeunes Algériens* was the surest path to creating an amalgam between the races without which the colons would unfailingly one day be thrown into the sea. The overwhelming majority of colons, however, feared the Young Algerians and rejected their program as a dangerous threat to the stability of French Algeria. For their part, this very narrow gallicized elite seemed to be more at home in the company of French liberals than with their own people. They never performed particularly well at the polls, a fact which they attributed to the conservative composition of the narrow electorate but which certainly reflects a degree of cultural and ideological disconnectedness.

It is probably because they sensed this isolation that Benthami and Bouderba thought it useful, in 1913, to enlist in their cause Emir Khaled, the prestigious grandson of ᶜAbd al Qadir. Khaled ibn Hashimi ibn Hajj ᶜAbd al Qadir, whom the Algerians called Emir, was born in 1875 in Syria, where he spent his entire childhood. Subsequently he studied at the elite Lycée Louis-le-Grand in Paris and was later admitted to the military academy at St-Cyr. His admission to St-Cyr was arranged "pending naturalization," a step which he subsequently refused to take. As an officer in the French army, he rose to the rank of captain and served with Marshal Lyautey in Morocco; but when he supported the former Moroccan Sultan Mawlay ᶜAbd al Aziz, after the French had begun to back his brother, ᶜAbd al Hafiz, his superiors became increasingly suspicious of his politics. Khaled signed his name to the Young Algerian charter of demands, pressed for them during talks in Paris in 1913, and the following year joined with Bouderba and Benthami in founding the *Union franco-algérienne,* which became the principal propaganda organization of the movement. In this period, Khaled proclaimed his loyalty to a French Algeria but complained that the settlers and the colonial government were the chief impediment to any program for the amelioration of the native condition. As

11. As quoted by Ageron, vol. 2 of *Histoire,* p. 235.

for the Muslims France singled out to represent Algerian interests, Khaled claimed that these "so-called representatives are really created to block our legitimate demands and serve their personal interests."[12] Because of such blunt talk, the colons in the last year before the war considered Emir Khaled the most disruptive and dangerous of the Young Algerians.

REFORM PROGRAMS, WORLD WAR I, AND THE JONNART LAW

The formation, in 1892, of a Senatorial Commission of Eighteen headed by Jules Ferry and the appointment in 1893 of his friend and colleague Jules Cambon to the Governor Generalship marked the beginning of a major effort on the part of the métropole to reform the Algerian system. For a while in 1892 and 1893, the issue of reform remained high on the agenda both of Parliament and the Parisian press. The colons, however, through their parliamentary representation and the Algerian press launched an acerbic and doggedly aggressive campaign to foil reform and eventually went on the offensive themselves. Once they had blunted the reformers' offensive, they launched the campaign mentioned earlier for greater autonomy from the métropole. A militant fringe in 1898 and 1899 was even talking insurrection and independence. One unpleasant aspect of the colon counterattack was a vitriolic and sometimes violent anti-Jewish movement. While the rhetoric invoked the Jews' influence over financial and business matters as well as their bloc voting in closely fought electoral contests, the main issue seems to have been that the enfranchisement of native Jewry, never popular with the colons, remained a symbol of the Republic's determination to impose its will on the colony. The Republic, within the context of the emerging victory of the pro-Dreyfus forces in France, never agreed to denaturalize the Algerian Jews. It did, however, as was noted earlier, accord a large measure of satisfaction to the colony by its policy of "dérattachements" and by granting it considerable financial autonomy. Finally, if there had still remained by the turn of the century any significant momentum for meaningful reform of native policy, this momentum was halted by the backlash from the Margueritte affair of 1901.

The reform movement acquired momentum again in 1907, a momentum that persisted until the outbreak of the First World War. Two factors account for the new thrust. One was the arrival on the scene of the organized and vocal Young Algeria movement; the other was the debate over and the ultimate imposition of compulsory military service on the natives. As France faced in this period the growing possibility of a war with a much more populous Germany, the notion of tapping Algeria's manpower through conscription became increasingly attractive. Ironically, the majority of colons and the majority of Muslims came together in opposition to this proposal. The colons

12. Ibid, p. 240.

feared that arming the natives could lead to insurrection or, alternatively, to inordinate native arrogance and political demands; Algerians saw little reason to fight or die for a Republic that had subjugated and humiliated them. The Young Algerians, however, perceived in conscription a vehicle through which to begin the process of extracting reforms. They were certain, as were many French liberals, that France would not long bear to ask men to die for France without according them basic civil rights.

In September 1908, Prime Minister Georges Clemenceau did, in fact, make one concession. He accorded Muslims the right they had been demanding for years of electing the Algerian members of the département general councils, who since the 1870s had been appointed. Since the population qualified to vote in département elections included only the same 5,000 who chose members of the Délégations financières, the reformers did not see Clemenceau's concession as one of overwhelming significance. A major Young Algeria delegation traveled to Paris again in 1912 to present a charter of reforms. Finally, in the winter of 1913 and 1914, several sessions of Parliament were devoted to debating the Algeria question. The only significant results were some lessening of penalties under the indigénat, the exemption from its provisions of certain categories of évolués, and the increase of Muslim representation in the municipal councils from one fourth to one third. In Algeria, both natives and settlers had been passionately interested in these debates; so in Paris was the daily press, led by the influential and usually proreform *Le Temps*. But metropolitan French politicians seemed far less concerned, since an average of only twenty or thirty of them attended the debate sessions. On most issues the colon deputies prevailed.

Further serious consideration of reform was put off until the last years of the war, partly because the Republic had other preoccupations but mainly because the sitting Governor General, Charles Lutaud, was one of the most persistent defenders of colon prerogatives. Contrary to the nervous expectations of Frenchmen who remembered 1871, Algeria remained fundamentally quiet and loyal through those difficult four years—in spite of German-Ottoman attempts to encourage sedition.[13] Including career soldiers, conscripts, and volunteers, more than 206,000 Algerians served under the tricolor during the war. Nearly 26,000 were killed or missing in action, and 72,000 were wounded, including 8,770 who were permanently disabled. Another 89,000 men were requisitioned for labor in France in addition to 30,000 who volunteered to work there. In all, more than a third of the male population between the ages of twenty and forty was in France during the war, a fact that would have enormous economic, cultural, and political consequences later.

When the philosophically anticolonialist Georges Clemenceau returned a final time to power in 1917, he determined to reward Algerians for their

13. André Nouschi, in *La naissance du nationalisme algérien*, pp. 24–28, presents discussion of aspects of German subversion and suggests that unrest in Algeria was more significant than allowed by most accounts.

contribution to the war effort. He recalled Lutaud from Algiers and replaced him with the sympathetic but paternalistic Charles Jonnart, who had already served two terms as Governor General. The cabinet's publication, in late 1917, of the reform program it intended to implement unleashed such a storm of settler protest that Jonnart eventually substituted a considerably more moderate program. In 1918, a plan to eliminate the impôts arabes was voted on June 21; and on 1 August the tribal jama^{c}as were restored and given jurisdiction over communal lands and other duwar resources. The bulk of the reforms were contained in the so-called Jonnart Law of 4 February 1919, however. This law expanded the Muslim electorate to about 425,000, or about 43 percent of the adult male population; and by instituting a separate college of non-French voters, it created, in effect, a kind of intermediate native citizenship. Empowered to vote in communal elections were all honorably discharged veterans, owners of land or businesses, active or retired civil servants, recipients of French decorations, graduates of elementary school, and members of chambers of commerce or agriculture. Muslim municipal councilmen could now participate in the election of mayors. The number of voters qualified to choose members of the general councils was raised to a little over 100,000.

Since the maximum representation of natives in the municipal councils was still limited to one-third and in the general councils to one-fourth, this newly qualified electorate was invited into a world of political activity designed to assure that most of its goals could be systematically frustrated by the representatives of the minority. At the same time the idea of a Council of Algeria seated in Paris to represent both Europeans and Muslims, which the Clemenceau cabinet had said in 1917 it favored, was dropped completely. The Jonnart legislation can be viewed in one sense as France's final rejection of the doctrine of assimilation[14] and in another as a fateful step in the direction of political instability.

In the area of personal status, all voters were exempted by the Jonnart Law from the jurisdiction of the indigénat and the tribunaux répressifs, and all Algerians were declared, in principle, eligible to hold any position in the civil service. On the critical issue of citizenship, however, no significant concessions were made, and the Jonnart Law was in some ways more restrictive than the sénatus-consulte of 1865.

Almost no one was satisfied with the reforms of 1918 and 1919. The colons thought far too much had been conceded. The widespread perception among natives was that France had promised much when accepting the tribute of Algerian lives in her hour of need, but that she had delivered little. The majority of Young Algerians, however, considering that progress had been made, decided to make the best of things. But Emir Khaled broke with his more gallicized compatriots. He called for a more thorough-going reform that included French citizenship with retention of Muslim personal status, Muslim

14. This is clearly the interpretation of Ageron, in vol. 2 of *Histoire,* p. 276.

representation in Parliament, abolition of the communes mixtes, and compulsory and free bilingual education for all Algerians. When a test of strength came in the Algiers municipal elections of 1919, the Emir's ticket won hands down. For the next four years, Khaled ibn Hashimi was the undisputed leader of the Algerian opposition movement.

THE ALGERIAN NATIONALIST MOVEMENT, 1919–1954

The settlement in Algeria of a European population determined to improve its standard of living had entailed the expropriation of the best of the country's productive resources, the progressive destructuration of the pre-1830 social order, and the reorientation of native energies toward the needs of a colonial economy, the most striking aspect of which was creation of a cheap labor pool in the countryside and later in the towns. Colonial apologetics all this time continued to insist upon the benefits that France's occupation conferred upon both land and people, a rhetoric which reached a crescendo in 1930 during the jubilant celebration of the centennial of the invasion. Young Algerians and their successors during the interwar period were to continue urging France to confirm those benefits by empowering and enfranchising the more advanced elements in society and by adopting programs to improve the abject economic condition of the masses. Yet, it is clear that survival of a colon society whose per capita income was seven times that of the Algerians depended upon the continued subordination of the majority. So it tenaciously resisted the establishment of mechanisms that would permit even the most gradual extension of rights to natives, lest they use those rights to erode European privilege. As they had since early in the century, the évolué leaders tried, between the wars, to circumvent colon intransigence by appealing to politicians of the metropolitan left, an effort which was to reach a dead end by 1938. In the meantime, a small group of separatists calling for an independent Algerian nation had made its appearance as an insignificant fringe group in the late 1920s. As their movement grew in the 1930s, it became the vocal extremist wing of the native opposition. Finally, in the 1940s, with the virtual collapse of the assimilationist program, nationalism in one form or another became the mainstream.

As the old Algerian society disintegrated, the new social formations appeared at different rates, often in isolation from each other and with few established patterns of communication amongst them horizontally or vertically. While all classes or subgroupings were profoundly touched by colonialism, they were touched by it in different ways and often had different perceptions of that reality. This meant that they developed different analyses of the colonial situation and different or only partially convergent agendas for remedy even after most accepted the basic concept of an Algerian nation. In this widely differentiated social setting, no leadership appeared before 1954 capable of building a broad consensus about either goals or tactics.

DISTORTED ECONOMIC DEVELOPMENT

The Algerian nationalist movement appeared and developed within the context of a progressively deteriorating economic situation which was caused by the conjuncture of negative world market forces, a series of bad crop years at home, and demographic pressures, all of which contributed to the growing disequilibrium within the economy as a whole. The war effort had produced a staggering rate of inflation which ate into the purchasing power of urban and some rural Algerians, leading to a period of labor unrest to which the authorities responded with sharp repression. At the same time, the index of industrial prices was rising far more rapidly than that of the agricultural products, which were the heart of the Algerian economy. Hardships caused by surpluses of unsold grain in 1919 were followed by failed harvests in 1920 that evoked for many the legendary famines of 1866 to 1870. Mortality rates soared, spurred on by the ravages of the lethal postwar epidemic of flu which the French-speaking world called *la grippe espagnole*. The harvest of 1922 was almost as bad as that of 1920, and the harvest of 1924 was the worst ever (see table 5.1).

It is worth noting that the native component of hard-wheat production, for instance, which fluctuated between four and six million quintals before the war (see table 4.4), now ranged between two and five million quintals. Yields from Algerian fields also varied more from one year to the next than did the European, reflecting the climatic vulnerability of the steppe and high plains locations onto which much native farming had been pushed, as well as minimal mechanization and backward technique. While population was growing in the period at between 1.6 percent and 2.2 percent annually, grain and most other basic food production was stagnating or regressing.

The brief period 1925 to 1930 was one of general economic recovery tied to metropolitan and world prosperity as well as to various water and other improvements undertaken by the government. A closer look at the period

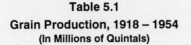

Table 5.1

Grain Production, 1918 – 1954

(In Millions of Quintals)

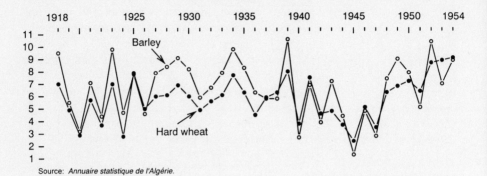

Source: *Annuaire statistique de l'Algérie.*

reveals, however, that the great bulk of the improvement was in the European sector, which benefited the Algerians largely through the consequent upturn in demand for their labor and services. Viticulture, the most profitable area of the agricultural sector, was 90 percent in European hands; vegetables and citrus production, almost as profitable, were 70 percent European. Even in the grain sector, traditionally left to the Algerians, colon entrepreneurs now accounted for 40 percent of production, including virtually all of the soft wheat. As will be seen later, this was a period of increasing marginalization of Algerian smallholders and of continuing difficulties in the southern agricultural zones which devastated native livestock herds. Sheep, which had numbered about 8,000,000 head in the prewar period, were down to 3,300,000 by 1926–27; cattle, which had numbered about 900,000 in 1914, were down to 707,000 the same year. By 1954, the cattle herd had returned to its 1914 size, but sheep had recovered only to the 6,000,000 level.

An important aspect of the agricultural recovery was the spectacular increase in wine production, which at more than 18,000,000 hectoliters annually in the mid-1930s made Algeria the third largest wine producer in the world, after only France and Italy (see table 5.2).

While viticulture was overwhelmingly a European enterprise, it was relatively labor intensive, absorbing between the wars a higher and higher percentage of the rural proletariat in pruning, various cultivation procedures, and harvesting. The business was clearly in competition with the French industry, which was the largest in the world. Algeria's flooding of already saturated French markets became a major political issue. As early as 1921, colons had to mobilize en masse to defeat a bill in the Chamber to curtail their exports to France. By the 1930s, metropolitan authorities came back on a different tack, however. They limited the size of new vineyards that could be planted first to ten and then to three hectares; by 1935, they implemented a program of

Table 5.2
Wine Production, 1918 – 1954
(In Millions of Hectoliters)

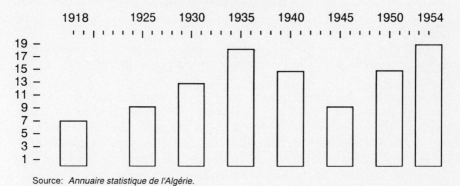

Source: *Annuaire statistique de l'Algérie.*

payments to landowners for voluntary destruction of vineyards, which may have been a factor in the leveling off of wine production thereafter.[1]

When the world depression reached Algeria in 1930, the country was particularly susceptible because of the primary nature of virtually all of its production. Iron and phosphates, both of which Algeria exported unrefined, were among the first industries hit. Between 1929 and 1932, iron ore production fell 75 percent; phosphate production in 1934 was half of what it had been in 1925. In the agricultural sector the price of a quintal of wheat dropped from 140 francs in 1929 to 80 francs in 1935–36. The bottom had fallen so completely out of the food-oil market that Kabyles could hardly earn enough from their olive harvests to buy the grains they needed, even at their historic low prices, reflecting an almost classic deflationary cycle. Unemployment and underemployment in the countryside and the cities reached critical levels, a phenomenon that was contributed to by a sharp decline in immigration to France, and, in 1933–34, an actual reversal of the flow.

The distortions in the Algerian economy, particularly its lack of the most elementary industrial base, would become painfully clear during the Second World War. Cut off from Europe, shortages of energy, machinery, and spare parts seriously curtailed productivity in almost every sector. Disappearance of the captive market for wine exports came close to ruining the entire viticulture sector. Observers at the time noted that an Algeria which exported wool had shortages of cloth; that even with its considerable reserves of phosphate rock, it was short of fertilizer; and that in spite of its huge iron deposits, it made no steel.

In 1936 Algerian industry, excluding building and public works, employed

1. The sharp drop in wine production during World War II was precipitated by the temporary disruption of the French market.

about 90,000 people, half of whom were Algerians. The average industrial concern employed only six people; in 1939 only 40,000 of the industrial labor force worked in establishments with twenty or more employees. Most were clustered around the ports and were in one way or another linked to agriculture (oil presses, breweries, cork factories, crate and box and barrel manufactories, etc.). But there were also sheet-iron works, cement factories, some metallurgy, and, of course, furniture manufacturers.

While the most obvious explanation for the minimal level of industrial development is that it reflected the economic logic of the classical colonial relationship, this relationship was, in fact, far from classical where settlers were concerned. For a century these settlers had demonstrated an uncommon ability to stand up to French politicians and to influence policy formation in their own favor. It seems more useful, therefore, to consider factors that are not necessarily specific to the colonial relationship. One such factor was that, lacking coal or major hydroelectric potential and before the crude-oil and natural-gas resources of the Sahara were discovered, energy cost 50 percent more in Algeria than it did in France. Added to this disincentive was the smallness of the 1936 Algerian market, which, in demographic terms, was not a fifth the size of the French market, and which, in terms of purchasing power, was much smaller yet. It should also be noted that the small landholding-colon oligarchy, which controlled the Délégations financières, consistently imposed heavier fiscal burdens on manufacturing and commerce than they did on agriculture. Metropolitan manufacturers did, in fact, perceive the economic advantages of cheap and less demanding Algerian manpower; but given the above factors, it was more efficient and profitable to bring that labor to France than to take the jobs to the labor.

In 1944, the central government embarked upon a program to attract light industry to the colony through various tax incentives and subsidies. Since the Assemblée financière[2] refused to grant the tax incentives, most of the encouragement took the form of borrowing or subsidies from the mother country. Some eighty-two companies employing 9,500 workers were created by 1948. The year 1949 saw the inauguration of the first of two four-year plans designed to build up the industrial infrastructure. It was in this period that some of the first heavier industry implanted itself in the country, mainly around Oran, Bône, and Algiers, at which many requisite raw materials arrived. By 1954, in spite of these efforts, only 146,000 Muslim and non-Muslim workers were employed by industry out of a total of 910,000 in the nonagricultural work force.

In the decades before the Revolution, the Algerian economy developed in a distorted and extremely unbalanced pattern, as table 5.3 illustrates.

The most striking observations about this evolution between 1880 and 1955 include the decline in the primary (agriculture and mining) sector's percentage of GDP from 46 to 31 and the increase in the secondary (industry,

2. Abolished during the war by the Pétain régime, the institution of the Délégations financières was reinstated after the coming of the Free French under this new name.

**Table 5.3   Algerian Gross Domestic Product, 1880–1955
(In Billions of 1955 Francs)[3]**

	1880	1910	1920	1930	1955
Agriculture (Including Stock Raising and Fishing)	78	138	162	194	210
Mining	—	4	10	14	19
Industry (Including Crafts)	12	17	22	31	91
Energy	—	1	1	2	13
Public works, Construction	5	8	11	13	47
Transport	1	5	8	12	16
Commerce	29	51	65	82	137
Services	32	59	62	75	116
Gross Domestic Production	155	285	340	425	650
Government Salaries	13	26	33	36	80
Gross Domestic Product	170	310	375	460	730

Source: Amin, *L'Economie du Maghreb,* vol. 1 (1966), p. 101.

energy, construction) sector's percentage from 10 to 21. Of secondary sector production, however, only two-thirds was industry per se and of that two-thirds, one-third was contributed by crafts, so that transforming industry itself accounted for only 8 percent of the gross domestic product. While the place of the tertiary sector grew more slowly, from 44 percent to 48 percent, the fact that nearly half of GDP came from sources other than the production of goods was a clear sign of a seriously underdeveloped economy.

DEMOGRAPHIC TRENDS

Two sets of contrasting phenomena best characterize the demographic changes in Algeria during the thirty-five years before the revolution: One is the slowing growth rate of the European community and the accelerating growth rate of the Muslim community. The other is the increasing over-population of many regions of the countryside coupled with almost explosive growth after 1936 of the urban Muslim population.

Except for a surge during the Spanish Civil War of 1936–39, European immigration had narrowed to a trickle by the Second World War, and most population growth was due to natural increase, which was much slower than that of the Muslims. After undergoing a net out-migration during World War II, European population stabilized and then grew to 984,000 by 1954 (see table

3. Between 1945 and 1960, the value of the French franc, eroded by World War II forces, stood at between 300 and 500 to the U.S. dollar.

4.4). On the other side, Muslim population reached 8,546,000 by 1954. Although apparent mortality and birth rates both fluctuate suspiciously, especially in the nineteenth and early twentieth centuries, this growth in population is clearly due to a conjuncture of declining death rates and increasing birth rates.

The colonial occupation had begun with years of brutal, life destroying conquest; but once it had succeeded, for all of its inequities, colonial rule established a level of security superior to that of the Ottoman period. It also created a market in which genuine famine had disappeared even if undernourishment was endemic. Colonial rule at the same time introduced in some areas rudimentary public health measures (e.g., small pox vaccination, water purification and quarantine measures). The infant mortality rate on the eve of World War II still stood at 160 per thousand live births and Algeria possessed only one hospital bed for each 4,581 people. Yet, plague had disappeared, and cholera and typhus, which had decimated whole villages and tribes in the nineteenth century, had been reduced to sporadic and limited outbreaks. These changes created an environment conducive to a general if uneven decline in death rates. Typical death rates which, between 1900 and 1910, ranged between 24 and 27 per thousand and still stood at nearly 20 per thousand during and immediately after World War I, declined into the teens during the 1920s and 1930s, only to peak again at a new high of 27.4 per thousand during World War II before declining to 17.5 per thousand by 1954.

At the same time, birth rates which stood in the range of 27 to 29 per thousand in the first decade of the century climbed during the entire 1919–54 period. Averaging 38 per thousand between the censuses of 1921 and 1926, the birth rate was 44 per thousand between 1926 and 1931 and went as high as 47 per thousand by 1954. The average annual growth of the Muslim population for the period 1886–1911 was 1.4 percent. For the period 1926–31, it had risen to 1.6 percent; for 1931–36, 2.2 percent; for 1936–48, 1.7 percent; and for 1948–54, 2 percent.

But this growth was not without posing its own problems, which is the second set of contrasts involved in this analysis. Table 5.4 illustrates the evolution of urban and rural populations for both communities.

These figures are far from perfect. There are particularly serious questions about the accuracy of the censuses of 1931 and 1936 in addition to problems around the definition of rural and urban. They nevertheless afford a clear idea of the enormous growth of the rural Muslim population, which in turn sparked the dramatic rush of Algerians toward the cities in the 1930s and especially in the 1940s and later. By 1936, Algerian rural population had reached an average density of 74.67 persons per arable square kilometer, while in some districts, such as Tizi Ouzou in the Grand Kabylia, it was more than 150. Observers have, in fact, suggested that given the physical environment and the level of technical development of the era, the countryside had probably reached saturation shortly before or after 1930. This overpopulation was accentuated by accelerating farm mechanization, which brought about a quad-

Table 5.4   Urban and Rural Population

	Urban Population					Rural Population				
	Non-Muslim	%	Muslim	%	Total	Non-Muslim	%	Muslim	%	Total
1886	297,305	57	226,126	43	523,431	167,515	5	3,061,091	95	3,228,606
1906	441,499	56	341,591	44	783,090	233,431	6	3,704,453	94	3,937,884
1926	591,908	54	508,235	46	1,100,143	236,672	5	4,107,546	95	4,344,218
1931	641,291	51	606,440	49	1,247,731	234,345	5	4,419,943	95	4,654,288
1936	709,220	50	722,293	50	1,431,513	230,311	5	4,847,814	95	5,078,125
1948	708,670	39	1,129,483	61	1,838,142	201,009	3	5,747,930	97	5,948,939
1954	788,031	37	1,398,563	63	2,186,594	196,000	3	7,147,437	97	7,343,437

Source: *Résultats statistiques du dénombrement de la population* (1948, 1954).

rupling in the number of tractors between 1934 and 1954 and a seven-fold increase in the number of harvest combines. Each of the latter could do the work of a hundred agricultural laborers.

At the same time the cities, which had for decades been predominantly and in many cases overwhelmingly European, began receiving from the mid-1930s an accelerating influx of rural migrants. While Algerian society was still only 16.6 percent urban by 1954, that figure represented a doubling in percentage terms since 1906 and at least a quadrupling numerically. Just as importantly, it marked the end of a hundred years of symbiosis, as it were, at arms reach. Until the second third of the twentieth century, most Algerians, while firmly integrated into the economic order created by colonialism and maintained there by the political power colonialism projected, lived socially and culturally at considerable distance from Europeans, who were concentrated in the cities, particularly in the larger ones. The city of Oran, only 12.7 percent Muslim in 1921 was 40.5 percent Algerian by 1954. Algiers which was about three-fourths European in 1926 was 45.5 percent Muslim by 1954. In most smaller towns, the Muslims were now small to substantial majorities. In the thirty towns where the great bulk of European population lived, the population was now 60.7 percent Muslim. Physical proximity within a framework of institutionalized inequality only heightened intercommunal tensions.

STRATIFICATION AND IMPOVERISHMENT IN RURAL SOCIETY

The social movement apparent in rural society before World War I continued and accelerated after that war. At the upper end of the scale, property continued to concentrate, while at the lower end, holdings fragmented even more and the agricultural proletariat and subproletariat swelled rapidly. In between the bottom and the top, there appeared more distinctly than before the war a class of middle-sized landowners. While the data series are difficult to correlate because of changes in categories after the war and because the information collected sometimes concerns the whole of Algeria and other times only the northern part, table 5.5, for the period from 1930 to 1950, indicates the direction of changes in landholding patterns along with ideas of their magnitude.[4]

Table 5.5   Muslim Algerian Landholding in 1930 and 1950

Size of Holding	1930	1950
100 or More Hectares		
Number of Properties	7,035	8,496
% of All Properties	1.1	1.3
Area of Land	1,593,498	1,688,800
% of All Land	21.1	23.0
50 to 99 Hectares		
Number of Properties	35,962	16,580
% of All Properties	5.8	2.6
Area of Land	1,595,398	1,096,100
% of All Land	21.0	14.9
10 to 49 Hectares		
Number of Properties	140,010	167,170
% of All Properties	22.7	26.5
Area of Land	2,635,275	3,185,800
% of All Land	34.8	43.3
Less Than 10 Hectares		
Number of Properties	434,537	437,647
% of All Properties	70.4	69.5
Area of Land	1,738,806	1,378,400
% of All Land	23.0	18.7
Total Number of Properties, 1930	617,544	
Total Number of Properties, 1950	630,732	
Total Land, 1930	7,562,877	
Total Land, 1950	7,349,100	

Source: Ageron, *Histoire de l'Algérie contemporaine,* vol. 2 (1979), p. 495.

4. These data were drawn by Charles-Robert Ageron from the respective editions of *Statistique quinquennale agricole.* Samir Amin, in vol. 1 of *L'économie du Maghreb,* also uses them. An indication of the kind of problems they posed is demonstrated in the 50 to 99 hectare category for 1930. If one divides the stated number of properties (35,962) into the total land area assigned to that category (1,595,398 ha), the average size of such a holding is only 44.4 ha, which is mathematically impossible.

While most specialists in twentieth-century Algerian social history have correctly stressed the impoverishment and proletarianization of rural society, this observation should not obscure the fact of a concomitant social stratification, as well.[5] By 1950, the 8,496 largest landowners controlled 23 percent of the land owned by Algerians, while 437,647 in the less-than-10-hectares category farmed only 18.7 percent. The average size of the holding in the richest category was 199 hectares, while the average size in the poorest category was only 3.1 hectares, far less than enough to live on in all but the richest and best watered soils. The average size of the smallest farms had shrunk 22 percent, from 4 hectares, in only twenty years. The large landholders employed tens of thousands of Algerian workers, while the smallholders were for the most part themselves blended into that labor pool, at least on an occasional or seasonal basis.

It was to the middle group that colonial apologists pointed with great pride, claiming that France's dismantling of ᶜarsh and jointly held mulk had permitted emergence on the land a comfortable native middle class which, given time, would become the mainstay of rural society. Since the average size of the holdings in the larger of the two middle groups, the 10-to-49-hectare category, is only 19 hectares (which in most Algerian soils must be considered the lower limit of "comfortable"),[6] it seems logical to conclude that half, at most, of this group could be considered well off. If this half is added to the category owning 50 to 99 hectares, this new rural middle class seems to number about 100,000, or 16 percent, of the 630,732 Algerian landowners counted in 1950.

But the significance of this "comfortable" class needs to be appreciated within the total rural context. Because of problems with definitions and the floating of individuals between categories, it is very difficult to discuss the agricultural proletariat in precise quantitative terms. Most analysts, however, indicate that the rural proletariat reached its greatest size in the 1920s or 1930s and then shrank somewhat as growth of agricultural production slowed and as European agriculture mechanized. Permanent employees in the agricultural sector, who are the easiest to count, were said to be 108,000 in 1954. Occasional or seasonal workers were estimated at between 400,000 and 500,000. What is most striking in the period, however, is a massive increase in rural unemployment, which in 1954 was put at 400,000. If one adds to this number 250,000 underemployed and a portion of the sharecroppers and herders, a total of nearly 1,000,000 workers appears usually to have been unemployed, about half of the rural population of working age. Studies from the 1930s indicated that between 65 percent and 75 percent of the rural population was at the time "poor" or "very poor."

Using categories significantly different from those in table 5.5, the economist Samir Amin developed the following figures to illustrate the unequal distribution of income in the countryside in the mid-1950s.

5. Amin, in vol. 1 of *L'économie*, pp. 121–31, was one of the first to stress this growing social differentiation.
6. The French word translated is *aisé*.

Table 5.6 Agricultural Income Distribution (In Thousands of 1955 Francs)

	Number of Persons	Total Income	Per Capita Income
Workers			
Permanent	100,000	10,000,000	100
Occasional &			
Seasonal	500,000	24,000,000	40–60
Landowners			
Small	210,000	13,000,000	60
Medium	210,000	42,000,000	200
Large	50,000	28,000,000	560
European	—	93,000,000	—
TOTALS	1,070,000	210,000,000	110

Source: Amin, *L'Economie du Maghreb,* vol. 1 (1966), p. 130.

THE NEW URBAN SOCIETY

The French historian Charles-Robert Ageron claimed that Algerian society changed more between the years 1920 and 1950 than it had in the preceding century.[7] Nowhere is this dramatic transformation more apparent than in the cities, which had held 5 percent of the Algerian population in 1830, held 8.5 percent just before World War I, and, as we have seen, 16.6 percent in 1954.

At the top of the urban social structure sat a small upper bourgeoisie of perhaps 5,000 to 6,000 economically active men. Because their path to power was blocked by the European ruling classes, this modernized native bourgeoisie could not be considered a true capitalist bourgeoisie in the Marxist sense. Yet, by standard of living, influence within the Muslim community, and social cohesiveness, they stood out as a successful elite on which other urban classes modelled. Members of this bourgeoisie were factory owners, proprietors of large commercial firms, high-level civil servants and managers, and the more affluent practitioners of the liberal professions. While not all had benefited from advanced levels of French education, it was the French educated intelligentsia who gave the bourgeoisie its dominant tone. Mostly, they lived in French style homes, adopted or adapted to many French customs and values, and supported assimilationist programs of the Young Algerians and their successors. In 1920, they wore the fez as a sign of cultural inheritance and class distinction; by 1954 they dressed completely in the European style. With

7. Ageron, vol. 2 of *Histoire de l'Algérie contemporaine,* p. 517.

some exceptions the upper bourgeoisie affiliated with conservative to moderate political movements through which, in the years before World War II, they dominated Muslim electoral politics in the cities.

Much larger and more significant for the future political evolution of the country was the middle class,[8] whose economically active component numbered around 200,000.[9] This class included less affluent members of the liberal professions, craftsmen, small and middle businessmen, middle-level civil servants, technicians, white-collar workers, and the best paid skilled workers. Sandwiched between the Muslim upper bourgeoisie (whose life-style they alternately emulated and railed against) and the privileged European middle classes (level for level much better off materially than they and whom they bitterly resented), this class presented, by the 1940s, a fertile field for the recruitment of nationalist militants. After World War II, they would come to dominate the urban political scene, slowly relegating most of the upper bourgeoisie to the political sidelines.

The proletariat, the third important component of urban society, was composed of three distinct elements: At the bottom, was a mass of unemployed, officially counted in 1954 at 133,000, or 28 percent of the urban work force, but which one specialist claims ranged, in the 1950s, between 150,000 and 230,000.[10] Piled up as they were in the old Arab quarters and the swelling *bidonvilles* that had first begun to appear on the edges of the Algerian cities in the 1920s, this lumpenproletariat represented the human surplus pushed out of the overcrowded and impoverished countryside, and they were notoriously difficult to count. Counting dependents, the lumpen represented a mass of about 600,000 people without visible regular means of support.

At the next level were the workers themselves, the largest group, consisting of 146,000 unskilled laborers scattered through the construction industry, dock work, manufacturing, and the services. There were additionally, in 1954, some 72,000 skilled workers distributed through a broad range of trades.

The third level of the Algerian urban proletariat did not live in Algeria at all. Reflecting the dependence of the Algerian economy upon industrial production located in the métropole, nearly 300,000 Algerian workers were employed in France in 1954, significantly more than the 228,000 who had found jobs in Algerian cities. Mostly bachelors who rotated in and out of the French work force, these young workers had a profound impact on cultural and political life in Algeria, both because of the nature of their experiences in Europe and because of the leavening their ideas and attitudes provided once they came home again.

8. French sociology normally distinguishes *bourgeoisie* from *classes moyennes* on the basis, first, of capital controlled, and, second, of levels of consumption.
9. Amin, in vol. 1 of *L'économie*, p. 156, finds 225,000 in this class. His data, however, refer to the "non-agricultural" population, which is considerably larger than the "urban" population. Ageron, in vol. 2 of *Histoire*, refers to about 181,000 in cities per se, but here he also includes the better paid skilled workers.
10. Amin, vol. 1 of *L'économie*, p. 155.

EDUCATION FROM 1919 TO 1954

By 1919, Muslim resistance to French education had for practical purposes disappeared and had been replaced by a growing chorus of demands for the building and upgrading of schools. Yet all through the interwar years the Délégations financières resisted those demands, partly for financial and partly for ideological reasons. During the period, 10 percent to 12 percent of the colonial operating budget went to education, but of those funds, only 20 percent was devoted to educating Muslims, who were 86 percent of the population. In 1921, the number of Muslims in primary schools was 46,000; in 1931, it was 69,000. Finally, by 1944, the primary school enrollment had reached 110,000, which was not quite 9 percent of the children between the ages of seven and fourteen. The great majority were taught in special native schools or in separate classes attached to the European schools, which were characterized by very high student-teacher ratios, physical overcrowding, and lowered academic standards.

In 1944, the Provisional Government of the French Republic, then located in Algiers, took several pressing matters, including education, directly into its own hands. Over vocal colon objections, it ordered an increase of the education expenditures to 18 percent of the operating budget and an accelerated program of school-building. In the next ten years, the number of classrooms grew from 6,500 to nearly 12,000 and the number of primary school pupils to 397,000, nearly a fourfold increase over 1939 but still representing only 12.75 percent of the elementary-age group.

During the same era, Muslim enrollment in secondary schools grew from 690 in 1927 to 1,358 in 1940 and then to 5,308 in the fall of 1954. The University of Algiers matriculated 47 Muslims in 1920, 94 in 1939, and 686 in 1954.

In spite of the restricted access to the colonial education establishment, the influence of French ideas, particularly the liberal and liberating ideologies of the Enlightenment and the French Revolution, was to influence enormously the way Algerian elites shaped the movement toward national liberation. But when the War of National Independence broke out, 86 percent of Algerian men and 95 percent of Algerian women were still illiterate, a monumental indictment of a system that for more than a century had claimed to be civilizing the uncivilized.

ALGERIAN WOMEN

While the status of women differed somewhat in the various types of Algerian communities, law and custom in all of them insisted upon a high degree of segregation of the sexes. Women and men were viewed as occupying two separate spheres: the internal procreative, nurturing one for the former; the external, civic, political one for the latter. Men knew their mothers as parents who doted on them and derived pride and status from the fact of their existence; later they knew women as wives, who satisfied their sexual urges and produced sons for them. Other than in these two relationships, there was little communication between the sexes.

Both the Maliki rite of Islamic law and Berber customary law tended to assure not only the segregation of the sexes but, to the extent they could, the subordination of the female to the male. That subordination was social and economic as well as legal. While such subordination is found throughout the Islamic world, it clearly reflects patterns antedating the coming of Islam. One can find it in Catholic Sicily, fifth-century Athens, orthodox Judaism, and Kabyle custom. The latter accords women even less protection than does the shari^{c}a. The French ethnologist Germaine Tillion, using data collected mainly in Algeria, suggests that the segregation/subordination pattern is essentially Mediterranean and the product of a continuing transition of populations from nomadic or seminomadic tribal organization to that of towns or cities.[11] One's clan (firq), viewed as a single large family, represented the most noble and pure of people. One sought to preserve that nobility by assuring the purity of its bloodlines through instituting a system of endogamy that favored the marriage of brothers' children to each other. Members of the firq were mutually pledged to uphold and defend the lives, property, *and* the purity of the bloodline of all of their kinsmen. Women within this system, according to Tillion's hypothesis, were a man's property, but the entire clan respected and defended that property. Because of the security of the environment, women enjoyed great freedom in the ways they circulated, communicated, and related to other members of the community. As nomadic and seminomadic peoples moved to towns and cities, however, the protections of the firq disappeared. To compensate, men devised other measures to protect their honor and the purity of their bloodlines. These included growing restraints upon the liberty of women as demonstrated in the Algerian case by the restrictions found in Berber qanuns and in Maliki law. Many scholars have argued, incidentally, that the Qur'an and Muhammad's authentic teachings put far fewer restraints on women than does the mature shari^{c}a, which was formulated during a period of rapid urbanization.

Women in towns and in many villages are more restricted in movement and in dress than they are in the traditional tribal setting. But the most important Maliki restraint upon a woman's freedom is found in a series of provisions which make her a ward of males throughout her life. As an unmarried female she is the ward of her father, grandfather, or brother; as a married woman she is the ward of her husband.[12] In most cases the guardian may give her in marriage without consulting her. Once she is married, she is required to obey her husband, who may punish her physically for conduct he finds offensive and may divorce her without cause. A husband is permitted up to four wives simultaneously. A wife, on the other hand, is permitted only one

11. Germaine Tillion, *Le harem et les cousins.*
12. In many instances, however, the divorced or widowed woman is free from such guardianship.

husband at a time and may divorce only in certain narrowly defined circumstances. It should be noted, however, that since most Algerian marriages tended through the period considered here to remain endogamous, family considerations limited to some extent the mistreatment of wives and unjustified divorce.

Islamic law, however, provides certain benefits to women that are absent in some of the Berber codes. These are especially evident in the economic sphere. The husband is required to support his wife at a material level comparable to that she enjoyed in her father's house. The *mahr,* or dowry, remains the wife's property throughout the marriage and provides her with a certain financial security. In many instances it serves as a guarantee against divorce, particularly if she has lent any of it to her husband, since he is required to repay it in the event the marriage dissolves. The shari^{c}a leaves very little individual choice to Muslims in the distribution of their estates. It provides that females receive only half of the inheritance due a male in the same degree of relationship. But these inheritances, which women of the middle and upper classes may expect to receive periodically over the course of their lives, are solely their property.

The colonial authorities did not attempt major alterations of Algerian family law. A Royal Ordinance of 26 September 1842 established a dual judiciary that formally made Muslim justice a branch of the French legal system. For generations, qadis trained in state madrasas handed down Islamic justice in the name of the French Republic. The only major innovation in family law, one that was frequently ignored, was a twentieth-century provision that forbade the marriage of girls under the age of fifteen. But, law aside, the presence of France over many generations was having an effect upon the status of women and the perceptions of that status.

French influence worked in opposite directions. In one direction, it actually favored the pattern of segregation and the subordination of women by dismantling the tribal system and accelerating the process of urbanization. Furthermore the cosmopolitan nature, racially and morally, of the centers to which many tribespeople were displaced certainly exacerbated the anxieties referred to by Tillion in her model. Studies also suggest that some male Algerians denied access and recognition by the colon system took out their frustrations by turning into tyrants at home.

But the French models, values, and institutions that were affecting other aspects of Algerian life could not fail to make some Algerians, particularly those who lived in the cities, question family values and the structure of gender relations. Surveys showed that the marriage of very young girls was increasingly frowned upon. With regard to polygamy, French figures, which may or may not be accurate, showed that while 16 percent of married Algerian males had more than one wife in 1886, only 3 percent did in 1948, and the average age of these men was more than sixty-five years. It is unclear, of course which factors weighed most heavily in the decline of polygamy: French disapproval (which was continuous and vocal), changing economic realities and housing patterns, or changing attitudes toward the practice in the broader Arab world. French education clearly influenced the attitudes of many men toward women. It also influenced the attitudes of the girls who had access to it. In 1907–08, 2,667 Muslim girls were attending French primary schools; but by 1953–54, there were 76,610 female primary pupils, 952 secondary students, and 22 university students. While still only a small minority of all girls had access to schooling of any kind, attitudes toward the education of girls clearly changed substantially during the first half of the twentieth century. Such changes reflected a readiness in many families to consider different roles for their daughters than those their mothers had filled, and they also began producing a generation of young women who would want different roles for themselves. At the same time, however, as key sectors of the public sphere that traditionally belonged to males came under control of the French, the inner, women's sphere was perceived by men, as well as by many women, as the last redoubt of cultural authenticity that must be preserved from change at all costs.

THE ALGERIAN OPPOSITION
AFTER WORLD WAR I

After enactment of the Jonnart laws of February 1919, the Young Algerian opposition split into two broad groupings. One, whose nominal leader continued to be Dr. Benthami, largely resigned itself to the equivocal nature of the new legislation and began to devote itself mainly to the pursuit of specific goals of interest to their various district constituencies. The other, headed by the Emir Khaled, determined to keep campaigning for full realization of the Young Algeria program. The central elements of the Emir's program were his continuing call both for citizenship without renunciation of personal status and for Muslim representation in Paris equal to that of the Europeans. When, during the summer of 1920, the colon delegation in Parliament persuaded the legislature to reinstate the indigénat (on a "temporary" basis that lasted until 1944), abolition of the exceptive laws became the third major element of the Emir's program.

By broadening the franchise of the second, or Muslim, college, the Jonnart Law had created a new political climate in Algeria. The existence of a Muslim electorate of 500,000 led to much more overt political discourse and activity than before the war. In the long run, this expanded body of voters, whom some planners had envisioned serving as a body of communicators between French and Algerian communities, became the most visible victims of a blocked system organically incapable of permitting the merger of the two peoples. In the short run, they provided a basis for a considerable broadening and popularization of politics, which redounded mostly to the benefit of Khaled, who was by now the most popular politician in the country. In the spring 1920 municipal elections at Algiers, his slate overwhelmed a more moderate Young Algerian slate organized by Benthami. When the prefectural council subsequently invalidated the results on the grounds that Khaled's campaign had appealed to "religious fanaticism," the electorate proceeded later the same year to return him to the General Council of the département by an even larger margin.

The colons, in the meantime, determined to foil the Algerian "nationalists" and "trouble-makers," had organized a conference of mayors which in turn galvanized the Délégations financières, whose principal victory was engineering the reinstatement of the code de l'indigénat. Their most eloquent and, in many ways, most influential spokesman was a Deputy from Constantine, Morinaud, who, in a 1920 speech, elaborated most succinctly the basis of colon opposition to assimilation of the natives. In the same 1920 speech, he offered his analysis of the "native problem," which is a classic of the genre:

> The colons are the best friends of the natives. That is the truth. They know our natives, their faults and their virtues . . . and they treat them as they should be treated, believe me. The good native, hardworking and honest— this is the majority—is their friend, their protégé. That is the truth. . . . To represent France as their adversary, as their exploiter or as a sort of slave driver who crossed the Mediterranean to enrich himself at the expense of the natives, is not only to commit an enormous error, but to commit an injustice and an odious calumny.[13]

The principal troublemaker, from the colon point of view, was Khaled, who in spite of constant attacks from official and unofficial elements of the colon establishment, continued to press for his program. When President Alexandre Millerand visited Algeria in 1922, the Emir took the occasion to declare unequivocally to the chief of state that "the people of Algeria are all, without distinction as to religion or race, equally children of France and have an equal right in her home." He went on to argue that "the desire we have to create within the bosom of France a status worthy of us and worthy of France is the best proof that we are good Frenchmen and wish only to strengthen the bonds that attach us to the mother country." In spite of such explicit evidence of Khaled's assimilationist vision, a number of Algerian as well as French writers have tried to portray Khaled ibn Hashimi as the first Algerian nationalist.[14] This argument rests partly in the false accusations the establishment made against him and partly in the fact that the French Communist party, searching for the "bourgeois nationalist" elements with which Lenin had recommended alliance, claimed for a while to have found such a nationalist in him. In 1924, in fact, after Khaled had been exiled from Algeria, he accepted a Communist invitation to lecture before their Union intercoloniale at

13. As quoted by André Nouschi, in La naissance du nationalisme algérien, pp. 57–58.
14. See, for instance, Mahfoud Kaddache, vol. 1 of Histoire du nationalisme algérien pp. 182–86. See also Charles-André Julien, L'Afrique du Nord en marche. Nationalismes musulmans et souveraineté française, 3d ed, pp. 100–1.

Paris. There he came into contact with some of the same émigré workers who were shortly to found the *Etoile nord-africaine,* the first explicitly nationalist movement. But even though he permitted his name to be used by the Communists because, at the time, they represented the only French movement willing to speak out against colonial injustice, there is no evidence that he ever made the long leap from aspiring son of France to nationalism.

By 1923, Khaled was becoming frustrated and bitter at French intransigence while, at the same time, the colonial government was encountering considerable success at isolating him from his colleagues, who came to fear personal and career consequences of close association with his brand of "radicalism." In April, Khaled abruptly withdrew from the race for the Conseil Général of the Algérois and halted publication of *Ikdam,* his newspaper. Then, at the end of July, he left Algeria for the last time, embarking into exile first at Alexandria and then in Damascus. Some contemporaries claimed he had been brutally expelled, others that French political and tactical successes had impelled him to make the decision himself. But pressures other than the political were involved, because Khaled was seriously in debt and was therefore personally vulnerable. It appears the government agreed to pay off his debts, to pay for his passage to the Near East, and to increase both his military pension and his pension as a descendant of ʿAbd al Qadir. He pressed his program for another year or two from the Near East and from Paris, but as time passed, his activity and his influence declined. A decade later in January 1936, when news reached Algeria of his death at Damascus, Algerians across the whole political spectrum rose up to mourn his passing and extol his legacy. They lionized him to such an extent that Khaled ibn Hashimi became, from that time onward, one of the sainted ancestors in the Algerian national tradition.

THE FÉDÉRATION DES ÉLUS INDIGÈNES

In the 1920s, four movements emerged to give voice in four different idioms to Algerian dissatisfaction with the status quo. The fact that these movements all sprang into life within a year or two of each other is clearly symptomatic of a decisive *prise de conscience* within the country. Of differing size and constituency, each movement went through important mutations over the decades, but among them, sometimes in competition and sometimes in collaboration, they provided the framework through which increasingly frustrated Algerian elites sought to use the political process to change or abolish the colonial system. But the fact that their analyses of the Algeria problem and their programs for solution differed so markedly from each other did not augur well for the creation of a unified national movement. These movements were the *Fédération des élus indigènes,* the Islamic Reform movement, the Etoile nord-africaine, and the Algerian Communist movement, which will be discussed in turn.

At least until the middle 1930s, it was the évolués wielding the Young

Algerian reform program who dominated the native side of the Franco-Algerian political dialogue. While they never inspired or spoke for more than a small minority of their compatriots, these gallicized elites held their prominent place as long as they did because of the superior skills with which French education had equipped them, because they had been the first natives to enter the political arena, because of the encouragement they received from French liberals, and because other groups until the 1930s remained insufficiently politicized.

In 1926, the Young Algerians most involved in political life, having drawn lessons from the superior organization of French elected officials, determined to try to increase their effectiveness by forming the Fédération des élus indigènes. The gallicized and moderate Benthami ould Hamida, who at the time was editor of the principal Young Algerian weekly, *Attakadoum,* was the first president of the organization and remained in that position until he was unseated in 1930. With 150 men in attendance, the Fédération held its first Congress at Algiers in September 1927, adopting a program that called for native representation in Parliament, equal payment for equal work in the bureaucracy, equality in length of military service,[15] free travel between Algeria and France, abolition of the indigénat, development of academic and vocational education, extension of metropolitan social legislation to Algeria, and reorganization of electoral procedures in the communes mixtes. While it is still possible in this period to find an articulate minority of very Europeanized élus whose main goal was unqualified assimilation into France, by the late 1920s, the key concept for most was no longer assimilation but equality—civilly, politically, juridically, and in professional and economic access. For most of the élus, being French did not connote the negation of Algerian or Muslim identity but, rather, a freer, nondiscriminatory environment within which to pursue their individual paths and fortunes. Algerian culture and personality should remain intact while the smaller Algerian fatherland moved progressively toward the greater French fatherland or, as the 1920s student leader Ferhat Abbas put it in the title of his collected essays, while Algeria moved "from colony to province."[16]

From the beginning, the Fédération des élus was beset by divisions both vertical and horizonal which translated into tactical, personal, and occasionally ideological quarrels. A significant majority in the organization were officials in the communes mixtes, who by and large stayed closer to the day-to-day native reality and were consequently unable to share totally the vision of the Europeanized politicians of the communes de plein exercice. There were also regional differences. More populous, more urban, and of deeper intellectual tradition, the Constantinois throughout the twentieth century supplied Algeria with even more than its share of intellectual and political leadership. With the exception of Tlemcen, Oranie, whose nomadic and seminomadic society

15. Muslims were liable by this time for two years of compulsory military service; Europeans for only one.
16. Ferhat Abbas, *De la colonie vers la province. Le jeune algérien,* 2d ed. The original edition was published in 1931.

had propelled it to such prominence during the phase of armed resistance, contributed far fewer leaders to the new political phase of struggle. The Algiers département swung between the two tendencies. Partly owing to these structural anomalies and partly owing to dissatisfaction with the leadership of Benthami, whose moderation made him appear to some as almost an administration candidate, the Federation, in 1930, divided itself into three departmental federations, which occasionally met together in congress but which henceforward eschewed permanent colony-wide organization.

From this reorganization the Fédération des élus indigènes of Constantine emerged in a clear position of leadership, and from it emerged the two most prominent leaders of the movement. The most influential of these, from 1933 through 1936, was Mohamed Salah Bendjelloul of Constantine. Born in 1898 into a middle-class family of modest means, he attended lycée in his native city, earned an M.D. degree from the University of Algiers, and became a public health service physician in 1924. Entering politics in the early thirties, he distinguished himself initially by his victories against proadministration candidates, and he seemed to presage a significant radicalization of the Young Algerian-élu movement. The major instrument for projecting his programs was the newspaper *La Voix indigène* in which, down until 1942, he tirelessly promoted the advantages of assimilation to France. While he was an effective orator and the most visible and powerful leader in the élu movement for several years, Bendjelloul's personal ambition in time seemed to take precedence over ideological commitment, and eventually Algerian political discourse left him behind.

The most famous and durable leader to emerge from the élu movement was Ferhat Abbas (1899–1985). He was born at Taher in the Lesser Kabylia, the son of an appointed qa'id who had been decorated with the Legion of honor and whose own father had been one of the victims of the Kabylia repression of 1871. Abbas, by climbing through the French educational system and earning a degree in pharmacy, represents one of the best examples of the track followed by the minority of traditional Algerian families that successfully made the transition into the colonial system. Head of the Muslim student organization at the University of Algiers, he became passionately involved in the issues of equality and assimilation that energized his class in the period. After opening a pharmacy in Sétif in 1931, he entered local politics, winning election to the General Council of the Constantinois in 1933, the Municipal Council of Sétif in 1935, and the Délégations financières in 1936. In 1935, he founded *L'Entente franco-musulmane* at Constantine, the organ of the Fédération des élus, which stood out as the most influential évolué publication during the rest of the decade.

THE ISLAMIC REFORM MOVEMENT

It was noted in chapter 4 that the Islamic Reform movement, inspired by Muhammad ʿAbduh and his pupil Muhammad Rashid Rida, had already attracted a certain Algerian following during the first decade of the century. It was not until the 1920s, however, that the movement began to create the kind of organization that would permit it to exert significant cultural and political influence.

Undisputed leader of the reformist movement until his death in 1940 was Shaykh ʿAbd al-Hamid Ben Badis. Born in 1889 at Constantine, of a patrician family whose grandfather and father had both held high office in the colonial administration and whose brother was a French educated lawyer, Ben Badis chose a different route. After a private traditional education in Algeria, he completed his studies at the venerable Zituna mosque university in Tunis, made the hajj, and then visited the major Near Eastern cities. While a man of deep personal, almost mystic faith, he proceeded upon his return to Algeria to devote the rest of his life to the very public work of the renaissance and purification of Algerian Islam.

Other figures in the movement included Bashir Ibrahimi of Bougie (1880–1965), who spent ten years in the Arab east, studying at Medina and teaching at Damascus, and who eventually became leader of the movement at Tlemcen. Shaykh Tayyib al-ʿUqbi of Biskra (1888–1960) spent most of his formative years in the Hijaz, where he was greatly influenced by neo-Wahhabi doctrine. Finally, the most intellectually powerful of the group was Mubarak al Mili, who, after studying with Ben Badis in Algeria, followed in his steps by completing his education at the Zituna.

In 1924, under Ben Badis's leadership, these and other reformists met to lay the plans which culminated in the creation of the periodical al-Muntaquid in July 1925. When this publication was shut down, in 1926, for including an article judged sympathetic to the Moroccan Rif rebellion, the ʿulama replaced it with al-Shihab (The Meteor), a monthly which remained their principal organ until its suppression on security grounds at the advent of World War II.

The program of the reformers, which called for a purification of Islam by returning to its roots in the Qur'an and the early Sunna of the Prophet, stressed additionally the necessity of opening the Islamic community to the spirit of modern scholarly inquiry and scientific method. By invoking the example of the salafs or earliest Arab Muslims, the reformers' program also promoted allegiance to Arab ancestors, to the Arab "métropole" in the east and to the Arabic language, thus explicitly repudiating the évolué notion that salvation for Algerian Muslims lay in merger with or into France. Between 1928 and 1932, Mubarak al Mili produced in two volumes the first national history in Arabic, Ta'rikh al jaza'ir fi l qadim wa l hadith (History of Algeria in Antiquity and in Modern Times). In his discussion of the discipline of history, al Mili sees it not only as the mirror of the past but as the creator of the present, the proof of nationhood, and the prerequisite of national recovery. Even more remarkable was the history of Ahmad Tawfiq al-Madani, another of the Shihab group, which was published in 1932. His work, Kitab al jaza'ir (Book of Algeria), begins with a preface in which he points to the absurdity of supposing that two peoples with totally different customs, language, and history can ever be one. The preface concludes with the appeal to his readers to adopt both in word and in deed the slogan "Islam is my religion; Arabic is my language; Algeria is my fatherland." This slogan, recited for years by pupils in the Qur'anic schools founded by the reformist movement, eventually became the official motto of the independent Algerian Republic.

From the beginning, the reformist ʿulama vigorously attacked the marabouts and brotherhoods for their promotion of destructive heterodoxy and superstition. They clearly saw them as anachronistic survivals of a rural aristocracy long since subverted by the colonial exploiters. Nor did they spare in their attacks much of the official religious establishment, which in its espousal of the narrowest forms of malikism and in its self-serving subordination to colonial authority seemed almost as responsible as the marabouts for the deplorable state into which Algerian Islam had fallen. By 1931, zawiya chiefs, smarting under the barrage of attacks, sought an agreement with the more moderate elements of reformism on the basis of a common program of religious and moral renewal. Discussions resulted the same year in creation of the Association of Muslim Algerian ʿUlama under the presidency of Shaykh Ben Badis and the vice presidency of Bashir Ibrahimi. After a year of very uneasy cohabitation and conflict, the reformists expelled the tariqa representatives, who went on to form a separate movement. A veritable war of religion ensued, which saw the reformists increasingly using the mosques as fora to attack the obscurantism and subservience of the other side. The colonial government, which had at first considered the Ben Badis people a narrowly intellectual movement of little political consequence, now began to react. The Desmichels Circular of 1933 forbade access to official mosques to all but official imams, an initiative that provoked such widespread outrage throughout the country that it is said to have contributed materially to the wave of agitation and unrest that soon surged up and lasted for years. At the same time, the so-called war of religion, with its scarcely concealed political overtones, reached a crescendo in 1936. In July of that year, the Maliki Mufti of Algiers, Bendali Mahmoud, sent a telegram to Paris protesting the credentials of a group of reformist ʿulama members of a wider delegation carrying the Algerian agenda to the recently installed Popular Front government. Two weeks later the Mufti was assassinated. Suspecting reformist complicity, the police arrested Shaykh Tayyib al-ʿUqbi, who was freed only after a long period of litigation. Many saw in the whole affair the manipulative hand of an administration determined to preserve the official religious institution, support cooperative marabouts, and undermine their challengers.

History's evaluation of the contribution of the reformist ʿulama movement is mixed. While it did much to stimulate the renewal of Algerian Islam in a formal sense, it never attracted a broad following. It has been argued, furthermore, that, to the extent the reformers were successful in undermining the credibility of rural preachers and detaching rural believers from the popular, indigenous forms of their religion, they may actually have contributed to a lessening of religious observance. In the cities, it has been observed that many young people, listening intently to the ʿulama's blazing indictments of their parents' religion, and witnessing the brutal internecine religious infighting, came to reject religion entirely.

On the positive side, the main contribution of the reformist ʿulama was that they were the first to articulate with clarity and eloquence the proposition that Algerians belonged to a distinct nation with its own specific culture and glorious past, which could never be confounded in another. In a celebrated 1936 *Entente* article, Ferhat Abbas wrote that after questioning history, the living and the dead, and visiting the cemeteries, he had concluded that the Algerian fatherland did not exist and that therefore one should link one's future definitively with that of France.[17] Ben Badis responded two months later in *al-Shihab* that the Algerian nation indeed existed and that that nation "is not France, cannot be France, and does not wish to be France."[18]

In spite of such examples of ideological clarity, however, the reformist movement always seemed torn between its cultural and religious vocation on the one hand and what many of its leaders considered as the secondary and potentially corrupting distraction of political activism. Sometimes its leaders sounded like nationalists and other times they feared being labeled radicals; still other times they sent telegrams of loyalty to the head of the French Republic. Such ambiguities in the long run limited the contributions the movement could make to growth of the national movement.

THE ETOILE NORD-AFRICAINE

While the Islamic reformers were trying to return religion to the true path and évolués through their fédérations des élus were campaigning for the rights of Frenchmen, Algerian workers in Paris were creating a national movement. By the middle 1920s, the North African worker community in France, which was overwhelmingly Algerian, had grown to about 100,000. Culturally isolated and confronted with numerous material problems, the workers discovered that only the French far left, the anarchists and especially the Communists, demonstrated much interest in their issues or their welfare. A small group of Algerians joined the French Communist party and a somewhat larger group the *Confédération générale du travail unitaire* (CGTU), the party's labor confederation. The Communists' *Union intercoloniale,* where the exiled Emir Khaled had already lectured, apparently encouraged the convening of a congress of Maghribi workers in December 1924. That congress, in addition to taking up the Emir Khaled's agenda, also drafted a detailed list of economic and social demands. Eventually, in a series of meetings between March and July

17. Not as often cited, however, is Abbas's admonition five paragraphs later that "without emancipation of the natives there is no durable French Algeria." Quoted in Claude Collot and Jean-Robert Henry, *Le mouvement national algérien* p. 67.
18. *Al-Shihab,* April 1936, as translated from the French in Collot and Henry, *Le mouvement,* p. 69.

1926, the Etoile nord-africaine was founded, the first permanent Maghribi political organization in France. It was governed by a board of directors composed principally of Communist party or CGTU members of which Hadj Ali Abd al Qadir was president and Messali Hadj secretary general.

Messali Hadj, who for a quarter of a century would personify the most radical and nationalistic wing of the Algerian opposition, first hired out in France as a day laborer, then as a delivery boy, and finally, between 1926 and 1933, kept a stall in a market. Born in Tlemcen in 1898 of a lower middle-class Kouloughli family, he attended a kuttab operated by Darqawa brethren and earned an elementary school diploma at a colonial school. He served three years in the French army in the Bordeaux region. Shortly after his discharge from the service in Algeria, he returned to France to work in 1923, married a French Communist activist, joined the party himself, and became increasingly involved in émigré affairs while at the same time auditing classes in classical Arabic at the *Ecole des langues orientales*.

In the Etoile's formative years, the Communist party provided meeting places, budgetary subsidies, and the printing facilities through which it published its first newspapers. It appears that from the beginning, however, there was tension between the party, which was trying to co-opt the émigrés for its own purposes, and many of the Algerian militants who were less interested in the universal proletarian cause and Marxist-Leninist revolutionary theory than in the specific grievances of their colonized society. Specifically, the official Komintern line at this time, while favoring tactical alliances with bourgeois nationalist parties for the purpose of weakening imperialist governments, saw actual independence for colonies as a diversion from the class struggle.

In February 1927, Messali delivered the Etoile's first list of "Algerian demands" to a conference organized by a so-called League Against Colonial Oppression at Brussels. The list's political agenda called for the independence of Algeria, withdrawal of the army of occupation, building of a national army, abolition of the code de l'indigénat, freedom of press and association, an Algerian parliament chosen via universal suffrage, and municipal councils chosen via universal suffrage. Economically and culturally, the agenda called for confiscation of large estates, the extension of French social legislation to Algeria, the expansion of credit facilities for fellahs, access to education at every level, and creation of Arabic language schools. An expanded version of the program, adopted in May 1933, added a number of the egalitarian themes popularized by the élus, called for the nationalization of banks and large industry, and identified additional programs to benefit the peasantry, such as irrigation projects, better rural communications, and more generous rural relief measures. Three themes from the start clearly separate the Etoile from other native opposition movements. The first is its concern with the plight of rural Algerians, the second is its openly anticapitalist campaign, and the third is the demand for independence. In time, these themes were to become central to the revolutionary ideology. But it is noteworthy that the breathtaking demand for independence is not followed by a coherent list of steps for achievement of that goal but, rather, by a series of demands many of which (such as equal access, educational and administrative reform, extension of metropolitan welfare benefits) clearly imply continuation of colonial rule. It is as if Messali and his colleagues realized that independence would be far down the road and so concluded that, if they wanted to attract a following, they would have to address more immediate concerns.

By 1928, the Etoile nord-africaine may have recruited as many as 4,000 members in France. Labelled subversive by the police, the organization was banned in 1929, and functioned semiclandestinely until 1933, when it reappeared as *La glorieuse étoile nord-africaine,* only to be banned again until an appellate court reversed the order. In spite of harassment, the Etoile continued to attract members in France where its newspaper, *El Ouma,* reached a circulation of 43,500 by 1934, a very significant percentage of the émigré community. As it grew it identified increasingly with the culturally specific interests of the émigrés. Messali Hadj had remained uncomfortably suspended for several years between Marxist-Leninist orthodoxy and nationalism. After an eight-month exile in Geneva, however, where he came under the influence of the Arab nationalist Shakib Arslan, he finally tilted definitively to the latter. This transformation in turn precipitated a final break with the French Communist party which subsequently condemned the Etoile with increasing virulence.

It was not until after the middle 1930s, however, that Messali began to attract a significant following in Algeria itself. The fact that the Algerian national movement was born on foreign soil, surprising at first glance, is not difficult to explain. It was in France, especially in Paris, that a modern Algerian community, largely leveled socially and economically because of its proletarian status and pressed into tightly knit groupings by its cultural isolation from the French majority, began to develop group solidarity and to perceive itself as a separate national entity. It was also in France that it encountered for the first time nationalist and Marxist ideologies that helped it to define that identity and articulate programs for changing unacceptable conditions. The movement's growth was furthered in the last instance by the fact, that in spite of police surveillance and periodic repression, France with its traditional republican protections and provisions for judicial due process provided a far freer environment than colonial Algeria for development of a movement challenging French North African sovereignty.

THE COMMUNIST PARTY

The Communist party was less a direct participant in the nationalist movement than a fermenting or leavening agent. Around and within it swirled debates about class and nation, evolution and revolution, collaboration or confrontation with moderate or conservative indigenous movements. It also provided the banners and the organization under which many Algerians first took to the streets to demonstrate their opposition to the status quo. But communism in this colonial context generated contradictions that proved ultimately unresolvable. The Communist federations, which represented Bolshevism in Algeria, were extensions of the French Communist party until 1936 when a change of tactics led to the creation of the Algerian Communist party. But even then real autonomy proved more theoretical than actual.

The early party membership was predominantly European, and while they had voted to accept the twenty-one conditions of August 1920 of the Communist International, it is clear most never fundamentally questioned the appropriateness of their own superior position in a colonial society. To the extent they were able, they would enlist native collaboration in the struggle to undermine bourgeois government, but they could not envisage replacing French government with Algerian government. In the early 1930s, orders came from the Komintern via Paris to work at Arabizing the party, which provoked wholesale defections of Europeans for a time. When the Communist party joined Léon Blum's Popular Front in 1936, however, Europeans began to filter back into its ranks, in spite of the Front's support of moderate reform measures. But because of the party's persistent condemnation of the nationalist demands of the Etoile and its successor, the *Parti du peuple algérien,* it then began to lose ground again amongst the Algerians. Algerian nationalists never forgave the Communists for consistently putting the interests of France or Frenchmen above those of their own community.

THE CRISIS OF THE 1930s AND THE BLUM-VIOLLETTE BILL

Just as the various organizations in the 1920s were beginning to give Algerians a range of voices within which to protest their condition, an event occurred that was bound to set aflame the tinder of native outrage. This was the self-congratulatory, insensitive celebration of the centennial, which reopened old wounds and rubbed salt in them by trumpeting the glories of 1830, reenacting French victories and native defeats in full period costume, churning out shelves full of pseudoscholarship justifying the occupation, and systematically refusing all suggested gestures of reconciliation to the native community. From 1933 to 1936, Algeria traversed a period of political crisis that represents a watershed in the nation's history and is the beginning of a process that led eventually to revolution and to independence. This time lower middle-class, working-class, and even poor rural Algerians joined alongside the elites for the first time in challenging the status quo. Algerians became political activists. This was a period of overwhelming voter turnout in support of opposition candidates, large public parades and demonstrations, strikes, boycotts of European merchants, snubbing of Bastille Day observances, resignations by elected officials, and multiplying incidents of violence. Morinaud's "good natives—hardworking and honest" seemed to have gone crazy. While the protests were undertaken on behalf of a range of disparate and often discordant goals, it is clear that this sudden political awakening of the Algerian natives was a reflection of the emergence of the new if still highly fragmented social order we have previously described. Serving as a catalyst to that *prise de conscience* was the never ending economic depression whose deflationary cycle left virtually no segment of Algerian society untouched and whose effect was to accentuate most of the inadequacies and inequities of colonial society.

Thousands of Muslims marched through the streets of Algiers crying "Vive les Soviets!" Ben Badis led rallies to protest the absence of freedom of religion. After measures were taken to muzzle the native press, Bendjelloul led rallies to demand freedom of expression. A low point in this period of crisis was reached in August 1934 when, in retaliation for a drunken Jewish soldier's defiling of a mosque at Constantine, Muslim mobs descended upon Jewish neighborhoods and businesses, instigating riots that left twenty-three Jews and five Muslims dead. Algerian and liberal French analysts have both concluded that the authorities purposely delayed intervening in a worsening crisis for more than a day in order to demonstrate the need for much more stringent security measures. Such measures in fact followed swiftly. The most infamous of them was the so-called Régnier decree of March 1935, which, in a further extension of the exceptive principles of the indigénat, provided prison terms of up to two years and fines up to 5,000 francs for natives or foreigners found guilty of inciting to civil disorder or of organizing demonstrations against French rule. The Régnier Decree, along with the earlier Desmichels Circular limiting access to official mosques, now became prime targets of the continuing Algerian protests, which did not, in fact, lessen as a result of either measure.

In these tumultuous circumstances, Algerian leaders began to talk about organizing a united opposition party or front, a strategy first proposed by the Emir Khaled in the early 1920s. But the ideological gaps separating assimilationists like Mohamed Bendjelloul from the religiosity or implied nationalism of the Islamists and the class revolution of the Communists proved unbridgeable for two years. Then, in the spring of 1936, Léon Blum and the Popular Front came to power in France, pledging more conciliatory colonial policies in Algeria and elsewhere in the French Empire. Especially heartening for the Algerians was Blum's appointment as Minister of State of Maurice Viollette, a prominent liberal Deputy who had been Governor General in the mid-1920s and who had worked then and afterward for legislation granting citizenship without change of personal status to thousands more Muslims. Overnight the political climate changed, because the ʿulama, perceiving for the first time opportunities for progress through a collaborative relationship with government that they had not seen before, moved closer to the reforming and assimilationist theses of the élus. They were finally able to coax the Fédération des élus indigènes of Constantine into joining them in what was designed to be a grand coalition in the form of an Algerian Muslim Congress. Their success at luring hesitant élus into the Congress owed much to the fact that they promised the movement's presidency to Dr. Bendjelloul. The Communists, whose party was part of the Popular Front, naturally joined the Congress as well, but Messali and the Etoile were excluded. Fearing their nationalist extremism, the organizers permitted Etoile militants to attend as individuals but kept them off the board of directors and managed the agenda so as to exclude their concerns.

In an atmosphere of enthusiastic optimism, the first Algerian Muslim Congress met at Algiers in June 1936, and by the following month, it had adopted an official program which it labeled the Charter of Demands of the Muslim Algerian People. The Charter of Demands was divided into civil, political, cultural, social, and economic sections. The civil demands included recision of all laws of exception, maintenance of Muslim civil status, complete administrative assimilation to France, and suppression of the Délégations financières, communes mixtes, and Government General. Politically, the Charter asked for universal suffrage, a single electoral college, representation in Parliament, and amnesty for political prisoners. Cultural demands centered on separating church and state, restitution of confiscated buildings and properties, and removal of restrictions tending to limit the teaching of the Arabic language or to categorize it as a foreign language. The social agenda called for compulsory free education for both sexes, merger of French and Algerian curricula, and improvement and extension of public assistance, health, and unemployment legislation. Economic demands included equal pay for equal work, aid to all needful economic sectors without distinction as to race, peasant agricultural cooperative and education centers, an end to judicial land expropriation, distribution of uncultivated estates to needy peasants, and abolition of the forest code. Later in the same month, Bendjelloul led a Muslim Congress delegation to Paris to present the Charter to the government where, much to the consternation of the colonial administration, they were received by Blum and Viollette with great cordiality and an open-ended commitment to satisfy a large number of their wishes.

In the meantime, the Popular Front cabinet had agreed to promote a proposal worked on for years by Maurice Viollette which would have granted citizenship to about 25,000 Algerian évolués. Although this Blum-Viollette Bill was a very modest offer compared to the very comprehensive reform of the Charter, it assumed enormous symbolic importance both for the Algerian opposition and the colon administration that was trying to hold the line. The élus and the Communists welcomed it enthusiastically, the reformist ᶜulama supported it on tactical grounds, and it became overnight a litmus test of the Popular Front's intentions regarding the Algeria question. The cabinet could have promulgated Blum-Viollette by decree in the way of so much other Algerian legislation over the past hundred years. But when the colons, in their first line of defense, convinced the government that this was too important a matter not to undergo a full airing in the halls of parliament, they slowed the reforming momentum.

Making matters easier for the right was the fact that the social unrest showed no signs of diminishing with the advent of the Popular Front, and some said it even worsened because of the unrealistic expectations to which its leftist rhetoric had given rise. The Mufti of Algiers was assassinated, and strikes, riots, and dangerous demonstrations seemed to multiply.

Messali Hadj, who had taken advantage in May of a Popular Front amnesty to return from exile in Switzerland, presented a separate Etoile "Plan of Immediate Demands" to the Ministry of the Interior in Paris. Then he went on to Algiers to begin the process of transferring his nationalist movement to native soil. The first stage in that process took the form of a remarkable and memorable speech. The Muslim Congress had organized a huge rally in the Algiers Municipal Stadium for August 2, 1936, to hear the enthusiastic report of their delegation returning from Paris. Invited as a courtesy to address the gathering briefly, Messali in a ten minute address, stole the show and electrified the crowd.[19] Speaking of the Charter of Demands on behalf of the Etoile brethren in Europe, he told his audience:

> We approve the immediate demands that are modest and legitimate. But we say frankly and categorically that we disapprove the Charter of Demands on the question of the attachment of our country to France and of parliamentary representation.
>
> Our country is in reality administratively attached to France today. . . . But this attachment is the consequence of a brutal conquest followed by a military occupation that presently rests on the 19th Army Corps to which the people had never given its consent.
>
> We [of the Etoile nord-africaine] are also children of the Algerian people and we will never accept our country's being attached to another against its will; we do not wish, under any pretext, to jeopardize the future, the hope for national freedom of the Algerian people.
>
> I conclude by shouting: down with the code de l'indigénat! down with the laws of exception and racial hatred! long live the Algerian people! long live the brotherhood of peoples and long live the Etoile nord-africaine![20]

For the first time, the national question had been publicly raised on Algerian soil. Messali began touring the country giving speeches, organizing Etoile chapters, and claiming that the Blum-Viollette Bill was no more than an attempt to co-opt the Algerian bourgeoisie while leaving six million peasants in ignorance and misery. He met with phenomenal success, particularly in his hometown of Tlemcen, and by October 1936, he claimed to have created thirty-six chapters with 11,000 members. But his program and style were frightening the Algerian native establishment, who did not want to be associated with what was then considered extremist adventurism and rightly feared

19. Earlier, Messali, meeting members of the delegation in Paris, had expressed his opposition to the attachment of Algeria to France and to the notion of Algerian representation in another country's parliament. The delegates are said to have told him that while his brand of radical nationalism might serve him well in France, he should not criticize them for practicing the art of the possible under the constraints imposed by the colonial administration. It appears they more or less dared him to air the same nationalist proposals in Algiers that he championed in Paris. See Kaddache, vol. 2 of *Histoire*, p. 471.
20. Collot and Henry, *Le mouvement*, pp. 83–85.

that Messali's talk of independence provided ammunition for the opponents of Blum-Viollette and the Charter of Demands. By October 1936, when Messali agreed to substitute a campaign for democratic freedoms for his demand for independence, it was already too late. The élus, not unexpectedly, were horrified; the Communists condemned him and, after some wavering, so did the reformist ᶜulama. The government dissolved the Etoile in January 1937, but two months later Messali founded the *Parti du peuple algérien* (PPA) with a more modest program, which both enemies and supporters assumed had been formulated more as a tactical than a philosophical retreat. Its motto was now: "Neither assimilation nor separation, but emancipation." But that July 14, 3,000 PPA members marched, chanting through Algiers under the green and white flag he had created for them. The next month Messali and five directors of the PPA were arrested and sentenced, under the Régnier decree, to the maximum two years imprisonment. Released in August 1939, he was rearrested soon afterward and, after refusing repeated overtures to cooperate with the government, was condemned, in March 1941, to sixteen years at hard labor. But his party remained the most popular and active of the Algerian movements until it was banned in September 1939. It attracted increasing numbers of urban workers and more and more younger members of the urban middle and lower middle classes. It functioned underground at reduced levels during World War II both in Algeria and in France.

But before this, the fragility of the Algerian Muslim Congress itself had been amply demonstrated. Apprehensive about what they saw as the radicalism of the ᶜulama and the Communists, the élus began a progressive defection from the Congress in fall 1936. Clearly, the united movement had brought together two fundamentally antithetical movements: the one anxious to accelerate the process of gallicization, and the other anxious to avoid it at all costs. The process of disintegration accelerated during the winter of 1936–37 as the Islamic reformers began to voice second thoughts about much of the Charter of Demands as well as the implications of the Blum-Viollette Bill. The position of the Algerian Communist party, ideologically as incompatible with the social conservatism of the Islamic movement as it was from the bourgeois évolués, was weakened by its obvious interest in keeping in step with the French party, which was more concerned with the escalating struggle against European fascism than in Algerian programs that might weaken anti-Fascist France. A second convention of the Algerian Muslim Congress was held during July 1937, but by 1938, the Congress was moribund and the first attempt at creating a grand native coalition had clearly failed.

Bendjelloul, who had earlier considered using his base in the Fédération des élus indigènes to found a political party, now proceeded to create a kind of electoral coalition of political clubs and associations. Ferhat Abbas, originally allied with Bendjelloul in this enterprise, was convinced, however, that the assimilationist movement needed to expand its base of support by creating a truly popular movement. This led him, in July 1938, to found the *Union populaire algérienne,* whose stated goal was to work for emancipation within the framework of an Algeria reconstituted as a French province. But in spite of his not inconsiderable efforts over the next year, the party failed to develop significantly; and when World War II broke out, in a gesture of solidarity with France, he suspended his political activity and volunteered for military service.

Before this, in 1938, the colons' Federation of Mayors had gone on strike to express its opposition to the Blum-Viollette Bill, and the Blum government, smarting under accusations that its policies were contributing to Algerian unrest jeopardizing the national security, refused to press its own legislation. Even though elected Algerian politicians also resorted to strikes, the bill was buried in a Chamber committee and, in the Senate where it did come to a vote, it was defeated. Disappointed and embittered, those assimilationists who survived the debacle politically were to do so by joining the more moderate wing of the nationalist movement in the 1940s. This evolution seemed to fulfill the February 1926 prediction of Maurice Viollette, who had written to the Minister of the Interior that he found in Algeria 100,000 educated and pro-ductive évolués who felt they belonged no place. "Six out of ten of these," he contended, "are ready to adopt the French fatherland without second thoughts, but if the French fatherland rejects them, raises itself so high that they cannot reach it, they will make their own fatherland, and we will have willed it."[21]

After France had, in fact, rejected the évolués, French liberals created a whole interpretive school which made of interwar Algerian history a tragic sequence of lost opportunities. Such analysis has been rejected by Marxist and nationalist historiography, both of which believe it implies that there could exist such a thing as "good colonialism." Marxist thought sees revolution as the only possible outcome of the colonial juxtaposition of classes, while some Algerian nationalist historiography, by positing the existential distinction between French and Algerian cultures and national spirits, insists upon the absolute inassimilability of the two. The latter thinking is peculiarly reminis-cent of the French colonialist school which earlier had insisted upon the absolute distinction between Oriental and Occidental in its own rejection of assimilation. While the historian who is neither a Marxist nor a nationalist is not inclined to accept the concept of historical inevitability, it is difficult to imagine the scenario in which 25,000 enfranchised Algerians could have turned back the forces of economic deprivation, social inequity, and psychological alienation that colonial success had created and set in motion. In any event, 1938 saw the final defeat of the Young Algeria program conceived thirty years earlier which sought salvation through the extension to Algerian shores of the Rights of Man and the Citizen.

THE SECOND WORLD WAR AND
THE MANIFESTO OF THE ALGERIAN PEOPLE

The Algerian opposition entered the difficult years of World War II divided and demoralized. Those opposition newspapers and movements which did not

21. As quoted by Ageron, vol. 2 of *Histoire*, p. 392.

voluntarily close down were banned on security grounds. Yet, most of the conditions which had led to their protest not only continued but worsened during the war. The economic situation in particular worsened from year to year owing to bad harvests, requisitions of grain for Europe, the closure of European markets, the virtual cessation of transfers from overseas workers, and shortages of the most elementary imports. Inflation, unemployment, and hunger all worsened from one year to the next.

It was the Allied landing in North Africa, in November 1942, that propelled the nationalist movement once again into the center of the political arena. Algerian leaders drew new hope and greater confidence from the perception that a greatly weakened France was now dependent upon a far more powerful United States; that United States had coauthored the Atlantic Charter, which called for the liberation of subject peoples. When the Government General began preparing to conscript Algerian men for the continuing war against Fascism, twenty-four Algerian leaders headed by Ferhat Abbas saw the opportunity to reopen their case. In December 1942, they drafted a "Message from the Algerian Muslim Representatives to the Responsible Authorities" recalling the American President's commitment to the liberation of peoples, drawing attention to the unfree status of Algerians, and calling for a Muslim conference to draft a new economic, social, and political status for Algeria. In return for its implementation, the authors committed Algerians to sacrifice themselves whole heartedly for the liberation of metropolitan France. But it was only after the Algerians had readdressed their message to the "*French* authorities" and specified that they sought liberation within an "essentially French framework" that Admiral François Darlan, de facto head of government, agreed to accept his copy of the message.

Government responses even to the reformulated message were hostile or evasive, however; so a small, but representative group of Algerian notables, including representatives of the banned PPA, met, in early February, and authorized Abbas to draft the document that became the Manifesto of the Algerian People. After more than a month of arduous negotiations, which resulted in modification of some of the first draft's more direct and radical positions, Abbas secured the signatures of the majority of the élu leadership and presented the document to Governor General Peyrouton at the end of March 1943. While still moderate in tone, The Manifesto of the Algerian People marked a major milestone in the progression of Algerian protest from assimilationism to separatism. After a nine-page historical and analytical exposé of the Algerian condition, the Manifesto reveals its program:

a) The condemnation and abolition of colonization, that is, the annexation and exploitation of one people by another. . . .

b) The application to all peoples small and large of the right to determine their own fate.

c) The endowment of Algeria with its own constitution guaranteeing:

1) The absolute freedom and equality of all its inhabitants without distinction as to race or religion.

2) The abolition of feudal property by a major agrarian reform and the right to well being of the immense agricultural proletariat.

3) The recognition of the Arabic language as official on the same basis as French.

4) Freedom of press and association.

5) Free compulsory education for children of both sexes.

6) Freedom of religion for all inhabitants and the application to all religions of the principle of separation of church and state.

d) The immediate and effective participation of Algerian Muslims in the government of their country. . . . Only this government will be able to realize in a climate of perfect unity participation of the Algerian people in the common struggle.

e) The release of all political prisoners and detainees regardless of party.[22]

The Governor General accepted the Manifesto as a "basis for future reforms"; and he asked that the Muslim officials draft a list of concrete, immediately realizable proposals, promising to appoint himself a commission to study Muslim economic and social reforms. The commission he named, on April 13, was heavily weighted in favor of conservative administration candidates sitting with some moderates. Abbas, seeing the government's approach as one of delay rather than real acceptance of the Manifesto, now took the offensive by persuading twenty-one of the twenty-four Arab and Kabyle Financial Delegates to sponsor an *Additif au Manifeste,* which was much more radical than the original document. It called for the recognition after the war of "the political autonomy of Algeria as a sovereign nation with *droit de regard*[23] by France and Allied military assistance in case of conflict." It demanded in the interim a long list of social, economic, and political reforms, the centerpiece of which was the erection of an interim government based upon equal participation of the French and Muslim communities. Messali Hadj, still interned, had orally approved but not signed this Additif, which represented the conversion of most of the élus, at least for the moment, to virtually the entirety of his separatist program.

On June 1, 1943, General Charles de Gaulle assumed power in Algeria as head of the *Comité français de libération nationale* and, four days later, appointed General Georges Catroux to the governorship of Algeria. Unwilling to entertain any discussion about French sovereignty, De Gaulle told Catroux to order the reform commission, then wavering between the nationalist proposals and its original mandate, to concentrate on immediate social and economic reforms and to get back on track. In the battle of wills between the Additif people and the new French leadership, the latter prevailed; Bendjelloul and the more conservative élus retreated from their support even of the original Manifesto. When Abbas and fourteen of the other delegates boycotted the September session of the Délégations financières, he and Sayah Abdelkader, President of

22. Collot and Henry, *Le mouvement,* pp. 163–64.
23. A juridical term meaning "right of inspection," which seems to imply some vague French interest short of sovereignty.

the Arab section, were placed under house arrest. In December, when Abbas was released, he, too, though not to the extent of other élus, moderated his position, pressing thereafter for an autonomous Algeria freely federated to France.

While de Gaulle and Catroux had succeeded by their harsh tactics in pushing the level of official Franco-Algerian discourse back from the independence issue, they became convinced that France was facing a very serious native problem that needed attention. In a speech at Constantine, de Gaulle announced his intention to proceed with reforms which, in sum, amounted to a remarkably generous and forthcoming version of the assimilationist program. Catroux appointed a new reform commission, this time representing the spectrum of native opinion from Communists and PPA to reformist ʿulama and élus, to draft details of such a reform. As divergent in viewpoint as ever, the commissioners could come to agreement only on a few issues; so the discussions dragged on. Wanting to get ahead of the nationalists, the government unilaterally promulgated the Ordinance of 7 March 1944, the first alteration of Algerian fundamental law since the Jonnart Law. It granted French citizenship without change of personal status to about 65,000 more Algerians in sixteen different categories. Other Muslims were to receive citizenship on terms to be specified by a national constituent assembly to be convened after the liberation of the métropole, but in the meantime all adult males could vote in the second, Muslim, college. Muslim representation in all elected bodies, including the Délégations financières, was raised to 40 percent. Finally, juridical equality with Europeans was established by abolition of the entirety of the code de l'indigénat.

Welcomed by Bendjelloul and the conservative wing of the élus as well as by the socialists and Communists, the Ordinance of 7 March 1944 was rejected by the Messalists and by most of the reformist ʿulama. It was also rejected by Ferhat Abbas and his followers, who henceforward constituted a middle ground of moderate nationalism or autonomism between the radical nationalism of the PPA to their left and the assimilationism of the old guard to their right. The de Gaulle concessions, which the great majority of Algerian elites would have joyfully welcomed in 1936, were too little too late for that majority eight years later.

THE AMIS DU MANIFESTE ET DE LA LIBERTÉ
AND THE INSURRECTION OF MAY 1945

A week after promulgation of the 7 March Ordinance, Ferhat Abbas decided to take his cause to the masses by organizing a political movement called the *Amis du Manifeste et de la Liberté* (AML). Not quite a political party, because it welcomed members of collaborating movements whose parent organizations stayed intact, the main goals of the AML were (1) to enlighten both Algerian and French opinion about the benefits of the Manifesto, (2) to unmask the reactionary maneuvering of both French and native feudalist forces, (3) to propagate the idea of an Algerian nation federated with a renovated and anti-imperialist France, (4) to wage war against the privileges of the ruling class, and (5) to preach human equality and the Algerian people's right to the pursuit of happiness and national life. The reformist ⁽ulama, led by Shaykh Ibrahimi, gave their enthusiastic endorsement while continuing separately to press their own religious and cultural agenda. Messali Hadj, who had by now been moved from prison to house arrest, also supported the AML, although with some reservations, and advised his followers to join. But Bendjelloul's assimilationists and the Communists condemned the new initiative.

Within months the AML had proved a sensational popular success. Its weekly newspaper, *Egalité,* attracted 500,000 subscribers, a circulation that no native or European publication had ever enjoyed. The illegal PPA, in the meantime, copying Communist organizational techniques, started creating networks of clandestine political cells across the country. It was especially successful at recruiting young middle-class men. It completely took over the Muslim Scouts and established a network of cells at the University and in secondary schools. In a campaign to convince young men to resist conscription, it made enough progress to worry the authorities. Most significantly of all, however, the PPA started establishing paramilitary cells of six to eight men in the Kabylia and the Constantinois.

More publicly during the winter of 1944–45, PPA loyalists were flocking to the AML, and they soon overwhelmed it by their numbers. Tensions between them and the Abbas faction soon began to surface and reached a critical stage during the AML Congress convened in March. While Abbas's ally, Ahmad Saadane, was elected president at that meeting, the PPA succeeded in pushing through resolutions clearly favoring the independence theses of Messali over the autonomist positions of the founders. In a clear affront to Abbas and the moderate leadership, the majority attached to a resolution calling for the liberation of Messali Hadj a statement qualifying him as "the uncontested leader of the Algerian people."

In the meantime, conditions conspired to aggravate the average Algerian's sense of deprivation and hopelessness. The winter of 1944–45 was one of the driest in memory. Only a fraction of the seed grain had germinated, and the harvest of 1945 was to be only one-third that of 1944. Shortages of most manufactured goods had reached critical proportions, while unemployment in many regions was catastrophic. As signs of social unrest multiplied through the month of April, police began to predict serious trouble. As a precautionary measure, Messali Hadj was removed from his residence to the Sahara and then, on April 30, was transported to the French Congo. In May Day demonstrations coordinated by the AML in twenty-one large and small towns across the country, crowds of Muslims marched under the green and white flag with the red star and crescent to demand freedom for Messali and independence for Algeria. Demonstrations led to violence that in Algiers, Oran, and other places left scores of wounded and took three lives. After these bloody confrontations, a kind of grim determination settled over the nationalist leadership; and as the day approached when the final liberation of Europe would be celebrated, they determined that the day should be the occasion for Algerians to demonstrate for their own liberation and to fly their own flag along with those of the victorious allies. Both AML and PPA leaders set about organizing marches and parades all over the country.

V–E Day was May 8, 1945. In most cities the demonstrations and marches went off without major incident. But this was not the case at Guelma and at Sétif in the Constantinois. At Sétif, organizers had been told they could demonstrate only if national flags and provocative placards were not displayed. May 8 happened to be market day at Sétif, so that the majority of marchers, organized early in the morning by AML representatives, were country folk come to town for the weekly marketing. Shortly after the march began, about 8:30, the forbidden flag and placards were unfurled contrary to orders, police charged to break up the demonstrations, some Muslims fought back, and others took out after hapless European civilians or attacked buildings that stood as symbols of colonial authority. By 11:00, some forty Muslims and Europeans were dead. As word of the violence in town spread to the countryside, villagers armed themselves and began attacking colon settlements, post offices, and government buildings. Open insurrection soon swept over the region between Sétif and the sea and in the areas surrounding Guelma to the northeast where a second demonstration had run afoul of the authorities. With the police overwhelmed, more than 10,000 troops had to be called in; planes bombed and strafed Arab and Kabyle villages, and a cruiser bombarded coastal mountain settlements. After a week, the worst of the insurrection in the northern Constantinois was controlled, though cleanup operations continued until the last week of May. But, totally out of phase with these events, attacks on government property were launched in Oranie on May 18 and in Kabylia on May 23, and a plot to seize military headquarters at Cherchell was uncovered. To compound the violence and confusion, PPA leaders in the Algiers département, responding belatedly to calls for help from the Constantinois, issued a call for general insurrection several days after it was already evident that the colonial forces had passed onto the offensive, a miscalculation that contributed needlessly to the suffering. In all, about 100 European men, women, and children had died in the insurrection, some brutally mutilated. But the number of Muslim lives taken in retaliation was out of all proportion to that toll. French government estimates spoke of 1,500 dead, the army of 6,000 to 8,000, American sources of from 7,000 to 40,000, and some Algerian nationalists of 45,000. Before the end of the year, 5,560 Muslims had been arrested, ninety-nine of whom were condemned to death and several hundred to life imprisonment. The most celebrated prisoner was the moderate Ferhat Abbas, who had been waiting in the anteroom of the Governor General to offer his congratulations on the Allied victory when word of the violence arrived and he was taken into custody. The government dissolved the AML one week later, ending the second and last effort before the Revolution to create a broadly based national movement.

Interpretations concerning the origin of the May 1945 uprising vary widely. A pair of early interpretations saw it as a provocation engineered either by right-wing colonial elements or by the French army; another school still sees it as an unintended accident resulting from demonstrations getting out of hand and subsequent police response; still a third views it as a preplanned insurrection that went awry because of faulty planning and inadequate communications and leadership. Further investigation concerning the origins is clearly called for.[24] What appears most probable in the present state of research is that the PPA had issued instructions of a generalized nature to local leaderships in some areas to be prepared for insurrection. Because the party's constantly harassed communications and command structures were very faulty, some local cell chiefs, ready to react violently, were not equipped to know when H-hour had actually come. In the case of the events of May 8, the central leadership probably wanted no more than demonstrations. When, in fact, these turned violent, local leaders in the Constantinois sent out the call for insurrection. Quite apart from the PPA, peasant villagers, seeing the outbreak of warfare and the startling breakdown of French authority, descended on colonial settlements to begin wreaking vengeance on their tormentors, much in the manner of their ancestors a century earlier. Later Algerian historiography, while condemning the overwhelming brutality of the colonialist reaction, has not always been forgiving of incompetent leaderships that sent men prematurely and unnecessarily to their deaths. Far more significantly, however, the events in northern Constantinois marked the first time the dispossessed and pauperized masses of the countryside, the principal victims of the colonial system, had linked up for meaningful action with a nationalist movement that urban Algerians had created and which had been spreading in the cities for fifteen years.

THE ORGANIC LAW OF ALGERIA

The violence and bloodshed of May 1945 served further to polarize the European and Algerian communities, the former convincing itself that central government concessions to the Muslims had emboldened them to the point of insurrection and the latter, embittered by the low price France attached to Algerian life, more determined than ever to push for separation. As postwar France embarked over the next two years on a search for new national and imperial institutions, the Algerians strove to make their case in the three successive assemblies that were created for that purpose and to which Algerians were now entitled to elect the same number of delegates as the colons. The thirteen Muslim members of the first Constituent Assembly, elected in

24. The most compelling analysis at this writing is found in Radouane Ainad-Tabet, *Le mouvement du 8 mai 1945 en Algérie*.

October 1945, were all government candidates or assimilationists like Mohamed Bendjelloul. They were swept into office largely because Messali Hadj and Ferhat Abbas, who were still under arrest, both urged their followers to abstain from the voting. About half of the Algerian electors, both in the first and second colleges, did, in fact, abstain. In Paris, Bendjelloul and his colleagues pressed unsuccessfully for the creation of an Algeria directly bound to France and represented in parliament by a unified Algerian delegation. In any case, the point became moot when the French electorate, in May 1946, rejected the constitution submitted to it by the first Constituent.

A second Constituent Assembly was elected in June. By this time Ferhat Abbas, who had been freed in March, had created a new party, the *Union démocratique du manifeste algérien* (UDMA). With the PPA boycott continuing, the UDMA easily overwhelmed the assimilationists, winning eleven of the thirteen seats. In August, standing at last in the Palais Bourbon, Abbas submitted a proposal to transform Algeria into an autonomous Republic within the framework of a newly created French Union, which would have responsibility for defense and foreign affairs. When this proposal went down to defeat, his and his party's prestige were considerably diminished.

The second Constituent eventually adopted an organic law that perpetuated the two separate electorates for choosing Algerian representatives in parliament, permitting thirty Algerians in the National Assembly of the Fourth Republic and fourteen in the upper house or Council of the Republic. Half of each were to be chosen by the second college. Unable to agree on other aspects of the organic law, the Constituent left the task to the first National Assembly of the Fourth Republic, which was chosen in November 1946. By then Messali Hadj had been released from internment and, after consultations with colleagues at Paris and in Algeria, hastily organized a movement to front for the outlawed PPA, the *Mouvement pour le triomphe des libertés démocratiques* (MTLD). In spite of the fact that several MTLD candidates were disqualified, the new party managed to win five of the fifteen second-college seats in the National Assembly. The true significance of this showing under less than ideal circumstances is obscured by the fact that the UDMA, embittered by the failure of its autonomist initiative, boycotted the Assembly elections and ran no candidates. The fact that, in the subsequent elections to the Council of the Republic, Abbas's partisans nevertheless took four of the seven Muslim seats indicates that support of this middle ground may have remained considerable in spite of the 1946 setbacks.

During the drawn out parliamentary debates on the organic law that extended intermittently from March into September 1947, the majority of Algerian deputies pressed for an autonomous Algerian Republic federated with Tunisia and Morocco within the framework of the French Union. The MTLD minority, however, steadfastly denied the competence of the French parliament to determine the status of Algeria. For their part, the colon representatives stood firmly against any modification in the basic statutes at all. The Organic Statute of Algeria that finally passed the National Assembly on 20

September 1947 was enacted with the abstention of the entire Communist bloc and over the nays of all but four Europeans in the thirty-member Algerian delegation. While it declared all residents of Algeria citizens of France without distinction as to origin, race, language, or religion, it perpetuated the Jonnart Law principle of separate electoral colleges by authorizing 510,000 voters of "French civil status" to elect the same number of representatives as the 1,500,000 voters of "local civil status." The law substituted an Algerian "parliament," named the Algerian Assembly, for the Délégations financières.[25] But the competence of the Assembly was explicitly limited by excluding a sizeable list of vital sectors such as defense, elections, local government, administrative and judicial organization, civil and penal procedure, determination of felonies and misdemeanors, land policy, and customs. Its bills required promulgation by decree of the Governor General, who was appointed by the French government. Budgets needed not only his approval but the signature of the Ministers of the Interior and Finance. Other clauses of the Organic Statute looked to the abolition of the communes mixtes and the Southern Territories administration as well as to the extension of Arabic language education. The timing and procedures for implementing these latter changes were left to the Government General, which, in fact, did nothing. In most respects the long awaited Organic Statute was simply a reconfiguration of the old status quo.

Algerian reaction to the new law was reflected in the next month's elections. To French alarm, they proved a spectacular victory for nationalist candidates, most notably those of the MTLD, which swept all the large cities and carried a total of 110 municipal councils. In response, Paris, in February 1948, appointed as Governor General the hard-liner Marcel-Edmond Naegelen, who came into office determined to wage war on the nationalists. Besides police and judicial powers, that war employed as a key tool a systematic campaign to control the electoral process. Elections for the new Algerian Assembly were scheduled for April. It was mathematically possible, given recent growth of Muslim representation in the first college and its enhanced potential for alliance with small European liberal elements there, that Algerians could control the legislative agenda. This was a possibility the colons were determined to prevent. More than a third of MTLD candidates were under arrest by the eve of the elections. Armed forces were everywhere, voters were intimidated, and ballot boxes were either stuffed or mysteriously carried off. The result, after the second, runoff round, was that forty-one of the sixty Muslim assemblymen were administration candidates. The MTLD, which, in spite of harassment and repression, had garnered 31 percent of the vote on the first round, elected only nine men in the final round. Criminal proceedings prevented four of these nine from taking their seats.

The same pattern of election rigging tainted the Assembly elections of 1951 and 1954 as well as the cantonal elections of 1949 and the municipal elections of 1953. While many Algerians across the political spectrum continued to participate in electoral politics, a growing number of younger men understood the message the colon establishment was attempting to communicate: natives need not look to representative institutions for improvement of their condition or for a shift in the power balance.

THE PPA-MTLD AND THE MARCH TOWARD REVOLUTION

Messali's abrupt decision to present slates of candidates in the parliamentary elections of 1946, after years of urging Algerians to boycott elections, spread confusion within the PPA and among other Algerians who looked to it for direction. Was the PPA preparing to seize Algerian rights by direct action or was it to engage in the electoral games promoted by the rulers? Its first party congress, held clandestinely in February 1947, decided that it was to do both. The newly created MTLD was to pursue the route of electoral politics, making whatever rhetorical or tactical compromises were necessary to be effective in that arena. But it was decided to continue the PPA at a secret level for the purposes of cultivating the movement's nationalistic purity and quietly communicating to Algerians that, although public statements might of necessity change from time to time, the goal of absolute independence within an Arab-Islamic framework remained unaltered. Finally, parallel to the PPA, a secret paramilitary structure was created known as the *Organisation spéciale* (OS). Its mission was to explore the possibilities for revolutionary action. Early leaders of the OS included Hocine Ait Ahmed of the Kabylia and Ahmed Ben Bella from Marnia, near the Moroccan frontier, who became the first President of independent Algeria. The object was to recruit young men of little or no political connection in order not to compromise the political action of the movement. Between 1947 and the end of 1949, the OS had enlisted between 1,000 and 1,500 fighters, including a significant number who assumed key roles in the forthcoming revolution. Its most notable exploit was the robbery, in 1949, of the Oran Post Office, from which it seized 3,000,000 francs with which to build up its treasury. In March 1950, however, the colonial police were able to break the movement, arresting 363 members and sending off to prison Ben Bella and 196 other militants.

During the late 1940s the PPA-MTLD grew rapidly, attracting broad-based membership from rural peasantries, the urban proletariat, and younger sons of the middle and lower middle classes. About 1950, it probably had 20,000 active members as compared to the UDMA membership of 3,000, and it clearly represented the most vital and popularly based of Algerian opposition movements. But it was riven with dissensions that multiplied and deepened as the years went on.

While appreciations of the internal dynamics of the PPA-MTLD in the late forties vary, it seems apparent that the movement was torn during these years between the partisans of legalistic and revolutionary strategies. The "politicals" could point to the disasters of Sétif and Guelma in support of their position, while the "revolutionaries" could point to French electoral fraud from 1948 onward in justification of theirs. One American scholar has suggested that it was the inability of the PPA-MTLD to resolve this fundamental conflict that lay at the root of a series of internal crises that progressively sapped its effectiveness.[26] A possible explanation for the widening gulf could lie in the movement's extraordinary success in attracting younger middle-class men who eventually dominated the leadership of what had started as a proletarian movement. Many such individuals had too great a stake in the existing order to seriously promote its complete and violent overturn.

In 1948 and 1949, the PPA-MTLD was weakened by a so-called Berber crisis which pitted Ait Ahmed and other Kabyle militants against Messali and the Central Committee. While not all Berber members followed them by any means, many objected to qualifying the movement as "Arab," insisting instead upon the more inclusive term "Algerian." At the same time, they objected to the increasingly Islamic rhetoric of the movement, preferring instead more secular, and particularly Marxist, frames of analysis. While these problems were eventually papered over, they were not resolved and would resurface from time to time as major issues in Algerian politics.

No sooner had the Berber crisis moderated than the unravelling of the OS network by the police set off a new one. Messali and the majority of the Central Committee, seeing in the massive arrests and crackdowns one more proof that revolutionary methods could not work, declared the OS dissolved and rejected all appeals by members who had escaped the dragnet to reconstitute it. After this, some of the most militant elements in Algerian society began to desert the MTLD. The weakening of the party was hastened, in 1951 and 1952, by an escalating conflict between the Central Committee and Messali Hadj, who was widely accused of authoritarianism and attempting to impose the cult of his own personality. Others condemned him for irresponsible rhetoric and agitation that led to senseless violence to the detriment of the people involved and the party's interests; ultimately, they condemned him as indecisive and ineffective. In spring 1953, a party congress convened to resolve these issues attempted to bridge the gap between revolutionary and political elements by authorizing reconstitution of the OS while, at the same time, adopting a policy of cooperation with liberal French elements within the municipal and other elected bodies. But the reconciliation broke down over Messali's attempts to retain personal control. Banned from Algerian territory in 1952 for inciting violence, Messali sparred from France with the executive committee and central committee in Algeria. After winning solid control of the émigré wing of the movement that was historically his home base, he called a congress at Hornu, Belgium, in July 1954, that accorded him presidency for life and authorized him to dissolve the central committee. The central committee, led by Benyoucef Benkhedda, Hocine Lahouel, and Abderrahmane Kiouane, reconstituted itself, designated a new executive committee, called another congress, in August of 1954, and expelled Messali Hadj and his supporters, thus sundering the nationalist party down the middle.

During the spring of 1954, as the dispute between the centralists and the

26. See William B. Quandt, *Revolution and Political Leadership,* pp. 60–61.

Messalists increasingly drained the energies of the MTLD, a group of young nationalists, many of whom had belonged to or sympathized with the OS, determined to create a "third force" between the two factions. At least some of this third force, which adopted the ambiguous name *Comité révolutionnaire d'unité et d'action* (CRUA), hoped initially to mediate between the factions and reunify the demoralized nationalist party. By summer, when it became clear that the MTLD was irretrievably split, they concluded that the political route to independence had reached a dead end, and began to plan the revolution that they finally launched on November 1, 1954.[27]

It is evident from the material presented in this chapter that, in the period since 1919, a new Algerian society had come progressively to realize its own national identity. It is equally evident that, by 1954, a clear majority of the politically active members of that society favored some form of national independence within which to express that identity. The quest for consensus on the parameters of that nationhood or the means to achieve it met with repeated and ultimate failure, however, so that Algerians entered upon the violent and exhausting period of revolutionary warfare without, as a majority, having either determined on that course or reached consensus about what the content of independence would be once they had won it. The kind of grand nationalist coalition that succeeded in bringing Tunisia and Morocco to independence with only a minimum of bloodshed was never achieved in Algeria. One reason it was not may have been the unbearable pressure placed on Algerian society at all levels by a colon authority willing to use every maneuver and every kind of force to inhibit the progression of the nationalist movement. An equally important explanation can be found in comparing the state of development of the different middle classes, which, in the twentieth century, have provided the leadership of many nationalist movements. At the center of the Neo-Destourian movement in Tunisia (which eventually allied with labor, peasant, women's and other movements), was a self confident, relatively cohesive bourgeoisie that, while modern in outlook, had roots extending back centuries and the wider societal recognition attaching to such longevity. In Morocco, the nationalist movement was led by a combination of traditional and modernist bourgeoisies which allied with aristocracies to oppose the prerogatives of the three-century-old ⁽Alawi sultanate to French pretensions. In Algeria, the old tribal and religious leaderships had long since disappeared, as had all but a very small part the traditional urban elites. The new middle classes did not enjoy the internal cohesion, the self-confidence, the patronage networks, or the tradition of leadership which the task of mobilizing a nation called for. Undergoing as they were a profound identity crisis that kept them torn between the polls of Gallicism, Arabism, and Islamism, they were unable to draw themselves together or to serve as a poll of attraction for other classes.

27. Mohamed Boudiaf, in *Où va l'Algérie?*, pp. 70ff., holds that the CRUA attempted until August 1954 to mediate and then dissolved. Ageron, in vol. 2 of *Histoire*, p. 594, repeats the substance of this version, claiming that the CRUA began planning insurrection only after attempts at mediation had failed. Alistair Horne, in *A Savage War of Peace*, p. 76, sees the CRUA as bent on revolution from March 1954.

CHAPTER
6

THE WAR OF INDEPENDENCE, 1954–1962

O f the several violent independence struggles that accompanied the decolonization process in the years after World War II, that of the Algerians stands out as the longest, the costliest, and arguably the most poignant in terms of the human issues it juxtaposed. On November 12, 1954, twelve days after the rebellion broke out, Prime Minister Pierre Mendès-France assured France, Algeria, and the world at large that the Algerian départements were irrevocably French, that no secession from the rest of France was possible, and that no French government of any political leaning would ever yield on this fundamental principle. Yet, against all reasonable odds, the profoundly disadvantaged Algerians, in eight years of determined struggle, wore down a people immensely more numerous, wealthy, and powerful than themselves, extracting at the end unqualified recognition of their independence. This stunning accomplishment provided the young Algerian nation with a self-confidence and sense of moral purpose that legitimized the radical campaign for national reconstruction that lay ahead and established it both as a model and as a persuasive advocate for peoples still struggling for liberation.

It has been a major premise of the present study that the colonial dialectic was the principal motor of modern Algerian history; a second premise has been that it was that dialectical process that created something approximating a national community; finally, it is concluded that a dispossessed community, to whom peaceful avenues of redress had been repeatedly closed, was ready, by 1954, to consider the use of force to liberate itself. But 8,500,000 people do not simultaneously initiate any enterprise. On November 1, 1954, all but a few thousand Algerians still accepted the inevitability of the colonial situation even if they despised it. Even one year later, though the revolution was spreading, the men and women willing to make the dangerous leap into revolutionary activism still constituted a small minority of the population. The task of the revolutionary leadership was first to convince the Algerian people of its existence, then to give it confidence in its capacities, and finally to create structures through which those capacities could overcome French power and within which the people could begin to express its nationhood. This chapter explores how the rebels managed progressively to rally layer after layer of Algerian society, starting with disillusioned small-town youth and impoverished peasants and ending up eventually with most of the privileged urbanites. At the same time, it examines the continuing impact of the colonial dialectic, of the political evolution in France, and of growing international awareness upon the processes of that mobilization. Along the way it traces the evolution of Algerian military, political, and social institutions which at first competed with the colonial institutions and ultimately replaced them.

THE INSURRECTION

By the summer of 1954, the CRUA was composed of twenty-two younger men, most of whom had been members of the Organisation spéciale. While the social backgrounds of these men exhibit considerable diversity, it is clear that most had far less of a stake culturally or economically in the colonial regime than the political activists who preceded them in the 1930s and 1940s. A few were of peasant or worker background, more came from the lower middle classes, and the great majority had only elementary or secondary educations. All but a handful of these revolutionaries lived in small towns or villages, which put most of them in closer touch with the interests and attitudes of the rural poor than the typical big-city politician.

During the summer and fall of 1954, the CRUA erected a revolutionary structure that continued and developed with modifications the clandestine organization of the PPA of the early 1940s and of the later OS. It divided the territory into five and later six military districts, which, by 1956, came to be known as *wilaya*s. While the internal organization and subdivision of each wilaya was still far from complete on the day the insurrection was launched, the plan called for dividing them into subsidiary units called *mantaqa*s (zones), which in turn contained *nahaya*s (regions), *qasma*s (sectors), and *duwwar*s (circles) in descending order. The wilaya was headed by a colonel supported by three assistants, one each for political affairs, logistics, and liaison and information. The smaller units were supposed to replicate the same four-headed organization with officers of lower rank. But neither at the start of the insurrection nor later was total symmetry achieved over more than a part of the territory.

The Committee of Twenty-Two chose six of their number to constitute a leadership committee. Led and coordinated by Mohamed Boudiaf of M'sila,

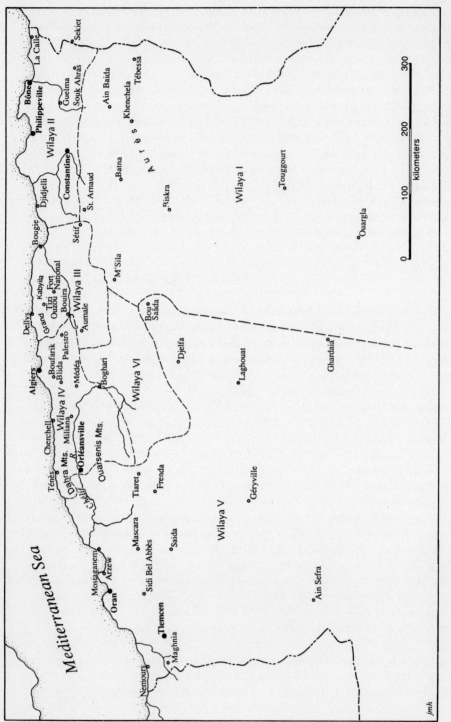

Mediterranean Sea

La Calle
Sekiet
Bône
Philippeville
Wilaya II
Guelma
Souk Ahrás
Ain Baida
Tébessa
Khenchela
Djidjelli
Constantine
St. Arnaud
Batna
A u r è s
Biskra
Bougie
Sétif
M'Sila
Wilaya I
Touggourt
Ouargla
Dellys
Kabylia
Fort
Tizi National
Grand Ouzou Bouira
Wilaya III
Aumale
Bou
Saáda
Ghardaïa
Algiers
Boufarik
Blida
Palestro
Médéa
Boghari
Wilaya IV Miliana
Cherchell
Orléansville
Ouarsenis Mts.
Djelfa
Laghouat
Ténès
Dahra Mts.
Chélif R.
Wilaya VI
Tiaret
Frenda
Géryville
Mascara
Saïda
Wilaya V
Mostaganem
Arzew
Sidi Bel Abbès
Oran
Ain Sefra
Tlemcen
Maghnia
Nemours

0   100   200   300
kilometers

MAP 6 The Wilayas, 1956

jmh

this executive group also included the five colonels in charge of the wilayas. These were Moustapha Ben Boulaid for Wilaya One in the Aurès and Nementcha; Mourad Didouche for Wilaya Two, the northern Constantinois; Belkacem Krim for Wilaya Three, the Kabylia; Rabah Bitat for Wilaya Four, the Algiers district; and Larbi Ben M'hidi for Wilaya Five, which covered Oran département (see map 6).[1] These six internals, as they came to be called, early established contact with three ex-OS exiles who had set up a bureau in Cairo to marshal Arab support for the Algerian movement. These externals were Ahmed Ben Bella, who had escaped from the Blida Prison in 1952, the Kabyle Hocine Ait Ahmed, and Mohamed Khider. These three externals along with the six internals are considered the nine *chefs historiques* of the Algerian Revolution.

Participants' estimates of the number of guerrillas committed to insurrection by November 1, 1954, range from a low of 900 to a high of about 3,000. Only about half actually possessed firearms, however, reflecting a weapons problem that hampered the internals in varying degrees throughout the war. The internal historiques determined the timing of the insurrection, which was to begin simultaneously in all five wilayas at 3:00 on the morning of All Saints Day. The most successful operations were carried out by Ben Boulaid and his men in the Aurès, where several Europeans and a qa'id were killed, roads and telephone lines cut, and French installations attacked. Krim also encountered some successes in Kabylia. But in the Algérois and the Oranie, almost everything misfired. By and large, because of poor planning, faulty synchronization, and superior French intelligence and communications, the beginning of Algeria's armed struggle was far from auspicious.

Given the limitations on human and material resources and the fact that most of the leadership was driven more by desperation than by rational hope for what insurrection could accomplish, CRUA's October 31 proclamation calling Algerians to arms was breathtaking in its ambition. After rehearsing the gains of the Moroccan and Tunisian national movements and the failures of the political gamesmanship that had caused Algeria's national movement to lag behind those of its neighbors, the authors announced the birth of a revolutionary movement, called the *Front de libération nationale* (FLN), which would welcome Algerians of all social classes and members of all purely Algerian parties and movements.

> Goal:
> National independence through:
> 1. The restoration of the sovereign, democratic, and social Algerian state within the framework of Islamic principles;
> 2. Respect of basic liberties without distinction as to race or religion.
>
> Interior objectives:
> 1. Political house-cleaning through re-directing the national revolutionary movement into the right path and in this to eliminate all vestiges of corruption and reformism which are the reasons for our present regression;

1. Wilaya Six, the South, was not yet organized in 1954.

2. Concentration and organization of all the wholesome energies of the Algerian people for the liquidation of the colonial system.

External objectives:
1. Internationalization of the Algerian problem;
2. Achievement of North African unity within its natural Arabo-Muslim framework;
3. Affirmation through the United Nations Charter of our sympathy for all nations who support our liberation effort;

Means of struggle:
In conformity with revolutionary principles and taking into account internal and external conditions, to continue the struggle by all means until the achievement of our goal.

To reach these ends the National Liberation Front will have two simultaneous tasks: an internal effort both on the political and direct action levels and an external effort aimed at making the Algerian problem a reality for the whole world with the support of our natural allies.

That is the overwhelming task that requires the mobilization of all national energies and resources. It is true that the struggle will be long, but the outcome is certain.

. . . We propose an honorable platform for discussion with the French authorities if . . . they recognize once and for all the right of subjugated peoples to decide their own fate:
1. The opening of negotiations with the authorized spokesmen of the Algerian people on the basis of the one and indivisible Algerian sovereignty;
2. . . . The freeing of all political prisoners, the abolition of all exceptional measures, and the cessation of all prosecutions against fighting forces;
3. Recognition of Algerian nationality by an official declaration abrogating the edicts, decrees and laws making Algeria a French land in denial of the history, the geography, the language, the religion, and the customs of the Algerian people.
In return:
1. French cultural and economic interests honestly acquired will be respected as will persons and families;
2. All Frenchmen wishing to stay in Algeria will have the choice between their original nationality in which case they will be considered foreigners . . . or can choose Algerian nationality. . . .
3. The links between France and Algeria will be defined . . . by an agreement between the two powers upon the basis of equality and mutual respect.

Algerian!
We invite you to meditate on our Charter above. Your duty is to associate yourself with it to save our country and give it back its freedom. The National Liberation Front is your front. As for us, determined to continue the fight in the certainty of your strong anti-imperialist feelings and your support, we are giving the best of ourselves for the fatherland.[2]

2. Mohamed Harbi, *Les archives de la révolution algérienne*, pp. 101–3.

The winter of 1954–55 in Algeria was one of the coldest on record and, except for the Aurès, whose wild topography favored hit and run guerrilla tactics, the insurrection's gains were few and its costs enormous. The second in command of Wilaya Five (Oran) had been killed on the first day of the insurrection. The police cracked Wilaya Four's organization within the first ten days, and by spring, both Rabah Bitat and his associate Zoubir Bouadjadj were in prison. Mourad Didouche, the leader of the northern Constantinois, was killed in January. In the next month, the French captured Ben Boulaid of Wilaya One, and though he subsequently escaped to return to the fight in the Aurès, he died there, in March 1956, when a booby-trapped radio blew up in his face. In the Kabylia, Belkacem Krim's forces were still able to assassinate some Muslim office holders and occasionally to cut telegraph and phone lines; but as the winter wore on, their welcome wore thin in many villages, and they were increasingly confined to the remotest and least populated mountain areas.

For their part, the colonial authorities had responded with a massive show of force that utilized not only police but also conventional armored units (of limited value in guerrilla warfare) and crack paratroop regiments, which eventually became the most effective counterinsurgency units. Among the repressive techniques the French employed were mass arrests on little or no evidence, destructive and punishing military sweeps through the countryside, and collective punishment of communities where attacks or sabotage had occurred. But indiscriminate and often grossly disproportionate sanctions were unwittingly driving many victims into the arms of the FLN. When the arrival of spring showed that, battered and depleted as it was, the FLN had not disintegrated, alienated young men began to replenish its ranks. In a major blunder, the authorities arrested the bulk of the guiltless MTLD centralists during the fall of 1954; released some months later, many of them, including Benyoussef Benkhedda and Saad Dahlab, rallied to the FLN, the first of the political class to turn revolutionary.

Pierre Mendès-France, the liberal leader of the often illiberal Radical Socialist Party, had successfully extricated France from Indo-China and was in the process of coming to terms with Tunisian and Moroccan nationalism. While he perceived Algeria in a totally different light and insisted upon absolute restoration of order as the first priority, his liberal instincts told him that for permanency, a forcible restoration of order must be accompanied by reforms addressing basic Algerian grievances. To formulate a reform package, he sent Jacques Soustelle, a prominent anti-Fascist intellectual, to Algiers. Arriving there early in 1955, Soustelle encountered a reception from the colon establishment that ranged from mistrust to open hostility. The heart of his program was implementation at long last of the provisions of the Organic Law of 1947, the majority of which had remained inoperative because of the resistance of the Algerian Assembly and the Government General. But now the ultimate goal was defined not in the time-worn language of assimilation but, rather, as "integration" of Algeria as a province to France, a scenario that recognized an Algerian personality distinct from that of the métropole but one which was still nevertheless French. Integration made little progress, however, partly because of the delaying tactics of the Algerian Assembly and partly because of the coolness of the conservative Faure government that succeeded Mendès-France in Paris even before Soustelle arrived in Algiers. But at the same time, a modest agrarian renewal program aimed at alleviating some of the worst aspects of rural poverty did encounter some success. Placed under the direction of a *Section administrative spécialisée* (SAS), the rural effort eventually organized some 400 separate detachments of corpsmen spread across the countryside. Their function was to train peasants in modern agricultural techniques and to help them launch cooperative ventures. While the SAS corpsmen were frequently welcomed by villagers, the tumultuous conditions under which they went about their work limited their overall effectiveness. One negative factor was the fact that they and Algerians who cooperated with them were highly visible targets for FLN retaliation. An even more important factor was the devastating impact of many of the military's pacification tactics.

FROM INSURRECTION TO REVOLUTION

The Philippeville massacres of August 20, 1955, were a major turning point in the Algerian War of Independence, after which there was little likelihood of turning back either for the Algerians or for the European community. The FLN's initial orders to its *mujahids* (fighters) strictly forbade violence against European civilians. While not unfailingly observed, and while the campaign against Algerian "collaborators," which escalated during the spring of 1955, gradually blurred the combattant-civilian distinction, the war had little impact upon the settlers who, with only a few exceptions, continued their lives as usual. The war was intellectually and emotionally important, but physically an abstraction. For Youssef Zighout, who had inherited the command of Wilaya Two upon the death of Didouche, this was an unacceptable situation. In consultation with his second in command, Lakhdar Ben Tobbal, he determined to widen the conflict by provoking a massive popular uprising that would show the settlers a real revolution was afoot. There is no doubt that Zighout's and Ben Tobbal's decision to carry the war to civilians was the result of a cold strategic calculation that heightening the level of intercommunal violence would accelerate the process of mass mobilization, upon which the turning of an insurrection into a revolution depended. Yet the new initiative was formally framed in defensive terms, a response to colonialism's brutal collective reprisals against the Algerian people. On Zighout's and Ben Tobbal's command, popular forces went on the offensive on August 20, 1955, in some twenty-six localities of the Constantinois, including the capital city itself and the beautiful resort-like coastal town of Philippeville. The most horrible events took place in the small pyrite mining town of El-Halia, a suburb of Philippeville, where, at noon, some eighty guerrillas fell on the village and slaughtered the inhabitants without regard to sex or age. Victims ranged from a seventy-three-year old grandmother to a five-day-old baby. Soustelle claimed that FLN-led mobs killed 123 people that day, including 71 Europeans and several Muslim office holders.

The French riposte was predictable and pitiless. Official government figures claim that 1,273 insurgents died in the attacks and the subsequent repression, but the FLN claimed at least 12,000 Muslim deaths resulted from a wild and indiscriminate reaction that involved police, troops, and settler vigilantes. Zighout's calculation was correct. From this time onward, the communities became irreversibly polarized; what some observers up to that time had dubbed a *"drôle de rébellion"* became overnight a full-fledged war. Wilaya Two, whose effectives in the spring had fallen to no more than 200, claimed 1,400 men under arms by October. It seems also to have been this bloodletting that transformed Jacques Soustelle from a reforming liberal into an intransigent hard liner. Philippeville and its aftermath also rendered impossible the already uncomfortable position of the assimilationist and moderate nationalist politicians. Mohamed Salah Bendjelloul, the leader of the former Fédération des élus, convoked a meeting of native deputies to the Algerian Assembly which, on September 26, issued a "Declaration of the Sixty-One." Adopted by a majority but acceded to unanimously, this declaration condemned the policies of blind repression and collective punishment and rejected the concept of integration, claiming that "the overwhelming majority of the population now supports the Algerian national idea." Thus, the only class that could conceivably have welcomed Soustelle's program of political reform had now rejected it out of hand and began moving rapidly into the revolutionary camp.

What had begun in 1954 as the desperate gamble of a handful of alienated and frustrated patriots was transformed by late 1955 and 1956 into an authentic revolution attracting the loyalties tacitly or actively of hundreds of thousands of Algerians. Two years after the All Saints Day insurrection, Muslim society throughout most of the national territory was organized into a vast network of clandestine institutions that included not only military command but elementary judicial structures, civil and tax authority, rudimentary pension, and family assistance programs—all of which competed with the legal institutions for the loyalty of the masses. While the clandestine organization was not equally effective in every region, its creation and expansion was staggering in both scope and implications, because it represented the institutional birth of a nation which neither the French nor outside observers were more than vaguely aware of at the time. While the successful implantation of the revolutionary organization is ultimately the response of a pauperized and rejected society to the conditions of its bondage, the trigger of that response lies in two more immediate factors: The first is the reaction to the counterinsurgency campaign itself, which, even when it did not indiscriminately target the innocent, tended for every authentic revolutionary it killed or imprisoned to multiply the alienation factor by turning that person's family and friends into revolutionaries. The second is the impact of the FLN campaign against the colonial Muslim establishment. Like most revolutionaries, the Algerians confronted not only the oppressor himself but also the compatriots who were willing to serve or tolerate him. From the first night, the revolution had targeted qa'ids and bachaghas in the communes mixtes; as the months wore on, they added to their list appointed and elected municipal officers, tax collectors, Muslims who paid taxes, Muslims who served in the French army, and even the families of those who did. In time, whole communities that refused to cooperate with the FLN were subject to the most severe sanctions. During the first two and one-half years of the war, the FLN killed only one European for every six Muslims it liquidated.

It was not only with collaborators, however, that the FLN found itself in disagreement. It was also with the existing Algerian political parties. Messali Hadj, who had already split from the central committee of the MTLD in the summer of 1954, was not amused by the further competition represented by the FLN. Shortly after the insurrection began, Messali's branch of the MTLD was renamed the *Mouvement national algérien* (MNA). Particularly strong among the émigré community, which was its historic base, the MNA also maintained strong support in parts of Algeria, most notably in the Kabylia. There it set up a rival militia of about 500 men, which, in the summer of 1955, suffered grievous casualties in a pitched battle with FLN forces under the leadership of Ait Ould Hamouda Amirouche, the most fearsome of the rising guerrilla leaders in the Djurdjura. The latter was also responsible for a grisly massacre of villagers, in May 1957, at the pro MNA settlement of Mélouza in the barren slopes of the southern Kabylia. Partly because of the blows it suffered from FLN forces and partly because of French success in co-opting various factions, the MNA as a guerrilla force ceased to pose a major threat to the FLN from mid-1957. It continued, however, to exercise major influence for the rest of the decade over the expatriate community, competition for whose financial support generated increasing violence on French soil itself.

By mid-1956, Messali Hadj's was the only important political movement that still continued to resist the FLN's call to unity in the common struggle. It has already been seen that the bulk of the MTLD centralists began to switch to the FLN as they were released from prison in 1955. As early as the spring of that same year, FLN agents were making discreet contacts with Abbas and other UDMA politicians, initiating a process of rapprochement that the Philippeville massacres accelerated. While several moderates, including Abbas, continued working during the winter of 1955–56 to engineer a negotiated solution, neither side seriously wanted to talk. By March 1956, UDMA and other Algerian deputies, concluding that political communication had reached the end of its road, requested the dissolution of the Algerian Assembly. The Governor General did so on April 11, effectively terminating attempts to implement the Organic Law of 1947 as well as the newer program of integration. That same month, Abbas, after consulting with Ben Bella in Switzerland, flew to Cairo, where he announced the dissolution of the UDMA and his own adhesion to the FLN.

The Algerian Communist party, as we have been seen, had been perennially disabled by its connections with the parent French party, whose priorities on domestic French politics and broader geopolitical issues regularly drove it to adopt positions embarrassing to the Algerian branch. As late as the spring of 1956, when the Socialist Guy Mollet was in power, the French Communist party voted for special repressive legislation and explicitly supported the concept of *Algérie française*. Still trapped in such hopeless contradictions as the revolution gathered momentum, the PCA sought to join the FLN as a coalition partner. While the FLN agreed to accept PCA members as individuals, it continued to insist upon the dismantling of the Communist party just as it did all others. When finally, on July 1, 1956, the PCA capitulated and voted itself out of existence, the FLN, after only twenty-one months of life, held the field to itself.

As early as the time of Emir Khaled, some Algerian politicians had begun to perceive the advantages of internationalizing their struggle. Internationalization became a major theme of Messali Hadj in the 1930s, of the AML in the 1940s, and was finally picked up again by the CRUA and the FLN. Most, if not all, FLN leaders realized from the start that it was naive to think 8,000,000 impoverished and undereducated Algerians could defeat a great power without outside help. Generation of international support was, therefore, along with arms procurement, the primary mission of the external delegation headquartered in Cairo. While Ben Bella's success as an arms procurer was limited, progress on the diplomatic front was cause for great optimism. Delegates to the Bandung Conference of nonaligned nations in Indonesia, in April 1955, unanimously adopted an Egyptian resolution upholding Algeria's right to independence. Even more significantly, the United Nations General Assembly, in its 1955 fall meeting, agreed by a one-vote majority to place the Algerian question on its agenda. France, claiming an intrusion into its internal affairs prohibited by the Charter, immediately walked out. But as months and years went by, France was able less and less to contain the process of internationalization—partly because the FLN entrusted the UN task to unusually capable and persuasive young diplomats, partly because the escalation of violence in Algeria made it harder and harder for the world to ignore the issue. Even more importantly, the accession of Tunisia and Morocco to independence, in March 1956, converted the bordering countries into important staging grounds for Algerian revolutionary forces. The new geographic reality greatly complicated France's pacification effort tactically and materially while, at the same time, it enmeshed two sovereign members of the UN in the Algerian war to a degree no state had previously experienced.

In spite of their remarkable successes at mobilizing a nation and drawing international attention to its plight, the revolutionaries had little success in maintaining effective command structures or in building meaningful political institutions. As the year 1956 advanced, it became clear to most of the leadership that the FLN's policy-making and executive institutions were not adequate to the enormous and complex tasks it faced. One issue was the problem of coordination among the guerrillas themselves. FLN efforts on the ground were weakened by interpersonal or intergroup conflicts largely irrelevant to the national struggle; they were hampered by the bewildering turnover provoked by the terrible toll of lives; French counterinsurgency tactics were increasingly effective at isolating the wilayas from each other. It was clear as well that the rapid expansion of the movement in 1956 called for institutions capable of accommodating the new, wider spectrum of classes, interests, and opinion. Finally, the relationship between the external and internal leaderships was in urgent need of clarification. The latter denounced Ben Bella and the Cairo Bureau for the inadequacy of their weapons effort, for claiming a policy role superior to that of the men physically bearing the burden of the revolution, and for negotiating behind their backs with the French.

The upshot was the Soummam Valley Congress of August–September 1956. Near Akbou, high in the forested mountains overlooking the Soummam Valley that separates the Greater from the Lesser Kabylia, some fifty internal leaders of the revolution met for twenty days under the very noses of French security forces to restructure the FLN. The forty-page platform they drafted clarified the objectives of the revolution, formalized the military structures that had been evolving ad hoc, and gave the revolution for the first time a set of overall political institutions.

Most notable among the objectives identified was the reaffirmation of the goal of complete independence and the pledge never to accept a cease-fire until France recognized the principle of independence. The Soummam Congress created a body called the *Conseil national de la révolution algérienne* (CNRA), which was in effect Algeria's first sovereign parliament. Although with its initial personnel the first CNRA never formally met as a whole, its creation marked a major step both in defining political institutions and in broadening the revolutionary leadership. While seventeen members of the CNRA were carried over from the CRUA, the body also included two members of the former UDMA, six former MTLD centralists, and two of the Reformist ʿUlama. As an executive cabinet, the conferees created a *Comité de coordination et d'exécution* (CCE), the five members of which were Benyoussef Benkhedda, Saad Dahlab, Belkacem Krim, Larbi Ben M'Hidi, and Abane Ramdane. Ramdane was a Kabyle who had risen rapidly in the internal leadership in 1955 and who, by the time of the Soummam Valley Congress, had become the most powerful internal FLN figure.

The platform condemned tendencies toward regionalism and the pursuit of personal power while affirming the principle of collegial decision-making as well as the authority of the political leadership over the military. It also affirmed the primacy of the internal leadership over the external, a position which was easy to take since none of the external leaders had made it to the Soummam Valley. Notified that a meeting was to take place, Ben Bella and his colleagues waited first at San Remo then at Tripoli for the escorts who were to guide them into the country. They were still waiting at Tripoli when word arrived the Congress had convened, met for twenty days, and then adjourned.

Brahim Mezhoudi, one of the conferees, claims he went to the Tunisian frontier to escort Ben Bella to the meeting but that the latter never appeared. Whether the absence of the externals was due to logistical problems or was by design of Ramdane Abane and the internals, the Cairo revolutionaries thought they had been the victims of a veritable coup and were left livid with anger. It should be noted as well that, since Abane and a disproportionate number of the conferees at the Kabylia forester's cottage had been Kabyles, this split contains hints of the unresolved issues separating Arabs from Kabyles that had already surfaced within the Organisation spéciale in 1949.

The schism might easily have dealt a mortal blow to the movement had not French action a month later inadvertently resolved the crisis of authority, at least temporarily. On October 22, 1956, a Moroccan DC-3 carrying Ben Bella, Boudiaf, Khider, Ait Ahmed, and Moustapha Lacheraf, a prominent Algerian intellectual, took off from Rabat en route to Tunis, where the Algerians hoped to discuss with Habib Bourguiba some French peace feelers. As it was flying over international waters, the DC-3 was ordered by the French Air Force to land at Oran, where the five passengers were taken into custody and subsequently shipped off to prison in France. The four political leaders, along with Rabah Bitat, the Wilaya Four leader who had already been arrested, remained under French detention until a few months before Algeria was granted its independence. While as time went on, Ben Bella and his colleagues found ways to communicate with other FLN leaders, the immediate effect of their imprisonment was to leave the Soummam Platform with its resounding affirmation of internal authority unchallenged.

THE BATTLE OF ALGIERS AND ITS REPERCUSSIONS

Decisions made by that internal authority would soon transform the physical map of the war. In spite of the popular and infrastructural successes of the FLN, the fall of 1956 was a period when French successes more and more limited its military effectiveness. French forces that had totalled 80,000 in 1954 were built up to over 400,000. Their effectiveness against *mujahidin* was maximized by deploying them into hundreds of small units defined by a system of *quadrillage,* which divided the bulk of the territory into small quadrants of a hundred or a few hundred square kilometers. The French were also beginning a policy of *regroupement,* or resettlement, of populations outside of regions where the FLN was most active in order to rob the rebels of revenue, supply, and shelter—in effect "taking the water away from the fish." Under these circumstances the new CCE, impelled by the analyses of Ramdane Abane, made two major decisions: One was to demonstrate to France and the world the FLN's authority over the Algerian population by calling for an eight-day general strike throughout the country. The other was to carry the battle from the countryside, where the outside world scarcely noticed what was going on, into the colonial capital by means of urban terrorism. A sinister dictum attributed to Abane was that "one corpse in a jacket is always worth more than twenty in uniform."[3] To skeptical militants who required justification for such a bloody course, Abane and Ben M'Hidi could point to a multiplication of incidents of urban violence that had already taken place in Algiers. In the summer of 1956, the FLN had already responded to the French execution of two rebel prisoners with a wave of random killings of European civilians in Algiers, which in turn had led to random reprisals against innocent Muslims by European mobs.

The actual Battle of Algiers as a planned campaign was launched on Sunday evening, September 30, 1956, when three young middle-class women placed bombs in a student dance spot, the fashionable Milk Bar on the Place Bugeaud, and in the downtown terminal of Air France. Three Europeans were killed and scores were seriously wounded, including many children. Orchestrated by Saadi Yacef, commander of the Autonomous Region of Algiers from a hideout in the heart of the Casbah, bombings and other outrages specifically aimed at the most innocent of the city's population succeeded each other month after bloody month into the winter and spring of 1957. On the French side, the countermeasures were the responsibility of Commander in Chief Raoul Salan and General Jacques Massu, commander of the elite Tenth Paratroop Regiment. The latter broke up the eight-day general strike—timed by the FLN to coincide with a UN Political Commission debate on Algeria—by forcibly opening and wrecking shuttered places of business, rounding up strikers in army trucks and herding them to their workplaces, and shooting strikers who resisted. By isolating the Muslim populations and their neighborhoods, by subjecting them to massive pressure and harassment, and by projecting intelligence operations into every corner of the city, Massu slowly made progress against the terrorists. Most notably he instituted widespread and systematic use of torture as an aid to interrogation. Hundreds and perhaps thousands were tortured in the campaign to uncover the murderous clandestine networks. A significant though uncountable number of suspects died under interrogation, including a number of prominent personalities. Among the latter were Maurice Audin, an assistant professor of political science who was collaborating with the nationalists, and Mohammed Larbi Ben M'Hidi, commander of Wilaya Four and member of the CCE. Through a combination of methods, Massu got the upper hand in the battle. By summer 1957, the main spokes of the terror network had been found and cut; by the fall, Saadi Yacef was taken into custody, and his principal lieutenant, the nationalist hero Ali la Pointe, was gunned down in a shoot-out with paratroopers. The Battle of Algiers was over.

What were its effects? With regard to whether it strengthened or weakened the FLN's authority among Algerians, judgments are mixed. Many Muslims were appalled at their side's resort to terrorism against the innocent and at the price equally innocent Algerians were called upon to pay in the French reac-

---

3. As quoted by Alistair Horne, *A Savage War of Peace*, p. 132.

tion. Others, up to then on the sidelines, were driven into resistance by Massu's counterterrorist excesses. The Battle's impact upon revolutionary structures and organization was, on the other hand, completely negative. The overwhelming, multifaceted repression further disrupted already fragile communications and command structures. By February 1957, the rebels' situation had become so dangerous that, with Ben M'Hidi already in prison, the rest of the CCE—Abane, Krim, Benkhedda, and Dahlab—were compelled to flee the country. Subsequently, they reconstituted the central FLN organization in Tunis. It was one of the more ironic twists of the War of Independence that, only five months after proclaiming the primacy of the internal over the external, the men who determined that policy were themselves transformed into externals. Once in Tunis they found themselves bitterly criticized for many decisions they had made. These included having called a general strike that failed; having launched a campaign of urban terrorism that broke the historic link between the revolution and its rural habitat; and having unleashed forces of repression that greatly strengthened the colonialist hand and weakened the arm of the mujahidin. From a longer perspective, however, it is clear that it was the Battle of Algiers that really riveted world attention for the first time upon the Algerian struggle and that, for the first time, brought many of its issues home to the public in France. In the long run, international pressures and a disillusioned French public opinion would be the key factors forcing the French state to accept Algerian independence.

But in the shorter term, the outlook for the FLN appeared bleaker than at any time since the first winter of insurrection. The system of quadrillages increasingly limited the military options of the *Armée de libération nationale* (ALN), as the revolutionary forces were now called. Algerians by the hundreds of thousands were being forced into *centres de regroupement,* bleak resettlement camps surrounded with barbed wire, where peasants whiled away the months in the most penurious and demoralized circumstances. Other villagers, to escape resettlement and intimidation by French search-and-destroy missions or by FLN activists, fled to the cities. Still others poured across the borders into Tunisia and Morocco.

During the same period, the French moved vigorously to secure the borders of newly independent Tunisia and Morocco, across which flowed the bulk of rebel weapons and beyond which rebel forces fleeing French units were free to regroup for renewed attacks into Algeria. To secure the borders, they systematically interdicted their sides of the frontiers to depths of from ten to sixty kilometers, often driving the inhabitants before them across the borders rather than resettling them inside Algeria. At the same time, they erected, at great expense, sophisticated physical barriers which, by late 1957, were strikingly effective in limiting border crossings. The Morice Line was the most famous. It was a 200-mile fence erected along the Tunisian border, charged with 5,000 volts of electricity and flanked by rolled barbed wire and lethal mine fields. The fighters inside Algeria, always in a lonely a vulnerable situation, were now more isolated than ever from the constituted leadership of the FLN.

Given all these negatives, that leadership and the decisions it made were increasingly called into question by other elements in the FLN. Principal of the critics, in 1957 and early 1958, were men still loyal to Ahmed Ben Bella and his fellow prisoners, typified best by ᶜAli Mahsas, a comrade from Ben Bella's OS days. Next to these was a rising class of military men who had gradually taken over direction of the war as death, imprisonment, or demonstrated incompetence thinned the ranks of the original revolutionaries. The first formal session of the CNRA, meeting in Cairo in July 1957, essentially reversed Soummam Valley decisions establishing the primacy of the interior and the superiority of the political over the military. It created an expanded CCE, which included Abbas, Debaghine, and Abdelhamid Mehri of the older political class, but which was dominated by five wilaya colonels. Most significant for the future was the appearance among the latter of Abdelhafid Boussouf, commander of Wilaya Five who, with his assistant, Houari Boumediene, had created the most disciplined and coherent military apparatus in the interior. Only Krim and Abane of the original CCE survived the reorganization. So bitter was the struggle of Abane to maintain his crumbling authority in the months following the reorganization that his opponents finally determined to dispose of him. In December 1957, under circumstances that are not yet totally clear, he was lured to Morocco and assassinated in the countryside not far from Tetouan, the former capital of Spanish Morocco. Poignancy is added to the spectacle of Abane's violent end when it is realized that he was one of the few top leaders whose revolutionary credentials went back to the very beginning— to the Sétif insurrection of May 8, 1945. But in spite of the endemic conflict which characterized intra-FLN relations all through the war, Abane's elimination was one of only a handful of cases where top leaders actually killed other top leaders.

CHARLES DE GAULLE AND THE GPRA

After September 1957, when the French completed the formidable Morice Line, the heaviest fighting shifted to the frontier, where wave after wave of Algerians spent itself trying to break through the barrier. With their failure, the operational balance of the war more and more favored the colonialists by the spring of 1958. Urban terrorism had been quelled, operational successes in the interior countryside were few and small, and the war on the frontiers had stagnated. It was precisely at this moment, however, that inherent contradictions on the colonial side began to destabilize the French political system. The oldest of these contradictions were those which had always separated the narrow goals of the Algerian colons from the broader interests of France. France's interest in a system equitable enough to insure the long-term loyalty of the Algerian Muslims had, for more than a century, been overridden by that of settlers determined to guarantee their own monopoly of political and economic power. When, under increasing pressure from the Algerian Revolution, the costs to the French nation of maintaining the colon monopoly began to mount—morally, materially, and in human lives—then the always tenuous trans-Mediterranean European alliance began to crack. Since 1871, it had been the institutionalized instability of the multiparty French parliamentary system that had permitted a single-minded colon minority almost always to have its way. But the system that could evade difficult moral choices interminably when pressured by a determined colon side became paralyzed and ultimately fell apart when confronted with an equally determined Algerian nationalism, by disillusioned French public opinion, and by mounting international pressure.

The buildup of French military forces to nearly half a million men had necessitated assigning a large number of conscripts to Algeria. While the loss of Foreign Legionnaires went largely unnoticed and the deaths of French career soldiers attracted only a little more attention, the growing toll of young citizen soldiers from 1956 onward brought the war home to the métropole in a personal way. While some conscripts who survived Algeria came home partisans of Algérie française, more returned with grave questions about brutality they had witnessed and the pacification methods they had participated in or heard about. In any of these cases, French families more and more questioned why their boys should pay such a price for maintaining France's colonial position.

A second and even more decisive factor in raising French public consciousness was the incontrovertible evidence of official and widespread resort to torture. The deaths by torture of French leftists, of gallicized Algerians well known in French intellectual circles, and the firsthand testimony of Henri Alleg, a French Communist who had survived interrogation, caused a French opinion, which was still reeling from the trauma of Nazi wartime excesses, to start grappling for the first time with the question of what it was that France was fighting for across the Mediterranean. A French economy still not totally recovered from World War II and still awaiting the infusion of life the Common Market would bring was in the grips of a debilitating inflation, only exacerbated by the mounting costs of the Algerian war.

Further complicating the picture was the wounded and still unhealed state of the French army. Smarting from a series of humiliations stretching from the debacle of 1940 to the defeat at Dien Bien Phu, in 1954, and the abortive mission to Suez, in 1956, it was an institution bent upon proving its worth to itself and the world. As the ability of revolving-door governments in Paris to make difficult decisions came increasingly into question, the officer corps turned more and more truculent. Because their distrust of the politicians was shared by the colons, who saw in a succession of reform proposals aimed at weaning Algerians from the FLN a slackening of the national will, an uneasy alliance between colons and military took shape.

In early 1958, the hottest armed conflict was along the Morice Line, which the Algerian ALN was at that moment still trying to breech. After Algerians based in the Tunisian border town of Sakiet twice shot at French aircraft, three

French bombers retaliated by leveling the town on February 8, 1958, killing some eighty people, including many Tunisian women and children. The Sakiet raid created overnight a major international incident, thrust the Algeria war onto center stage at the UN, and motivated both Britain and America to attempt mediation between France and an aggrieved Tunisia. But the raid had taken place without civilian authorization. The army, which had been delighted with the tactical results of Sakiet, was stunned at the international uproar it elicited and at the reprimands to which the government subjected it. By the spring of 1958, leading officers believed that, thanks to their newer counterinsurgency tactics and the effectiveness of the Morice Line, military victory was clearly in sight. But they feared incompetent and weak-willed politicians might well snatch that victory away.

When a government crisis occurred late in April 1958, Pierre Pflimin, an Alsatian moderate who was rumored to favor a negotiated settlement, received the presidential mandate to attempt forming the Fourth Republic's thirteenth government. Just at this time, events in Algeria reach the crisis stage. When the French executed three men convicted of terrorism and the FLN retaliated by executing three French prisoners, settler Algeria rose in revolt. On May 13, a massive crowd of colons assembled at Algiers' *Monument aux Morts* in the steeply terraced park that spread down the hill from the palace of the Government General above. There they proclaimed a Committee of Public Safety with General Massu as its president, while mobs invaded and overran the seat of government. Overnight the insurrection seemed on the verge of spreading back into France itself and the fate of the Republic hung in the balance as France faced the threat of its first military coup against a legitimate government since 1799. The newly invested Pflimin government was unable to cope. All eyes turned to General Charles de Gaulle who, out of power since 1946, seemed like the only person with the stature and credibility to save the nation and extricate it from the Algerian embroglio. De Gaulle was admired by many Frenchmen because of his heroic wartime role, was untainted by the political infighting of the Fourth Republic, and enjoyed the confidence of the army, which could not imagine one of its own doing anything dishonorable. He accepted President René Coty's invitation to form a government, which was approved by Parliament on June 1, 1958. As conditions of his acceptance, he had won power to rule by decree for six months and to submit a new constitution before the end of that time. That constitution, duly ratified in September 1958 by a national plebiscite, created the Fifth Republic, which adjusted the balance of governmental power in favor of the executive branch and ended the long ordeal of France's postwar instability.

On June 4, de Gaulle flew to Algeria, where he began a three-day tour with an emotional speech in the capital, where he raised his arms in a V sign and exclaimed to the enthralled crowd, "Je vous ai compris!"[4] He went on to praise

4. "I have understood you."

the discipline and dedication of the army, to assure his audience that from this day onward all of the inhabitants of Algeria were Frenchmen in the full sense of the word, and to open the door of reconciliation to the "Muslim Frenchmen" who, out of exasperation and hopelessness, had gone astray. In June 1958, the army, the settlers, and a considerable number of war-weary Algerians were convinced that de Gaulle really did understand them and that he really could bring about a solution according with their interests and needs. But it seems evident in retrospect that the de Gaulle of June 1958 did not comprehend the essence of the problem tearing Algeria apart. He failed to understand the degree to which the notion of Algerian national identity had seized the Muslims. He also failed to understand that the concept of a reconciliation based upon the equality of all inhabitants flew in the face of the century of institutionalized inequality which the Europeans of 1958 were still determined to prolong. The concrete proposals he finally submitted in September and October included measures for accelerating Algerian integration into France by granting universal adult suffrage, instituting a single electoral college, and assuring that a minimum of two-thirds of Algerian representatives in the Parliament of the Fifth Republic would be Muslims. The social and economic aspects of de Gaulle's proposals were contained in the Constantine Plan unveiled on October 3. In this the General inaugurated an ambitious five-year development program, the most conspicuous features of which were a crash program of educational expansion, redistribution of 250,000 hectares of state lands, and a program of industrial investment designed to create 400,000 new jobs.

During the first months of the de Gaulle era, when the spell of his legend and the power of his ambiguous rhetoric still kept many Muslims mesmerized, some FLN leaders began to fear they were losing their hold over the masses and that the magician might be able to damage the movement seriously. In September, as the date approached for the newly enfranchised Algerians to vote on the constitutional referendum, the size of the turnout became a test of wills between France and the FLN. In spite of an FLN ordered boycott, 79.9 percent of Muslim men and women came to the polls; of these, 96.6 percent voted approval of the constitution of the Fifth Republic.

Earlier in the same month, the CNRA launched a three-part offensive to counteract the Gaullist initiatives. The offensive included transporting the revolution to French soil in an attempt to tighten control over the émigré community, much of which was still loyal to Messali's MNA, launching a new diplomatic offensive designed to turn East–West rivalries to Algerian advantage, and forming a Provisional Government. The first, which unleashed a wave of intracommunal violence in France, was counterproductive in its impact on French opinion, but it was a financial success to the extent that it diverted more money into FLN coffers. The diplomatic offensive, which saw Ben Khedda lead the first FLN visit to China in December, was of great psychological and diplomatic importance and also stimulated what would eventually become a major flow of East-bloc arms to the revolution.

Finally, in unequivocal rejection of de Gaulle's program of integration, the FLN announced, in a Cairo press conference on September 19, 1958, the creation of the *Gouvernement provisoire de la République algérienne* (GPRA) with its capital at Tunis. In composition, the GPRA represented the most broadly based executive yet created by the FLN. Ferhat Abbas was named President, a masterly stroke designed to capitalize upon the reputation for statesmanship and moderation he enjoyed abroad. Ben Bella became a Vice President, and his four fellow prisoners were all made Ministers of State. Lamine Debaghine, the former MTLD centralist, became Foreign Minister, and Tewfik el-Madani, of the Reformist ʿUlama, became Minister of Culture. For all of its breadth, however, the main power positions remained in the hands of the militant triumvirate who had dominated the second CCE: Belkacem Krim as Vice President and Minister of War, Lakhdar Ben Tobbal as Minister of the Interior, and Abdelhafid Boussouf as Minister of Communications.

EXTERNALIZATION AND POLITICIZATION OF THE CONFLICT

Most analysts agree that the so-called heroic years of the Algerian Revolution, which extend from November 1954 to September 1958, constitute a synchronous whole centered upon the primary task of converting and mobilizing the Algerian people and proving the authenticity of the revolution and its institutions. These tasks could only be accomplished by interaction inside the country among the FLN, the Algerians, and the colonial system. The second phase of the revolution extends from late 1958 until independence. While the internal interaction certainly continued in the second phase, the principal processes that determined the subsequent course of the struggle were predominantly political and diplomatic in nature and unfolded mainly outside the country. The large Muslim turnout for the September 1958 plebiscite represented a serious blow to the FLN's prestige and was the high point of de Gaulle's campaign to lure the Algerians away from it. As the fall wore on, however, the contradictions in the General's program were increasingly apparent to colons and Muslims alike. At the same time, the steadfastness of the FLN and the new prestige it won by creating a Provisional Government whose representatives were received with respect and even enthusiasm in distant capitals helped it to build back from September's low point.

The turning of the tide was clear from October onward when the GPRA summarily rejected the Constantine Plan and then the so-called "paix des braves" in which de Gaulle, in a stunning misreading of the causes and psychology of conflict, offered reconciliation without recrimination on the basis of the unconditional surrender of all FLN forces. In the November elections to choose Algeria's forty-six deputies to the first parliament of the Fifth Republic, only 65 percent of eligible voters turned out. Even more significantly, not a single Algerian of political consequence had agreed to stand for election. While it would be some months yet before de Gaulle realized or admitted it, integration was a dead issue. If he wanted peace he would some day have to talk with the spokesmen of the Algerian people, and these were, almost without exception, affiliated with the FLN.

In the meantime, Massu and other officers were required to resign from the Committee of Public Safety and de Gaulle reassigned the activist General Salan to France, turning the governorship over to the civilian Paul Delouvrier and the army command over to Maurice Challe. Under Challe's leadership, France, in 1959, came as close as it ever would to ending the Algerian war in a military sense. So intense was his pressure that ALN units, which had occasionally still functioned at the company level, were reduced first to platoon and then to squad or even smaller operations. More than one general pronounced the war won. General Challe's military operations and the astute manipulation of French counterintelligence were so successful that the organization and operations of Wilayas Two, Three, and Four were thrown into complete disarray. Yet, in the absence of a political solution, only persistent and overwhelming military presence could keep the fragmented rebel units from reforming whenever vigilance was relaxed. But this potential for major eruption, along with the ability to maintain a steady stream of smaller but still provocative incidents, was all the FLN now required, because it was precisely at this time that the building of armies on Algeria's borders was becoming more important than the magnitude of the internal military struggle.

The growth in size and influence of the external army represented an evolutionary process that reflected the changing logic of the struggle. With increasing French military success inside Algeria and the fragmentation of the internal organization, Tunisia and Morocco served as refuges both for ALN guerrillas on the run and for recruitable civilian refugees. In these bordering countries, the movement could establish far more orderly training and command structures than at home. They also had first choice of the widening flow of sophisticated arms flowing from East-bloc countries. As the months and years passed, the external ALN weighed more and more heavily, not only in the direction of military matters but in the political and diplomatic processes as well.

DE GAULLE'S SLOW CONVERSION AND THE DEFECTION OF THE ULTRAS

As military success persistently failed to translate into a political solution, the French public was growing restless. At the same time, international pressures on France kept mounting. Finally, in a watershed proposal delivered to the nation via radio and television on September 16, 1959, de Gaulle, for the first time, uttered the words "self-determination." Peace must come first. But four years, at the latest, after peace had been restored, the Algerians would be called upon to choose independence, integration with France, or a relationship of association. De Gaulle clearly favored the latter solution. But in seeking to determine the will of the Algerian people, he insisted that France would deal with them only as individuals and never with the FLN, which he labeled "a group of ambitious agitators determined to set up by raw force and terror their totalitarian dictatorship."

While the people of France were broadly supportive of what, in a French context, was a bold initiative, the FLN found it unacceptable for obvious reasons. But because it represented the first real crack in the colonialist armor, the September 16 speech gave a tremendous boost to revolutionary morale. For the French army, by contrast, the prospect of continuing to fight and die for a country the government seemed willing, in the end, to give away was thoroughly unacceptable. Finally, for the colons, the September 16 proposal spelled nothing less than the loss of their birthright. The alliance of settlers and soldiers, which was first manifested in May 1958 and which triggered de Gaulle's rise to power, now began to reform as it became clear that the new Chief of State was no more willing than his predecessors to do what was necessary to preserve Algérie française. In November 1959, the colons organized a *Front national français* to defend their interests. By January 1960, they had raised barricades in the heart of the capital and were firing on gendarmes while the army looked on. After a week of disorder and open collusion between rebellious settlers and elements of crack paratroop units, the uprising was brought to an end by the appearance of General de Gaulle on radio and television. In one of the most effective addresses of his career, de Gaulle was able to tip the teetering balance of military loyalties back in favor of republican authority and legitimacy. The barricades came down, but for the next two years, it was colon intransigence and, even more importantly, the specter of losing control of the army that provided the greatest impediment to France's coming to terms with the reality of Algeria's will to independence.

Similar splits between accommodationists and maximalists slowed the progress toward negotiation on the FLN side. It appears that Abbas, Ahmed Francis, Ahmed Boumendjel, and a number of other politicians, along with many internal leaders, were prepared to make concessions in order to get negotiations started. They were regularly dissuaded from this path by Krim and others of the external revolutionaries, by some of the more radical politicians, and especially, in a strange parallelism, by the Algerians' growing army, the ALN, which consistently pressed the hardest and most uncompromising stance. These observations are not meant to suggest that an outcome short of total independence was at all probable at this stage. They mean only that, had intransigents on both sides not been in a position for two years to slow the process of accommodation, meaningful negotiations might have started earlier and many lives might have been spared.

During the spring of 1960, relations between the government and the army remained tense. At the same time, Abdelhafid Boussouf, Ahmed Francis, and Belkacem Krim led a second and highly successful delegation to Peking and Moscow, which added to the international pressures de Gaulle felt weighing on him. In hindsight, France had less to fear from superpower pressures than seemed apparent at the time. The United States feared that too much pressure on such a politically sensitive issue might contribute to the destabilization of a state that was NATO's continental linchpin. The Soviets, for their part, were loathe to embarrass the French Communists and were anxious to encourage de Gaulle's moves toward greater independence from NATO. But these priorities were not as clear in 1960 as they later appeared. Moreover, France's attempt to maintain influence in the Third World (including, then, decolonizing sub-Saharan Africa) or to pursue interests elsewhere were not advanced by constantly having to defend its Algeria policy.

In March 1960, the search for non–FLN negotiating partners began to show promise for the first time when French counterintelligence established contacts with representatives of the Wilaya Four leadership south of Algiers. These men were disillusioned with the rigidity of the GPRA, perceived by many internals as high-living bureaucrats and power-hungry officers playing games for their own advancement while compatriots inside were bleeding to death. From their point of view, those who were bearing the brunt of the struggle should be the ones to determine the timing and conditions of negotiations. By June 10, the French had secretly flown the top three Algérois leaders to Paris, where they met with de Gaulle in the Elysée Palace. The President told the Algerians that he was now ready to offer the GPRA the opportunity to negotiate a cease-fire and that, in case the latter remained unresponsive, they would become France's negotiating partners. On June 14, de Gaulle broadcast an invitation to the GPRA to come to France to discuss a cease-fire. Eleven days later, the first official FLN delegation ever to come to France began meetings with French counterparts at the town of Melun south of Paris. There the French repeated their scenario for a cease-fire to precede any further steps toward resolution, while the Algerian delegates insisted, as they had since 1954, that a cease-fire could only be accepted as part of a total settlement, including unequivocal French recognition of their independence. On June 29, the talks broke off without any substantive progress having been made. It is possible that the French had deliberately leaked news of the clandestine overtures to the Wilaya Four dissidents in order to pressure the GPRA to the negotiating table. Within a year, at any rate, all of the internals involved in the secret negotiations had been liquidated either by the FLN or by the French. Military and intelligence circles were convinced that, in deciding not to negotiate substantively with the Wilaya Four dissidents, de Gaulle had missed a golden opportunity to split the FLN. However this may be, he had made no progress toward peace, but by extending de facto to the GPRA in June the recognition he had sworn in September never to grant, he had provided the FLN with its second stunning diplomatic victory in less than a year.

Even after the Melun talks failed, moderates within the GPRA—Abbas, Francis, and others—continued to incline toward accommodation, and some back-channel contacts did take place. But the dominant hard-liners were convinced more than ever that effective strategy now consisted in sitting back and waiting for their opponents to crumble. During the same year, the FLN succeeded in restoring to a modest extent the network in Algiers and its suburbs that had been shattered in the Battle of Algiers. It then launched a high visibility campaign of hit-and-run terrorist attacks against largely civilian targets. While these attacks were of minimal value militarily, they had the effect not only of infuriating the colon population but also of keeping the pressure on the military and the colonial government.

This increased the pressure on de Gaulle to find a solution, and on November 4, 1960, he took another major step in his gradual accommodation to the idea of Algerian independence. In one more of his celebrated addresses, the General explained that, when he had taken over the leadership of France, he had embarked upon a new course leading "from government of Algeria by metropolitan France to an Algerian Algeria. That means an emancipated Algeria . . . an Algeria which, if Algerians so wish—and I believe this to be the case—will have its own government, its own institutions, its own laws."[5] He then went on to startle many viewers by referring to the "Algerian Republic" which he saw in the future. On November 16, he called for a referendum of the Algerian and French electorates on the idea of self-determination and began preparing a swing through Algeria to promote his new program.

In the meantime, the ultra resistance, which had been thrown off balance in the crackdown that followed Barricades Week, had begun to reconstitute itself as the year 1960 progressed. The *Front de l'Algérie française* (FAF), as the movement now called itself, claimed more than a million members by late summer and enjoyed close ties with the colonialist establishment in France, which included Jacques Soustelle, the centrist political leader Georges Bidault, and the right-wing activist Jean-Marie Le Pen. More importantly, the FAF was attracting even greater support from middle-level officers of paratrooper and other units than it had the year before. During the summer and fall, General Raoul Salan, who had just retired from the army, and General Edmond Jouhaud, a native of Oran who had also recently retired, both joined the movement. The result was that, from the fall of 1960 until April 1961, the ultra movement fell more and more clearly under the leadership of defecting French officers.

It was the "Algérie algérienne" speech that galvanized the FAF into concrete action. They almost literally drove the Delegate General, Paul Delouvrier, out of office. When news spread of de Gaulle's impending tour, scheduled for December 9–12, to promote the self-determination referendum, no fewer than four separate plots were laid to assassinate or detain him. Most were badly conceived and coordinated. The most serious was at Algiers where the FAF planned to paralyze the city by calling a general strike and then to respond to the predictable disorder by marching dissident military units into the city to seize and detain de Gaulle. But this plan collapsed when de Gaulle wisely decided not to visit Algiers but to concentrate on lesser cities (e.g., Tlemcen, Orléansville, and Tizi Ouzou). At most of his stops, the President

5. As quoted by Horne, *Savage War,* p. 422.

was loudly booed by colons, but he was received politely and occasionally with enthusiasm by Muslims—a difficult position for a French head of state to be in. The most dramatic events of the month took place on December 11, when the Algiers FLN leaders managed to bring thousands of Muslims into the street to counter FAF demonstrations of the preceding two days. Countless hand-sown green and white national flags appeared spontaneously all over the city as marching, chanting Algerians poured out of their poorer quarters into the central districts of the capital. It was by far the most massive and dramatic demonstration of Algerian nationalism the capital had yet seen.

The referendum, held on schedule January 8, 1961, asked citizens if they approved of "the plan submitted to the French people by the President of the Republic concerning the self-determination of the Algerian population and the organization of the public powers in Algeria prior to self-determination." The result was an apparently convincing affirmative vote of 75 percent. Only 60 percent of the electorate had gone to the polls, however. In Algeria itself, the FLN, not wanting to surrender the initiative on the question of independence to de Gaulle, urged a Muslim boycott, with the result that the measure carried there by a bare 55 percent.

In January 1961, the FAF was banned for its seditious activities, but the next month, the ultras created the final and, ultimately, the most destructive of their organizations. This was the *Organisation armée secrète* (OAS), sparked by the colon extremists Pierre Lagaillarde and Jean-Jacques Susini. Its military leadership was provided by Raoul Salan, by this time in exile in Madrid, and by Marie-André Zeller, a retired chief of staff, as well as by Edmond Jouhaud. It received an enormous boost with the adhesion of Maurice Challe, who, disillusioned with the self-determination program, took early retirement and flew clandestinely to Algiers in April. There he agreed to coordinate a military putsch the OAS had been organizing for several weeks before his arrival. On the night of April 21 1961, using the First Foreign Legion Parachute Regiment as their main instrument, the OAS took over all of the key governmental, communications and security facilities in Algiers and detained the military commander and governor. On the morning of April 22, Challe went on the radio to announce that he and his colleagues had assumed full powers in Algeria and the Sahara so that both French Algeria and France itself could live. Unfortunately for the conspirators, only the unit commanders of the capital region were clearly on their side. The commander of the Oranie rejected the OAS appeal and the commander of the Constantinois temporized. While many frightened contemporaries expected disaffected units in France to join the putsch and Parisians kept watching the skies for paratroopers, the army in France maintained its loyalty. After the evening of April 23, when de Gaulle made yet another of his stirring pleas to the troops, the movement began to unravel. By April 25, the coup had failed, Challe surrendered, and other putchists were arrested or fled into hiding. There followed a widespread purge of disloyal and questionable elements in the officer corps. While this purge finally assured the security of the Republic and its constitution, it effectively crippled the military instrument with which France had for so long been trying to contain the Algerian drive toward independence. As a colon organization reflecting the fury and despair of a dying society, the OAS continued in ever more destructive paths as the movement toward independence accelerated,[6] but it had lost hope of changing the regime in France or altering the course of history.

CONFLICT IN THE FLN

It was observed in chapter 5 that Algeria alone among France's North African possessions failed to develop a broad-based nationalist movement capable of articulating national goals or coherent strategies for achieving them. At least one explanation for this failure lies in the success of the colonial system in preventing the emergence of any class with sufficient self-confidence and popular credibility to articulate the goals and lead the movement. The Algerian insurrection was less an expression of a national consensus than of frustration with the national inability to forge a consensus. In the early years, the FLN proved remarkably successful at mobilizing popular resistance and at integrating representatives of the various political tendencies into its institutional framework. But it experienced great difficulty in building consensus about revolutionary resistance strategies and institutions, still more in outlining the shape of the new social and economic order it envisaged or the nature of the political institutions it wanted to give the independent nation. The Algerian political elite was extraordinarily heterogeneous and became more so as it strove to broaden itself and as the differing wartime experiences differentiated one faction from another. One model suggests that much of the difficulty lay in the progression of elites that succeeded to the movement's leadership, a progression that took place because each group that came to the top perceived its predecessor as having been inadequate to its task. Messali Hadj and the PPA/MTLD seized the initiative from Abbas's assimilationist/autonomist moderates because they believed the latter to be faulty in their analysis of the Algerian condition, mindless of the needs of the masses, and ineffective in attempts to extract concessions from the colonials. The CRUA and early FLN revolutionaries rejected in turn the leaderships of both parties for continuing to play self-serving political games long after it was proven that the national interest could not be served by such activity. Later, the officers of the ALN rejected the leadership of the historic revolutionaries on the grounds, among others, that many were pursuing the cult of personality and attempting to divide the country into individually dominated fiefdoms. Still later, as the government in exile expanded, a class of bureaucrats and technicians emerged, generally better educated than either the guerrillas or the ALN officers, whose level of competence and understanding made them uncomfortable with the

6. Individual retired or renegade officers continued to participate in the OAS campaign of terror.

leadership claims of the former. Yet, all attempted to coexist within the inadequate institutions of the FLN and the result was continuing and worsening internal conflict.[7]

Attempts have been made to portray the intra-elite conflict in ideological terms, and it is clear that the FLN did contain a mixture of liberals, Marxists, Islamists and others whose world views differed markedly. But the majority of the leadership had little systematic exposure to or concern with the ideologies of the day. Aside from the fact that most, because of their modest backgrounds, rejected the middle-class orientation of what they called "Bourguibism," it seems that the compartmentalization of experience and interest imposed by circumstances as well as interpersonal conflict and pure pursuit of power were the causes of most of the dissension. By the early 1960s, thousands of Algerians who had played leadership roles of many different kinds in the revolution could lay claim to a share of political power but no mechanism had been created to adjudicate and apportion such claims. If the years 1954–56 witnessed a progressive coming together of nationalist leadership, the years 1957–62 witnessed an ever greater segmentation of the elites. This was in contrast to the society as a whole, which, through the shared experiences of war and repression, had developed the clear sense of identity referred to earlier and demonstrated so dramatically in the events of December 1960.

From 1958 onward, one axis of conflict was dissension between the moderates of the former UDMA (such as Ferhat Abbas, Ahmed Francis, and Ahmed Boumendjel) and the more Marxist radicals (such as Benyoussef Benkhedda, M'Hammed Yazid, and Lamine Debaghine). Another and more important axis of conflict was between the GPRA and the military. The leaders of the interior Wilayas (Two, Three, and Four) were increasingly alienated from the political leadership that claimed to speak for the nation. The defection, in spring 1960, of the Wilaya Four leadership was one symptom of that conflict.

In the long run, internal military opposition proved less significant than that of the external ALN. As the political institutions of the FLN in Tunis, Tripoli, and Cairo were weakening due to personality and other conflicts, the external ALN, almost by default, was becoming the most cohesive institution within the Algerian movement and therefore its most powerful. During the early stages of its formation, it competed for influence with wilaya leaders or those still attached to them such as Krim. Next, it faced the formidable logistical problems caused by its division into Tunisian and Moroccan wings. But in time, attracting numerous experienced veterans from the French army and profiting from the freedom to establish regular training programs and coherent command structures, the ALN created an impressive force of disciplined and responsive soldiers commanded by a corps of professional and equally disciplined officers.

7. This is the basic model of William B. Quandt in *Revolution and Political Leadership: Algeria, 1954–1968.*

Rising by steps to the top of the external army during the years 1957 to 1960 was Colonel Houari Boumediene, who later became the second President of Algeria. Born Mohammed Ben Brahim Boukharouba at Clauzel near Guelma in the Constantinois, Boumediene had attended both French and Quranic primary schools as well as a conservative madrasa. A participant in the 1945 insurrection who fortunately emerged unscathed, Boumediene later chose to flee the country rather than fulfill his military obligation to the French army. While in exile in Cairo, he broadened and deepened his Islamic education by enrolling at Al Azhar. While essentially a secularist, his attachment to the Arabo-Islamic heritage was more profound than that of other top FLN leaders. Serving after the rebellion began as Boussouf's assistant in Wilaya Five, he rose to command the Moroccan wing of the ALN under the second CCE. In 1959, when a group of ALN colonels in Tunisia were apprehended plotting the overthrow of the GPRA, it was Boumediene who presided over their court martial, thus establishing himself as the most prominent officer in the emerging army. But his summary handling of the rebels appears to have been less a sign of loyalty to the politicians than of concern for military discipline.

When the third meeting of the CNRA convened at Tripoli on December 13, 1959, for what turned out to be an acrimonious thirty-three day session, one of the most difficult issues it faced was widespread dissatisfaction with the conduct of the war. Belkacem Krim came under withering attack for his stewardship of the Ministry of War. Eventually, his ministry was dismantled and a unified General Staff was created that assumed not only operational but policy responsibility as well. An interministerial committee of three maintained a fiction of GPRA oversight, but real authority had passed to the General Staff. The retiring but determined Colonel Boumediene was chief of that General Staff. In spite of the fact that many fighters of the beleaguered interior wilayas rejected Boumediene's authority, his strong base in the external ALN and the border wilayas was such that he rapidly became a force that no one could ignore.

After weeks of CNRA infighting, a new GPRA was formed, in January 1960, which saw Krim demoted to the Foreign Ministry and the radical politicians Debaghine and Benkhedda eliminated—apparently because of their close relationship to Krim and the other revolutionaries the ALN was unhappy with. While Abbas was reconfirmed as President, he was hardly more than a figurehead in this second GPRA, which retained him more for his international stature than because of any internal power base. The moderates' proposals for positive response to de Gaulle's self-determination speech were soundly defeated. A pivotal achievement during the long meeting was drafting and ratification of a constitution which, for the first time, affirmed that Algeria was conducting not only a war of national liberation but also a revolution. For the first time, the FLN was specifically designated the single party responsible for carrying out that revolution. Considering the depth and pervasiveness of the conflict that tore at the very heart of the Algerian independence movement through these crucial years, it is surprising that virtually none of it ever became public and that the FLN continued, with apparently monolithic determination, to pursue its all-or-nothing strategy in dealing with the colonial power.

THE EVIAN AGREEMENT

The hard-liners' strategy of waiting for France to cave in had slowly yielded dividends. From his white flags and "peace of the brave" offer in 1958, de Gaulle had moved, by 1959, first to a vague right of self-determination excluding the FLN, then to inviting its representatives to Melun, and finally, by the fall of 1960, to a "république algérienne." In the late winter of 1961, Georges Pompidou, a trusted confidant of the General's, conducted a series of secret meetings in Switzerland with the Algerian lawyer Ahmed Boumendjel to pave the way for peace talks. Eventually the GPRA and the government of France began negotiations, on May 20, at Evian on the French side of Lac Léman, to which Belkacem Krim and the Algerian delegation traveled daily from their accommodations on the Swiss side. While the French, in hopes of eliciting a conciliatory attitude on the part of the Algerians, had ordered a unilateral cease-fire and released several thousand Algerian prisoners, the chasm between the two sides gapped as broad and deep as ever when they sat down to talk. Casting long shadows over the negotiations from the beginning were the questions of guarantees for the French minority that was expected to remain in an independent Algeria; sovereignty over the Sahara, where major petroleum deposits had been discovered in 1956; the status of French military, air, and naval bases on Algerian soil; and a formula for association between France and Algeria. The distance between the two sides was so great on the first two issues that the negotiators never got around to serious consideration of the last two. The French negotiators sought assurances that settlers in an independent Algeria would have a right to dual citizenship, that they would enjoy normal civil and political rights, and that their property rights would be guaranteed. The Algerians argued that such arrangements could only be made once a sovereign Algerian state was in place and in a position to negotiate on the basis of equality with the government of France. It is especially worth noting in regard to property rights that land reform, which had been a stated goal of the FLN since its inception, had become increasingly focal as the revolutionary goals of the struggle became more explicit. With regard to the Sahara, whose oil resources many Frenchman saw as the key to their economic future, France argued that the great desert had never been a part of Algeria, had only been pacified and developed thanks to French effort and investment, and could therefore never be ceded to an independent Algeria. The Algerians, on the other hand, maintained since the Soummam Valley Conference that the Sahara was an integral and inalienable part of their homeland. After thirteen sessions, the meetings broke down in June. The negotiators reconvened, in July, at Lugrin in the mountains above Evian, but, after six more fruitless sessions, they recessed indefinitely.

These negotiations took place against a disheartening background of OAS terror-bombings and assassinations, which the FLN finally, though reluctantly, decided to counter with its own campaign of violence. In the meantime, behind the scenes, the FLN was undergoing its greatest leadership crisis to date. As the second round of negotiations was limping toward impasse at Evian, Boumediene and his key aides sent a bitter letter of protest and resignation to the GPRA. While at one level the General Staff's accusations against the GPRA concerned substance (alleged corruption, alleged softness at Evian, too many bourgeois ideas), at a more fundamental level the dispute was about power, specifically about the GPRA's authority over the ALN. These were the issues that preoccupied the fourth CNRA when it convened at Tripoli on August 5, 1961.

While the members of the GPRA continued to indulge their own internal conflicts, they were virtually unanimous in resisting any further transfer of power to the General Staff; many even wanted to discipline the officers. But support for Boumediene came from a different direction—that of Ahmed Ben Bella and the other prisoners France had been holding since 1956 and 1957. The five had become an increasingly important factor both diplomatically, as the two sides began creeping toward a settlement, and politically, as the internal conflicts in the FLN sharpened. The fact of their incarceration and the circumstances of any release became major agenda items in Franco-Algerian dialogue from Melun onward. Through all the years of their imprisonment, the ideological and personality conflicts that characterized the men's relationships before their apprehension persisted and even worsened. This was particularly true of the relationship between Ben Bella and Ait Ahmed. But few, if any, outsiders knew this. As the luster of the active FLN leaders became progressively tarnished by the rough and tumble of politics, by varying degrees of incompetence, and by the consequences of making hard decisions in difficult times, the untainted prisoners in far-off France assumed greater and greater symbolic importance. The most physically arduous years for Ben Bella and his colleagues were those spent in La Santé prison in Paris until March 1959. But as the French government attempted to send positive signals to the Algerians and the international community, they were transferred to a series of more comfortable accommodations, ending up ultimately in the luxurious Château d'Aulnoy. As their conditions of internment improved, so did their access to the outside world; before long Ben Bella, in particular, was becoming again a major political force.

It was to Ben Bella that Boumediene turned, in 1961, in his struggle with the old line politicians and revolutionaries, and it was largely because of Ben Bella's support that the fourth CNRA was able to make enough changes to induce the staff officers to withdraw their resignations. That meeting also reshuffled membership of the GPRA one more time. To a considerable extent, the reshuffling reflected the ALN's hostility to Krim, who was now demoted still further to the Interior Ministry on the questionable grounds that his negotiating stance lacked firmness. The reshuffling also resulted in the expulsion of Abbas and the moderates and the return of Benkhedda and the radical politicians who had been excluded from the second GPRA—not because the military found them more congenial but because, after arguing so strenuously for firmness, they could hardly reject the candidacies of men with whom firmness was a byword. When the fourth CNRA concluded, differences had been papered over; but the major question, that of authority, was as far from resolution as ever.

As the fall of 1961 went on, urban Algeria, thanks to the OAS and its so-called *plastiques,* was collapsing into bloody anarchy; regional and international pressures on France were becoming unbearable; and the French people overwhelmingly wanted out of Algeria. De Gaulle finally broke the dam by announcing his willingness to give up the Sahara, a concession which left only the status of the settlers as a major potential stumbling block. The overwhelming majority of the GPRA, alarmed by the breakdown of order and what it might portend, wanted to return to the bargaining table. Though Boumediene remained as adamant as ever, Ben Bella this time sent word that he, too, thought the time to settle had arrived. With this, the Algerians agreed to go back to Evian.

Preliminary talks took place at Yéti, in the Jura Alps, during February 1962, but for the official negotiations the full delegations reassembled once again at Evian, where the final agreement was signed on March 18. The ninety-three page document began with the formal recognition of the independence of Algeria over its entire territory. It called for an immediate cease-fire, which went into effect the next day but which did not end the violence because the OAS responded by launching the bloodiest phase yet of its campaign of nihilism. Measures were taken for the immediate release of prisoners. France was assured leases on key air and naval facilities. On economic questions, Algeria agreed to remain in the franc zone, Algerian workers could remain in France, preferential trade arrangements were established, and France agreed to continue funding the Constantine Plan and other aid projects at 1962 levels for a minimum of three years. With regard to the important oil sector, the agreement recognized Algeria's ownership of its subsoil resources, but it confirmed all exploration, production, and transport rights previously granted to French companies and gave French firms preference in new contracts for a period of six years. The agreement also made arrangements for a binational Provisional Executive to manage the transition to independence. This government assumed power on April 7.

The French negotiators had labored long and hard to secure the best possible deal for the European community, but in the long run, the concessions they won proved largely unnecessary. Already in February, Europeans were beginning to head for the ports and airdromes. The exodus accelerated after March 18, and in June alone, more than 300,000 departed in an exodus which reached panic proportions. By the end of 1962, nine-tenths had departed; ultimately, not more than 30,000 settlers, many of them too old or poor to move on, remained in Algeria. During the last phases, departing

colons methodically and vindictively destroyed libraries, hospitals, government buildings, factories, machinery, and whatever else was within their reach
that they could not take with them. It was the violent, cataclysmic demise of a
community, many of whose members could claim roots in Algeria going back
four and even five generations. But most were clearly unready to remain in an
Algeria without the monopoly of power and means of production which had
assured their superior standard of living or in which the values and styles of the
long subordinate culture would become normative.

IMPACT OF WAR ON ALGERIAN SOCIETY AND ECONOMY

As noted in chapter 5, the Algerian economy entered a period of crisis after
the First World War from which it was only starting to recover by the early
1950s, thanks to improving postwar performance of the metropolitan economy and the investment stimulated by the two four-year plans. But recovery
and growth did not affect all sectors equally, as table 6.1 shows.

Table 6.1   Gross Domestic Product, 1930–1955

	Value in Billions of 1955 Francs		Annual Rate of Growth
	1930	1955	
Agriculture	194	210	.3%
Mining	14	19	1.2%
Manufacturing, Energy	33	104	4.6%
Building and Public Works	13	47	5.4%
Transport, Business and Services	169	269	1.9%
Civil Administration	36	80	3.3%
Gross Domestic Product	460	730	1.8%

Source: Amin: *L'Economie du Maghreb,* vol. 1 (1966), p. 190.

Both mining and agriculture were stagnating; the minor growth in the
latter was located exclusively within the modern sector dominated by the
colons. Traditional agriculture, which still provided the economic base for
the majority of the population, was continuing to regress as it had for sixty
years. Grain production had scarcely increased since the turn of the century;
the livestock herd had shrunk measurably. In 1953, the colon earned 34,000
francs for an average hectare cultivated, and the fellah, 6,400 francs. The
annual per capita income of the 5,840,000 fellahin was 19,200 francs; that of the
middle classes, which were 92 percent European, was 227,000 francs; and that
of the upper classes (bourgeoisie) was 1,500,000 francs.

But while the primary economic sector was stagnating, growth of the other sectors was accelerating. Between 1950 and 1954, the secondary grew at an average annual rate of 3.8 percent, moving up, between 1954 and 1958, at 6.4 percent. The tertiary sector averaged growth of 5 percent a year during the first period and speeded up to 11.6 percent during 1954–58. These growth rates reflected, in the first instance, the investment from the two four-year plans begun in 1949, capital committed almost entirely from the public sector. Second, much of the growth after 1954 was generated by the demand for services occasioned by the enormous military buildup. In either case, the beneficiaries were primarily city dwellers, mostly, if not exclusively, European. Finally, the emerging hydrocarbon sector attracted very substantial public and private investment from 1956 onward, and soon afterward it began contributing substantially to the GNP.

The opening bell in what was to become a rush for oil and gas in the Sahara was sounded in 1952 when the government's *Bureau de Recherches de Pétrole* began letting five-year exploration contracts to a series of companies. The most active of these companies were S. N. Repal *(Société nationale de Recherches de Pétrole en Algérie),* the Algerian affiliate of C. F. P. *(Compagnie française des Pétroles),* and C. R. E. S. P. *(Compagnie de Recherches et d'Exploitation de Pétrole au Sahara),* all of which were mixed-capital corporations. But by 1961, more than a dozen firms were involved, including affiliates of Royal Dutch Shell, Socony Mobil, and Standard Oil of New Jersey. While the Sahara contains two million square kilometers of desert and steppe, only the broad northeastern basin, extending from the Atlas to the Hoggar and from Tanezrouft to the Tripolitania border, had been systematically explored before 1962.

By 1956, major oil deposits had been found first in the Edjeleh Basin near the Libyan frontier and a little later in the Hassi-Messaoud Basin east of the Ouargla Oasis. Large reserves of natural gas were discovered south of Lagouat at Hassi R'Mel and later at Gassi-Touil; lesser ones, to the south around In Salah (see map 7). By independence, the petroleum reserves at Hassi-Messaoud were estimated at between 300 and 500 million tons, those around Edjeleh at about 140 million. The gas reserves at Hassi R'Mel were placed at 800 billion cubic meters. Crude oil began to flow to market in 1959, production reaching 9 million tons in 1960 and 25 million by 1962. Annual natural gas production at independence exceeded 200 million cubic meters.

The news from the Sahara had stimulated, during the late 1950s, a frenetic rush of French businessmen, financiers, and investors hoping to share in the bonanza—a new commitment to Algeria that was totally out of phase with a politico-military reality that augured imminent disengagement. Between 1954 and 1961, the oil and gas sectors attracted 588 billion francs in investment, a fact that explains, even better than the real yearning for energy independence, the French government's insistence until the eleventh hour that the status of the Sahara was not negotiable. This impressive investment in oil and gas tended to mask the decline and then progressive liquidation of private investment in other sectors of the economy just as, after 1960, gas and oil production

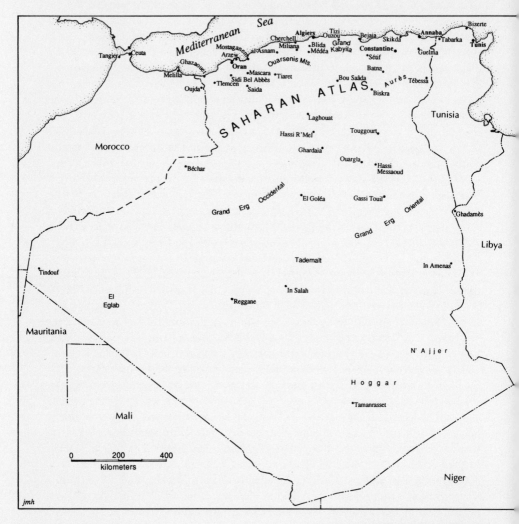

MAP 7 **Independent Algeria**

tended to mask the declines in productivity in the agricultural and industrial sectors.

The Constantine Plan, which was launched by Charles de Gaulle in October 1958 as the economic centerpiece of his campaign for an Algeria of equals, had actually been in the making since about 1955, when a group of French technocrats at Algiers became convinced that the key to financial stability for Algeria lay in thorough restructuring of a seriously unbalanced economy. Its investment priorities would target not only the anemic industrial sector but the long-neglected traditional agriculture and social infrastructure as well. This five-year plan, interrupted by the coming of independence in the middle of its fourth year, aimed at revolutionizing traditional agriculture by launching a crash program of education, by sending teams of agricultural experts into the field (one for each 200 farmers), by establishing cooperatives and democratic village institutions, and by draining marshes and extending irrigation. A massive program of industrialization from the ground up included basic steel and petrochemical industries as well as a great variety of manufacturing and processing ventures. The number of elementary school students was to reach 1,100,000 by 1963–64, and the number of secondary school students, 70,000.

Both the technocrats who designed the Constantine Plan and the President who promulgated it assumed an ending of the war to be imminent. In fact, the plan itself was supposed to hasten the reconciliation. But the political analysis was faulty, the war did not end as hoped, and the most fundamental premises underlying the plan were invalid. Schools, hospital beds, lodging, and some industries were built as planned. But as the war raged on and the mood of the country became more unsettled, private capital actually began to flee Algeria so that, in spite of new public investment, industrial production grew very little. Because of the army's spreading policy of regroupement, of transporting peasants away from farms and villages to vast resettlement camps, and of prohibiting or limiting access to large stretches of land on which they made their livings, traditional agricultural production plummeted.

The policy of concentrating Algerian peasants in centres de regroupement camps, with impeccable logic, the series of colonial policies that began with the sequestrations of the 1840s and proceeded to the cantonnement of the 1850s and to the sénatus-consulte of 1863 and the Warnier Law of 1873. By 1950–51, most Algerian peasants no longer owned land. But of those who did, 69 percent possessed fewer than ten hectares, and the average plot consisted of 3.1 hectares, far less than enough to support a family. Nevertheless, whether on their own land, or as workers on the land of colons and the better-off Muslim landlords or as casual laborers doing anything that was called for in the neighborhood, some 6,000,000 fellahin still clung precariously to the village way of life. The policy of regroupement and the effects of unending war, however, ended that way of life forever. By 1960, 2,157,000 Muslims were piled up in more than 2,000 internment centers under night and day surveillance of the French army. Several hundred thousand more had been driven across or fled across the borders of Tunisia and Morocco. Still others sought shelter and sustenance in the already overcrowded cities. By the time the war ended, more than 3,000,000 rural Algerians had been displaced from their homes, the majority of which had long since provided only a marginal standard of living. Hundreds of villages had been razed, fields, pastures and forests burned. When the war was over, fewer than half of the displaced peasants even tried to go home. Between 1954 and 1960 alone, the population of the cities increased by 67 percent, a destination which would attract nearly half of the displaced once the French gave up their internment centers in 1962. It was with millions of impoverished, uprooted, culturally deprived, and bewildered ex-peasants that independent Algeria would begin the difficult task of restructuring itself.

It is not only in its impact upon Algerian social structures and their relationship to land that French colonial policy displays a disturbing continuity for 130 years. That continuity is also seen in the recourse to violence to insure control and in the impact of that violence upon the Algerian people. As noted in chapters 3 and 4, the toll on human life extracted by the wars of conquest effected an absolute decline of population over the first forty years of colonial presence. In attempting to retain the colony, in the 1950s and 1960s, by the same recourse to force with which it had originally acquired it, the human cost was on an annual basis even greater. Fortunately, the War of Independence did not last as long as the wars of conquest.

The aggregate number of deaths, however, is the subject of a grisly debate in the literature. Beginning in 1962, Algerians claimed the War of Independence had cost 1,000,000 lives, and this figure has gained wide currency. Later, there were even claims that the death toll had reached 1,500,000. Supporters of Algérie française, for their part, admitted a maximum of 375,000 lives, claiming that at least half of these were victims of the FLN. Many Algerians suggest privately that the number of deaths should be either 500,000 or 600,000. A noted French demographer generally sympathetic to the Algerian national cause concluded, after a careful study of preindependence and postindependence census data, that there could not have been more than 300,000 deaths in excess of those that current mortality rates would have yielded.[8]

THE CRISIS OF INDEPENDENCE

Under the terms of the Evian Agreement, the Provisional Executive was required to hold a referendum on independence between three and six months after the cease fire. Since there was not a shade of doubt concerning the electorate's choice on the question, the struggle for power within the fractured FLN grew more frenetic as the clock ticked down toward the day of voting. In a last attempt to resolve the internal conflicts before independence, the CNRA

8. Xavier Yacono, "Les Pertes algériennes de 1954 à 1962," *Revue de l'Occident musulman et de la Méditerranée* no. 2 (1982).

met at Tripoli, in May and early June 1962, for what turned out to be its final session. While the Council had made some progress, during recent meetings, toward laying out in general ways the philosophy and goals of the revolution, it had made none at all toward establishing the political institutions that would govern an independent state or even mechanisms for creating them. Scarcely concealed behind the ideological and institutional questions was the ongoing struggle for power among individuals and factions. More than a dozen separate centers of contention can be identified: the GPRA; the moderate politicians; the radical politicians; the General Staff; six different wilaya commands; the financially important *Fédération de France du FLN* (FFFLN); the *Union générale des travailleurs algériens* (UGTA); and, most importantly, the prisoners of Aulnoy—or the *"purs"*, as some contemporaries called them—who had been released on the day the Evian Agreement was signed.

Discussions at Tripoli centered on two major questions: adoption of a political agenda, subsequently known as the Tripoli Program, and nomination of a Political Bureau. The Tripoli Program was written primarily by four leftist FLN intellectuals with the encouragement of Ahmed Ben Bella. It began with an analysis of the colonial legacy and discussion of the threat that the Franco-Algerian cooperation agreed to at Evian might end up projecting a neocolonialism. It dealt extensively with the problems of liquidating the OAS, which it claimed the Gaullists were doing too little to control, and also with the future status of the French minority, which still seemed a major issue in early June 1962. More striking, however, is its merciless criticism of the conduct of the war and the stewardship of the GPRA and wilaya leaders. While the FLN had clearly represented an advance over the leadership of the political parties it succeeded, its thinking during the war had scarcely moved beyond thoughts of national liberation. This intellectual immobilism contrasted with the thought of the masses themselves, who, faced with the brutal reaction of the dominant society, came to understand, if not clearly to articulate, the need for fundamental structural changes in the society. The leadership is criticized for lacking ideological firmness; for "formalism", "paternalism", and "petit bourgeois" attitudes; for being antirevolutionary; for "feudalism"; and for confusion of party and state—all practices and beliefs which, if not adjusted by "ideological combat," would lead to creation of an antipopular and mediocre bureaucracy. With regard to the future, the Tripoli Program called for a popular democratic revolution based upon the leadership of the rural masses, and assisted by the urban poor and middle class youth. It rejected both economic dependency and market economics in favor of a socialist system in which the large means of production would be collectivized and in which the state would play the major role in the economic planning process. Algerian culture was to be national, revolutionary, and scientific, as well as Islamic, in the modern and progressive sense of that term.

The fact that the Tripoli Program, with its elliptical but harsh indictment of the existing leadership, was adopted by a large majority of the CNRA speaks eloquently of the widespread disillusionment that must have existed within the FLN. But retrospective criticism and ideological pronouncement came more easily than decisions about political institutions or distribution of power. Ben Bella is said by many who knew him at the time to have had a greater craving for power than any of his extraordinarily competitive contemporaries. With the support of Boumediene and the General Staff, he now proposed that a Political Bureau be established to replace the GPRA and guide the nation in the creation of its political institutions. Membership of the Political Bureau was to include the five ex-prisoners, one wilaya leader, and only one member of the existing GPRA. This was tantamount to total repudiation of the leadership that had brought the war to a successful conclusion; and at such brashness, the CNRA balked. Many councilmen, including President Benkhedda, simply left Tripoli. In the long run, the CNRA refused to ratify either the concept or the membership of a Political Bureau, and the meeting adjourned without having taken any step at all toward the creation of political institutions.[9]

On July 1, 1962, the Algerians voted 5,975,581 to 16,534 for independence. At 10:30 A.M., on July 3, President de Gaulle proclaimed the independence of Algeria. The official celebration of independence took place on July 5, 132 years to the day from the time the white flag of the house of Bourbon had first flown over the Casbah.

In the meantime, the disarray within the FLN became public for the first time. On the eve of the referendum, the GPRA moved to assert its supremacy by firing the three top officers of the General Staff: Colonel Boumediene, Major Ahmed Kaid, and Major Ali Mendjli. The officers denied Benkhedda's authority to take such action, a position in which they were backed by Ben Bella within twenty-four hours. This was the signal for an open polarization of leadership along lines that had been developing behind the scenes for several years. The General Staff entered Algeria to consolidate its authority. On July 11 Ben Bella triumphantly entered the country from Morocco and established himself at Tlemcen in his home district. Here there coalesced a so-called "Tlemcen group" composed of the General Staff and the officers of the exterior wilayas; of the nominees to the Political Bureau, with the exception of Mohamed Boudiaf and Hocine Ait Ahmed, who refused to serve with their former prison mate; and of the disgruntled moderates Abbas, Boumendjel, and Francis, who were bitterly opposed to the GPRA that had ousted them the year before. Benkhedda and the GPRA settled in the capital of the Kabylia, where they formed the "Tizi Ouzou group" with the nearly solid support of Wilayas Two, Three, and Four, and that of the influential FFFLN. The fact that the Tlemcen group was almost totally Arab while the Tizi Ouzou group contained a substantial Berber representation and was based in the heart of the Kabylia, leaves one with the impression that ethnicity as well as power and personality questions were involved in the split. For several weeks the two

9. Ben Bella claimed that a majority of the CRUA supported the Political Bureau. But it is clear that the two-thirds support required by the constitution for such a change was not garnered, and it is equally true that the matter never came to a formal vote.

sides conducted a war of words, culminating in Ben Bella's announcement, on July 22, that the Political Bureau had decided to assume its responsibilities within the legal framework of the FLN and to begin leading the country in its search for institutions. With only five members, the Political Bureau seemed a particularly narrow body to be aspiring to a task of such scope. Besides the ambitious Ben Bella, its membership, in July 1962, included Mohamed Khider, the most skilled political operative in the group; Rabah Bitat, the former guerrilla; Colonel Hadj Ben Alla, a young colonel charged with military affairs; and Said Mohamedi, a Kabyle who may have been chosen as a concession to Berber opinion and who was the weakest member of the group. Narrow as it was, the Political Bureau could count on the all-important support of Boumediene and the ALN, whose forces were converging on the capital from Tunisia and Morocco. Having nothing with which to oppose the Tlemcen group's self-investiture and with its own solidarity beginning to crumble, the GPRA, on July 28, agreed to accept the composition of the Political Bureau as proposed at Tripoli.[10] Negotiations between the two sides resulted in an agreement to hold, late in August, the elections for the National Assembly called for by chapter 5 of the Evian Agreement and upon which the sovereign powers of the Provisional Executive were supposed to devolve. A single list of 196 candidates was published that was a veritable who's who of the Algerian Revolution.[11]

This agreement could not be carried out, however, because the fate of Algeria was not entirely in the hands of either the Tlemcen or the Tizi Ouzou group. Most of the leaders of the Wilayas Two, Three, and Four remained adamantly opposed to the Political Bureau and especially to Boumediene and the General Staff. They were especially worried about the Tripoli Program's plan for the "reconversion" of the ALN and its transformation into a new *Armée nationale populaire* (ANP). According to the Program's scenario, the internal forces were either to disarm and become part of the civilian leadership of the FLN or to merge into the ANP—meaning, of course, to submit to the authority of the General Staff. While much of the wilayas' opposition to "reconversion" represents a natural wish to conserve personal authority and fiefdoms, it is obvious that the subordination of the forces who had borne the brunt of the fighting to leaders, many of whom had seen none, was in many eyes almost counterrevolutionary.

The Political Bureau first tried negotiations. It succeeded in neutralizing Wilaya Four for a few days but, more significantly, in winning over Saout el-Arab, commander of Wilaya Two, by offering him military command of his district. But Mohand ou el-Hadj and ultimately Si Hassan, commanders of Wilayas Three and Four respectively, remained adamant. On August 30, Mohamed Khider, in Algiers, issued a call to the ANP and the allied wilayas

10. One of the nominees, Ait Ahmed, never agreed to serve on the Political Bureau. Boudiaf agreed to participate on August 2, but he resigned three weeks later.
11. In accordance with a ruling of the Provisional Executive, the list also included sixteen Europeans.

to help the Political Bureau pacify the dissidents. To the dismay of the Algerian people, full-scale war broke out in which hundreds and perhaps thousands of Algerians were killed by other Algerians. On the night of September 1, some twenty thousand people demonstrated in the capital crying *"baraka saba'a sanin"* ("seven years is enough"). But Boumediene's forces were advancing steadily through the Algérois. On September 4, Ben Bella arrived in Algiers. The next day, the dissident wilayas capitulated to the authority of his Political Bureau, and on September 9, Boumediene's forces sealed the capitulation militarily by marching into Algiers. The long delayed election for a National Constituent Assembly could now be held. Ben Bella, Khider, and the Political Bureau drew up a new list of 196 candidates, which was now narrower than the one it had fielded in August in collaboration with the GPRA. On September 20, 5,285,000 of Algeria's 6,504,000 registered voters ratified that list. Five days later, both the GPRA and the Provisional Executive formally remitted their powers to the National Constituent Assembly. On that same day, the Assembly proclaimed the existence of the Democratic and Popular Republic of Algeria.

CHAPTER

7

THE CHALLENGES OF
INDEPENDENCE, 1962–1978

Most native Algerian social and economic structures had been dismantled in the nineteenth century and reshaped over three generations to meet the needs of the colonial occupation. These new structures themselves were then destabilized by more than seven years of revolutionary war. They underwent one final traumatic shock as the colonial system collapsed. As 90 percent of the Europeans fled the country, many acted out their despair by wantonly destroying hospitals, schools, libraries, communications facilities, factories, and other valuable infrastructure. Their departure also deprived Algeria of the largest part of its professional, technical, and managerial expertise. Finally, the flight of private capital that began during the war accelerated to 500 million francs a month in 1962 and totalled a further 4.5 billion dinars[1] between 1963 and 1965. Between 1960 and 1963, GNP contracted by 35 percent, with especially precipitous declines in manufacturing, construction, and public works, at the precise moment when uprooted peasantries were flooding the cities looking for work. It has been estimated that up to 70 percent of the active male labor force was unemployed or underemployed by 1963.

A historically distorted and now barely functioning economy urgently required revolutionary transformation if it was to cope with the needs of an impoverished and disoriented population and give material content to political independence. But such an economic revolution could not be carried out

1. In April 1964, the Algerian dinar was created on a par with the French franc, then averaging 4.85 to the U.S. dollar. In subsequent years its value diverged from that of the franc.

195

without strong political leadership capable of formulating appropriate economic policies, imposing them upon a society where many interests remained vested in the economic status quo, and mobilizing disparate populations for their implementation. Despite much revolutionary, socialist, and populist rhetoric, Ben Bella, until 1965, and then Boumediene, until 1967, were primarily occupied with the painful process of consolidating their political power.

It was only beginning in 1967 that the Boumediene regime was able to launch its first economic plan and inaugurate the process of economic restructuring. During the next eleven years, Algeria moved rapidly down a state-capitalist road that gave highest priority to the hydrocarbon sector and heavy industry, deemphasizing the agricultural sector which the Tripoli Program of 1962 had singled out for top priority. GNP grew rapidly but with great sectoral disparity. In the meantime, as Boumediene and his colleagues consolidated their position, meaningful political participation in the country virtually disappeared, and most major policy decisions were made either by his small closed circle or by bureaucrats and technocrats. By 1976, the government sought to increase popular involvement and to regularize itself by putting to a successful referendum a National Charter that set down in great detail Algeria's socialist past and its pathway to the future. Next, the voters overwhelmingly approved a constitution that, theoretically, vested much power in a single party and an elected parliament but that, in fact, legitimized the enormous power already concentrated in the executive branch by confirming the president as chief of state, head of government, secretary-general of the party, and commander of the armed forces. By 1978, some Algerian intellectuals and politicians were beginning to question the unbalanced model of development the regime had pioneered; and when Houari Boumediene fell ill and died at the end of the year, the stage was set for significant readjustment of structures and priorities.

BEN BELLA'S CONSOLIDATION OF POWER

The absence of political consensus which had splintered the nationalist movement before 1954 and the revolutionary leadership afterward threatened to plunge the country into chaos once independence was won and Algerians were faced with the actual responsibility of governing themselves. Conflict was expressed ideologically as a struggle between socialists of various tendencies on the one hand, who viewed independence as the beginning of a revolution, and liberals on the other, who viewed it as the culmination of one. Liberals, who in general favored a multiparty political system and a market economy, represented, in the first instance, that portion of the Algerian middle class that had survived the material and political perils of the war; second, they also included a large number of *nouveaux riches* who, in an ironic reverse reenactment of the events of 1830, had swooped down on the property of fleeing colons and appropriated it either at bargain prices or by outright seizure; finally, they included some individuals who had risen in the colonial civil service pursuant to French attempts at Algerianization or who had secured high position there with the departure of the French. The socialists included heirs of the PPA and PCA traditions, the UGTA leadership, some students, and middle-class intellectuals, as well as much of the historic revolutionary leadership. Socialists were divided between partisans of state or party centralism and partisans of decentralized socialism who looked to the revolutionary fervor and leadership of the working masses. All factions invoked the name and interests of the "people" to justify their proposals, infusing Algerian political culture with a populist vocabulary that did not begin to recede until the rise of Islamic fundamentalism in the 1980s.

Some of this populist discourse, particularly that of the democratic socialists, appears to have been shared by urban workers, especially those affiliated with the UGTA. But the 70 percent of the population that still lived in the countryside either never heard or did not comprehend this discourse. While politicians invoked the revolutionary instincts and will of the rural masses, the most tangible manifestation of peasant will was an outpouring of communal energy to build and renovate mosques and other religious buildings. The fundamentally Islamic caste of hinterland Algeria, which seeped toward the coast with the flow of the unemployed to the cities, was reflected in repeated demands by the ʿulama for the inclusion of Islam in political programs. For years these demands resulted more in verbal than in substantive modifications to secularly inspired programs.

It was not primarily ideological conflict, however, that caused Algeria's political instability over the first five years of independence. With the exception of the bourgeois liberals who were more economically than politically influential, most of the political elite, including all six surviving historic chiefs, espoused socialist goals for the revolution. What differences separated them as to the best paths to achieve those goals are insufficient to explain the intensity of the infighting in which they engaged. They served instead as ideological cover for conflict grounded in personal ambition and the interests of "clans" gathered about ambitious men. These "clans" seldom represented ongoing family or regional loyalties, as in the Arab East, because the generations-long detribalization of Algeria had been too thorough. Rather, they represented relationships based on school, wartime, or other networking.

Ben Bella and his Tlemcen group had won supreme power by buying off or militarily defeating the leaders of the interior wilayas who commanded the only military forces more or less on the side of Benkhedda and the GPRA. It was the five-man Political Bureau he had created that nominated the deputies to the National Assembly who, when elected, naturally asked him to form a government. For some time after his victory over the Tizi Ouzou group and its offshoots, Ben Bella's main political troubles would come not from the men he had defeated but from the UGTA, which had stood on the sidelines during the summer power struggle, and especially from within the heterogeneous Tlemcen group itself. In addition to men Ben Bella could more or less control, the Tlemcen group included many he could not. Most prominent among these were Boumediene and his supporters, the core of which was made up of the so-called Oujda Clan, five officers who had served on his staff in Morocco;[2] the prestigious Ferhat Abbas, spokesman for the liberals who was President of the National Assembly; and the ambitious Mohamed Khider, who was Secretary-General of the Political Bureau.

During the first year, the power struggle revolved around efforts to draft a constitution establishing the nation's political institutions and defining the powers of government, assembly, and party. Abbas believed that only the Assembly was empowered to draft and vote a constitution. Khider held that policy making as well as constituent authority lay with the party. The Assembly promptly bogged down in debating its rules and procedures so that, well into 1963, it could not pass a single statute much less deal with the fundamental law. At the same time, the FLN as a party separate from the wartime military and bureaucratic apparatus scarcely existed; institutionally, in 1962, it was the five-man Political Bureau.

As head of government, Ben Bella was in the best position to strengthen his power base against these various competitors. Through the fall and into the winter, he ruled by decree, seldom consulting the parliament. In January, he and Khider, still working together though sparring, managed to bring the 300,000 member UGTA under party (i.e., Political Bureau) control by packing its congress with their supporters. More importantly, Ben Bella was taking steps to put himself at the head of the most important grass-roots movement to have sprung up since independence. This was the *autogestion,* or self-management, movement.

As their exodus from Algeria accelerated in late spring and early summer 1962, colons began to sell off their properties at ludicrously low prices to enterprising Algerians with a little cash, to members of the state bureaucracy, and even to guerrilla and ALN officers. Other hastily vacated properties— houses, apartments, shops, small farms—were simply seized by adventurous individuals without any form of payment. But when it came to the larger farms or factories, workers there usually would not tolerate individual usurpation. Instead, with crops ripening in the fields, employees on many estates organized themselves to bring in the harvest, to see to its marketing, and to provide for upkeep of the facilities. To a lesser extent, workers organized committees to operate factories that had been abandoned, but here problems of worker management were more complex. While there is evidence that, in some instances, the worker takeovers were encouraged by UGTA leadership, for the most part, the organization of the management committees was a

2. The clan included Ahmed Kaid, Ahmed Medeghri, Cherif Belkacem, Abdelaziz Bouteflika, and Mohamed Tayebi.

spontaneous grass-roots response to the totally unexpected disappearance of European owners and managers.

One of Ben Bella's first acts after election was to create a *Bureau national des biens vacants* (BNBV) to study ways of protecting and regularizing the workers' committees and the popularly based system of production they represented. Because autogestion early on captivated the national imagination, the politician who could position himself as its champion stood to make major gains in the struggle against political opponents. By late winter 1963, Ben Bella and Mohamed Khider, who had collaborated in reducing the power of the UGTA, were themselves locked in an unseemly struggle for power in which Khider, as head of the party, seemed to be positioning that party to begin limiting Ben Bella's freedom of action. It was in this context that Ben Bella issued the March Decrees prepared for him by the BNBV. The March Decrees created a legal definition of vacant property, established a detailed system of worker self-management to be applied to all such properties, and provided for a system of profit sharing within each enterprise. Promulgation of the decrees significantly increased Ben Bella's popularity and strengthened his power base. A few weeks later, Khider resigned as Secretary-General of the Political Bureau, leaving the FLN essentially in control of the President.

In the meantime, autogestion rapidly assumed the proportions of a national myth, a symbol of revolutionary Algeria's determination to complete its struggle for political liberation with a truly popular revolt against the capitalist system which had been colonialism's most dehumanizing tool. Even on the international scene, Algeria's reputation as a Third World leader and model became somehow tied to its famous experiment in self-management. After the nationalization, in October 1963, of remaining French farms and the recovery of some of the lands that had passed illegally to private Algerians, the self-managed sector contained some 2,300,000 hectares, or about one-fourth of the farmland in the country. The property was divided, by late 1964, into 2,284 farms employing about 200,000 workers, or about one-eighth of the active rural work force. Several hundred factories and service establishments were also included in the self-managed sector.

But autogestion proved little more than a myth. The advisors who drew up the March Decrees included a number of Trotskyites—some of them foreign—who honestly believed they had found in Algeria the ideal situation in which to implement for the first time a truly decentralized and democratic socialism. But others of the commissioners, many of whom were holdovers from SASs and other agricultural organizations associated with Lacoste's agrarian reform program, believed firmly in state control of the agricultural sector. The result was a compromise package of overlapping jurisdictions and confusing institutional directions which were almost impossible of implementation by the largely illiterate rural workers. While the president of the management committee, which in turn represented a workers' council and an elected general assembly, was supposed to be the chief manager of the enterprise, authority soon fell in most cases to an on-site director who was the representative of the *Office national de la réforme agraire* (ONRA) which the decrees had set up to provide for guidance and coordination. Within a month of issuing the March Decrees, the ONRA took control both of credit and marketing. With the key inputs and the ultimate outputs firmly in the hands of the bureaucracy, the self-managed units soon became state farms in all but name. Some analysts have interpreted this development in class terms, as reflecting the determination of bourgeois agents in the bureaucracy to keep peasants and workers from taking control of the means of production. Others have seen it as a part of a wider instinct to rein in an Algerian society that many saw spinning toward chaos with the collapse of colonial control. Still others have seen it as primarily a reflection of Ben Bella's drive to personal power. In any event, autogestion soon proved economically counterproductive. While unusually favorable climatic conditions made 1964 a bumper crop year, production in the self-managed sector, which included the bulk of the richest lands in the country, began to decline thereafter.

During the winter of 1962–63, Ben Bella had increasingly disputed the legislative authority of the National Assembly. Khider, at the same time, had been arguing the party's superiority over both government and Assembly. While not in principle opposed to this proposition, Ben Bella declined to press it as long as Khider was in charge of the FLN. But with Khider gone by April, Ben Bella began to press his thesis that drafting of the constitution was the prerogative of the party. Ferhat Abbas argued vehemently against this proposition, but since neither of the two draft constitutions under consideration had even reached the floor of the Assembly by summer, he was not in a strong position to argue the parliamentary prerogative. Under these circumstances, the Political Bureau, which was now totally under Ahmed Ben Bella's control, drafted its own constitution. In July, this document was submitted to party officials around the country and then ratified at a gathering of FLN and government officials at a meeting in the Majestic cinema in downtown Algiers. On August 12, Abbas, knowing he had nowhere near the votes to resist Ben Bella's initiative, resigned as president of the National Assembly. He claimed with some justification that the party in a legal sense separate from government and bureaucracy did not actually exist and that the Political Bureau was so small and unrepresentative as to make it no more than a tool of the President. Later that month, the Assembly ratified the constitution by a vote of 139 to 23, with 8 abstentions.

The Constitution of 1963 declared Algeria a socialist state, established Arabic as the official language and Islam as the official religion. It dedicated Algeria to continuing the antiimperialist struggle at home and abroad and proclaimed autogestion as a major arm in the battle against poverty and economic dependency. It made the FLN the sole legal party of the country, the people's monitor of government, and the principal policy-making body. Institutions of government were heavily weighted toward the executive branch while the National Assembly's role was one of elaboration and ratification. On

September 8, the constitution was approved by 96.8 percent of those voting in a national referendum. The next week, running unopposed, Ben Bella was elected to the presidency by popular vote.[3] The heterogeneous alliance of 1962 had now been replaced with a power structure clearly dominated by Ben Bella. As head of state, head of government, and Secretary-General of the FLN, and with the backing of the army, Ben Bella was clearly the man in charge. Of the six historic chiefs who had survived the war, Khider, Belkacem Krim, and Rabah Bitat were in exile; Mohamed Boudiaf was under arrest in the Sahara for organizing an unlawful party; and Ait Ahmed, who had deserted the National Assembly in June, had retired to the Kabylia to organize opposition.

While liberal observers inside and outside Algeria had hoped to see a pluralistic multiparty system take root in Algeria, other analysts argued that pluralism would have led to the creation of as many parties as there were ambitious politicians and that the only possible solution was a centralized and more or less authoritarian state. In fact, the extraordinary proliferation of parties in 1989 and 1990, when the third Algerian constitution at last opened the way to a multiparty system, suggests that Algerian political culture even by then had not mastered the art of coalition-building, upon which viable multiparty systems depend.

GUERRILLA RESISTANCE AND THE CONGRESSES

During the year it took Ben Bella to shunt aside the dissident elements of the coalition he had ridden to power, much disorder continued in the countryside where numerous guerrilla leaders had set up personal fiefdoms, sometimes financed like real fiefs by the exploitation of abandoned colon estates. In time, many of these dissidents were tenuously rallied to the regime by appointments to regional commands of the ALN, which often did little to assure actual government control of their regions. In the Kabylia guerrilla resistance to government intrusion was reinforced by traditional ethnic antipathy to Arab control. When Ait Ahmed concluded that a parliamentary seat was an ineffective position from which to challenge Ben Bella's growing power monopoly, he returned to Kabylia and began mobilizing guerrillas. He urged Algerians to boycott the constitutional referendum and the presidential election and was gratified with an impressive rate of abstention. Then, on September 29, in Tizi Ouzou, with guerrilla Colonel Mohand ou el-Hadj at his side, he proclaimed the *Front des forces socialistes* (FFS) and called upon Algerians to fight with him against the imposition of a fascist dictatorship. But there were major inconsistencies and weaknesses in his position and program that limited his appeal. He claimed to be the leader of a more authentic socialist

3. From this point on, Ben Bella (who had previously been only the head of government, or Prime Minister) was both Chief of State and head of government (Président de la République and Président du Conseil).

movement than Ben Bella's, but the ways in which this was true eluded most socialists. At the same time, his espousal of any socialism at all alienated the middle classes. While condemning Ben Bella's "fascism," he favored compromise with such "fascism" by proposing a collegial leadership of the chefs historiques that included both himself and Ben Bella.

Unfortunate timing also limited Ait Ahmed's chances for success. In October, a border war erupted between Algeria and Morocco. Morocco had long been dissatisfied with the frontier, the central and southern portions of which it considered to have been dictated by colonial France. Mohammed V and his successor, Hassan II, had been led to believe that in return for Morocco's support of the FLN's struggle, Algerians would sit down and negotiate frontier adjustments once independence came. When Algeria refused to do, Morocco launched a border incursion. Opportunistically, Ben Bella now charged Ait Ahmed with being an agent of the Moroccans who, as agents of international imperialism, were bent upon rolling back the Algerian revolution. As troops and volunteers rushed to the frontier in a wave of patriotic fervor, the FFS coalition began to disintegrate and Ait Ahmed was forced to call a truce.

When he ended the truce in February 1964, he triggered a period of hit-and-run raids against government forces and acts of sabotage; and, ultimately, a major assassination attempt was made on Ben Bella's life. But far from becoming a nationally based opposition, the FFS and allied factions were now limited primarily to Kabyles. While Kabyles did not universally support Ait Ahmed or related factions, only 40 percent turned out, in 1964, to vote in elections for the new National Assembly. By the fall, Boumediene had concentrated more than 50,000 troops in the Kabylia and eastern Algeria. Several thousand political prisoners had been taken, and even Abbas and Bitat were placed under house arrest. When Ait Ahmed and his closest aides were arrested on October 17, the insurrection lost steam. In 1965, Ait Ahmed was tried, found guilty, and sentenced to death. Ben Bella commuted the sentence to life imprisonment, however, and in 1966 he escaped and fled to Europe.

By the fall of 1963, Ben Bella's inner circle consisted entirely of men he could count on, whose political careers depended on him. But they spoke for no substantial constituencies themselves and did little to enhance his standing around the country. In these circumstances, Ben Bella resorted more and more to a politics of gestures designed to win over constituencies who perceived benefit from those gestures. Such a gesture was his abrupt nationalization, in fall 1963, of still occupied French farms. Next, he organized national congresses of agricultural workers in the self-managed sector and then in the industrial sector. Neither of these congresses addressed the growing dissatisfaction with the way this sector was functioning, but they helped make the workers believe they were politically important and that they had a stake in the Ben Bella regime. They also served to deflect criticism about problems in the sector away from Ben Bella and onto others.

Since independence, much of the Algerian political leadership had believed that only a congress of the FLN could resolve outstanding constitutional and leadership issues and legitimately point the direction of Algeria's revolution. But during 1962 and 1963, convening such a congress was delayed by the struggle for power itself. It was by no means clear who had the authority to convene it or to determine its membership, its rules of procedure, or its agenda. Men such as Mohamed Khider and Ait Ahmed saw a party congress as the vehicle for limiting Ben Bella's drive to power. That is why Ben Bella, until he had consolidated his power, resisted summoning a congress. But after his popular election to the presidency, he felt sufficiently in control to begin preparations.

From Ben Bella's point of view the congress's principal objectives were (1) reshaping the FLN into a homogeneous avant-garde party that would be the motor of revolution and (2) sharpening the ideology and strategy of that revolution. Many others saw the congress as an opportunity to heal the rifts that had preoccupied the country since independence. While Ben Bella at times sounded as though he shared this goal, such a reconciliation process clearly went in the opposite direction from homogenization. The preparatory committee Ben Bella appointed, in November 1963, to lay the groundwork for a congress was dominated by his own men. This signalled the opposition that the deck would be stacked against them. The largest part of the draft platform was written by Mohamed Harbi and Abdelaziz Zerdani, two of Ben Bella's most leftist advisors, and was filled with the text-book rhetoric of class struggle.

The congress of 1,991 members convened in the Salle Ibn Khaldoun at Algiers between April 16 and April 21, 1964. Frozen out of the preparations, Ait Ahmed, Boudiaf, Abbas, Bitat, and Khider refused to participate. Only Belkacem Krim of the historic leadership attended. But many dissident wilaya leaders (e.g., Mohand ou el-Hadj, Saout el-Arab, and Mohamed Chaabani) did attend, along with some of the reformist ʿulama and many local and regional notables. The delegates also included about 250 persons identified primarily with Boumediene and the ANP so that, in spite of the boycott by the major opposition figures, the congress represented a rather wide cross-section of party leadership. The rules and the agenda were firmly controlled by the Ben Bella men, however, and in the end the delegates adopted the draft platform without modification.

This 176-page document is known as the Algiers Charter. It formalized the organization of the FLN that had been developing on an ad hoc basis since independence and defined, at least in theory, the relationship between party and state. It remained until 1976 the official statement of Algeria's political and ideological orientation. Continuing in the tradition of the Soummam Platform and the Tripoli Program, it begins with the most detailed historical and ideological analysis yet of the evolution of Algerian society and the revolution. After this, separate sections outline the fundamental problems of transition and development and then the specific programs or strategies for dealing with those problems.

Reaffirming Algeria's socialist option, the Charter declared socialism to be totally consistent with the nation's Arabo-Islamic heritage, especially when Islam is understood in its true progressive sense. It located the revolution's principal opposition in the small native bourgeoisie and even more importantly in the bourgeois elements that had infiltrated the bureaucracy determined to use their new positions of authority to keep power out of the hands of the working masses. The FLN was to be the catalyst and motor of the revolution. But since, for the purposes of national mobilization during the war, it had to enlist the support of all segments of the population, even nonrevolutionary segments, its task now was to purge itself of such elements in order that it could effectively serve as guarantor of the revolution.

The system of agricultural autogestion was to be completed by an agrarian revolution aimed at cooperativizing the still private farm sector. A major program of industrialization would have as primary goals creating jobs, fulfilling consumer demand, and absorbing certain agricultural products; and to assure its viability, any development of heavy industry would be contingent upon establishment of broader than national markets. The banking, insurance, transportation, and foreign-trade sectors were to be nationalized, along with all mineral and energy resources. Tourism and the artisanat should be developed. Finally, after sufficient data had been collected, Algeria should institute a system of central economic planning.

As a concession to delegates with continuing reservations about aspects of the platform—and there were many—the leadership permitted the congress to pass two lengthy final resolutions as a sort of postscript to the Charter. These resolutions addressed more than forty issues ranging from housing to vocational education to the administration of self-management. Very significantly, four of them dealt with the emotionally charged issue of Arabization.

Much dissatisfaction with the Charter had been expressed by Houari Boumediene and the large ANP delegation. Explanations of that dissatisfaction vary. One school holds that Boumediene was opposed to a strengthened party in principle because he saw it threatening the hegemony of the army which he was working to build and project. Another, contemporary school believed the military was hostile or lukewarm to the socialism because of the petit bourgeois backgrounds of many of its officers. Others believed that the principal problem lay in the secular Marxist tone of the analysis. This was a discourse totally alien to the Algerian cultural heritage. Last-minute editing of the draft had declared socialism compatible in every way with Islam, but many found such verbal changes superficial and perfunctory. For them, the road Algeria seemed poised to travel was a road laid out by foreigners. The final resolutions attempted to address this latter concern. They stressed the need to accelerate the Arabization of education, to strengthen ties with the Arab world, and to broaden Arab studies at the University. They called for a national commission to monitor Arabization "for the purpose of safeguarding and developing our cultural and spiritual values."[4] It is worth noting that from the beginning most Algerians believed Arabization to be inherently tied to Islamization and, inferentially, francophony to be tied to secularization.

A second cause for delegate uneasiness with the Charter, but one which was articulated far less openly, was the call to purge the party of nonrevolutionary elements. By 1964, the party rolls had swollen to more than 150,000 full and 600,000 aspirant members, representing a wide spectrum of class, economic, and regional interests. Such a party was inherently incapable of purging itself, nor could Ben Bella and his Marxist advisors effect the purge from on top without jeopardizing their hold on power.

The party did not become a homogeneous revolutionary avant-garde. After electing Ben Bella Secretary-General of the FLN,[5] the congress chose a 103-member Central Committee which, even without the historical opposition leaders, represented a study in heterogeneity. It was an odd amalgam of doctrinaire Marxists, military officers, wilaya strongmen, cooperative Kabyles, party hacks, and labor officials. The seventeen-man Political Bureau included nine of Ben Bella's men, four wilaya leaders and four of Boumediene's men. While some analysts hold that the 1964 congress finally gave Ben Bella the legitimacy he had lacked, others insist that his strong-armed overthrow of the GPRA and his rise to power on the arms of the ALN saddled Ben Bella with a usurper's image that he never outlived. At any rate, when the congress adjourned, Ben Bella was as far from establishing a homogeneous and reliable base for his rule as he had ever been.

But with the Algiers Charter there was created a myth: that the party, separate and distinct from government, was the guarantor of the nation's ideological purity and the articulator of its major policies. According to the myth, it was an avant-garde revolutionary elite expressing the will of the working masses, and as such, it bore responsibility for policing the bourgeois-infested state bureaucracy, one of the more unfortunate legacies of colonialism. Yet, by 1964, the FLN had itself become a major vehicle of upward mobility for Algerians anxious to improve their material and community standing. Instead of a single bureaucratic ladder to climb, ambitious Algerians could now choose from two: the ladder of the state or the ladder of party bureaucracy.

THE COUP OF JUNE 19, 1965

Over a period of two years, Ben Bella had defeated every serious challenge to his authority and presented the country with institutions of his own design. Yet, his rise to power and his determination to stay there left him without a

4. "Les résolutions finales," *Annuaire de l'Afrique du Nord,* vol. 3 (1964), pp. 570 and 572.
5. Previously he was Secretary General of the Political Bureau.

solid political base or major political allies. In many ways, Ben Bella's revolution was a revolution of form without substance. He was afraid to permit the political institutions he had created to function as they were intended. It was not the FLN that determined policy but Ben Bella and his inner circle. It was not the Central Committee or the Political Bureau that drew up the list of candidates for the second National Assembly but Ben Bella and the same inner circle. It was not the National Assembly that made the laws but Ben Bella who made them and the Assembly that rubber stamped them.

The economy, for all of the rhetorical attention it received, was in disarray. The March Decrees had not been permitted to function as intended and there was reason to believe they never would. Not even the planning for agrarian reform had begun. The few foreign designed and financed industrial projects were far behind schedule. By 1965, the bureaucracy still had not produced an economic development plan.

The only faction remaining inside the power structure that was not there on Ben Bella's terms was the military. Initially, it was left little time for politics because of its preoccupation with the so-called reconversion of the ANP and the unsettled situation in parts of the countryside. Nonetheless, in the summer of 1963, the Boumediene clan had complete control of the General Staff and held as many key government posts as the Ben Bella clan. These ministries in turn sat at the apex of important patronage networks by which the clan assured the loyalty of thousands of supporters. But after receiving his popular mandate in the fall of 1963, Ben Bella began whittling away at that power. In October 1963, he appointed the wilaya chief Tahar Zbiri to be Chief of the General Staff, as much to undermine Boumediene as to conciliate wilaya leaders leaning toward the FFS. When the new Politbureau was named, the Boumediene clan got less than a fourth of the seats. In the summer of 1964, Ben Bella forced Ahmed Medeghri, a close associate of Boumediene, out of the pivotal Interior Ministry, whose patronage network was one of the most extensive; later he eliminated Ahmed Kaid from the Ministry of Tourism and demoted Cherif Belkacem from the Education Ministry. By early 1965, only Boumediene in the War Ministry[6] and Abdelaziz Bouteflika in the Foreign Ministry survived as reminders of the considerable weight in government the Oujda Clan had once enjoyed. Ben Bella had also embarked upon a program to create popular militias, which the ANP saw as a tactic to undermine it in the field. At the same time, he was travelling the country attempting to rally support with more and more leftist rhetoric. He struck a new deal with radical elements of the UGTA and was also growing closer to the PCA.

During May and June 1965, the government was making preparations for Algiers to host a second Afro-Asian conference as a successor to the celebrated Bandung meeting a decade earlier. With the great flair for Third World politics Ben Bella had developed, he took more and more personal control of these negotiations, thereby undercutting the authority of Foreign Minister Boute-

6. Boumediene was also Vice President.

flika. When Boumediene intervened on behalf of his ally, Ben Bella threatened to dismiss them both. At this critical moment, rumors also began to spread that, without cabinet knowledge, the President was seeking an accommodation with the FFS and that Ait Ahmed, then in prison, had been offered the post of Foreign Minister. Early in the morning of June 19, 1965, as Boumediene's army moved swiftly to take over the country, a unit ironically under the personal command Tahar Zbiri descended on the President's residence and arrested him while he was still in bed. The coup was bloodless.

By June 1965, although Ben Bella enjoyed enormous prestige abroad, he had maneuvered himself into a position of precarious isolation at home. The youth and student organizations he had cultivated during his last year of power organized a series of demonstrations condemning his deposition, but these demonstrations failed to spread to the general public. A few dedicated leftists aside, the great majority of Algeria's political elites applauded his disappearance. Ben Bella himself remained imprisoned for fourteen years until President Chadli Bendjedid transferred him to house arrest, in July 1979, and then freed him the next year. A short time later he followed the path of other historic leaders of the revolution into European exile.

THE CONSOLIDATION OF STATE AUTHORITY

At midday on June 19, 1965, radio Algiers broadcast a proclamation from a body calling itself the Council of the Revolution telling the people what had taken place. It said the army had seized power because, after three years of independence, the government Algerians had sacrificed so much to bring into existence had fallen prey to "sordid calculations, political narcissism, and the morbid love of power best illustrated in the liquidation of the country's cadres and in the criminal attempt to discredit the *moujahidin* and resistance fighters." It promised an end to "personal power," which had exposed all of the national and regional institutions to the capriciousness of a single individual; and it promised to organize "a democratic and responsible state ordered by laws and founded in morality, a state capable of outliving governments and individuals."[7]

The coup had in fact been engineered by a small clique of officers. The Council of the Revolution in whose name the leaders spoke was not fully constituted until early July. Composed of twenty-six members, it included the General Staff, commanders of the five military regions, four former wilaya leaders no longer in the army, and two civilian defectors from the Ben Bella camp. The heart of the Council was the Oujda clan, which also took over the most sensitive posts in the cabinet (e.g., defense, interior, foreign affairs, and finance). Colonel Boumediene headed both the Council of the Revolution and the government.

7. Proclamation is found in *Annuaire de l'Afrique du Nord,* vol. 4 (1965), pp. 627–29.

Because of the heavy reliance on guerrilla leaders, the initial Council of the Revolution was as heterogeneous in its way as Ben Bella's earlier governments had been. Instead of trying to eliminate disparate elements in the first years, however, Boumediene, stressing "collegiality," attempted to win them over or to neutralize them. While he had to cope with a major revolt by Tahar Zbiri and his followers, at the end of 1967, he came to terms with other guerrilla leaders by gradually easing them into nongovernmental posts or into governmental slots without major clientages. At the same time, he was succeeding both in neutralizing leftist ministers who had continued from Ben Bella's last cabinet and in bringing both the student movement and the UGTA back under government control.

With his power base stabilizing, Boumediene and his team were able, by 1966 and 1967, to begin rationally addressing for the first time the pressing issues of economic development Algeria had mainly toyed with for four and a half years. As government focus shifted from the political to the developmental, its recruitment priorities began to shift to the scientific and technical. There emerged a new elite of technocrats who had spent the 1950s and 1960s in schools rather than in the maquis or in political infighting. Their relatively apolitical outlook added to the pragmatic approach of the military served further to stabilize the system. Finally, when the cleavages generated by the difficult development choices of the period began to generate differences among the remaining politicians in his entourage, Boumediene began to separate himself even from key members of the Oujda Clan. Between 1972 and 1975, Ahmed Kaid, Ahmed Medeghri, and Cherif Belkacem were driven out of government. By 1976, the twenty-six-man membership of the Council of the Revolution had been reduced to a compact and much more homogeneous nine.

When it assumed power, the Council of the Revolution suspended the constitution of 1963 and abolished the National Assembly along with the Central Committee and the Political Bureau of the FLN. Its primary goal was the construction of a strong state that would transcend and outlast personnel changes in government so that the state could get on with the real business of the revolution. Such a focus on the state had ominous implications for the role of the party as defined in the Algiers Charter. While Boumediene declared 1968 "the year of the party" and entrusted its revitalization to Ahmed Kaid, the fact was that none of the critical ministries would admit party organizers on their turf, nor would the army nor most of the state economic enterprises that mushroomed in this period. Though the party's ranks swelled during the Boumediene years—to around 300,000 regular members by the late 1970s—it had become a bureaucratized symbol of revolution whose main function was to recruit and indoctrinate members. It was emphatically not an agitational party. It had lost its militancy and had been completely subordinated to the uses of the military, administrative, or technocratic elites.

It was not until 1967 that Houari Boumediene began to sketch a picture of the political system he envisaged. The picture that emerged was one of political institutions rebuilt through a systematic process of political education at the base supervised from above. That education was grounded in popularly elected local and regional assemblies intimately in touch with the real world of ordinary citizens. The popular assemblies were counterbalanced and coordinated by a theoretically strong party and a well-established central administration. Though Boumediene warned against paralyzing bureaucracy and over-centralization, his vision had not been developed with particular clarity. The concept of a renewal from the base supervised from above was inherently contradictory.

In 1967, the first communal assemblies were elected from candidate slates prepared by the FLN. In 1969, the first wilaya[8] assemblies were chosen in the same way. For a variety of reasons, not the least of which was the fact that fiscal authority and access to credit were controlled by the central government and the central bank, these assemblies did not become the foundation of a popularly based political structure. Authority over even mundane matters still lodged in national government and in the party apparatus. Local government's role was essentially one of implementation.

With the streamlining and homogenization of the government, the growing authority of the technocracy, the bureaucratization of the party, and the harnessing of the labor, student, youth, and women's organizations, Algeria by the 1970s had become increasingly depoliticized. The professional bureaucrats, technocrats, and military officers who made policy functioned in increasing isolation from public opinion. They took decisions of enormous consequence, making vast commitments of human and material resources with little consultation beyond their own tight circles.

On June 19, 1975, the tenth anniversary of the "revolutionary readjustment" that had brought him to power, Boumediene announced plans for the drafting of a new National Charter to evaluate the nation's progress and plot its future course. The draft charter was published in 1976, and the public was invited to a wide-ranging national debate on its content. With a degree of freedom unparalleled in Algerian political life since the first year of independence, Algerians discussed and criticized the document over a period of months. After numerous amendments, of which none was particularly substantive, the 80,000-word National Charter was put to a referendum on June 27, 1976, from which it emerged with overwhelming approval.

Following in the tradition of the Tripoli Program and the Algiers Charter, the National Charter of 1976 began with an extensive historical overview of the Algerian people's path to the present. There followed seven chapters devoted to (1) an analysis of socialism as it applied to Algeria; (2) the party, the state, and the relations between the two; (3) the main areas and themes of socialistic development; (4) national defense; (5) foreign policy; (6) the main emphases of development policy; and (7) the principal objects of development.

---

8. *Wilaya* is an Arabic word for province. The provinces into which the Algerian Republic was subdivided were not identical to the military jurisdictions created during the War of Independence.

The Charter provided the conceptual framework for the second Algerian constitution, which was adopted in a separate referendum on November 22, 1976. The 1976 constitution affirmed that Islam was the religion of the state, republicanism the form of the government, and socialism the form of the economy. It guaranteed basic freedoms such as expression and assembly, the right of women to full participation in every facet of national life, and protection to private property that was not used to exploit the labor of others.

Technically, the FLN remained the guarantor of continuing revolution and through its revitalized Political Bureau and Central Committee it was supposed to draw up bills to be put to the Popular National Assembly (APN) for enactment into law. The 261 members of the APN were elected for five-year terms from a larger slate of candidates drawn up by the party. Theoretically all legislative power belonged to the APN, as did the power to adopt foreign policy resolutions, to ratify treaties, to conduct inquiry into any issue of public interest, and to amend the constitution. But legislative power was effectively constrained by the enormous authority given to the executive branch.

The President of the Republic was nominated by a full congress of the FLN and then elected by popular vote for a five-year term indefinitely renewable. He named the cabinet, which was not responsible to the legislature beyond answering its questions. If he wished, he could appoint a prime minister or a vice president and dismiss them at will, but he need not have either. He was Commander in Chief of the armed forces and Secretary-General of the FLN. He could rule by executive ordinance during parliamentary recess. Since the APN's regular sessions were limited to a duration of six months and its right to ratify ordinances after the fact was tightly circumscribed, the executive in fact retained the dominant role in legislation as in every other facet of national life.

Ultimately, the great political restructuring of 1976, trumpeted as the vehicle for readmitting the Algerian people to the political process, served to reinforce Boumediene's powers in the same way the constitution of 1963 and the Algiers Charter of 1964 had reinforced Ben Bella's. Two French scholars have suggested the Weberian term "sultanism" to describe an Algerian system in which the holder of power seeks "to make himself independent of any group having autonomous bases of power, be these institutional, political, administrative or social. The Algerian president . . . is not an arbitrary sovereign *depending only on himself,* but a sovereign free in his movements who takes care *not to depend on others* by leaning alternately or simultaneously on this or that group without becoming the prisoner of any."[9] One is, in fact, struck by how many times in different ways, during the first sixteen years of Algerian independence, both Boumediene and his predecessor announced the intention of allowing the people to share in power. Yet, it is clear that to the extent they

9. Jean Leca and Jean-Claude Vatin, "Le système politique algérien (1976–1978). Idéologie, institutions, et changement social," in *Développements politiques au Maghreb. Aménagements institutionels et processus électoraux* (Paris: CNRS, 1979), pp. 27–28.

were sincere in their intentions, which often they undoubtedly were, they were never prepared to share power in ways that would weaken their personal hold on it. They seem to have been willing to allow popular participation to limit the power of subordinates. But since these subordinates and those below them were equally reluctant to admit real limits within their own spheres, it is not difficult to understand why Algeria did not become a democracy in spite of the populist rhetoric that dominated its political discourse.

FOREIGN POLICY

During their long and costly struggle against colonialism, Algerians were dismayed to see the major world powers either supporting France or standing equivocally on the sidelines until the eleventh hour. The experience left Algerian elites with an extremely negative view of the existing international system. In many arenas and in many parts of the world, Algerians sought to undermine that world order and to work for a level playing field in which North and South, developed and underdeveloped would play the game of world politics according to new rules. At the same time, Algeria's stirring wartime victory and the determination with which it went about assuring and broadening its independence afterward caused emerging nations at all stages to heed Algeria's leadership.

Algeria became a respected leader in Third World politics, in North-South relations, and in the effort to create a new international economic order. It was also a key factor in reinvigorating the nonaligned movement that for a time, in the early 1960s, seemed to be losing its dynamism. As deep as Algeria's ideological commitment undoubtedly was, it eschewed most of the empty rhetoric characteristic of the times. The foreign policy it conducted was characterized by a degree of pragmatism and by a seriousness of purpose and business-like implementation that won the nation respect even from states with whom it had many differences.

Algeria's dogged pursuit of nonalignment followed from its conviction that a developing country could never hope to achieve genuine independence politically or economically if it was subordinate in any way to one of the advantaged powers. Its leaders reserved their strongest anti-imperialist attacks through the 1960s and 1970s for the United States. Conflict with the United States expressed itself in continuous support for Fidel Castro's Cuba, whose pluckiness in facing up to a great power reminded many Algerians of their own stand; in determination to support revolutionary over "neocolonial" regimes in Sub-Saharan Africa; in opposition to America's support for Israel against the Palestinians and the other Arabs; and in support of North Korea and the Viet Cong. But political conflict never seemed to hamper economic relationships between the United States and Algeria. As the program of industrialization accelerated, the United States became and remained, until the early 1980s, the principal customer for Algerian hydrocarbons and a major supplier of machinery, tools, and engineering and management expertise. American corporations were major participants in some of the most important industrial projects in the country.

During the Ben Bella years, when Algeria remained heavily dependent upon French financial and technical assistance and upon continuing economic cooperation with the former métropole, France was the target of far less anti-imperialist invective than the United States. But from 1967 until the early 1970s, as the Boumediene regime moved forward with a program of national-izations, Franco-Algerian relations deteriorated. In the same period, Algeria was insisting on phasing out French bases in the country, most notably the nuclear-testing facilities in the Sahara and the great naval base at Mers el Kébir. France retaliated by limiting wine and other Algerian imports and placing restrictions on immigration. Algeria managed to minimize to some extent the effects of French displeasure, however, by deftly playing off against her the nation's growing relationship with the Soviet Union. Initially torn in its East-bloc policy between a Chinese or a Soviet orientation, Ben Bella and his colleagues soon opted for the latter. While significant industrial cooperation developed, it was in the field of military supply and training that Soviet-Algerian cooperation ultimately became the most notable. Between 1966 and 1971, 90 percent of heavy military purchases were from the Soviet Union and two thousand Algerian pilots and other officers had been trained in the USSR. Several thousand Soviet military and technical advisors worked in the country. But Algeria never allowed foreign bases of any kind to be reestablished on its territory, and it jealously guarded its independence of action both in the military and industrial spheres.

After a brief period in which Algeria's Third World activism was con-centrated mainly in the inherently divided Afro-Asian movement, the coun-try's attention was absorbed by problems within the African, the Arab, and the broader Middle East systems, and by pursuit of the new economic order. Algeria's attention focused on the Congo, Mozambique, South Africa and other countries where Algeria perceived the forces of liberation still in con-frontation with those of colonialism. While not losing interest in Africa after the overthrow of Ben Bella, Algeria was drawn, under Boumediene, toward greater involvement in Mashriqi issues. Contemporary observers thought the shift occurred because Boumediene was more Arab than Ben Bella, given his traditional education and his studies in Egypt. It is probable, however, that, given the exacerbation of Arab-Israeli conflict after 1967 and the growing importance of OPEC and OAPEC, this reorientation would have occurred under any leadership. A militant supporter of the Palestinians and the Arab states against Israel, Algeria managed to remain largely neutral in other con-flicts that inflamed the Middle East and as such proved an important mediator in both intra-Arab and Arab-Iranian disputes.

As a major proponent of a new economics, Algeria hosted the Group of 77's first meeting, in October 1967, and a nonaligned conference, in 1974, devoted to the same subject. Later, in 1974, it was Boumediene who summoned and gave the opening address to the special session of the United Nations that issued the Declaration of the New International Economic Order. That Order's agenda called for more and easier credit terms for developing nations, better access to northern markets for goods manufactured in the Third World, and higher and more stable prices for the primary goods that constituted the developing world's main exports. In this regard, Algeria in OPEC early distinguished itself as a hard-liner on price and as an advocate of strict production quotas in order to maximize prices.

Algeria's relations with Tunisia and Morocco have often been characterized by tension and sometimes by open hostility. One explanation for this conflict holds that it represents the natural opposition of a radical Algeria to a moderate Tunisia and a conservative Morocco. Such perceptions combined with the unassailable fact that Algeria's major source of armament was the Soviet Union, led the United States and France to become the major suppliers of Tunisia and Morocco and to support them diplomatically, even by modest military posturing at times.

More important than ideological or globalistic concerns to understanding the dynamics of the Maghrib system, however, is Algeria's territorial heritage and a related power struggle with its Moroccan neighbor. It is ironic that one of the most vocal and militant opponents of imperialism and neo-imperialism should have been one of the greatest territorial beneficiaries of imperialism. The fact that Algeria is the second largest country in Africa is attributable solely to the military hegemony France enjoyed in Northwestern Africa for over a century. Securing recognition of the colonially drawn lines was a matter of highest priority to the Algerian Foreign Ministry. Ultimately it had no difficulty winning the assent of Mauritania, Mali, and Niger to the borders. Tunisia, however, resisted signing a formal border agreement until 1970 and Libya, which claimed a strip of territory between Ghat and Ghadames, until the 1980s.

The biggest problem was with Morocco. The 972-mile Algero-Moroccan border had been officially defined only as far as Figuig. The rest had been established de facto by the superiority of French arms in the nineteenth and twentieth centuries. Morocco was particularly insistent in claiming the Béchar region, Touat, and iron rich Tindouf and its environs. Hassan II actually signed an agreement relinquishing his claims to the disputed regions in 1972, but he later declared the accord void because parliament had not been in session to ratify it. Morocco also had historically based claims to the thinly populated Western Sahara, which Spain was preparing to relinquish in the early 1970s. Morocco's claims conflicted with those of a group of Sahraouis who desired an independent state. When Morocco occupied the northern part of the territory late in 1975 and Mauritania the southern, the Sahraoui resistance movement, the Polisario,[10] moved to Tindouf, in Algerian territory. When Algeria recognized the independence of the Saharan Arab Democratic Republic, in February 1976, Morocco broke diplomatic relations, the border was closed, and the two states became involved in a costly proxy war for the next ten years.

Algeria's support of the Polisario was based formally on her policy of encouraging national liberation movements, especially revolutionary ones, and upon the World Court's finding that Morocco must accept as legitimate the boundaries drawn by Spanish imperialism. More fundamentally, however, the conflict over the Sahara reflected a struggle for regional hegemony. With almost equal populations, the two states between them account for about 80 percent of the total population of the Greater Maghrib. Morocco, presided over by a centuries old monarchy and political tradition, had historically dominated the politics of this part of the world. Algeria—revolutionary, oil-rich, and economically dynamic—represented a clear challenge to the traditional hegemony of its neighbor. The battle for the Sahara was a struggle for dominance of the Maghrib regional system and for influence that would inevitably radiate southward and southeastward through the African continent.

SOCIETY AND THE ECONOMY

At independence, about 30 percent of Algerian society was living in the cities. This population included an upper middle class (bourgeoisie) of about 50,000 entrepreneurs, landlords, upper managers, and professionals. The lower middle class (petite bourgeoisie) was composed of small shopkeepers, artisans, civil servants, and other service employees, and it numbered about 180,000. The urban proletariat included about 110,000 full-time workers, although 400,000 Algerians worked in Europe. By far the largest component of urban society was the subproletariat that had been driven out of the countryside by the endemic stagnation of the agricultural sector and by the war. Numbering at least 2,000,000, this unemployed and underemployed mass of uprooted peasants spread out into *bidonvilles* around the coastal cities or into the overcrowded traditional medinas with only the most elemental of infrastructure and social services. They were fully 55 percent of the urban population.[11]

In the countryside, where most Algerians still lived, 25,000 families with estates larger than 100 hectares owned half of the country's arable land. About

10. *Frente popular para la liberación de Saguia el Hamra y Río de Oro.*
11. The figure for the subproletariat is a global one that includes wage earners or potential wage earners as well as dependents. Figures for the other classes refer to active work force only. By assuming an urban household to consist of five people, the working- and middle-class categories total 1,600,000; and the overall urban population is 3,600,000. Mahfoud Bennoune, in *The Making of Contemporary Algeria, 1830–1987*, p. 93, places the urban subproletariat at 65 percent.

170,000 middle peasant households farmed holdings of from 10 to 50 hectares. Some 450,000 families farmed holdings smaller than 10 hectares and of these, about 120,000 owned less than 1 hectare. There were another 450,000 seasonal and about 130,000 permanent agricultural laborers. Some of the seasonal laborers came from families with small holdings of their own.

Per capita GDP during the first years of independence hovered around 1,000 dinars, but with gross distributional disparities among the classes. While 60 percent of the active work force earned its living from agriculture, estimates of per capita income on an average traditional farm range from 200 dinars to 350 dinars. Given the disruption of markets, flight of expertise and capital, and the general collapse of the colonial economy, many economic indicators were negative during the first four years of independence. Economic stagnation and regression combined with administrative disorder limited tax and fee collections so that, in 1964, government revenues covered only 60 percent of expenditures. Algeria was heavily dependent upon foreign aid—Soviet, Arab, and especially French, which continued at a level of more than a billion francs annually. As the economy worsened, the exodus of workers overseas accelerated and their transfers—thought to have totalled around $200 million by 1964—became the margin of survival for many families and for some whole communities.

Managerial confusion, the disappearing markets, breakdowns in equipment, and shortage of credit brought declines in agricultural productivity after the climate-induced success of 1963. The only sector of the economy whose growth was not negatively affected by the crisis of independence was the hydrocarbon sector, whose revenues grew from $54 million in 1963 to $128.6 million in 1966. In the industrial and mining sectors, productivity was affected by the flight of technicians, by mismanagement and shortage of credit in the self-managed enterprises, and by declining confidence about the security of private investment. Most industrial growth was the result of French financed projects contained in the Constantine Plan (e.g., a petrochemical plant at Arzew and an iron and steel plant at el-Hadjar). While the decline in aggregate GDP turned around in 1964, investment remained negative; and after three years of independence, unemployment still stood at 45 percent, with many more underemployed.

During the unstable Ben Bella years, advocates of a decentralized, worker-managed approach to economic development occupied the ideological high ground of national debate. Against them was the weight of the propertied middle classes, many of whom had dramatically increased their capital in the unseemly scramble for colon assets. Given the smallness of their class and the poverty of the masses, the free-enterprise position did not generate much political enthusiasm, however. The middle ground between the Trotskyites and the capitalists was occupied by the proponents of state capitalism who dominated the bureaucracy. Class analysis has laid the ultimate victory of the state capitalists to the petit bourgeois backgrounds of bureaucrats determined to block access of the working classes to the means of production.[12] Others see the victory of state capitalism as an example of the universal need of bureaucrats to control. Still others see it tied to the radical nationalism of the Algerian political elites.[13] The latter analysis holds that, after the great price they had paid for independence, Algerians were frustrated and humiliated by the continuing economic, financial, and technical dependence upon the former métropole. Nationalizing French assets was a politically popular thing to do, but many believed that Ben Bella, for fear of alienating de Gaulle who was the country's biggest benefactor, had been too timid in this area. Boumediene and his entourage were convinced that genuine independence could only be realized through control of all of the country's natural resources, especially its hydrocarbons, and through rapid industrialization. Furthermore, given the outreach of the advanced industrial economies, this industrialization could only be achieved through nationalization of the large means of production and state control of the economic processes.

THE RACE TO INDUSTRIALIZE

Between 1966 and 1971, Algeria moved decisively to take control of its economic future. It progressively nationalized one foreign sector after another—minerals, banking, insurance, manufacturing. The process culminated, in 1971, in acquisition of 51 percent of the oil sector and 100 percent of the gas sector, an initiative that put Algeria far ahead of other OPEC countries in winning control of the industry. A majority of the enterprises in the self-managed industrial sector were also nationalized in this period. To absorb these nationalized enterprises, expand their operations, and create new ones, the state gradually erected a network of forty-five national industrial corporations, eight banking and financial organizations, and nineteen national offices. Each company was responsible for a specific branch of the economy and exercised a virtual monopoly over every facet of that branch. The most influential and best financed of the state corporations was SONATRACH *(Société nationale de transports et de commercialisation des hydrocarbons)*, which operated the oil and gas industry in all of its aspects and which attracted many of the best scientists, technicians, and managers in the country. Other important corporations were SNS *(Société nationale de sidérurgie)*, the steel company; SNIC *(Société nationale des industries chimiques)*, in charge of petrochemicals; SONACOME *(Société nationale des constructions mécaniques)*, for machinery of all kinds; and ESDNC *(Entreprise socialiste pour le développement national de la construction)*.

The basic Algerian development strategy was formulated between 1966

---

12. One of the most persuasive examples of this argument is Rachid Tlemcani, *State and Revolution in Algeria*.
13. See John P. Entelis, *Algeria: The Revolution Institutionalized*, p. 112.

and 1967 within the circle of Abdessalam Belaid, the very influential Minister of Industry from 1965 to 1978. It was a strategy designed to break the cycle of economic dependency through rapid industrialization based upon integration and introversion. The goal was to achieve, hopefully by 1990, a mostly self-contained economic sector that would satisfy society's basic consumption needs while at the same time making maximum utilization of local raw material and manpower. Capital to build the infrastructure would be provided by the rapidly expanding hydrocarbon sector. Access to these earnings helped Algeria avoid the classical Third World dilemma of choosing between foreign investment or reduced consumption as a source of capital. But even so, the choice was not easy, given the marginal living standards of most Algerians. Those standards would rise only minimally in order to maximize the rates of industrial investment. Since hydrocarbon resources were finite, these must be converted into economic infrastructure and the Rostowian point of economic take-off reached before they were exhausted.

Just as the strategy emphasized investment over consumption, it also emphasized industry over agriculture. This was an abrupt departure from the vision of the Tripoli Program. But the economists of 1966 used very different tools of analysis from the ideologues of 1962. Being in a Mediterranean climate, the agricultural potential of Algerian land was inherently limited. The majority of the nation's farmlands were marginal in quality and had been subdivided to the point they were losing their economic viability. With population growing at 3.2 to 3.4 percent per year and with 175,000 applicants entering the job market annually, a program of industrialization now seemed the only logical alternative.

The strategy of sectorally unbalanced growth grew out of the thinking of a number of French economic advisors, most notably of Gérard Destanne de Bernis. In addition to being the godfather of much of the preceding analysis, he was the originator of the concept of *industries industrialisantes*. These were a group of industries believed to stimulate further industrialization automatically. Industrializing industries include energy-related activities, notably for Algeria the hydrocarbon sector, iron metallurgy and other mineral processing, organic and inorganic chemicals, and heavy machinery. These are huge, capital-intensive industries, which then act as a motor of economic growth, producing raw materials and machinery for other industries and, at the same time, absorbing minerals and agricultural products from the primary sector. Products of the new industry will contribute to the modernization of backward sectors, notably agriculture, by supplying inputs such as pumps, machinery, and fertilizers and by stimulating demand for outputs both in the form of industrial crops and food for the growing industrial work force. By deliberate decision, the strategy deemphasized development of light industry and minimized the production of consumer goods until the basic infrastructure was in place. A deliberate choice was also made to deemphasize agricultural investment on the theory that the stimulus from the burgeoning industrial sector would generate increased productivity.

Implementation of this economic strategy began with a modest "pre-plan" in 1967–1969. It was during these three years that the nationalization of most foreign assets occurred and that the basic structures of the state-directed economy were created, including the major industrial corporations, financial institutions, purchasing and marketing agencies, and the central planning apparatus. There followed two consecutive four-year plans. Industrialization began in earnest during the first four-year plan in 1970–73 and accelerated dramatically with the overnight quadrupling of crude oil prices at the start of the 1974–77 plan. Concerns and conflict about anomalies and inefficiencies that developed as the economy expanded led the government to fall back to a single year plan for 1978.

Public sector investment grew dramatically over the life of the first three plans. Targeted investment was 9.6 billion dinars in the pre-plan, 27.75 billion dinars in the first four-year plan, and 119 billion dinars in the second four-year plan. Table 7.1 indicates the success achieved in investing those funds, as well as the sectoral distribution.

Table 7.1   Planned and Actual Investment, 1967–1977

| | 1967–69 | | 1970–73 | | 1974–77 | |
	Planned %	Actual %	Planned %	Actual %	Planned %	Actual %
Hydrocarbons	41.9	50.9	36.9	47.1	40.6	48.6
Capital and Intermediate Goods	47.0	40.6	48.9	46.2	47.6	44.5
Consumer Goods	11.1	8.5	14.2	6.7	11.8	6.9
Total Industry	48.7	55.3	44.7	57	43.6	62.0
Agriculture	16.9	16.4	14.9	13	13.2	4.7
Infrastructure	34.4	28.3	40.4	30	43.2	33.3
TOTAL	100	100	100	100	100	100

Source: Lawless, "Algeria: The Contradictions of Rapid Industrialization," in *North Africa: Contemporary Politics and Economic Development* (1984), p. 165.

The figures for planned investment illustrate the sectoral imbalance central to the development strategy. The columns for actual investment show that the imbalances were actually greater than planned, because agriculture and social infrastructure were experiencing difficulties utilizing their shares, while the large state corporations were absorbing more than theirs. Furthermore, as economic growth accelerated and as funds available for investment grew, the limitations inherent in a bureaucratized, centrally planned system made it increasingly difficult for most sectors and branches to reach their targets. By

Table 7.2   Industrial Growth, 1967–1978 (In Billions of 1978 Dinars)

Branch	1967	1973	1977	1978
Basic Industry	1.6	3.3	4.9	5.9
Light Industry	2.3	4.3	4.7	4.8
Mining and Electricity	0.4	0.8	1.5	1.6
Total without Hydrocarbons	4.3	8.4	11.1	12.3
Hydrocarbons	14.2	21.2	22.5	24.6
TOTAL	18.5	29.6	33.6	36.9

Source: Bennoune, *The Making of Contemporary Algeria, 1830–1987* (1988), p. 142.

1978, for instance, the public industrial sector achieved less than 60 percent of its investment goal. Nevertheless, average annual growth of the Algerian economy between 1967 and 1978 was an impressive 7.2 percent. In constant prices, Algerian industrial production had doubled in the twelve years since the launching of the first plan. Factoring out the hydrocarbon sector, industrial production had tripled. The basic industries that were the top priority of the planners had nearly quadrupled.

During the same period, total industrial employment had grown to about 460,000, two-thirds of which was in the state sector; and 73 percent of industry's contribution to GDP also came from the public sector. Heavy industry was almost exclusively under state control while somewhat more than half of consumer products were produced by a rapidly expanding private light industry sector.

Table 7.3   Population and Labor Force, 1966–1977

	1966	1977	Ratio of 1977 : 1966
Total Population	12,420,000	17,660,000	1.4
Abroad	600,000	800,000	1.3
Urban	3,900,000	7,060,000	1.8
Rural	7,920,000	9,800,000	1.2
Agricultural	5,700,000	7,150,000	1.3
Non-agricultural	2,220,000	2,750,000	1.2
Total Labor Force	2,450,000	3,740,000	1.5
Agricultural	1,270,000	1,545,000	1.2
Full-time	450,000	570,000	1.3
Part-time	820,000	975,000	1.2
Non-agricultural	1,180,000	2,085,000	1.9

Source: Pfeifer, *Agrarian Reform Under State Capitalism in Algeria* (1985), p. 30.

In spite of its achievements, it was clear, by 1977, that the Algerian economy was in serious trouble. While the program of rapid industrialization had reduced official unemployment since 1969 from 30 percent to 22 percent, Algerians had been led to expect far better results. But relatively slow job creation was one of the prices paid for concentrating on capital intensive basic industry. Even for those who were employed, moreover, there were many reasons for dissatisfaction. Between 1969 and 1979, the purchasing power of the average worker increased by only 20 percent. The number of strikes in 1969 had totalled seventy-two; but by 1977, there were more than 500, almost all for higher wages.

The reasons for poor performance of the economy were manifold and interconnected, but most were related either to the frenetic speed of development or to the sectoral and branch imbalances that kept it from nearing the goals of introversion and integration. As pressures grew to meet unrealistic targets, the central planning office and the larger state corporations were frequently overwhelmed by the magnitude of their tasks. Programs were subject to long delays and escalating costs. State corporations let contracts to foreign companies to build complex turnkey enterprises, which greatly increased development costs and at the same time created new dependency on foreign suppliers and expertise. The avoidance of such dependency had been one of the primary goals of the national economic strategy. The process also stamped the emerging industrial infrastructure with a technological incoherence that inhibited integration. Pressures to meet targets also created capital demands beyond the earnings capacity of SONATRACH, on which the economy depended for 95 percent of its foreign currency. To meet these demands, Algeria turned to international banks, which considered Algeria an excellent credit risk because of its profitable oil and gas resources and because of the business-like reputation the country's managers acquired during the decade. By 1980, the nation's external debt had risen to $16.3 billion and its servicing absorbed about 25 percent of foreign currency earnings.

A further problem related to pell-mell industrialization was low productivity. Productivity suffered because of the low level of managerial, technical, and vocational skills, which was to be expected in a society that fifteen years earlier was 85 percent illiterate. At the same time, many Algerian industries operated at 10 percent to 65 percent of capacity, either because sufficient inputs were not yet available or because markets for their products had yet to develop. A third factor in low productivity was the impossibility of realizing economies of scale because of the smallness of the domestic market. Penetrating overseas markets, on the other hand, was virtually impossible because of global gluts of basic products, such as steel, and because Algerian costs were often double those of European or Japanese competitors.

Though each of the four-year plans raised the investment quotas of light industry, state corporations proved unable to meet the burgeoning consumer demand generated by rapid industrialization, urbanization, and growth in well-paid governmental and other service employment. The private sector moved in to fill part of this demand, absorbing products produced at great cost by the core sectors. But even so, demand for consumer goods in many areas outstripped supply, resulting in a widening outflow of foreign currency earnings. Though hard data are unavailable, it is believed that the great bulk of transfers from overseas workers went ultimately to pay for Japanese and European electronics, household appliances, vehicles, and other consumer necessities. While development strategy was predicated upon popular willingness to accept two to three decades of austerity, rising incomes in the favored sectors created demand that essentially vitiated the austerity premise.

Investment in social infrastructure also failed to meet planned targets. Medical services, educational plant and equipment, and especially housing remained in desperately short supply during the 1970s. In this area, the result was deepening social malaise and growing pressures on decision-makers to adjust investment priorities. By far the most serious difficulty encountered by the economy, however, was the crisis caused by the slow growth of agriculture at a time when population growth and rising urban incomes were causing demand to soar. Between 1967 and 1978, as GDP grew at an average annual rate of 7.2 percent, agriculture grew at 2.4 percent.

AGRICULTURAL CRISIS AND
THE AGRARIAN REFORM

To some extent, the agricultural crisis was a function of the marginality of much of Algeria's soil and the fact that the country could fall back on virtually no uncultivated reserves. Even taking into account these physical limitations, however, Algeria's agricultural sector seriously under produced. Its failure to respond as predicted to the demand created by industrialization and urbanization is related to three factors: asymmetry of the sector, insufficiency of investment, and government pricing policies.

The agricultural dualism characteristic of the colonial period continued after independence, when the self-managed sector continued the modern colon sector under a different name and management. It continued to receive the bulk of state attention and public investment, and its employees earned the best salaries in agriculture. Yet, it failed to realize anything like its full potential. One reason for this failure was the difficulty it encountered in readjusting to new market realities, especially the decline of viticulture, the most profitable sector, whose markets in France contracted sharply after the middle 1960s. It is also clear that bureaucratization and central control impeded productivity as did the absence of personal incentives for the workers in this sector. Personal productivity and salary level were not correlated, and the sharing of profits among the workers foreseen by the March Decrees rarely occurred since few state farms ever showed a profit. In the private sector, which still encompassed nearly 75 percent of the arable soil, much of the land was of extremely marginal quality and much was hopelessly subdivided. These factors added to technical archaism and the absence of modern equipment meant that private agriculture was largely incapable of responding to demand emanating from the city. Nevertheless, it was on this sector, as in colonial times, that Algerians still depended for the bulk of their subsistence crops.

Algerian planning never targeted agriculture for more than 16.9 percent of public investment. But even with such low projections, actual investment never reached the targets and actually declined as the years went by. While data on private sector agricultural investment are fragmentary, the state monopoly of the credit institutions made it extremely difficult for private farmers to finance improvements.

Finally, government pricing was a major factor keeping the agricultural sector from responding in the ways authors of the development strategy had foreseen. As rising urban per capita income increased demand for food, the government refused to let most producer prices rise or to subsidize them, thus removing the incentive to increase production. Only uncontrolled products, such as poultry and vegetables, responded well to the stimulus of the market. Like governments in many parts of the world before and since, when it came to food, the government of Houari Boumediene pursued social rather than economic objectives. The result was that imports of food from abroad grew dramatically. A country that in net terms was self-sufficent in food in 1962 was only 70 percent self-sufficient in 1969 and 35 percent self-sufficient by 1978. Food's contribution to the drain on reserves grew disturbingly.

By 1970, as the inability of the agricultural sector to fulfill its role in the national development strategy was becoming very evident, pressures grew to implement the agrarian reform repeatedly promised since 1962. After much internal debate, the Charter of the Agrarian Revolution was finally promulgated in 1971. The most important of its goals was a rehabilitation of the private agricultural sector, enabling it to produce the foods and raw materials required by the growing population and expanding industry. A related goal was maximum commercialization of agriculture so that rural populations with money in their pockets would provide markets for the products of expanding industry. Finally, it was hoped that, by making life in the countryside more remunerative and attractive, the accelerating exodus of peasants to the city could be brought under control.

Land was to be distributed to poor peasants in tenures whose permanency was contingent upon their working them themselves and which did not include the right of resale. They would share equipment and achieve economies of scale by membership in production cooperatives. The production units would be supported by a smaller number of service cooperatives to provide input-output and marketing services. The Charter also called for building a thousand "socialist villages" as rural magnets to provide urban style amenities and services for the rural populations. Land for the program was to come from the public domain and from the larger private estates. Absentee owners of more than five hectares were to be expropriated, but resident owners were permitted to keep land sufficient to produce an annual income per family of 13,500 dinars, about triple the wage in the self-managed sector. During the first phase of the reform, from January 1972 to June 1973, the khammisat was abolished, sharecroppers' debts were forgiven, and 700,000 hectares of state land were distributed to 54,000 peasants. During the second phase, June 1973 to June 1975, 650,000 hectares of expropriated land was distributed to 60,000 more landless families. The average plot distributed in these two phases was 14.7 hectares in area. Finally, in a third phase, beginning in 1975, an attempt was made to cooperativize some of the country's herdsmen.

In the long run, the agrarian "revolution" failed to revolutionize the agricultural sector. Of the registered arable land in 1977, 2,064,360 hectares were in the autogestion sector,[14] 4,472,220 hectares were still in the private sector, and only 1,000,600 hectares had moved to the reform sector.[15] Very little privately held land had actually changed hands, due to the massive resistance of middle and larger landholders. In anticipation of expropriation, many landlords had subdivided holdings among family members. Others were able to adjust accounts to make earnings on their holdings appear lower than they actually were. While some observers see the reform's failure to expropriate any but a small fraction of private land as the result of landlords' ability to thwart the state, others believe it resulted more from collusion of the bureaucrats with close ties to these families. Still others believe the Charter of the Agrarian Revolution was purposely framed from the beginning to include penetrable loopholes.

By 1980, agrarian reform had created 5,966 production cooperatives, 177 service cooperatives, and 670 socialist villages. But employment, production, and earnings of the sector were far short of what had been expected. Very few showed a profit. The reform sector covered only 13 percent of the arable land and showed little or no growth, and 59 percent of cultivable land remained under private ownership and supported 1.5 million families on 800,000 farms. More than half were smaller than five hectares and only 23 percent of the tractors were located in this sector. Yet the private farms produced 95 percent of the livestock, 60 percent of vegetables, 44 percent of winter cereals, and 18 percent of industrial crops. Receiving practically no government assistance, it still was the locus of most of the country's agricultural growth. But still the agricultural crisis deepened. The ratios of production in 1978–81 relative to 1962–65 for key cereals were as follows: hard wheat, 0.75; soft wheat, 1.60; barley, 1.95; oats, 1.23. Meat and most vegetable production was keeping up with population growth but not with demand.

14. Excludes about 300,000 hectares of grazing and unproductive land in the self-managed sector. Also, expansion of urban housing and industrial plant had resulted, since the middle 1960s, in this sector's losing some 250,000 hectares—some of it prime land.
15. Including grazing lands and unproductive lands, the sector officially included 1,412,920 hectares.

SOCIETY AND CULTURE IN TRANSITION

At least as formidable as the political and economic tasks independent Algeria faced was that of building a consensus about the nature of Algerian culture. One model of nation building, as discussed in the introduction, suggests that the most fundamental process underlying the creation of a nation-state is the transition from segmentation to integration. Integration is geographic, economic, sociological, and political, but the framework that enables and interprets it is cultural. It is the sense of cultural identity that explains one's participation in the social, economic, and political systems functioning on the national territory and rationalizes the particular forms they have taken. Without general agreement on the shape of the cultural system and its values, national integration at all levels is in jeopardy.

The FLN had adopted as its credo reformist Islam's profession that "Islam is our religion, Arabic is our language, Algeria is our fatherland." The credo reflected in broad terms a sense of cultural identity shared by a great majority of Algerians. But it left unsaid the ways in which each of its statements was true. Was the Islam referred to official, reformist, puritanical, maraboutic? What was the relationship of Islam to political and economic spheres that had long since been preempted by the secular or to social areas influenced by it? Was the Arabic referred to classical or modern literary, which few could read and hardly anyone could speak, or was it dialectal which 99 percent of Algerians could speak? If Arabic was the language of Algeria, what were Kabyle and the other Berber languages? What was French? In what way was the Algerian fatherland different from the greater Maghrib, the Arab nation, or the Islamic *umma?* Did the Algerian fatherland have room for non-Arabs? For non-Muslims? For any of the cultural inputs Europe had supplied over five generations?

The problem of defining Algeria's identity within the framework of Islamism, Arabism, and Algerianism was made all the more difficult by the cultural disjuncture between the national political leadership and the rural or recently urbanized masses. As much as 95 percent of the political leadership and virtually all of the technical and scientific leadership had been educated in French and shaped by wide exposure to European values, systems, and ideologies. The rhetoric of class conflict jarred Islamists, for whom the ideal community is one of brothers; assuring the rights of women ran counter to deeply ingrained patriarchal tradition; invoking individual rights threatened the authority of the group, especially the family.

Throughout the first thirteen years of independence, the leadership worked assiduously to demonstrate the philosophical compatibility of Islam and socialism, even going so far as to claim on occasion that Muhammad himself was the founder of socialism. It devoted substantial resources to religious building, Islamic education, and training and remuneration of the clergy while, at the same time, it moved vigorously to appropriate religious symbols by incorporating public religious observance into official life. At the same time, government maneuvered through the Ministry of Religious Affairs to keep the clergy under its control, delivering weekly suggestions for Friday sermon topics and signalling displeasure when mosques became overly politicized. While dissident Muslim voices were heard increasingly through the 1970s, the government managed by judicious use of incentives and disincentives to keep them from getting out of hand.

Closely related to the religious question, but going even beyond it in its implications, was that of Arabization. The affirmation of Algerian national identity had early carried with it the affirmation of the national language. The language of the colonizer had to be rejected if the nation was to recuperate its Arabo-Islamic heritage. Yet, French was in fact the written language of the Algerian Revolution, the medium through which it expressed its ideology and goals. It maintained its position through the 1960s and 1970s as the principal language of government and industry. To a great extent, the continuing primacy of French reflected the educational legacy and historical momentum of the colonial period. Yet, even as the majority of Algerian elites affirmed the need to Arabize, they were caught on the horns of two different dilemmas: The first was the inconsistency between the cultural goal of recuperating a heritage and the developmental goal of rapid technological and economic change. In the Arab East, Arabic had become the medium for a range of modernist and progressive movements. In Algeria, however, the return to Arabic was closely associated in everyone's mind with a return to Islam and clearly prioritized traditional and conservative values. The maintenance and expansion of francophony was just as clearly the most direct route to the scientific and technological insights necessary for rapid industrialization. The first strengthened ties to an Arab and Islamic East whose greatest achievements seemed mainly in the past; the second opened the door to a West whose achievements had dominated the modern era.

The other major dilemma posed by Arabization was that the return to Arabic, which many Algerians viewed as a sine qua non of societal integration, was viewed as a major threat to the identity of the Kabyle community and thus it promoted division rather than integration. Kabyles saw the Arabization campaign as a threat to their culture, a negation of the rights they had earned by their wartime sacrifices, and an ill-disguised attempt by Arabs to impose themselves culturally and politically on their region. Kabyles disputed the notion that Algeria was or should be exclusively Arab. While they accepted the primacy of classical Arabic in the religious sphere and most recognized the utility of the vulgate in day to day communication, they stubbornly resisted imposition of written Arabic as the exclusive national language.

In spite of the disadvantages of Arabization and in spite of the attachment of political and intellectual elites to the French language, irresistible sociopolitical forces after independence favored Arabization. Proficiency in French was associated with privilege. Whether it was the bureaucrat, businessman, or professional who had prospered under the French, the revolutionary Marxist who had fought them, or the new generation technocrat in SONATRACH or SONACOME who was building Algeria's future, the individual who could read and write French was almost invariably better off than the one who could not. For reasons explored earlier, Kabyles also belonged to that group. They exhibited higher rates of francophony than the rest of the population and, while there were poor Kabyles, as a group they enjoyed higher living standards than Arabs. They were disproportionately represented in the central bureaucracy and in better paid private jobs, especially in Algiers.

In a decolonizing society whose formal goal was socialism and whose dominant political discourse was populism, Arabization was not only ideologically correct; it became a major political tool. By advocating Arabization, the politician identified himself simultaneously with revolutionary orthodoxy, Arabo-Muslim authenticity, and the aspirations of the economically disadvantaged majority. At the same time he was implicitly taking shots at the privileged: the avaricious middle class, the haughty bureaucrats, and the cosmopolitan Kabyles.

EDUCATION, CULTURE, AND DEVELOPMENT

The most visible national arena within which the debate about cultural identity played itself out was the field of education. As early as 1963, Algeria committed itself to progressive Algerianization, universalization, democratization, and Arabization of education. Planning also gave priority to scientific, technical, and vocational education.

The problems the country faced implementing these goals were enormous. In 1961, only 300,000 of an estimated 1,800,000 primary-age children were actually attending school. Only 30 percent of secondary students and 10 percent of university students were Algerian; 90 percent of the European teachers fled the country at independence; and plant and equipment were in desperately short supply.

Staffing the schools the first years of independence required heroic recruiting efforts targeted at both foreigners and Algerians and resulted in considerable lowering of professional standards. Overflow classes were housed in a great variety of abandoned colon buildings, and double sessions were the norm. Somehow, however, during the academic year 1962–63, 778,636 pupils were enrolled in primary schools and 51,000 in secondary. During several years in the 1970s and early 1980s, the regime devoted more than 30 percent of state budget and 11 percent of GDP to education. Table 7.4 illustrates the spectacular growth in school enrollments.

The percentage of elementary-age children actually attending school rose from 25 percent in the first year of independence to 71 percent in 1977–78 (83.8 percent for boys and 58.3 percent for girls). The breakdown by sex reflected the society's male bias. In 1977–78, the female percentage of primary enroll-

Table 7.4 Educational Enrollments, 1962–1963 to 1977–1978

Level	1962–63	1969–70	1977–78
Primary	777,636	1,689,023	2,894,084
Secondary	50,789	233,847	741,718
Intermediate	30,790	199,708	596,652
Upper	19,999	34,139	145,066
University	3,718	18,150	51,850
TOTAL	832,143	1,941,020	3,687,652

Source: Bennoune, *The Making of Contemporary Algeria, 1830–1987* (1988), pp. 220, 225, 228, 229.

ment was 41 percent and of secondary enrollment, 36 percent. The decline in female enrollment at secondary was even more pronounced at the upper-school level, reflecting the widespread opinion that basic skills were all most women needed to perform the functions expected of them in society. The most striking overall increases were in the secondary schools and at the universities. While elementary enrollments more than tripled, those for the higher levels grew by a multiple of fifteen. The difference reflected the transition from colonialism's policy that most Algerians needed basic education at most to the independent regime's goal of rapid modernization and industrialization.

Algerianization of faculty proceeded most rapidly at the primary level, being virtually completed by 1978. At the more advanced levels the process was slower. By 1978, 82 percent of secondary teachers were Algerian as were 60 percent of university faculty. In the senior ranks of the university, however, foreigners still outnumbered Algerians. Algerianization of subject matter, particularly important in the humanities and social sciences, moved forward fitfully on an ad hoc basis as the country coped with the daunting task of conceptualizing and then producing texts and other teaching aids appropriate to a new nation.

During the entire period, the structure of the Algerian education system remained a modified version of the French. French education was designed to provide basic verbal and quantitative skills for the majority while offering opportunities for the very talented to climb higher up a sharply pitched educational pyramid. From first grade onward, promotion to the next class depended upon passing a year-end examination. At the end of each level of schooling, award of the appropriate diploma depended upon passing a rigorous comprehensive examination. Failure rates for the *diplôme d'études primaires,* the *brevet,* and the *baccalauréat* ranged from 48 percent to 75 percent. The failure rates built into this elitist system generated much dissatisfaction in a society that had been taught to think of itself as democratic, revolutionary, and populist. It was for this reason that a reformed system was instituted in 1979–80. This system consolidated the primary and intermediate schools into a single, upgraded nine-year *école polytechnique fondamentale,* graduation from which was the guaranteed right of every Algerian child who would work for it. A choice of technical or academic tracks lay beyond for those who qualified.

Arabization of primary education began in the first year of independence, when the teaching of Arabic was made compulsory in all programs at every level. In the academic year 1964–65, the first grade was entirely Arabized. Subsequently, the second grade was also Arabized, while in the third and fourth grades, French and Arabic were used about equally as languages of instruction. Until the reform of 1979, the fifth and sixth grades continued to be taught in French. At the secondary level, by the 1970s, there emerged a two-track system: an Arabic track and a bilingual track. In the former, all subjects were taught in Arabic and French was taught as a foreign language; in the latter, scientific subjects were taught in French and others in Arabic. But the two-track secondary proved costly and disruptive in human, social, and economic terms. The quality of the textbooks and the preparation of the teachers in the Arabic sections were generally inferior to those in the bilingual section. The result was that students from the former found it difficult to qualify for the better jobs in government and the burgeoning industrial sector, which in all events continued to function in French. Given the limited professional success of Arabized science and technology graduates, the number of Arabized students electing to major in math and science declined from 42.5 percent in 1974 to 28.8 percent in 1977, which further emphasized the apparent job-market discrimination against the Arabized. It is also evident that students choosing the Arabic track came disproportionately from rural or recently urbanized strata, while those in the bilingual track tended to be Kabyles or children of the middle class. Thus, the way Arabization was carried out only widened the social cleavages it was designed to bridge and exacerbated the tensions tearing at a still very fragmented society.

Conflicting societal goals hampered Algeria's attempt to assemble the pool of trained minds and skilled arms its development made imperative. Beyond the substantive malfunction of the system, however, lay a potentially more serious one. The educational policy forged after independence was the product of a dialogue between protagonists of a patriarchal Islamic worldview and protagonists of a one party, quasi-authoritarian state. The aim of the system was to produce "a participant but obedient public, trained to assume the technical requirements of a scientifically developing society although maintaining, indeed reinforcing, the Arab-Islamic identity."[16] Even at its highest levels, the system was better geared to turning out technicians than scientists, organizers than creators, doers than thinkers.

WOMEN IN INDEPENDENT ALGERIA

Nowhere was the legacy of the Algerian Revolution more ambiguous than in the question of gender relations. On the one hand, the rhetoric of national

16. Entelis, *Algeria,* p. 92.

liberation appeared to imply the liberation of *all* Algerians from colonial oppression, and the heroic roles played by many women during the war added substance to that interpretation. On the other hand, since that struggle was an explicit affirmation of Arabo-Muslim values, it also implied the continuing subordination of women and perhaps even the return to submission of the small minority for whom Western presence had meant greater personal freedom. The fact that the majority of FLN militants were country people reinforced the conservative interpretation. FLN cells during the war were strictly segregated by gender, and the mujahidin set themselves up as guardians of male-female propriety. Amidst the euphoria of liberation during the summer of 1962, FLN militants roamed the streets intimidating single women. A woman accompanied in public by a man other than a relative was liable to be hurried off to a forced marriage or jailed if she refused.

Nevertheless, emancipation was what socialism meant to many urban women who attended Ben Bella's rallies in impressive numbers. At the organizational meeting of the *Union nationale des femmes algériennes* (UNFA), Amar Bentoumi thrilled his audience by stating that "The Algerian woman has, because of her effective contribution to the struggle for national liberation, earned her *droit de cité*. . . . The role of women is no longer a matter of debate."[17] The constitution of 1963 guaranteed equality between the sexes, and ten women were elected to the new National Assembly.

Much of the energy of the feminist movement over the next decade and a half was spent in trying to secure passage of a liberalized family code that would project the constitutional guarantees into law. At independence, the position of women was defined by Islamic law as locally interpreted, but which had been modified over the years by a number of extensions of the French *code civil*. The earliest project was in the form of a draft that, in 1963–64, never made it to the floor of the Assembly. Other legislation advanced in 1966, 1973, and 1980 also failed. Government repeatedly capitulated to the wishes of conservative males where women's issues were concerned. It is evident, moreover, that Boumediene and even Ben Bella, for all of their socialist rhetoric, remained deeply conservative in their own attitudes toward women. It is evident as well that there existed great ambiguity amongst women themselves. As in many societies, women were considered and considered themselves the primary custodians of religious and family values, roles explicitly accepted by the constitution of UNFA itself. Outside of Algiers and the major cities, UNFA did not even exist and its membership never grew to more than a few thousand.

Nevertheless, women made some progress. They won a few seats in the communal and provincial elections of 1967 and 1969, and they secured nine seats in the new National Assembly of 1977. In spite of the fact that nagging problems of unemployment and underemployment created very difficult conditions for job-seeking women, more than 180,000 women were in the work

17. As quoted by Peter R. Knauss, in *The Persistence of Patriarchy*, p. 99.

force by 1977, double the number employed in 1966. By the end of the Boumediene era, more than 1.5 million girls and young women were attending school. The development process was markedly increasing the percentage of Algerian women prepared to press for the dismantling of patriarchy.

CHAPTER 8

THE BENDJEDID YEARS—
READJUSTMENT AND CRISIS

In December 1978, when Houari Boumediene died of a rare blood disease, a reevaluation of the 1966–77 development record was already in progress. Chadli Bendjedid, who was elected president on February 7, 1979, presided over the drafting of a five-year plan for 1980–1984 that re-oriented economic priorities away from basic industry toward greater sectoral balance and the needs of consumers. A second five-year plan in 1985–89 continued the priorities of the first but also stressed the private sector and the need for greater efficiency. Implementation of the second five-year plan had hardly begun when the price of crude oil plunged by more than two-thirds on world markets and the Algerian economy, hard put to satisfy the needs of a rapidly growing population, was plunged into a profound crisis which led to increasing social unrest. Social tensions already evident in the late 1970s worsened through the 1980s, expressing themselves increasingly in opposition to the FLN's monopoly of power and to the philosophy of Algeria's revolution. This opposition came from liberal and leftist factions but even more importantly from a growing base of Islamic fundamentalism.

A progression of protests ranging from student demonstrations, strikes, and attacks on public buildings, to sporadic guerrilla assaults culminated in October 1988 in an unprecedented wave of demonstrations and rioting that brought labor unionists, students, and fundamentalists into violent clashes with security forces in Algiers and other cities. Hundreds of deaths resulted. In an attempt to get out ahead of the protests Chadli Bendjedid proposed and secured legislation and con-stitutional changes that lifted overnight the controls on political expression with which the country had been shackled since independence and authorized transition toward a multi-party system. By 1990 and 1991 secular parties of the center and left were challenging the FLN's generation-long hold on power, as were the Islamists of the *Front islamique du salut* (FIS). Partially because of the bewildering divisions amongst the secularists, but also because of a sense of disenfranchisement of major segments of the population, the FIS swept the local elections of June 1990, the first genuinely free elections Algerians had seen since independence. Then, when the FIS appeared certain to win a run-off round of parliamentary elections in January 1992, the military-dominated High Security Council forced Bendjedid to resign and annulled the elections.

"TOWARD A BETTER LIFE"

It appears that a part of Boumediene's long-range strategy had been a social restructuring and a rejuvenation of the increasingly bureaucratized FLN. In preparation for a party congress designed to advance these goals, youth, labor, veterans, and women's organizations had met over the course of several months in 1978. When the congress finally met in January 1979, however, its major business turned out not to be revitalization, but the divisive problem of nominating a successor to Houari Boumediene. The two major contenders for the presidency were Mohamed Salah Yahiaoui and Abdelaziz Bouteflika. Boumediene had appointed Yahiaoui Coordinator of the Party in 1977 with the express mandate to accomplish the proposed rejuvenation and restructuring. Generally considered a Boumediene loyalist who would continue most of his policies while moving to develop party control over the administrative apparatus, he enjoyed the support of labor, leftist youth, many proponents of Arabization, and sections of the army. Bouteflika, Boumediene's long-time foreign minister, who enjoyed support of much of the bureaucratic and technocratic elite and of the private economic sector, was thought to favor some degree of liberalization of the system. When the Yahiaoui and Bouteflika sides deadlocked, the army delegates emerged as arbiters and proposed Colonel Chadli Bendjedid, commander of the Oran military district, one of the ANP's most senior and respected officers. With military support, Chadli's nomination was a foregone conclusion and it was ratified the next month by 95 percent of the national electorate that went to the polls.

Algeria's third president was born in 1929 to a farm family of modest resources in northeastern Algeria. Because of the family's connections to Tunisia and because he was educated in Annaba (Bône), it is said that Chadli shared much of the cosmopolitan, Mediterranean outlook for which residents of Tunisia's north coast are noted. Joining the resistance in 1955 in Wilaya Two, he subsequently became an officer in the external ALN in Tunisia and a loyal supporter of Houari Boumediene.

He participated in the repression of the summer 1964 uprising, supported the 1965 coup that overthrew Ben Bella, and helped to put down Tahar Zbiri's revolt in 1967. Chadli was appointed commander of the Oran military district in 1964 and remained there until his election to the presidency. He was also a member of the pivotal Council of the Revolution from its formation until the death of Boumediene. His reputation was that of a loyal, business-like, and competent professional.

As a candidate of the establishment, Bendjedid's election naturally connoted continuity rather than abrupt change and such was the rhetoric of the new regime. Yet only six of the twenty-eight members of the last Boumediene government retained the same portfolios in the new cabinet. He marginalized and then eliminated Bouteflika and Yahiaoui and then moved step by step to assure control of the FLN Central Committee and other key institutions. By the end of his first five-year term, Algeria's power structure had been quietly but thoroughly "de-Boumedienized."

Exercising his constitutional prerogative, Bendjedid appointed Colonel Mohamed Benahmed Abdelghani, a business-like administrator, as prime minister, a position which under the constitution of 1976 the president was permitted but not obliged to fill. Later in 1979 the National Assembly adopted a constitutional amendment mandating the position. With this the Algerian presidency, while losing none of its impressive power, took a step toward insulating itself from the day to day infighting of government and projecting an image of greater authority and serenity.

In spite of the rhetoric of continuity, it subsequently became clear that Chadli from the beginning was determined to distance himself from many of Boumediene's economic policies. The critique of the Boumediene economic legacy went to the heart of the nation's development strategy by calling into question the validity of the deliberately unbalanced model. SONATRACH, SNS, SNIC, SONACOME and the other basic industries were accused of monopolizing investment capital to the detriment of other sectors, running up external debt by their voracious cash demands, and operating bloated, bureaucratized enterprises at such low levels of productivity that they weighed down the whole economy. They had failed to create jobs in the numbers expected and those created were concentrated in three or four privileged northern towns while most of the country remained an economic backwater. Such industrial concentration exacerbated geographical disparities in wealth distribution while saddling the infrastructures of the affected municipalities with almost insuperable burdens. Finally, lack of attention to agriculture and consumer industry generated demand for imports that wasted foreign currency reserves and threatened the ability of the economy to capitalize growth in the future.

An extraordinary congress of the FLN in the summer of 1980 adopted the first five-year plan aimed at rectifying many of these problems. By adopting the theme "Toward a Better Life" the planners and the congress signaled a new concern with agriculture, social infrastructure, and light industry and a relaxation of the austerity theme of the Boumediene years. Industry, which had absorbed an average of 59 percent of total investment under the Boumediene plans, was assigned only 38.6 percent of the total. Within that category (see table 8.1), the hydrocarbon sector was cut by three quarters. The largest part of industrial investment was committed to completing ongoing heavy industry projects rather than to starting new ones; the funds available for finished and consumer products doubled. The agricultural sector, where actual investment had fallen to an abysmal 4.7 percent of the total during the 1974–77 plan, was given 11.7 percent of the total if water development is included. Investment in housing, health, and other social infrastructure increased significantly.

It was noted in chapter 7 that in spite of a hostile political environment the private sector had grown considerably in the late 1970s, monopolizing retail trade and many light industries downstream from the basic state industries. In August

Table 8.1 Projected Investment, 1980–1984

Sector	Dinars (billion)	Percentage
Industry	154.5	38.6
(of which hydrocarbons)	63.0	15.7
Agriculture, water	47.1	11.8
Vegetable and animal	20.0	5.0
Forestry	3.2	0.8
Water resources	23.0	5.7
Fishing	0.9	0.2
Transport	13.0	3.2
Economic Infrastructure	37.9	9.5
Social Infrastructure	118.5	29.6
Public health	7.0	1.7
Housing	60.0	15.0
Education	42.2	10.5
Other	9.3	1.9
Collective equipment	9.6	2.4
Means of implementation	20.0	5.0

Source: Marc Ollivier, "L'économie algérienne vingt ans après 1966: l'indépendance nationale en question," *Annuaire de l'Afrique du Nord* XXIV (1985), (Paris: 1987): 451.

1982 new legislation was enacted to encourage and focus this sector. It did not grow as rapidly as expected, however, due to the difficulty of operating in an environment dominated by massive state corporations and administrative bureaucracies and because of difficult access to credit and imports. About 27 percent of the industrial work force was privately employed and about a third of industrial production during the first Bendjedid term came from private manufacturing which held a good share of construction and public works and which predominated in food processing and textiles.

While much was made at the time of the new regime's interest in economic liberalization, it is clear that Chadli and his advisors had no intention of relinquishing a significant share of state economic control to the private sector. Their principal objective, rather, was to decentralize and deconcentrate the system in order to make the institutions of state capitalism more reactive to economic forces and more responsive to the needs of the society. Parliamentary and party investigations had uncovered widespread mismanagement and much corruption in state companies. Beginning in 1982 the 66 public corporations were systematically broken down into 474 smaller enterprises; the 19 huge state industries were divided functionally into 120 smaller ones spread throughout the country far beyond the industrial hubs of Oran, Algiers, and Constantine. SONATRACH, which with its 100,000 employees and its great financial resources constituted almost a state within a state, was broken into 13 smaller companies. The ESDNC became 25 new companies; SNS became 17.

Presiding over much of this readjustment and re-structuring was Abdelhamid Brahimi, the minister of planning, who was long the head of SONATRACH's American office and was widely viewed as an advocate of economic liberalization. While excellent economic and managerial arguments were advanced for the policy of decentralization and deconcentration, it is clear that the policy also served political goals. The large state corporations with their huge budgets and incestuous ties to responsible ministries had become centers of power and patronage increasingly resistant to central authority. Their budgets, managers, and eventually their entire kingdoms became targets of would-be reformers or of politicians who needed scapegoats.[1] It is significant that some of the first men to lose position during the Chadli era were those associated with such enterprises. Belaïd Abdessalam, founder of SONATRACH and the powerful minister of industry who from 1968 to 1979 presided over the nation's economic development, was pressed out step by step between 1979 and 1981. Sid Ahmed Ghozali, his successor at SONATRACH, who subsequently became minister of energy, was unceremoniously sacked in fall 1979. At the same time the selection of the sites to host the spun-off smaller enterprises was itself an exercise in patronage of enormous political significance.

Unlike Tunisia and Morocco, which were forced by circumstances to rely on a variety of sources for foreign currency earnings, Algeria limited its earnings to the production and sale of hydrocarbons. Because its oil and gas were paid for in dollars, central planners pegged the dinar at an artificially high rate in order to exert downward pressure on the price of imports. While savings in some areas were realized by this policy, a side effect was virtually to preclude the possibility of earnings from other sectors. In contrast to its neighbors, Algeria refused to bid for a share of the lucrative European tourist market. But even the casual visitor was discouraged by the high prices he or she encountered in Algeria. Already noncompetitive prices of potential manufactured exports were made more so by the artificial exchange rate. Naturally almost none of the foreign currency transferred home by Algerian workers abroad went through the national banking system.

About 98 percent of the country's foreign exchange earnings were generated by hydrocarbon sales. These earnings were vulnerable not only because of the volatility of world hydrocarbon markets, but also because petroleum reserves proved far less extensive than originally thought. From the late 1970s planners began to lay out strategies for reducing this vulnerability. Algerian natural gas reserves were the fifth largest in the world. So the first of these strategies was to give urgent priority to their development. This involved the building of massive LNG plants and port facilities at Arzew and Bejaïa, and the completion in 1983 of a 1,600-mile natural

---

1. A class analysis of the destructuring of the state corporations maintains that what was primarily involved was an attack on the increasingly independent technocracy. Orchestrators and beneficiaries of this attack were the petit bourgeois bureaucracy and the private business sector. Cf. Mahfoud Bennoune, *The Making of Contemporary Algeria, 1830–1987,* 262ff, and Rabah Abdoun, "Crise, politique économique et transnationalisation en Algérie," pp. 5–7.

gas pipeline from Hassi R'Mel through Tunisia and under the Mediterranean to Europe. The second was a decision to include escalator clauses tied to the price of crude oil in new long-term natural gas contracts and an often acrimonious campaign to renegotiate existing contracts to procure the same escalators.[2] The third strategy involved concentrating more on refined petroleum products than crude oil, whose price was subject to wider market swings.

The results of the first five-year plan were disappointing. In spite of the fact that oil prices more than doubled in 1979–80, investment in productive capacity lagged. Only 40 percent of GDP was invested in the 1980–84 period as opposed to 47 percent in the 1970s. Jobs were created at an annual rate of only 4.2 percent at a time when 700,000 people each year were entering the work force. The agricultural work force shrank slightly while industrial employment expanded by 25 percent. But services grew by 22 percent and the bureaucracy expanded by 37 percent, accounting for nearly a third of the non-agricultural work force in 1984. Between 1979 and 1984 GDP adjusted for inflation grew by an average of only 4.3 percent per annum, which, given the rate of demographic increase, meant barely staying ahead (see table 8.2).

The fact that industrial production grew at a healthy 9.5 percent annually was due mostly to either the opening or the fuller utilization of plants begun in the preceding decade. The old problems in agriculture were complicated by a series of droughts and other climatic adversities, so that production in this critical sector continued to fall behind demand. Performance in social infrastructure was equally dismal. Because an average of 9.5 individuals occupied each unit of housing in 1979 this section of the plan gave highest priority to building 500,000 lodgings over its five years; but half that number were actually constructed.

Industry was able to absorb only 68.1 percent of its projected investment, while agriculture and other sectors fell even farther short of their targets. This meant that industry, accused by its detractors of having monopolized resources in the preceding decade now fell back to the performance levels of the other sectors, while those targeted for faster growth showed little or no improvement. Partisans of the *industries industrialisantes* approach argued that the strategy had been given less than a decade to prove itself, not nearly long enough by any standard to produce results. They argued that given the underdeveloped nature of the industrial environment—technically, socio-culturally, and administratively—as well as the hostile international order, industrial take-off could not rationally have been expected at this stage. What was required was a concerted effort to identify and remedy the structural and environmental problems. Instead, without serious study or trial, the public enterprises were dismantled and deconcentrated, leaving technical and managerial confusion in their wake. The most dynamic sector of the economy was starved of the capital it needed in order to become the engine of growth. By failing to hold the course, apologists

2. From the perspective of 1980, long-term natural gas contracts negotiated in the early 1970s seemed like very poor business. But tying gas contracts to the price of crude oil seemed like a better policy between 1979 and 1984 than it did after crude prices began to plummet in 1985.

Table 8.2 Sectoral Growth of GDP, 1979–1984 (Billions of Constant Dinars)

	1979		1984		Average Annual Variation	Variation of Added Value
	Value	%	Value	%		
Agriculture	10,776	9.36	12,101	10.4	2.4	1,325
Industry	13,570	11.79	21,400	18.4	9.5	7,830
Hydrocarbons	53,535	46.52	33,072	28.4	-6.7	20,463
Construction and Public Works	6,726	5.8	8,758	7.5	5.4	2,032
Transportation and Communication	nd	nd	nd	nd	nd	nd
Trade	16,790	14.6	20,744	17.8	4.3	3,954
Services	5,105	4.4	6,395	5.5	4.6	1,291
Total Added Value	104,621	92.5	125,848	88.0	0.6	4,032
Taxes	6,072	5.3	9,544	8.2	9.5	3,472
Customs Duties	2,514	2.2	4,414	3.8	11.9	1,900
TOTAL GDP	113,207	100.0	116,428	100.0	4.3	1,340

Source: Bennoune, *The Making of Contemporary Algeria* (1988), p. 280.

maintain, Algeria created economic confusion and abandoned hope of creating an economy independent of the core economies of the world.[3]

Given the problems encountered by other command economies, it is hard to know why Algeria's version would have succeeded even if allowed the time its designers said it needed. Even more importantly, the way the development strategy was arrived at and the way it was abruptly changed in the 1980s, constitutes a telling argument in favor of a participatory political system. The ability to generate broad national debate and consensus on matters of such magnitude is not only the best guarantor of their feasibility but also the best guarantor of their durability.

3. Such is the "Boumedienist" argument of Bennoune, in *Making of Contemporary Algeria,* pp. 262–96.

FOREIGN POLICY

It was observed in chapter 7 that although Soviet-Algerian cooperation was close, particularly in the field of military supply and training, Algeria never allowed foreign bases on its soil and jealously guarded its independent status as a player in the international system. Yet almost inevitably, given the fact that Algeria and the Soviet Union found themselves on the same side of many issues in the formerly colonized world, Algeria's non-alignment was a non-alignment much of the world saw tilted toward the East Bloc. In the 1980s, Chadli Bendjedid became increasingly concerned about the burden such perceptions entailed for the pursuit of national objectives. There were major concerns about the quality of Soviet military hardware and also about dependency on this single source of military supply. Equally as important, the perception of Algeria as "radical" or pro-Soviet overlaid intra-Maghrib relations with troubling global complications. Whenever Algeria, for instance, had a dispute with Tunisia or Morocco, it had to expect that France or the United States or both would weigh in on the neighbor's side. Though economic and technical cooperation with the West were not usually affected by such perceptions, they occasionally were. With all of these issues in mind, Chadli from 1980 onward slowly implemented a process of *recentrage* which eventually brought about a warming of relations both with France and the United States.

In late 1980 and early 1981, it was the Algerian government which negotiated the release of the American hostages from the United States embassy in Teheran, where they had been held by Islamic militants for more than a year. France and especially the United States continued to give technical and military support to the Moroccan cause in the Western Sahara, but the climate improved slowly. Vice President George Bush visited Algiers in September 1983. A major barrier was breached the next November when Chadli became the first Algerian president to make a state visit to France. The chance to seal the better relationship with the United States appeared in 1984 when Morocco shocked the White House and the State Department by entering into a "union of states" with Libya, a country the United States believed was a sponsor of international terrorism. This Arab-African Union, as it was called, survived barely two years, but during its lifetime the United States signaled its displeasure with King Hassan II in several ways, including inviting Chadli Bendjedid for a state visit to Washington in April 1985. Algeria was able to buy some American military hardware and more importantly to acquire American wheat at very favorable prices.

In the meantime, in February 1983, Chadli surprised many observers by meeting with Hassan II at the frontier village of Akid-Lotsi in an effort to find a solution to the Western Sahara conflict and bring about a rapprochement between the two countries. He offered a number of economic incentives, including the construction of a gas pipeline to Iberia through Morocco, in return for which Hassan agreed to open direct negotiations with Polisario leaders. The next month Chadli signaled that there could also be diplomatic disincentives attaching to non-cooperation. In March 1983 at Tunis he signed a *Traité de fraternité et de concorde* that was designed to be the framework for a Pan-Maghrib movement of cooperation. All Maghrib states that agreed first to resolve outstanding territorial disputes with their neighbors were invited to become members of the treaty organization. Mauritania adhered to the treaty later in 1983. But Libya and Morocco, both of which had outstanding territorial disputes with Algeria, saw the new initiative as an Algerian ploy to force agreement on Algeria's terms and to erect a system she could dominate. The effect of Chadli's initiative was to throw Libya, which up to 1983 had cooperated with Algeria on the Western Sahara issue, into the arms of Morocco in the union of 1984.

In the meantime Polisario-Moroccan negotiations had never got off the ground and the conflict in the Western Sahara continued. But by the middle of the decade the tactical situation on the ground had changed and the power relationship between the Maghrib's two large states was also changing. Over the years the Moroccans had created a series of berms and other defenses radiating out from the Saharan capital of Al-Ayoun which in time gave them effective control of almost all of the disputed territory, leaving the Polisario in the main only Algerian and Mauritanian territory on which to maneuver. Then, when world oil prices began to collapse at the end of 1985, the economic disparity between Morocco and Algeria began to attenuate. Algeria's economic situation from 1986 onward was becoming desperate, while that of Morocco, which was 80 percent energy dependent, improved significantly. The result was a series of bilateral negotiations during 1987 and early 1988 that by May 1988 led to the restoration of diplomatic relations that had been broken for twelve years and the reopening of the Morocco-Algerian frontier. In February 1989 Algeria joined Morocco and its other neighbors in a new Arab Maghrib Union that it was hoped would lead to a customs union and eventually to some federative or confederative political system. It is worth noting that Algeria reconciled with Morocco with the latter still in occupation of the Sahara and pledged to a future referendum on the wishes of Sahraouis to be held under conditions that were not at all clearly spelled out. Morocco did agree at length to accept the French-drawn frontier between itself and Algeria. But the impression in many circles was that in the struggle for ownership of the former Spanish Sahara, Algeria had implicitly conceded victory to Morocco.

OPPOSITION AND THE ISLAMISTS

The problems generated by rapid social change worsened in the Bendjedid years. The regime's inability to deliver to most citizens the "better life" it promised contributed to that worsening as did the continuing absence of consensus about the nature of Algerian culture.

During the winter of 1979–80 a major crisis erupted at the University of Algiers when Arabized students, who then constituted about 25 percent of the student body, launched a two-month strike to protest the favoritism shown the francophone students and the better career opportunities open to them. The fear that Islamic fundamentalists were about to capture this movement gave the crisis political urgency. In order to get out ahead of the movement Chadli took a number of initiatives. He Arabized the justice system with a stroke of the pen, a step that immediately provided job openings for several hundred monolingual law graduates who were up to then unemployed. He also appointed strong advocates of Arabization to the ministries of education and of higher education. Under their leadership Algeria accelerated the process of Arabization both at the secondary and university levels through a series of rapid curricular, organizational, and personnel changes. By 1985, 65 percent of general secondary students, 28 percent of technical school students, 32.5 percent of undergraduate college students, and 20 percent of graduate students were in Arabic tracks. The trend was clear and irreversible; the Arabic speakers were rising through the system, portending more clashes with the francophone elite before the process was completed. Most observers believe that the changes resulted in significant lowering of educational standards during the 1980s and that they severely hampered the ability of the system to provide the brains and skills required by the development program.

An immediate result of the regime's concessions to the Arabizers was a crisis of confidence in the Kabylia. A student strike that began in the University Center of Tizi Ouzou in March 1980 spread quickly to the high schools and by mid-April broadened its social base with a highly effective general strike. When tough security forces were brought in to clear the university premises, the city erupted in the most serious rioting seen in Algeria since independence. The protesters promptly baptized the events as "le printemps de Tizi Ouzou" in explicit recollection of the infamous Prague Spring twelve years earlier. The government made a few symbolic concessions to the Kabyles, but none of substance; and in May the FLN Central Committee resoundingly endorsed its commitment to Arabization. Demonstrations at Tizi Ouzou in commemoration of that spring or for other reasons continued all through the decade and many turned to violence.

The political strategy followed by the Bendjedid government is not difficult to discern. In its attempt to consolidate its power and to readjust the economic priorities, it had to overcome the resistance of men who at the time were rather loosely called leftists. These "Marxo-Boumedienists" were found in parts of the labor movement, on university campuses and in the youth movement. As allies in their campaign, the Bendjedid team turned to Arabists whose agenda was mainly cultural rather than economic and who as a rule were political conservatives in spite of the populist thrust of their agenda. Kabyles tended to have stronger ties than other groups to the left. These ties were demonstrated on university campuses throughout the country where francophone Berber students and faculty were heavily represented in everything secular or leftist. They were also demonstrated in the political arena. The clandestine *Parti de l'avant garde socialiste* (PAGS), successor to the PCA, was strongest in these mountains, as were other opposition movements, many with roots going back to the 1960s. But even if no Kabyles were linked to the so-called "left," the regime still would have supported the Arabizers to the detriment of Kabyle cultural interests because it needed their help in dismantling the house of Boumediene.

The emergence of Islamic fundamentalism, the most important movement of the 1980s, gave the government another incentive to take the road it did. Fundamentalism in the Islamic world had been on the rise since the early 1970s and had actually been encouraged by secular politicians such as Anwar Sadat and Habib Bourguiba as a counterweight to the Marxist left. Its appearance can be attributed to several different factors. In the broadest sense the late twentieth century recrudescence of Islamic political discourse and Islamism is the continuation of a centuries-old effort by Muslims to conform social and political institutions to the will of God as expressed in scripture, tradition, and the holy law, shari'a. Islam has no parallel to the Augustinian distinction between the earthly and the heavenly cities; the only city is God's.

More immediately Islamism flowed from the belief that the nationalist leaders who led their countries to independence after World War II did not deliver to most people the better lives they promised; they and their foreign ideologies had failed. This perception of failure cut to a considerable extent along generational lines. As older people rested on the laurels of victories past, younger people were looking for victories over present problems which their elders seemed unable or unwilling to produce. Their dissatisfaction was reinforced by the fact that slow economic growth limited their upward mobility. Those who had made and profited from the revolution could not now make room for their own children, or at least for the children of those who had not profited. Unemployment, underemployment, and inappropriate employment were greatest among the young, most of whom ironically now boasted better educations than their parents. Rapid urbanization and disconnection from networks that provided material and psychological support within the framework of unquestioned value systems begot alienation and bewilderment. Finally, political systems which almost universally failed to institutionalize mechanisms for voicing opposition, unwittingly left the mosques as the only fora for such expression.

As early as 1979 militant Muslims clearly distinguishable from mere Arabizers clashed with "Berberists" and "Marxists" on university campuses. Female students were intimidated for failure to abide by Muslim standards of dress or propriety. Soon student and non-student fundamentalists undertook campaigns to ransack cafés, restaurants, and other establishments that served alcoholic beverages. Amongst the leaders of the emerging fundamentalists were Shaykh Abdelatif Sultani and Shaykh Ahmed Sahnoun, organizers and theoreticians of the Islamic *da'wa* movement. One of their understudies was Abassi Madani, a former FLN loyalist who had broken with them after independence, eventually gone off to London to earn a Ph.D., and came back to teach sociology at the University of Algiers. By 1981, much to the concern of the authorities, fundamentalists began to organize street-side and other informal mosques and even went so far as to evict official imams from regular mosques. While government had given rein to Arabizers in educational matters, it had taken great pains to assign the Ministry of Religious Affairs to loyal organization men so that the pulpits and seminaries would not go out of control. Now they were beginning to do so.

During 1982 an increasing number of Islamist tracts on and off campus began demanding abrogation of the National Charter and the institution of an Islamic government. Connected with these demands were calls for radical changes in the universities, elimination of secondary and higher education for females, prohibition of alcohol, and so forth. Fundamentalists used physical as well as moral means of persuasion. During October violent clashes multiplied on the campuses. Then in early

November, after fundamentalists killed a leftist student at a suburban Algiers campus, the police cracked down and arrested 400 of them. In response to the crack-down some 100,000 shouting, banner-waving Muslim demonstrators converged for Friday prayers on the downtown university mosque. Governors and people were astounded at the magnitude and passion of what they saw. It was the greatest challenge to state authority since independence. Several hundred militants were arrested, including Shaykhs Sahnoun and Sultani as well as Abassi Madani, who by now was well known for his eloquent lecture hall condemnations of the secular university curriculum. Some of the arrested were tried and convicted while many others, including Madani, spent eighteen months or more in jail without trial. But in time, in attempts to conciliate, the government began to parole convicted fundamentalists in 1983 and 1984 and gradually to release those irregularly detained. Most militants were sufficiently impressed by the crack-down to keep future activity within legal bounds. Nevertheless, the continuing vitality of the movement was demonstrated by the turnout for the funeral of Shaykh Abdelatif Sultani in March 1984. The seventy-nine-year-old Shaykh had been incarcerated along with other activists in the 1982 crack-down but then died shortly after he was released to house arrest. Militants claimed 400,000 faithful participated in the emotional funeral and rally to honor him. At another level, a small number of activists joined a guerrilla movement founded by Moustapha Bouyali, an ex-Wilaya Four moujahid who had become disillusioned with the corruption and favoritism of the FLN and the state corporation he worked for and who had founded an organization called the Group for Defense Against the Illicit. After his parole he fled into the countryside bent on stirring up armed insurrection. During 1984 and the first half of 1985 the movement eluded extraordinary efforts to track it down in the mountains south of Algiers. During the fall of 1985 most of Bouyali's followers were killed or captured and finally in March 1987 Bouyali, himself, was tracked down and killed by a patrol in the Larbaa region. But some of his group would survive and reappear during the insurgency of the 1990s.

As was noted earlier, the need to outflank Islamists entered into government calculations when it acceded to demands from Arabizers. The same concern accounts for dramatic increases in funding for religious education at all levels from Qur'anic schools to institutes of Islamic science. The government established Islamic cultural centers in each of the country's forty-eight wilayas. In fall 1984 it opened the massive Emir Abdelkader University of Islamic Sciences at Constantine, one of the largest mosque-universities in the world, as the premier Islamic academic institution in the country.

Another area in which the influence of the fundamentalists turned out to be determining was in the divisive struggle to enact a national family code. Conservatives had managed for years to frustrate feminist efforts to liberalize women's status. One of the Justice Ministry's first acts after Bendjedid's election was to appoint a commission to draft the new legislation. The commission included no women and when versions of the bill began to leak out in 1981, female activists were appalled to find that contrary to constitutional guarantees of equal rights, the legislation would in many respects turn women into permanent minors. Because UNFA had been largely co-opted by the FLN by this time, ad hoc committees of women at Oran and

Algiers universities took the matter into their own hands. By December, when the bill reached the parliament, they mounted impressive protests in front of the Popular National Assembly, notable especially for the fact that the most celebrated heroines of the War of Independence were out in front. The government backed down and the women won a signal victory.

By July 1984, however, the influence of the fundamentalists and especially the government's fear of fundamentalists were much greater than they had been two and a half years earlier. The government presented new legislation that in most respects was more repressive than the 1981 bill. This time, however, there was very little female opposition. While reasons for this have not been thoroughly studied, several feminist activists were languishing in jail at this moment, a fact that may have helped intimidate women already fearful of fundamentalist harassment. The new Family Code, a blend of Islamic and traditional Algerian notions, was enacted with almost no opposition. A woman was the ward of her family until the consummation of marriage when she became the ward of her husband; women could not marry non-Muslims; divorce was almost totally a male prerogative; a woman's right to work outside the home was by implication subject to approval by her guardian.

In January 1986 Algerians went to the polls to approve an "enriched" charter, the fifth authoritative analysis of the national situation and goals since the Soummam platform. It reflected the readjustments in economic strategies and priorities of the early eighties, but it also represented an attempt to come to terms with the divisive ideological and social issues encountered in the Bendjedid years. The 1986 charter pointedly deleted most of the specific guarantees of women's rights contained in the 1964 and 1976 versions. It defined Algerians as an "Arab and Muslim people" and called for greater stress on religious education at all levels, but it also took pains to emphasize that the Islam referred to was not a formalistic one of rote religious observance but one that calls people to creative thinking. This was the first charter to specify that the Algerians were Arab as well as Muslim. But as a concession to the Berbers, it was also the first charter to trace the national history to the Berber kingdom of Numidia and Jurgurtha's heroic struggle against Roman imperialism.

A major force for liberalizing change was the Algerian human rights movement, an offshoot of the Berber opposition movement, spearheaded by Abdennour Ali Yahia. A founding member of the UGTA who had spent five years in detention during the War of Independence, this Kabyle militant was a follower in 1963 of the rebel Colonel Mohand Ou al-Hadj. He eventually agreed to serve in government but after a short time broke with the Boumediene regime over its heavy-handed policy of economic centralization. He went on to open shop as an attorney specializing in political cases and during the eighties achieved a reputation defending both Berberists and fundamentalists against what he saw as violations of rights guaranteed by the constitution. In and out of prison twice for his efforts, he organized, in June 1985, with forty intellectuals and Berber cultural movement activists an Algerian League of Human Rights pledged to defend the principles of the Universal Declaration of Human Rights of 1948 and the guarantees of the constitution. Ali Yahia applied for recognition of the League under terms of the 1971 ordinance on associations, but along with several co-founders he was jailed in July 1985 and given a new prison sentence of eleven months. Out of prison in 1986, Ali Yahia continued his campaign undeterred, attracting increasing international attention. Embarrassed, the regime eventually recognized a less militant rights organization, but permitted the original movement, now a member of the International Human Rights Federation, to function unofficially. It is clear that the League was a major factor nudging the Bendjedid government toward the spectacular liberalization that occurred beginning in 1988.

THE ECONOMIC CRISIS

During his first years in power Chadli Bendjedid resorted to frequent reshufflings, reassignments, and institutional reorganizations rather than outright confrontation to move his political opponents farther and farther from the center of power. By 1983 he enjoyed virtually complete control over government, the party, and the military. With this control he was reelected Secretary General of the FLN on December 22, which made him automatically the party's candidate for president of the Republic to which he was reelected for a second five-year term on January 12, 1984, by 95.36 percent of the votes cast. In the cabinet reshuffle that followed, Abdelhamid Brahimi became Algeria's second prime minister. Because as minister of planning he was closely associated with the destructuring of the national corporations, the emphasis on consumerism, and the tilt toward the private sector, Brahimi's choice as second in command clearly signaled that the priorities of the first five-year plan were not going to be abandoned.

The second five-year plan was adopted by the FLN Central Committee in May 1984 and by the cabinet in July. Its theme, "Work and discipline to guarantee the future," emphasized the planners' recognition that means of implementation were at least as important as goals themselves in achieving the better life. There was a new concern with economic integration, with fuller use of plants, with technical and vocational training, with efficiency, and with individual productivity. The plan assumed somewhat lower hydrocarbon earnings because of declining world oil prices and also because it hoped to accelerate retirement of external debt. Both of these limited capital formation. While the plan called for a 20 percent increase in non-hydrocarbon resources and for greater private investment, a considerable part of growth was expected to come out of better use of existing human and material resources. In effect Algerians were being told that the attempt to leave behind the austerity of the Boumediene years had been premature and that even though emphases on consumer goods and social infrastructure were to continue, a period of belt tightening and hard work lay ahead for everyone.

But time was running out. The import bill for food, capital goods, and consumer goods kept growing while attempts to reduce the debt service ratio, successful through 1983, had turned negative in 1984. By 1984, total external debt stood at $14,766,000,000 and the debt service ratio was an onerous 32.8 percent. Belt tightening and greater efficiency could only turn the economy around if earnings remained more or less stable and no large new demands were put upon that capacity. During

Table 8.3 Projected Investment, 1985–1989

	(Billion dinars)	Percentage
Industry	174.20	31.6
(of which hydrocarbons)	39.80	7.2
Agriculture, water	79.00	14.4
Vegetable and animal	30.00	5.5
Water	41.00	7.4
Forestry	7.00	1.3
Fishing	1.00	0.2
Transports	15.00	2.7
Economic Infrastructure	69.35	12.6
Social Infrastructure	149.45	27.2
Housing	86.46	15.7
Education	45.00	8.2
Public Health	10.00	1.8
Other	8.00	1.5
Collective equipment	44.00	8.0
Means of implementation	19.00	3.5

Source: Abdelkader Djeghloul, "Chronique algérienne," *Annuaire de l'Afrique du Nord* XXIV (1985): 597.

1985 the price of crude oil, which had been hovering around $30 per barrel began to slip. Then in December the prices stopped slipping and started to plummet. By summer of 1986 the barrel had fallen below $10, recovering only slightly by early 1987. The catastrophe was compounded by the rapid fall of the dollar which lost more than 40 percent of its value against European currencies. It was these currencies that Algeria depended upon for the roughly two thirds of its imports that came from the Common Market.

A partial and temporary cushion was provided by a spectacular cereal harvest in 1984–85 and a very satisfactory one the following year. Nevertheless, the country was forced into a desperate campaign of import slashing. In 1986 imports were cut 15 percent by value over 1984 levels and by 1987 they were off 28 percent (see table 8.4). While it was impossible in the interests of social peace to cut basic food imports, "luxury" foods, e.g., coffee, tea, and meats as well as consumer durables were cut to the bone, and capital goods, while theoretically protected, became harder and harder for industry to get. Investment for 1986 was reduced by a third. Still there was a balance of payments gap and foreign debt soared. The percentage of foreign earnings needed to service the debt was 51 percent in 1986, 54 percent in 1987, and 87 percent in 1988. Unlike many developing countries, Algeria was able to avoid rescheduling by frantically maneuvering to refinance shorter with longer term debt. In the meantime, however, the economy was a shambles.

Table 8.4 Imports, Exports, and External Debt 1984–1988 (in billions of U.S. dollars)

Year	Imports	Exports	External Debt	Debt Service Ratio
1984	9,234	12,792	14,766	32.8
1985	8,811	13,034	17,069	32.5
1986	7,879	8,065	20,566	51.0
1987	6,616	9,029	24,601	54.0
1988	6,675	7,620	25,041	87.0

Source: IMF, *International Financial Statistics,* 1989; Banque centrale d'Algérie, 1990; *Economist Intelligence Unit. Algeria Country Profile,* 1989–90, p. 45.

The growth of GDP slowed and then turned negative (see table 8.5). State budgets fell into chronic deficit beginning in 1986, averaging about 5 percent of GDP for the rest of the decade. This helped trigger double-digit inflation that was worsening as the decade ended. Unemployment grew by 1988 to an estimated 25 percent. Shortages of even basic commodities became endemic as Algerians began scampering from queue to queue in pursuit of semolina, oil, tomato paste, coffee, and tea. Per capita consumption fell.

Facing a crisis of almost unmanageable proportions, Algeria, with the encouragement of IMF (International Monetary Fund) advisors, began in late 1987 dismantling the structures of state capitalism and moving in the direction of a market economy. As a signal of this sea change in economic policy, Chadli announced abolition of the Ministry of Planning. It was replaced in 1988 by a National Planning Council responsible only for general economic policy. Beginning with agriculture, the reforms were to move gradually to the state corporations, the banks, and the pricing system. In agriculture the state began the process of dismantling the socialist sector and creating thousands of *exploitations agricoles individuelles* and *exploitations agricoles collectives* (three or more operators). While the land was still owned by the state, the state disengaged itself completely from the production on it. Buildings, equipment, and livestock were to be privately owned. Even more importantly, the operators were given permanent right of usufruct that was both heritable and marketable after a tenure of five years. It was expected that by 1993 a major market in farm land would therefore come into existence.

Table 8.5 Percentage Growth of GDP

1984	1985	1986	1987	1988
5.2	2.7	0.6	–1.4	–2.7

Source: IMF, *International Financial Statistics,* 1989.

Legislation promulgated early in 1988 was designed to set the public industrial enterprises free from bureaucratic control and to coax them into profitability. The state corporations were transformed into *entreprises publiques économiques* (EPEs) managed by independent boards of directors. Shares in the EPEs were owned by one or more of nine *fonds de participation,* which were essentially trusts holding capital for the state but independent of it. Except for the basic core industries—energy, steel, petrochemicals, etc.—EPEs unable to become economically viable in three years could be liquidated at the discretion of the share-holding funds.

In 1988 the banking system was cut loose from the Banque Centrale d'Algérie. The function of the banks was to accumulate funds and lend them at a profit to private and public enterprises. Under the new rules banks provided capital only for investments they believed profitable, assuming commercial risk without possibility of rescue by the central bank. While the former banking system featured institutions specializing in the various sectors of the economy, the new autonomous institutions were free to place funds wherever they wished and each enterprise was free to shop the banks for the best deal.

Legislation of April 1990 effectively terminated the state monopoly on credit, banking, and financial institutions by permitting domestic and foreign private investment in all of these sectors. Foreign investment, previously limited to minority share of enterprises, was now encouraged in all fields and the right of repatriation of profits was guaranteed. Legislation of August 1990 terminated the state monopoly over export-import trade that had been in place since 1978. During the same year a new wage and salary system was instituted, ending the policy of nationwide parity of remuneration for similar work. In what was perhaps the most profound repudiation of socialist orthodoxy the country had seen, wage levels henceforward were subject to the same market forces as other factors of production.

THE UPRISING OF 1988

Long before it was known if any of these reforms could turn the economy around, Algerian society was reacting in violence to the economy's inability to perform. In 1985 there was serious rioting in the Casbah. The return to classes of 1986 was marked by a series of strikes, demonstrations, and riots at Algiers, Oran, Skikda, and especially at Constantine and Sétif where the regime faced the most serious challenge to its authority since 1982. On November 5 in Constantine lycée students launched a protest against new requirements in religion and politics. The disorder spread quickly to university students at suburban Zouaghi, where security forces responded with great brutality. The next day tens of thousands of students and other young people started a silent march down the main street of Constantine to protest the violence. But when the authorities unleashed even greater force on this demonstration, the participants erupted in fury, targeting for destruction every visible symbol of state authority: party headquarters, the *Galeries algériennes* department store, offices of *Air Algérie,* and municipal vehicles. Similar riots took place at Sétif on November 11 and 12 just as authorities were beginning to bring Constantine back under control. Neither the government nor the controlled press portrayed any of these events as other than the vandalistic action of social misfits and common criminals.

The protests of 1986 involved primarily students, spreading only occasionally to wider segments of the population. Although 1987 saw a continuation of student unrest, it also saw labor unrest spreading rapidly from one sector to another. By 1988 a combination of factors came together to produce a crisis that shook and transformed the regime. The economy in 1988 was still shrinking; wages were frozen while prices soared; even basic foodstuffs were becoming hard to find; unemployment was at its highest in more than a decade; the new campaign for efficiency and profitability multiplied factory lay-offs and even more importantly spread fear of future lay-offs. In the midst of austerity and anxiety the Algerian masses were confronted with the increasing affluence of merchants and other entrepreneurs for whom recent liberalization measures had opened profitable avenues. Government encouragement of private investment had not by the late 1980s attracted a great deal of new capital into the industrial sector, principally because it was difficult to build confidence in long-term investment after the wave of nationalizations and anti-capitalist rhetoric the country had only recently passed through. Private entrepreneurs preferred more speculative investments where turnover was rapid and returns high. The widespread belief that government and party apparatchiks were enriching themselves as voraciously as the "speculators" compounded the feelings of alienation and bitterness.

During September 1988 strikes became endemic in the country, but especially in the Algérois industrial zones of Rouiba-Reghaia, El-Harrach, and Bouira where police repression was especially severe. The strikes reached Algiers itself on October 2 when the postal employees went on strike, and scattered disorder was reported. On October 4 the rumor mill spread calls to a general strike the next day. While such a strike did not officially materialize, secondary school students did walk out and their movement spread rapidly amongst laborers and unemployed young people. October 5 saw young men by the thousands storming through the center of Algiers and many residential quarters destroying government and party property as well as property associated with profiteers and the lifestyle of the well off. At least two ministries were sacked the first day. In the next two days the movement was spreading like wild fire; rioting spread to Oran, Mostaganem, Blida, Annaba, and many other cities and towns. With little initial organization, it seems that the movement came soon to involve student groups, unionists, leftists of the PAGS, and large numbers of fundamentalists. On October 6, the government declared a state of siege and the repression began in earnest. In addition to billy clubs and tear gas, the security forces began using live fire and ultimately resorted to several kinds of automatic weapons. Before order was more or less restored on October 10 hundreds of Algerians—mostly young men—had died;[4] and thousands had been taken into custody where many were tortured.

4. The government admitted 156 deaths. Other estimates range between 250 and 500.

The country was first stunned and then infuriated. Its anger was directed especially at the forces of order and particularly at military security for the brutality they had displayed. The army, whose officers permeated every major political institution of the country, and which had long been viewed not only as the maker of the revolution but as its guarantor, came out of "Black October" with a seriously diminished reputation. But popular anger was directed too at the broader system—a system perceived as an inbred monopoly of power by government and party that in the people's name had led the people to the brink of the precipice. The violent repression did not, as in previous years, silence the opposition. This time the reverse happened and the opposition swelled and spread with unprecedented determination. Algerians of many classes and conditions began to clamor for justice and for change. Illegal independent organizations mushroomed—of students, professors, journalists, lawyers, physicians—to demand both accountability for the events of October and fundamental transformations in the system. In many neighborhoods Islamic activists were clearly in control of the streets, and others offered assistance to the bereaved and the wounded. On October 10, President Bendjedid, in a television address, had already promised economic, educational, and political reforms. By the end of October he had fired Mohamed Chérif Massaadia, second in command (after himself) of the FLN and who had become a particular target of popular anger, as well as Medjoub Lakhal-Ayat, the commander of the hated military security force. He also outlined a strategy for reform that included making the government for the first time responsible to parliament, summoning a party congress to consider other constitutional reforms, and finally asking for a popular referendum on the reforms themselves.

On November 3, the voters approved a constitutional amendment making the prime minister and his cabinet responsible to the APN. Chadli now asked Colonel Kasdi Merbah, who had served as Security Chief in the Boumediene years and later in a number of cabinet posts, to become the country's third prime minister. Merbah had a reputation for efficiency but not for liberalism, and he may have been chosen to head a reform government in the hope that conservatives in parliament and the party would find his leadership acceptable. After approval by the parliament, Merbah submitted a program of economic stabilization and popular legislation designed to "soak the rich" by assuring a more equitable distribution of the burdens of economic austerity.

During the sixth regular party congress that met in late November and early December Chadli's program of political reforms ran into considerable opposition because many of them would inevitably undercut the privileged position of the single party. He nevertheless won FLN nomination to a third presidential term to which he was elected on December 22 by 81 percent of the 88 percent of registered voters who went to the polls. While both of these percentages were significantly lower than those in any preceding presidential election, Chadli nevertheless came away with a mandate to take his reform program directly to the people and to preside over its implementation through the next five years.

THE CONSTITUTION OF 1989

In the months after Black October, observers watched with fascination as Algerian civil society, rarely glimpsed since the first year of independence, began boisterously making its presence known. That civil society was clamoring for more meaningful participation in the political process. But it was the existing political establishment that was called upon to manage its transition to participation. At the beginning of 1989 the FLN was still firmly in control of the country. As the nominee of the party congress, Chadli Bendjedid had just run unopposed for a third five-year term as president. Members of the APN, who were returned in February 1987, were without exception members of the FLN and their terms would not expire until 1992 unless the president decided to advance the elections.

In February 1989 voters overwhelmingly approved a new constitution conceived by the president's office that was designed to open the road toward pluralism. Algeria's third constitution represented a major break with the past in several key areas. While the 1976 constitution defined Algeria as a socialist state, the new one defined Algeria only as the Democratic and Popular Republic of Algeria. The 1976 constitution guaranteed "the rights and basic freedoms of the people." The 1989 constitution, in a swing toward Western conceptions of individual rights that would have been unacceptable a year or two earlier, guaranteed "the freedoms and basic rights of man and the citizen." Article 39 guaranteed freedom of expression, association, and meeting. These guarantees represented an enormous victory for Abdennour Ali Yahia and the other liberals who had sacrificed throughout the decade for such principles. But the other track of Algeria's evolution was represented in new and more explicit language about the Islamic nature of the Algerian state and society. The explicit guarantees of female rights contained in the 1976 constitution had disappeared completely.

During the 1980s, the three principal centers of power were the presidency, the army, and the party, with the first clearly dominant. The new constitution left only the presidency unscathed. It made no mention at all of the FLN and the army was dealt with strictly as a military institution for the defense of the unity and sovereignty of the nation. In March, the army withdrew officially from participation in all political bodies, although, as subsequent events demonstrated, its interest in Algeria's political development remained very much alive. But the constitution pointed the way toward political pluralism by recognizing the right of citizens to found "associations of a political character."

During the year 1989 a stream of enabling legislation flowed out of a sometimes balky parliament as the country moved rapidly down the road toward pluralism and democracy. In succession the APN produced a new law on political associations, a new electoral law, and a new public information act. Along the way it abolished the State Security Court whose principal function had been the punishment of political deviation. While the electronic media still tended to reflect official interests, the written press during 1989 became the most free and most politically varied in the Arab world. During this heady period of political and economic liberalization, however, material conditions for the average Algerian continued to deteriorate. Shortages were as great as ever, rampant inflation cut more and more deeply into purchasing power, and the country was plagued by an unending series of strikes that affected almost every major town. In September, Chadli Bendjedid fired Prime Minister Kasdi Merbah for moving too slowly with reform and replaced him with Mouloud Hamrouche, who up to then had been Secretary General of the Presidency.[5]

As soon as the provisions of the new constitution were known, Algerians began to organize political associations. After the passage of enabling legislation on July 5, these associations began applying for recognition as political parties and by early 1991 thirty-three parties had obtained official recognition. These included three religious parties and thirty secular groupings of diverse tendencies.

The majority of the secular parties represented very narrow personal or regional interests. In addition to the FLN, those with broader appeal included the *Front des forces socialistes,* which had never completely disappeared, and which was now legalized. It was given a new lease on life with the return after twenty-three years of exile of Hocine Aït Ahmed who toured the country flaunting cultural pluralism by speaking interchangeably in Tamazight (Kabyle), Arabic, and French. Of about the same size was the *Rassemblement pour la culture et la démocratie* (RCD), headed by Dr. Saïd Saadi, which was the political expression of the Printemps Kabyle movement and which saw itself as a major defender not only of Berber cultural rights but of individual rights in general—both female and male. The *Parti social-démocrate,* led by Abderrahmane Adjérid, was composed primarily of entrepreneurs, academics, and members of the liberal professions; it saw itself as the party of the center. Finally, the PAGS, led by Sadek Hadjeres, which had operated for years just beyond the fringe of legality, maintained important connections within the UGTA and hence a relatively broad network of support.

More important than any of the secular opposition parties was the *Front islamique du salut.* The FIS was a coalition of organized and informal Islamist groups whose leaders came together on February 18, 1989, to discuss unification and political participation. After much discussion and dissension, the organization publicly proclaimed its existence on March 10 at the Ben Badis mosque of Kouba. From an ideological perspective, the FIS coalition was composed of two main currents, radical *salafis* and *djazarist*s. The radical salafis were offshoots of the reformist *salafism* of ʿAbd al-Hamid Ben Badis, the political dimensions of whose thought were considerably enhanced after independence by the teachings of Abdelatif Sultani and Shaykh Sahnoun. Most of these radical salafis demanded rapid transformation of the Algerian state and society—some by more vigorous political participation and others by jihad. The majority of them were imams or preachers in popular districts with traditional Arabic language and Islamic education. The djazarists evolved from an informal, mostly francophone, group of Algiers University faculty and students that developed in the intellectual path laid out by Malek Bennabi, a French-educated

---

5. The incident led to a tense moment when Merbah denied the president's authority to dismiss him, claiming he was responsible only to the APN. While the constitution required the prime minister to seek and maintain the confidence of the legislature, it did not enjoin the president from dismissing him and choosing another person who could win that confidence.

professor and Director of Higher Education who died in 1973. Significant elements of his outlook included the necessity of change and the conditions for achieving it, informing the population about the relevance of Islam to modern life, and activism in spreading Islamic values and practices. The positions of many FIS loyalists fell between the djazarist and neo-salafi camps or could vary with circumstances.

The official declaration of the Front on March 10, 1989, highlighted seven key objectives or strategies: preservation of the unity of the Muslim *umma;* the substitution of Islamic for imported ideologies; movement via a middle path; tactical moderation; collective action; encouraging of the spirit of initiative; and safeguarding of the Islamic historical and civilizational heritage. These objectives and strategies clearly reflected the moderate approach of the djazarists, but examination of the list of the FIS's fifteen founding leaders shows they were extremely diverse ideologically, including radicals and moderates, young and old, and representing many regions of the country. Quite a few Islamists did not join the new coalition. These included Mahfoud Nahnah, who went on to form the HAMAS (The Movement for Islamic Society) party; Abdallah Djaballah, who founded *al-Nahda;* and militants who identified with the violent insurgency of the Bouyalists. The two founding leaders who became best known publicly were Abassi Madani, its president, who, as an educator at Algiers University, was generally seen as closer to the djazara faction and Ali Benhadj, imam of al-Sunna mosque in the popular Bab el-Oued quarter of Algiers. Benhadj was a young, charismatic, and extremely articulate preacher who is generally associated with the radical salafi group. Born in Tunis in 1956 of a family from Ouargla in the south of Algeria, he received a totally Arabic education in Islamic schools, taught by scholars such as Omar Arabaoui, Ahmed Sahnoun, and Abdelatif Sultani. He himself taught secondary school for a short period. Although Madani and Benhadj are generally viewed as holding very different perspectives on how to bring about an Islamic state, they nevertheless seemed to work well together.

Bendjedid's decision to recognize the FIS in September 1989 was viewed by some as a step contrary to the provisions of the new constitution, and also contrary to the July 5 act which prohibited the recognition of parties based exclusively on religion, language, or regionalism. Many analysts believe the president's decision was a tactical move aimed at splitting the fundamentalists and isolating their more revolutionary elements from those willing to work within the system. He may also have wanted to use the specter of Islamism to bring obstructionist elements of the FLN into line with his reform program.

FIS VICTORIES AND THE MILITARY COUP

While both secular and religious oppositions called repeatedly for election of a new National Assembly, Chadli exercised his constitutional authority to refuse early elections, instead scheduling local and provincial elections for June 1990. The law under which the elections were held was based upon a party list system for each district. If one party received a majority, the balance of seats would be distributed proportionally to others receiving at least 7 percent of the vote. But if no party received a majority, that with a plurality would receive 50 percent plus one of the seats, with the balance distributed proportionally to those receiving at least 7 percent. The law was clearly designed to favor the largest party which all presumed to be the FLN.

None of the new secular parties was able to develop a nationwide grassroots organization in preparation for these elections. Both Aït Ahmed and Ben Bella[6] called on Algerians to boycott elections they claimed were rigged against them. The FLN after its years of power maintained in effect a very impressive political organization. But the FIS, with linkages to 9,000 mosques large and small, benefited from instant and extraordinarily effective organization.

At least partly because most of the secular parties boycotted the elections, only 65 percent of the nation's 12,841,769 registered voters went to the polls on June 12, 1990. When the ballots were counted, the FIS had won 54 percent of the votes cast, compared to 28 percent for the FLN. Eight hundred fifty of the 1,500 municipal councils fell under FIS control, including those of Algiers, Oran, Constantine, and Annaba. The FLN won 480 of them, while the rest went to independents or smaller parties such as the RCD, which, in the Kabylia, *had* fielded slates. The FIS had taken control of thirty-two of the forty-eight wilayas against fourteen for the FLN, one for the RCD, and one for independents. Given its assets as the party in power, the results were a stunning repudiation of the FLN and its record.

Analysis of the areas where FIS votes were the strongest shows them to have been primarily in the sprawling slums around Algiers and other cities which were the product of massive population growth and urbanization. Its most devoted followers were militant Islamists, most of whom were young Arabic-educated individuals resentful of the status of the francophone elites. Many were unemployed or underemployed. They were joined by large numbers of unemployed, ill-housed young men without strong ideological commitment but filled as well with resentment and passion. Many small businessmen seeking freedom from the power of a state-run economy voted for the FIS.

As FIS politicians took over local and provincial governments, Islamists' ability to control political discourse in many parts of the country grew, as did their ability to raise funds from local entrepreneurs and *trabendistes*. They also promulgated and enforced elements of their Islamist agenda that at times clashed with constitutional and statutory requirements, e.g., closing coeducational schools, forbidding married women to work outside the home, requiring females to wear head scarves, prohibiting alcoholic beverages.

As the reality of multipartism began to sink in, major political figures increasingly left the FLN. At the same time, leaders of the victorious FIS kept pressing for parliamentary elections to replace the 1987 legislature installed before the new constitution and still dominated by that party. During the Gulf War of early 1991 the image of Iraqis defending themselves against Western aggressors became a major mobilizing issue for the FIS and thousands of its young activists began taking to the streets.

---

6. Ben Bella was still in exile at the time of the elections. One of the last of the major political exiles to be permitted to return, he returned to Algeria in September 1990.

Under more and more popular pressure, the FLN-dominated legislature, under the leadership of Prime Minister Mouloud Hamrouche, enacted in April 1991 a law establishing parliamentary election by districts. The districts were clearly gerrymandered to favor southern, eastern, and mostly rural regions where the once single party still retained status. Some such districts had populations only a fraction of those of urban districts. The law also banned campaigning in mosques or schools and forbade men to cast votes for their wives, which they frequently had done in 1990. The president declared that parliamentary elections would be held on June 27.

After considerable internal debate, the FIS decided to challenge the new law. It called a general strike for May 25, 1991, demanding its abrogation and also calling for new presidential elections to accompany the legislative elections. While the strike was not especially well organized or successful, demonstrations and the occupation of public places by FIS supporters looked more and more like a frontal assault on the authority of the state. The military was increasingly fearful of that assault and disturbed with the policies of the Hamrouche government, which it saw as too permissive. The critical figure in the military opposition was Major General Khaled Nezzar, who became defense minister in July 1990 and quickly appointed a close colleague, Mohamed Lamari, to command the ground forces. As the first individual other than the president to control the military since the overthrow of Ben Bella, Nezzar was in the best position to challenge the chief of state since that time. On June 4, under pressure from Nezzar, the president declared a state of siege. Troops moved in to drive militants away and struggles between Islamists and the military in Algiers and other cities resulted in approximately fifty deaths and hundreds of imprisonments. On June 5 Hamrouche resigned.

As next prime minister, Chadli chose now Foreign Minister Sid Ahmed Ghozali. In spite of long service as head of SONATRACH, Ghozali had gained a reputation as a critic of regime policies and as something of an outsider. The new government he selected, composed mainly of personalities peripheral to the FLN establishment, was meant to signal an attempt at national reconciliation. But he retained Nezzar as minister of defense and eventually appointed Major General Larby Belkheir minister of the interior, which was a position of great power during this period of national emergency. Ghozali postponed the June 27 legislative elections, promised revision of the controversial electoral law, and "free and clean" ones by the end of 1991.

While the FIS leadership at first appeared satisfied with the change of government and with Ghozali's concessions, the momentum of the mass movement they had created soon impelled them forward again. Before the end of the month, Ali Benhadj and Abassi Madani were both openly demanding establishment of an Islamic Republic and threatening to call for jihad. On June 30, the army moved in and arrested hundreds of militants, including both Madani and Benhadj. The FIS's consultative council (*Majlis al Shura*) named Abdelkader Hachani, a representative of the moderate djazarist wing, as interim head of the party. Under his diplomatic leadership and with security precautions tight, street activism declined markedly. Radical Islamists did in the late fall, however, attack a military post on the eastern border, killing several soldiers.

After intense negotiations, Ghozali, who apparently preferred proportional representation, ceded to the wishes of the APN and put forth a system based upon 430 electoral districts. Any candidate with a majority would win the district. If no candidate won a majority, a runoff would take place in three weeks between the two with the highest numbers of votes. The date for the first round was set for December 26. Partly because FIS leaders were still jailed in Blida and had been declared ineligible to run for office, Hachani withheld approval of the electoral law for many weeks, but on December 14 he announced that the FIS would participate in the elections and urged its supporters to go to the polls.

The results of the December 26 elections were a shock to the mostly Westernized elites who had ruled Algeria since independence. Although the balloting was characterized by an extraordinary abstention rate of 39 percent, 47.54 percent of people who did go to the polls voted for FIS candidates. The FIS won absolute majorities in 188 of the 430 electoral districts, while the FLN clinched only 15 races. It, in fact, ran behind Hocine Aït Ahmed's FFS, which swept the Kabylia with 26 seats. It was mathematically obvious that in the second round of elections, scheduled for January 16, 1992, the FIS would easily end up with a majority of seats in a new parliament. Government and FLN spokesmen immediately alleged massive voting irregularities. In many FIS-controlled areas, non-FIS supporters had trouble obtaining voting cards. It was claimed there had been more than 900,000 blank or spoiled ballots. More than 400 complaints were filed for investigation by the Constitutional Council. But even though flawed, the election was largely free by Algeria's historical standards.

Within the government, debate opened as to whether to permit the second round of elections or to forestall it. By the first days of January, it seemed that President Bendjedid had made up his mind to see through the program of political liberalization he had inaugurated three years earlier. Observers believed he hoped to use his position as chief of state to temper the more extreme programs and policies of a FIS-dominated parliament. At the same time Hachani announced the possibility of cooperating with Chadli and rumors spread of a secret meeting between the two, but members of the cabinet, including Ghozali and Generals Nezzar and Belkheir, concluded that ceding power to the FIS would spell disaster. Some were concerned about preserving the secular, nationalist traditions of the nation and others about maintaining its fragile transition to democracy. Still others were concerned about losing personal power and access to wealth, particularly that generated by the hydrocarbon industry.

During the second week in January, Chadli's opponents, backed by Chief of Staff Abdelmalek Guenaïza and other key military leaders confronted Chadli with their decision, but in order to maintain the appearance of legality, they did much scrambling. In a television appearance on January 11, 1992, Bendjedid announced his resignation. He also informed the audience that he had dissolved the parliament on January 4, thereby terminating the mandate of the speaker, who was his constitutional successor, a dissolution no one had heard of previously. Apparently the military would have accepted Abdelmalek Benhabilès, president of the

Constitutional Council, who would have been next in line, but he confounded them the next day when a council spokesman declared its head had declined the post. As a founder of the Algerian League of Human Rights, Benhabilès apparently did not wish to be viewed as a sponsor of the coup. Within hours of his refusal, on the evening of January 12, the coup leaders decided that power had devolved upon a presidential advisory committee called the *Haut Comité de Sécurité* (HCS). At this point its members included Prime Minister Ghozali and three generals—Nezzar, Belkheir, and Guenaïza—in addition to Foreign Minister Lakhdar Brahimi, and Justice Minister Hamdani Benkhelil. On January 13 the HCS declared the December 26 elections annulled and announced the creation of a High State Council (*Haut Comité d'Etat,* HCE) to serve as a collective presidency until the end of Bendjedid's term in December 1993.

INSURGENCY AND THE
PURSUIT OF DEMOCRACY

The military forced the resignation of Chadli Bendjedid in January 1992 in order to prevent Islamists from seizing control of a political system which it had controlled directly or indirectly since 1965. The High State Council (HCE), a collective executive which ruled for the next two years, outlawed the FIS, dismantled its structures, and arrested many of its leaders. This course triggered nearly a decade of conflict during which violent acts by Islamists and casualties inflicted by security forces caused as many as 150,000 deaths. While many observers termed the bloody struggle a civil war, it seems best characterized as an insurgency, since, in spite of its toll, only a small minority of Algerians supported the Islamists' resort to war and the number of their combatants peaked at no more than 25,000.

When Defense Minister Liamine Zéroual was designated interim president in 1994 to replace the collective executive, his two principal goals were restoring security and reestablishing the legitimacy of a government installed by coup. From its inception the military regime was torn between "eradicators" and "concilia-tors," so that while its forces pursued aggressive and often inhumane tactics, the government also worked behind the scenes to negotiate with elements of an Islamist movement which was also split between moderates and extremists. At the political level, Zéroual led a step by step return to political pluralism. The first step was a presidential election in which voters transformed his appointed presidency into an elected one. He then secured popular approval of Algeria's fourth constitution, aimed at strengthening the presidency and eliminating electoral problems encountered in 1990 and 1991. Finally he organized parliamentary, provincial, and local elections. All of the elections lacked the transparency many citizens desired, but open politi-cal discourse was definitely returning. At the same time, an economy which had been deteriorating since the 1980s was worsened by the dismal security situation.

By 1994 Algeria felt compelled to accept an IMF plan of economic restructuring, which, while stabilizing the government fiscally and gradually restoring growth of GDP, significantly lowered the already declining living standards of millions of its citizens. Income inequality grew, social support systems were dismantled or deprived of funds, and unemployment levels of 30 percent or more became the norm.

Former foreign minister Abdelaziz Bouteflika was elected Zéroual's successor in 1999 and through popular referendum enacted a Law of Civil Concord which conferred amnesty upon most insurgents willing to lay down their arms. Many Algerians questioned aspects of the law, but it set in motion a dynamic which saw the violence decline measurably during the first years of the new decade. While much progress was being made on the Islamist front, tensions between Kabyles and the state, which had first exploded in 1980, did so again in 2001. The conflict eventually led the Bouteflika government to make important concessions to Kabyle protesters, but they proved insufficient to heal the deep cleavages that had separated Arabs and Berbers for decades. Related to these issues were continuing problems over language, women's rights, and growing alienation of the demographic majority of youth and young adults.

It was clear as the 2000s proceeded that the multipartism whose life had been cut short in 1992 was returning with remarkable verve. Algeria's first civilian president had managed during his five years in office to wrest most power from the hands of the military, but then much of that power remained in his own. As Bouteflika began his second term in 2004, serious questions remained about the fairness of the electoral process, the maintenance of a state of emergency first proclaimed on a temporary basis in 1992, limits on freedom of the press, and frequent executive interference with judicial proceedings.

THE HIGH STATE COUNCIL
AND DESCENT INTO WAR

The elections of December 1991, though flawed, were clearly the freest national elections in Algeria's history to that time. Their annulment by a military-dominated security body left many citizens deeply troubled. Amongst the most troubled were the roughly 25 percent of voters who had cast ballots for the FIS. They had played by the rules and passionately believed that the second round, certain to accord them control of the parliament, should have proceeded. Equally troubled, however, were liberals who over the past two years had begun to hope that Algeria was on the track toward truly representative government. But liberals as well as Islamists were divided amongst themselves. Some supporters of the FIS still believed the political process was the best avenue to achieve their goals, while others, many of whom had always been skeptical, were convinced that revolutionary tactics were the only alternative. Many liberals, looking toward the djazarist wing of the FIS, believed the Islamist movement would be willing to work within a democratic system, but a majority feared a legislature dominated by Islamists would sooner or later force a theocratic model upon the country, ending all hopes for democracy. In addition to

Islamists and liberals, of course, there were still many adherents to the single party system long supported by the military who wanted neither a democratic nor an Islamist outcome.

The High State Council named on January 14, 1992, consisted of five members. They were Defense Minister Khaled Nezzar; Ali Kafi, who had been head of the *Office National des Anciens Moudjahidine;* Ali Haroun, minister of human rights in Ghozali's first government; Tedjini Haddam, a former minister of religious affairs; and Mohamed Boudiaf, its president. Boudiaf, a hero of the War of Independence, left the country after disputes with Ben Bella and had lived in exile since 1964. His choice as president was clearly an attempt by the coup leaders to confer legitimacy upon an invented, unconstitutional executive body. Prime Minister Sid Ahmed Ghozali and his cabinet remained in office, but were answerable to the collective presidency.

From the beginning the primary goal of the HCE and its president was repression of the FIS and its supporters. While Abdelkader Hachani and other FIS leaders called upon demonstrators to avoid violence and sought cooperation with other parties—such as the FFS and the FLN—the military began arresting suspected FIS supporters the day after the elections were canceled. News of arrests and violent measures taken by police brought dramatic increases in the number and size of protests, which ranged from street marches to blockades of public buildings, student strikes, and massive demonstrations outside mosques after Friday prayers. On January 22, security forces arrested Abdelkader Hachani on grounds that he was encouraging revolt within the army and on January 28 they arrested Rabah Kébir, one of the FIS's chief spokesmen. They also began limiting press coverage of their activities. By early February estimates of the number of Algerians killed ranged between 50 and 150 and of those wounded between 200 and 700. Several thousand had been imprisoned—many sent to internment camps in the Sahara. On February 9 the High State Council declared a state of siege which empowered the interior minister to take all actions necessary to maintain law and order. The next day Islamists killed six police officers in Algiers and two others during an arrest at Bordj Menaiel. Although there had been earlier attacks on security facilities, these were the first for which Islamists publicly claimed responsibility and are viewed by many as the launching point of the insurrection which plagued the nation for the rest of the decade.

The next month, the HCE began the process of dismantling the FIS as an organization. On March 4 the Algiers Judicial Council officially dissolved the party, a decision which, after appeal, was confirmed by the Supreme Court on April 27. In late March the government dismissed nearly half of the local and provincial councils controlled by the FIS since the 1990 elections, replacing them with government-appointed "executive delegations." More councils were dissolved later in the year. On July 15 a military court at Blida sentenced the already imprisoned Abassi Madani and Ali Benhadj to twelve years of prison, which they served until June 2003, with short intervals of house arrest and probation.

In the meantime, President Mohamed Boudiaf was becoming increasingly proactive. Determined to portray himself as a populist, he preferred to speak in Arabic vernacular rather than in formal Arabic or French. He claimed to be a unifier, helping his people bridge "artificial" gaps of culture, civilization, region, ethnicity, and language, and, as an ardent secularist, insisted that Islam was an integral part of Algerian national culture and could not be hijacked by a single movement or party. One aspect of his policy as a unifier was the key role he played in the nomination of a National Consultative Council. This body, officially installed on April 22, 1992, was designed to replace the dissolved parliament. Some said its role was purely advisory, while others argued it should become an interim legislature. At any rate, its membership of sixty mostly apolitical men and women was designed to appeal to a broad, though mostly progressive spectrum of Algerian society. Another aspect of Boudiaf's unity policy was his attempt to deal with the disfunctionality of the country's political pluralism which had led to the emergence of fifty-one different political parties between 1989 and 1991. He created an umbrella political entity named the *Rassemblement Patriotique National* (RPN, National Patriotic Rally) designed to bring together as many secular parties as possible. During the month of May ten agreed to join the RPN.

Closely connected to Boudiaf's effort to bring smaller secularist parties together was his visceral opposition to the FLN, which, with the dissolution of the FIS, was once again the largest national party, many of whose leaders still maintained positions of power. At the same time, in his most important presidential address, delivered on April 22, he pledged to address the question of institutional corruption. Such an initiative blended seamlessly with his populist approach, since the overwhelming majority of Algerians were convinced that political leaders and heads of state corporations had long been diverting public funds to their own accounts. An earlier assertion by former prime minister Abdelhamid Brahimi maintained that twenty-six billion dollars had been stolen. The anti-corruption plank of Boudiaf's platform was certainly threatening to a number of officers and many former or current FLN politicians.

On the morning of June 29, Boudiaf was giving a speech to businessmen at the House of Culture in Annaba when he was shot dead. The assassin was Second Lieutenant Boumarafi Lembarek, a member of the counterintelligence service not usually a part of the presidential bodyguard. He confessed to the crime, saying he did so "on his own initiative and because of religious conviction." An investigatory commission's first report on July 29 refuted the notion that it was an isolated act and accused the security services of criminal negligence. In September the commission demanded that the government conduct an internal investigation, which the government never did. On December 9 a spokesman for the commission modified its earlier findings, asserting that Lembarek had acted alone at the behest of "those whose path to power had been cut off" but also at the behest of "those who feel threatened by their status and privileges inside and outside of power."[1] Thus the lieutenant was seen as acting for Islamists, for the establishment, or for both.

On July 3, Ali Kafi became the new president of the High State Council and Redha Malek, Chairman of the National Consultative Council, was chosen to fill

1. *Annuaire de l'Afrique du Nord,* vol. XXXI, 1992, pp. 629–30.

the Council's fifth seat. Malek was celebrated for his distinguished diplomatic career, which included a key role in negotiating the Evian Accords. Kafi appointed Belaïd Abdessalam, minister of industry in the Boumediene era, to replace Ghozali as prime minister. As the security and political situation deteriorated, the fragile Algerian economy was weakening. External pressures for economic restructuring and debt rescheduling were growing, but the choice of Abdessalam signaled that the new government was very hesitant to move down the economic path Chadli had gingerly begun to open. Instead Abdessalam determined to freeze economic reform, impose greater economic austerity, and tighten state control. The new government also toned down the anti-corruption rhetoric of Boudiaf and in fact fired its new justice minister in November for suspending five officials charged with corruption.

As the months went by, Islamists launched more and more violent attacks. Most of their targets during 1992 were soldiers, police, or their facilities. But there were other targets as well, the most alarming of which was the Houari Boumediene Airport, where a bomb exploded on August 26 at the international terminal, taking ten lives and injuring at least a hundred. Attempts to thwart such acts did not reduce the violence, however, especially since security operations in suspicious neighborhoods often pursued the totally innocent, a tactic which generated still more opposition. By November, unofficial counts of deaths brought on by the insurgency ranged between 3,000 and 6,000. How many were attributable to insurgents or to the forces of order were unknown. In November the government imposed a curfew in the wilayas of Algiers, Blida, Boumerdès, Tipasa, Bouira, Médéa, and Aïn Delfa, which was later extended to other regions. In December special tribunals were established to try those accused of terrorist acts, a term which in the official view included all anti-regime violence.[2] It is evident that while these steps were being taken important divisions were developing within the military between the hardliners and those who favored dialogue with Islamist moderates—between the eradicators and conciliators, as they were called. Some observers believed, for instance, that the July sentences meted out to FIS leaders would have been considerably harsher had it not been for concerns of the conciliators. In October, in response to widespread public protest, about 1,000 prisoners were freed from detention in the Sahara where conditions were described as abominable. Also Kébir, the FIS spokesman arrested in January, was released to house arrest in April. When he turned up in Europe in August, many believed the authorities had consented to his expatriation. But then in 1993 a special tribunal in Constantine condemned him to death in absentia, a decision attributable in some eyes to eradicators.

During 1993 Islamists, while more than doubling the number of attacks on the military and police, were also aiming at more and more noncombatants. Victims included civil servants, academics, journalists, doctors, and foreigners. In October, three French consular officers were kidnapped and then released with a note demanding that all foreigners leave Algeria within a month. On the other side, while frequently responding to attacks, security forces sometimes launched preemptive

---

2. In this book the term *terrorist* is applied to individuals deliberately targeting noncombatants for ideological, political, or tactical reasons.

strikes which were extremely provocative. Many of these were initiated by special units trained in guerrilla warfare, which the army began assembling in 1992. Amnesty International claimed the military was presiding over a grave deterioration in human rights, including increasing resort to torture. Facts concerning military and police tactics became difficult to ascertain, because the print press, which had become extraordinarily free after 1989, was increasingly muzzled in its coverage of national security issues.

In the months after the 1992 coup many Western governments sent mixed signals. While promoting democracy and democratic processes, many deeply feared the spread of Islamism, convinced that a democratic Islamic state was an oxymoron. France was one such country. It was deeply concerned about the flood of refugees an Islamist victory might send pouring onto its shores and also at the impact of such a victory upon its own Muslim community. But concern for democracy and horror at the rising violence also generated substantial support for a conciliatory approach. Ultimately what mattered most to French policy makers was stability, however. Tight police and intelligence cooperation between the two governments subsisted from 1992 on. France continually replenished arms supplies and by 1994 it began sending helicopters and night vision material to be used in anti-guerrilla operations. It also provided significant financial aid and encouraged the Paris Club and the IMF to do the same. Support for the Algerian regime became especially strong in 1995 after the assassination of several French citizens in Algeria and a number of terrorist attacks on French soil. As the principal Western player in the Algeria crisis, France also played a critical role in the formulation of Algeria policies by the European Union, its member states, and by the United States, most of whose policies were similar, if not always identical.[3]

Faced with the explosion of violence, and perceptions both of inadequacy and disproportionality of its response, the military was also anxious to maintain its own internal unity. Mohamed Lamari replaced Abdelmalek Guenaïza as Chief of Staff. But the latter, considered an extreme eradicator, continued to command the special forces. Liamine Zéroual replaced Khaled Nezzar as minister of defense, although Nezzar retained his seat on the High State Council. Zéroual, aged fifty-two, had resigned from the army in 1989, ostensibly because of Nezzar's plans to restructure the military along French lines and because of Bendjedid's willingness to recognize the FIS. He was viewed by many as a conciliator, however, and may in fact have opened dialogue for a short time with the imprisoned FIS leaders.

In August, Belaïd Abdessalam, whose tenure was viewed by most as a failure, was replaced as prime minister by Redha Malek. Malek strongly believed that Algeria needed economic reform and accepted the necessity of debt rescheduling, deficit reduction, devaluing the currency, and trimming subsidies. A more immediate problem, however, was that the mandate of the HCE was set to expire at the end of 1993. In October a National Committee on Dialogue consisting of three military and five civilians was created in order to work through the issues. Talks with political

3. A senior state department official remarked to the author in 1996 that "Algeria is French territory."

leaders were almost continuous, but ultimately the two largest parties, the FLN and the FFS, refused to negotiate unless the outlawed FIS was reinstated. When the December 31 deadline passed, the High Security Council, which had created the HCE two years earlier, extended its mandate for a month and called for a broader Conference on National Dialogue, where debate extended for weeks. A position as interim president was offered to Abdelaziz Bouteflika, Boumediene's chosen successor in 1979, but he declined, reportedly because he was refused control over military appointments. Finally, on January 30, with the conference failed, the High Security Council appointed Defense Minister Zéroual to the presidency for a three-year transitional period and officially dissolved the High State Council.

THE INSURGENCY

While the main movements and many important leaders of the Islamist insurgency are known, it is often difficult to lay out with precision the internal dynamics of these movements and the interaction amongst them. Even before the 1992 military coup there existed several small groups of Islamists who totally rejected the FIS's political approach and believed jihad was the only way to achieve the goal of an Islamic state. Among these were *Amr bi'l ma'ruf* led by Noureddine Salamna and *Takfir wa'l hijra,* who were popularly known as "the Afghans." The latter were headed by former Bouyalist Mansouri Meliani who was condemned to death in 1987, but had been granted amnesty in 1990. It was his group that undertook the attack on the Tunisia frontier post of Guemmar in 1991.

More important and better organized than the smaller groups was the Armed Islamic Movement (*Mouvement Islamique Armée,* MIA) headed by Abdelkader Chébouti, also an amnestied Bouyalist. Chébouti, while not believing that the political route would prove successful, had promised elected FIS representatives not to engage in acts which would disrupt the parliamentary electoral process. Many of the smaller groups which were urban based were destroyed by security forces or disintegrated during the early months of the insurrection. The MIA, however, centered in the Blida Atlas south of the capital, was initially less vulnerable because of its location. It set about recruiting and training young militants escaping from the urban communes where the Algerian security forces were concentrating most of their attention. Eventually the MIA attracted some 2,000 fighters, and its units spread eastward through the mountains toward Constantine. For many young militants, the emir Chébouti became a mythical figure, known as "the lion of the mountains." However, disputes over recruiting strategies and military tactics soon arose. Chébouti was quite selective in his recruiting and demanded tight discipline. One of his associates, Saïd Makhloufi, ideologically more of a populist, favored mass recruitment. He broke off and established the *Mouvement pour l'Etat Islamique* (MEI, Movement for the Islamic State), which was most active to the east between Boumerdès and Djidjel. By 1993 and 1994, however, as the military was able increasingly to scour the hinterland, both of these movements were severely weakened and the maintenance of central command became impossible.

From the beginning of the crisis, new insurgent cells had continued to emerge as others disappeared and in 1993 many of them, along with a few veterans of the splintering MEI and MIA came together to form the *Groupement Islamique Armé* (GIA, Armed Islamic Group), which eventually became the most radical and violent wing of the Islamist movement. Although some GIA leaders had once been members of the FIS, most had not, and its leadership explicitly condemned the FIS and its overseas executive bureau headed by Kébir, which kept responding to peace overtures made by *dialoguistes* of the regime. The official slogan of the GIA as of 1994 was "no dialogue, no truce, no reconciliation." It specifically condemned all unbelievers and supporters of the "apostate" regime and declared that unless one was a jihadist or supported jihad one was a legitimate target of their war. Over the years it was headed by a number of different national emirs, amongst whom the earliest were Abdelhak Layada, Si Ahmed, and Chérif Gousmi. Functionally, however, the GIA was actually an agglomeration of armed groups, each with its own local emir. As some cells were eliminated by adversaries, others divided, and new ones emerged, the number in the mid-1990s approximated between thirty and forty.

While the GIA was developing in the greater Algiers region, other armed groups had been emerging in Oran, Tlemcen, Aïn Delfa, and other western regions of the country. Under the leadership of Ahmed Ben Aïcha some united in May 1994 to form the *Armée Islamique du Salut* (AIS, Islamic Salvation Army). In July an eastern region of the AIS led by Madani Mezraq also emerged. The movement attracted many FIS loyalists, some fighters from the MIA, and considerable numbers of army deserters. It proclaimed itself the armed wing of the FIS, thus placing itself in direct opposition to the GIA, which labeled the FIS and its supporters traitors. Significantly, while the AIS maintained that jihad could be a means of establishing an Islamic state, it did not consider jihad an imperative. In time the AIS also denounced deliberate targeting of innocent civilians as action contrary to the Qur'an and the Sunna.

The number of rebels in the various armed cells probably peaked in 1996 at about 25,000, although this figure does not account for the significantly larger numbers who voluntarily or through constraint provided economic or logistical support. Also, as the years went by, some of the cells became significantly better armed and equipped, so that their effectiveness improved even when numbers shrank. As noted earlier, while initial attacks mainly targeted security forces and their facilities, by 1995 more and more civilians became victims. Through a series of edicts issued by GIA terrorists, it became clear that anyone who collaborated with the "apostate" regime, attended its schools, followed lifestyles they deemed contrary to Islamic teaching, or failed to support the holy warriors was a legitimate target. Assassinations multiplied, bombs were set off in restaurants, post offices, markets, cinemas, and other public places. Public utilities and other infrastructures were damaged or destroyed. Militants along highways would stop travelers to assess their affiliations or extract payments and hundreds were killed. Communes and villages, often under death threats, were forced to pay fees to insurgents. By 1996 and 1997 warfare had deteriorated to a point where large-scale massacres in villages and neighborhoods were being carried out.

The violence to which Algerians were subjected was far more than the result of confrontation between Islamists and security forces. Islamists frequently attacked rival groups or their supporters, usually citing ideological disputes, but sometimes because of personal or clan rivalries. The tactics adopted by Algeria's police, gendarmerie, and army caused thousands of casualties. These included indiscriminate targeting of young males in communes supportive of the FIS as well as arrests, torture aimed at extracting information, and summary executions. The latter engendered bitterness amongst surviving family members that continued as a political issue well into the next decade. Widespread evidence exists that soldiers dressed as civilians would carry out village massacres that could then be blamed on terrorists. Another allegation is that attacks on civilians close to military outposts—some lasting for hours—often generated no response from a complicit army. A large number of the massacres in the countryside were perpetrated by "patriotic militias." Understanding that the majority of rural Algerians had never been pro-FIS, the military created and armed them to assist in the fight against Islamists grouped in nearby mountains or to oppose villagers supporting them willingly or unwillingly. Some of these confrontations in time blended with longstanding property or clan disputes.

ELECTIONS AND THE CONSTITUTION OF 1996

In one of his first addresses after his 1994 appointment to the presidency, General Liamine Zéroual stated that "the realization of national concord amongst Algerians must be our principal concern. . . . The achievement of this concord will depend upon our will to promote and pursue dialogue . . . and will depend also upon our will to extirpate violence from our society."[4] From then until he left office in 1998, he trod this difficult dialogue-extirpation path strewn with contradictions and pitfalls. Although the majority of Zéroual's cabinet were civilians, the most important members of his inner circle were generals, the most frequently mentioned of whom were Tewfiq Médiène, Mohamed Betchine, Mohamed Lamari, and Benabbès Gheziel. Lamari, Head of the Joint Chiefs of Staff and Gheziel, Chief of the National Gendarmerie, were both eradicators. Médiène and especially Betchine were more in favor of dialogue. It was very difficult for Zéroual to move toward reconciliation without the consensus of this inner circle. For instance, although dialogue with leaders of the outlawed FIS was carried on, Zéroual was limited in the actual concessions he could grant. Like the government, the FIS was divided between hardliners and moderates. Its principal demands were that, before it could ask its followers to renounce violence, the regime must acknowledge its role in initiating it, inaugurate a cease-fire, re-legitimize the party, and free its leaders from prison.

While the secret negotiations were taking place with little progress, representatives of seven Algerian political parties and movements agreed to meet with exiled

---

4. *Annuaire de l'Afrique du Nord,* vol. XXXIII, 1994, p. 454.

FIS leaders in Rome under the auspices of the Sant' Egidio Catholic lay community. Besides the FIS, organizations participating included the Algerian League for
the Defense of Human Rights, the FLN, the FFS, Ben Bella's small Movement for
Democracy in Algeria, the Trotskyist Workers' Party of Louisa Hanoune, al-Nahda,
and Contemporary Muslim Algeria. While the General Union of Algerian Workers,
the Communist Party, and Saïd Saadi's RCD declined to participate, those in Rome
who signed a Platform for a National Contract on January 13, 1995, represented a
broad spectrum of Algerian political opinion.

The Platform called for the convening of a national conference to create a short-
term transitional authority to oversee free and pluralistic elections that would permit
the Algerian people to choose a new government under rules established by the
constitution of 1989. It also outlined the basic values and principles underlying its
program and the system it wished to implement. These included the affirmation of
basic human rights, popular sovereignty, the rule of law, and the separation of powers. It rejected all forms of dictatorship and required the army to withdraw from the
political field. While guaranteeing freedom of religion to all, the Platform affirmed
Islam as an important element of Algerian identity as it did also the Tamazight and
Arabic languages. As measures to precede negotiations, it called for the liberation
of all political prisoners including leaders of the FIS, restoration of press freedoms,
and reopening of the political field to all parties, including the FIS. It called for
the ending of torture, capital executions, extra-judicial executions and reprisals
against civilians, implicitly a condemnation of security-force practices. But it also
demanded an end to attacks upon civilians, foreigners, and public property, implicitly
condemning terrorist tactics.

The Zéroual government quickly rejected the Sant' Egidio platform, claiming
that because of the auspices under which it was drafted, it represented unacceptable outside interference in Algeria's internal affairs. Despite this official rationale,
however, it appears that two other factors were more important in its decision. The
first was that acceptance of the platform might confirm that the military was, in
fact, guilty of acts of extreme violence which it was officially denying. The other
was that demand for the military to return to the barracks was unacceptable at this
time to hardliners of the inner circle and elsewhere.

In April, Zéroual decided to resume negotiations with imprisoned FIS leaders. Mohamed Betchine, chief of military security and minister-counselor to the
president, met several times with Madani, who in a sign of reconciliation had been
transferred to house arrest. These talks led to assemblage of a broader group of FIS
leaders in June who agreed to issue a call for an end to violence and to change the
name of their party so that it could participate in upcoming elections. Apparently
Benhadj and a few others refused to associate themselves with these concessions,
however. Without support of his closest colleague, Madani ultimately pulled back
and negotiations broke down. In retaliation, the government placed both of them
in solitary confinement, where they remained for the next two years. When news
of the secret negotiations was made public, GIA Emir Djamel Zitouni threatened all
FIS leaders who negotiated with the government with "physical elimination" and
expelled Benhadj and Madani from leadership roles in the GIA, which, of course,
they had never held.

Connected very closely to dialogue with the FIS was the question of elections, which lay at the heart of the appointed government's search for legitimacy. In November 1994, Zéroual announced that presidential elections would be held before the end of the next year and in January 1995, just as the Sant' Egidio platform was taking center stage, he installed a special commission to prepare for them. In March he began an arduous series of talks with leaders of political parties and other movements trying to win commitment to his plans, talks which dragged on until July. Many believed that presidential elections before parliamentary elections would only reinforce the power of a military-dominated executive. The major parties that had negotiated in Rome steadfastly opposed them. Nevertheless, in August the government announced that elections would be held on November 16 and invited candidates wishing to appear on the ballot to collect signatures. To qualify, 75,000, representing at least half of Algeria's provinces would be necessary. Those whose candidacies were accepted besides Zéroual were Saïd Saadi of the secularist RCD, Mahfoud Nahnah, head of the moderate Islamist HAMAS, and Nouredine Boukhrouh, leader of the Party for Algerian Reform (PRA), a liberal Islamic movement. The security situation was extraordinarily tense as election day approached. A tract issued by the GIA warned that "those who go to the polls" will finish "in a casket." The AIS cautioned Algerians against leaving their homes on election day, while the FIS called upon all to boycott the elections. Nevertheless, the turnout for Algeria's first free presidential elections was nearly 75 percent of registered voters. In balloting that international observers concluded was basically free and fair, about 61 percent voted for Zéroual, 25.6 percent for Nahnah, 9.6 percent for Saadi, and 3.8 percent for Boukhrouh.

Shortly after his inauguration, Zéroual appointed the relatively unknown Kabyle, Ahmed Ouyahia, as prime minister and he then selected a cabinet composed mostly of members of the preceding government, but he also assigned portfolios to HAMAS and the PRA. During January 1996, in which the month of Ramadan also began, violence, which had relented somewhat during the elections, exploded once more, with attacks on trains, buses, public utilities, and especially on individual civilians, including women venturing out without head scarves, journalists, civil servants, and artists. In spring seven monks from the monastery of Tibérhine were abducted and murdered. Later the Roman Catholic Archbishop of Oran was assassinated.

In spite of the turmoil, the government announced that parliamentary elections would be held the next year, but that before they could go forward a format needed to be created that would protect them from the problems encountered in 1990 and 1991. This required the drafting of a new constitution, which the government did during the spring and summer of 1996. After calling for consultations with many parties and movements during summer and early fall, the government's initial draft remained largely unchanged and a referendum on its ratification was held in November. In spite of the fact that several political parties asked their supporters to abstain, the new constitution was ratified on November 28 by what the government claimed was 80 percent of voters in an 80 percent turnout, numbers that raised many eyebrows.

While building upon the constitution of 1989, Algeria's fourth constitution did make significant changes. The most important was the strengthening of the executive branch. The 1996 constitution gave Algeria a bicameral legislature for the first time. The lower house, the Peoples National Assembly (APN), was to be chosen by popular vote every five years. Members of the upper house, the Council of the Nation, were selected two thirds by communal and wilaya councils and one third by the president of the Republic. Legislation was initiated in the APN, but in order to become law 75 percent of the Council of the Nation needed to approve it, which thus gave the president veto authority that was irreversible. The constitution invested the president with greater emergency powers than that of 1989 and continued his right to appoint and remove the prime ministers without parliamentary consent. It did, however, limit his tenure to two five-year terms.

Article 42 of the new constitution specifically addressed the party problems growing out of that of 1989. It recognized and guaranteed the right to create political parties but specifically forbade the use of this right for creation of parties hostile to the basic identity, liberty, or security of the nation. Furthermore, no political party could be founded on a "religious, linguistic, racial, sex, corporatist, or regional basis."[5]

In spite of the fact that 1997 was the bloodiest year the country had experienced since the start of the insurrection, General Zéroual moved forward with the parliamentary elections he considered essential to overcoming the sorry legacy of 1991–92. After two months of discussions with the National Transitional Council, which had replaced the National Consultative Council, and with leaders of various parties, the government in early March issued a law establishing electoral guidelines. It fixed the number of seats in the lower house at 380. In order to avoid the disparity between popular vote and seats won that had occurred in 1991, it assigned electoral districts to wilayas in proportion to their populations and then drew the borders of each. It also permitted voting by Algerians living abroad, but elections were still by party list. Recognized moderate religious parties were required to change their names. Nahnah's HAMAS became the *Mouvement pour la Société et de la Paix* (Movement for Society and Peace, MSP) and Abdallah Djaballah's Movement of the Islamic Renaissance (Nahda) became simply Ennahda.

Just before the new electoral laws were issued, supporters of the regime, including Prime Minister Ouyahia and Abdelkader Bensalah of the National Transitional Council, created their own party called the *Rassemblement Nationale Démocratique* (RND, National Democratic Rally). When the elections were held on June 5 the official reported turnout was 65 percent of registered voters. The RND, to no one's surprise, attracted the largest number of votes, 32 percent of the total, and took 156 of the parliament's 380 seats. Second was the MSP with 14 percent of the votes and 69 seats. Just below it was the FLN with nearly 14 percent but just 62 seats. Ennahda won 34, the FFS 19, the RCD 18, and Hanoune's Trotskyist Workers' Party 4. The rest went to independents or others. Not surprisingly most parties protested the outcome. All claimed that their access to electronic media was limited. Some claimed that ballot boxes were either stuffed or destroyed, others that votes from military bases were not monitored and far too large. The Joint International Observation Mission, which had dispatched 106 observers under the auspices of the

5. See the constitution of 1996 in *Annuaire de l'Afrique du Nord,* vol. XXXV, 1996, p. 450.

United Nations, reported that while some observers believed they had free access to the process many felt they had not; so it wrote that it could not comment officially on the correctness of process or its outcome. It was nevertheless significant that all of the Sant' Egidio parties, which had refused participation in the presidential elections, did participate in these.

After the elections Ouyahia was named prime minister again, and he organized a coalition government based on the RND, MSP, and FLN, distributing portfolios mainly according to party strength. In spite of continuing violence, the government in May 1996 began a secret process of negotiations with the AIS. General Boughaba, then commander of the Constantine military district, established the first contacts with Madani Mezrag, hoping to convince the AIS guerrillas that they could benefit from a law of clemency recently promulgated by Zéroual. Negotiations were then taken over by Smaïl Lamari, who was closer to the inner circle of generals. The military took several steps to accommodate the guerrillas. In July 1997, Benabbès Gheziel, the hardline chief of the National Gendarmerie, was removed; Abdelkader Hachani was freed from preventive detention, where he had been since 1992; and Abassi Madani was let out of prison. On August 20, Lamari and Mezrag signed a secret agreement, the principal element of which was a grant of amnesty to all guerrilla groups that would lay down their arms and enter into a truce.[6] In compliance with this secret accord, Mezrag the next month declared what officials termed a "unilateral" cease fire effective October 1.[7]

Completion of the parliamentary election process required selection of the Council of the Nation. Before this could be done, however, new communal and wilaya councils had to be elected to replace those of 1990, especially since many had been dissolved by government edict. These elections, held on October 23, brought an even more resounding victory for the RND than those in June. The government party took more than half of local and provincial seats, leading to massive protests in Algiers and other cities. When the indirect elections for the Council of the Nation took place in December, the councils gave eighty of the ninety-six seats to the RND. The other forty-eight, in accordance with the new constitution, were filled by the president. In spite of sincere efforts at several levels to reach out to Islamist and other opponents and to restore the political pluralism begun in 1989, the process conducted by Zéroual and his team had clearly been one from the top down. Many Algerians believed at the end of 1997 that the power of the presidency and of the military that controlled it had only been enhanced. Yet it was clear that political participation in Algeria was more dynamic and widespread than it had ever been, despite dissatisfaction with some outcomes.

In 1997 and 1998, concern about the responsibility of security forces for Algeria's mounting bloodshed led to more and more calls for independent international investigation into human rights abuses. Zéroual permitted a UN team with limited access to gather information, but most saw its mission as a sham. As Algeria's international stature declined and guerrilla attacks continued, accusations of regime corruption

---

6. Madani was soon placed under house arrest, apparently for violating terms of parole.
7. The written agreement was not made public until December 1999.

were also spreading, raising more and more questions about the president's record. Yet most Algerians were astonished when, in a televised address on September 11, he announced that there would be new presidential elections in February 1999, nearly a year and a half before expiration of his term, and that he would not be a candidate. Most observers were convinced that military hardliners, led by Chief of Staff Mohamed Lamari, had forced the resignation. Certainly deep resentment had developed amongst many eradicators over the creation of the National Democratic Rally and the power it had brought to the man *they* had raised to the presidency. They also resented his attempts to usurp military functions, such as authorizing a general in his group to negotiate the truce with the AIS. Many probably resented as well Ouyahia's and Betchine's diversion of financial assets away from them to their own entourage. Betchine, minister-counselor to the president, resigned on October 18 and Prime Minister Ouyahia stepped down on December 14. His successor, Smail Hamdani, a longtime aide of Houari Boumediene, promised free and fair elections and Chief of Staff Lamari pledged that the army would remain neutral.

FAILED ECONOMICS AND PARTIAL RESTRUCTURING

While ideological, political, generational, and clan factors are all critical to understanding Algeria's turmoil, the importance of economic realities cannot be overstressed. The failures of the "industrializing industries" policy that persistently invested massive hydrocarbon revenues in dysfunctional state corporations were discussed in chapters 7 and 8. Because of the devastating decline in agricultural production and the failure of the industrial sector to provide consumer products, an increasing share of hydrocarbon revenues was needed to pay for the importation of foods, pharmaceuticals, basic consumer goods, and equipment. Then, as gas and especially oil prices plummeted, the state had to resort increasingly to external borrowing. Realizing the dangers that lay ahead and with advice from the Paris Club and the IMF in 1987 and 1988, Bendjedid, as noted in the preceding chapter, launched a program of economic liberalization. But, for a variety of reasons, that program moved forward quite haltingly through most of the 1990s. Popular opposition to the termination of government jobs, subsidies, and support systems was widespread, but elites, too, were reluctant to dismantle institutions and networks from which they and their clients benefited enormously. Attracting private capital into long-term investment was also difficult, because of the poor security situation, mistrust of legal frameworks, and the less than supportive bank credit policies. By the late 1990s, after some restructuring, productivity began to improve, but by 2003 Algeria's per capita income of $1,890 ranked 115th in the world.[8]

One of the major problems Algeria had faced since independence was the rapid growth of population. While birth rates dropped from 4.5 percent in 1981 to 2.7 percent in 1994, death rates had also fallen significantly, so that population by the

8. World Bank figure using Atlas index. In purchasing power parity, per capita income was $5,800, ranking 105th.

mid-1990s was increasing at about 2.1 percent annually and more than 30 percent of that population was not yet of working age. The 1988 law that created hundreds of Public Economic Enterprises (EPEs) was expected to inaugurate an era of greater productivity in the industrial sector, but it failed to do so. Increasing amounts of public funds were, in fact, being used in the early 1990s to bail them out. Many retained the inefficiencies of the larger enterprises from which they had spun off, while the state still determined salary levels and forbade firing of employees. Evidence is also widespread that many executives were diverting resources to their own interests.

Another problem was inflation. In late 1989 the IMF had offered limited financial assistance contingent upon a number of reforms, the most critical of which was devaluation of the dinar so that Algerian products would become more attractive in international markets. Between 1989 and 1991 the value of the dinar in U.S. dollars was lowered by two thirds. But given the production constraints in place, devaluation did virtually nothing to stimulate non–hydrocarbon exports. Instead, it tripled the cost of critical imports, which sent inflation soaring, vastly increased the cost of government subsidies, and severely lowered the standard of living of the majority of Algerians. Table 9.1 details the virtual stagnation of the economy during the first half of the 1990s.

As per capita GDP was falling, Algeria was prevented from dealing with the economy's fundamental problems by the legacy of borrowing it had resorted to for importation of the basics. External debt had risen from $26.4 billion in 1989 to $28.7 by 1994, representing 67.8 percent of GDP, and its servicing had risen from 69 percent of export earnings to an estimated 92 percent. The problem of how to handle the debt generated spirited debate within the political establishment. Economic reformers such as Mouloud Hamrouche and Redha Malek favored working with the IMF to reschedule the debt, which they knew the IMF would consent to only if they agreed to serious steps toward liberalization. Traditional FLN leaders such as Belaïd Abdessalam strongly objected to such steps, not only because they still adhered to a considerable extent to the Boumedienist model, but also because, as dedicated nationalists, they resented the thought of Algeria being under the thumb of foreign bodies such as the IMF, the Paris Club, or the World Bank. The option traditionalists preferred was re-financing, particularly of short-term debt, which was a small but significant percentage of the whole. This they were able to

Table 9.1 Economic Growth Indicators (in percentages)

Average Annual Production	1980–1990	1990–1995
Agriculture	4.6	1.3
Industry	2.3	-1.1
Services	3.8	1.3
Exports, good & services	4.1	.2
Investment	-2.3	-4.7
Total GDP	2.8	.1

Source: Ahmed Dahmani, *Annuaire de l'Afrique du Nord* XXVII (1998): 145.

accomplish in March 1992 with American and French assistance under the aegis of the Crédit Lyonnais. When Belaïd Abdessalam became prime minister in July of that year, he declared that Algeria was now in the "war economy" that was needed to restore Algeria's national authority and international standing. Maintaining both the economy and finance portfolios himself, Abdessalam denounced the reforms of his predecessors, promised there could be no further devaluation of the dinar, and insisted that a prerequisite to any further liberalization would be protection of the internal market and restoration of national production to the extent that it could meet internal demand.

Abdessalam's policies proved an abject failure and by mid-1993 it appeared the country might soon be in default of its external debt. His successor, Redha Malek, quickly began discussions with the Paris Club and the IMF. The discussions slowed somewhat because of the difficult political transition underway, but in the spring of 1994, as a result of these discussions, Malek raised prices on several foods by 25 to 100 percent and devalued the dinar by 40 percent. The news of concessions and rescheduling sparked massive labor union protests. Nevertheless, Malek on April 13 delivered a letter of intent to the IMF. Two days later he resigned, a resignation which Zéroual accepted, reportedly in order to avoid personal responsibility for economic policies that were so unpopular. The new prime minister, Mokdad Sifi, however, was allowed to move forward with negotiations and on June 1 a standby agreement permitting the start of a rescheduling process was finally reached. International creditors gathered at the Paris Club agreed to a $5 billion debt service reduction, and initial cash assistance of more than $3 billion. With this accord, annual debt servicing, which might well have exceeded 1994 export earnings, fell to 55.3 percent.

In March 1995 more aid came as the Algerian government consented to a "program of stabilization" aimed at reducing inflation to 5 percent annually, limiting the state budget deficit to 5 percent of GDP, and striving for a growth rate of 6 percent. The agreement also foresaw the elimination of all price controls, the opening of Algerian markets, and the withdrawal of the state from economic sectors. The question of which economic sectors and at what time became subjects of ongoing debate with the IMF. The regime agreed to withdraw over the next three years from the sectors of tourism, distribution, public works, services, and road transport. Telecommunications was privatized in 2000 and cement and metallurgy in 2002, but privatization of the hydrocarbon industry was never on the table. By 2001, about 1,000 public enterprises had been shut down. Aside from SONATRACH, there were still 83 EPE's functioning in important sectors and 377 local companies, which together carried a debt burden of about $9 billion. As many state companies in fact disappeared and individual initiative was encouraged, it was expected that industrial investment would stimulate industrial production, but it did not. Instead, with the elimination of state control over external trade, importation became the most profitable business in the country with clientage networks emanating from the state-controlled energy sector supplying much of the funding they required. Many of the military played key roles in this new system. At the same time, *trabendo,* a sector which had first appeared in the 1980s for the sale of goods smuggled from Europe, was transformed into a much larger parallel economic sector for the distribution of goods of many provenances.

Although efforts to attract investment were unsuccessful in most sectors, foreign firms contributed billions of dollars to the hydrocarbon sector—in partnership, of course—with the dominant SONATRACH. Many new reserves of natural gas and petroleum were discovered and production and export of both expanded considerably. In 2003 Algeria had the fifth-largest natural gas reserves and was the second-largest gas exporter. In petroleum reserves, it ranked fourteenth and exports, though supposedly limited by OPEC quotas, rose to 1.1 million barrels per day.

The economy improved considerably after the start of structural re-adjustment, but it did so mostly because of increases in hydrocarbon exports; sharp rises in oil prices, which by 2004 reached the highest in history in nominal dollars, and the dramatic decline in debt servicing.

Table 9.2 Annual Economic Indicators

	1998	1999	2000	2001	2002
GDP (US $ bn)	47.8	48.3	54.2	53.9	55.7
Real GDP growth (percent)	5.1	3.2	2.4	2.2	4.1
Consumer price inflation (percent)	6.2	2.1	-0.6	3.5	2.3
Population (millions)	30.1	30.6	31.2	31.7	32.3
Exports (US $ bn)	10.14	12.32	21.71	19.09	19.71
Imports (US $ bn)	8.63	8.96	9.20	9.48	10.37
Total external debt (US $ bn)	30.7	28.0	25.3	22.5	21.7
Debt service ratio, paid	42.1	36.6	18.6	20.0	15.1

Source: *Economist Intelligence Unit Country Report, Algeria,* August 2003.

Structurally, as table 9.3 indicates, the Algerian economy had changed little over the decade, except for the significant decline in manufacturing.

Table 9.3 Algerian Economic Structure (percent of GDP)

	1992	2001	2002
Agriculture	12.1	10.7	10.0
Industry	49.7	53.0	52.7
Manufacturing	12.3	7.9	7.3
Services	38.2	36.2	37.3
Private consumption	51.8	43.6	44.3
General government consumption	16.0	14.7	15.3
Imports of goods and services	23.9	21.7	26.0

Source: World Bank, 2003.

While at the macroeconomic level Algeria's economy was growing by the late 1990s and early 2000s, the advent of structural readjustment had a mostly negative impact on the lives of ordinary Algerians, which had already been worsening materially for a decade. The closure of 1,000 public companies entailed the loss of about 400,000 jobs. The official unemployment rate in 1998 was 29.5 percent and in 2003 it was 28.4 percent, though many outside observers during these years placed it as high as 32 percent. The unemployment rate for Algerians aged sixteen to nineteen was 53.6 percent and that for those aged twenty to twenty-four was 55.6 percent, which contributed to the sense of hopelessness many had. Estimates were that, in order to meet the employment demands of a burgeoning population, 300,000 jobs per year would have to be created, something the economy was not close to achieving. By the late 1990s real income had fallen by 35 percent from its 1993 level and by 2001 roughly 40 percent of the population was living beneath the level of poverty. But income distribution was also becoming more inequitable. Income of the poorest 10 percent of Algerians was reckoned at 2.8 percent of GDP while that of the wealthiest 10 percent stood at 27 percent. The size of an average household, often within a two- or three-room apartment, was greater than seven, with surveys showing that in some of the poorer communes as many as three families together were crammed into the same apartment, with individuals forced to sleep in shifts. Nevertheless, under pressure from the IMF, spending on public housing was reduced 70 percent in 1995–96. In order to prevent further housing deterioration, it was estimated in 1999 that at least 100,000 units a year would have to be constructed, and that, for the situation to improve, at least double that number, a total of one million, would be required. With dramatic decreases in state funding, educational spending as a percentage of GDP fell to half of what it had been in the 1980s, as did declining expenditure on public health. The water situation was so poor that drinking water in certain urban neighborhoods was only available three or four times a week.

In the wake of mounting social tensions, the Benflis government, which came into power in 2000, inaugurated in 2001 an Emergency Reconstruction Program designed to reduce unemployment, improve infrastructures, and increase economic growth to 6 percent annually. To achieve these goals, the government pledged to allocate more than $6 billion through 2004 for labor-intensive housing, water, and road projects. But bureaucratic difficulties, disputes over priorities, regional competition, and funding problems kept the program from moving forward as rapidly as promised. With regard to the continuing privatization issue, while governments talked of progress, little was actually achieved.

ABDELAZIZ BOUTEFLIKA AND CIVIL CONCORD

President Zéroual had originally announced that elections for his replacement would take place in February 1999, but due apparently to requests from several parties for more preparation time, they were pushed back to April 15. Forty-eight individuals announced their candidacies, twelve presented petitions with the required 75,000 signatures, but ultimately the Constitutional Council was able to certify only seven of them. They were those of former prime ministers Mouloud Hamrouche and Mokdad Sifi, Hocine Aït Ahmed of the FFS, Youssef Khateb, who chaired the abortive national dialogue in 1994–95, moderate Islamists Abdallah Djaballah and Ahmed Taleb al Ibrahimi, and former foreign minister Abdelaziz Bouteflika.

Although Bouteflika was clearly the choice of the military, he and the six other candidates were all civilians. In spite of the authoritarian nature of key aspects of military rule since 1992, particularly where security was concerned, the growing candor of political discourse had led to open discussion of the role of the military in the Republic, a subject which had been totally taboo since independence. At the same time, the army itself, increasingly concerned about criticism from the international community and human rights groups, determined it wanted to reduce its visibility as much as possible, although most senior generals were not willing to relinquish ultimate power.

The campaign, which began officially on March 25, was open, free, and extremely demanding, requiring appearances from one end of the country to the other.[9] Although the military did not openly speak up for Bouteflika, he nevertheless held immense advantages over his competitors. He had far more money to spend on newspaper ads and public events and also managed through a variety of techniques to receive much greater coverage on state-owned radio and television. More importantly, the system was behind him. He enjoyed the support of four of the most important parties in parliament, of the powerful UGTA, and of an assortment of professional associations with deep roots in the Algerian bureaucracy. It was obvious from polling samples that Bouteflika would win a substantial plurality if not an absolute majority of votes cast.

By early April, several candidates began to express concerns about the mechanics of the election, one of which was the distribution of two separate forms for reporting results at each polling station. The vote tally was to be listed on one form, while the signatures of the officials certifying the tally were placed on a second one. On Tuesday, April 13, 703 mobile polling stations began collecting votes from Saharan nomads and isolated communities in the high plateaux and on Wednesday votes were taken in "special polling stations" reserved for the army and other security forces. As these polls began, the six opposition candidates claimed there were irregularities at the sites, demanded that ballots from both be excluded, and requested a meeting with the president of the Republic to discuss their concerns. When Zéroual declined their request on April 14, they issued a communiqué stating that, because the president would not hear their complaints, they had "decided upon collective withdrawal from the elections and non-recognition of the legitimacy of the results of the polls." They also asked all of their representatives engaged in administration and monitoring of the elections to leave. The withdrawal of the opposition less than twenty-four hours before the formal election day shocked observers inside and outside the country. The official turnout on April 15 was 60.3 percent of registered voters, many still voting for retired candidates, but 73.8 percent of the votes went to Bouteflika, who was inaugurated president on April 27.

---

9. Except for Aït Ahmed, who was hospitalized with a heart condition.

While not defining them carefully during the election, the main planks of Bouteflika's platform were economic growth, security, and national reconciliation. He chose soon after his election to launch national reconciliation as his first initiative. In spite of the misgivings of many eradicators, Bouteflika began consultation with Islamists and won support of Abdelkader Mezrag, Abassi Madani, and Kébir. On July 13 he issued the Law of Civil Concord and announced it would be submitted to a national referendum in September. The act was basically the inscription into law of certain aspects of the accord between the army and the AIS secretly signed by Smaïl Lamari and Mezrag two years earlier.

Article 1 of the Law of Civil Concord stated that:

> The present law is in keeping with the larger plan for reestablishing civil concord and has as its objective the institution of special measures to relieve from standard penalties persons involved or who have been involved in acts of terrorism or subversion who express in good faith their wish to cease their criminal activities and to grant them the opportunity to put in concrete form this wish through re-entry into society. In order to benefit from the provisions of the present law, the persons indicated above must inform the appropriate authorities that they are ceasing all terrorist activity and present themselves to these authorities.[10]

The law then specifies that individuals mentioned in Article 1 can be subject to three different levels of judicial treatment: exemption from prosecution, probation for three to twelve years, or imprisonment for not longer than ten years. It also calls for release of all previously incarcerated individuals subject to exemption from prosecution. The decision as to which individuals fit into which of the three categories was left up to provincial and state agencies. The law refers specifically to several types of crime: 1) homicide, 2) rape, 3) infliction of permanent disability, 4) collective massacres, and 5) setting off explosives at public places or in places frequented by the public. Only perpetrators of the last two do not qualify for relief of punishment and are, under the criminal code, subject to the death penalty. But Article 41 then states that "the dispositions mentioned are not applicable, except where needed, to people having belonged to organizations which have voluntarily and spontaneously decided to put an end to acts of violence and have placed themselves completely [at] the disposition of the state."[11] In a presidential decree of January 10, 2000, Bouteflika essentially elided the terms "except where needed" and declared that these individuals "shall have full possession of their civil rights and shall benefit from the status of exemption from prosecution."[12] Basically this article and the ensuing decree granted total amnesty to the fighters of the AIS.

In promoting his policy of reconciliation, Bouteflika argued that although there would certainly be many bumps along the way, failing to deal with a tragedy that

10. *Journal Officiel de la République Algérienne.*
11. Ibid.
12. Luis Martinez, "Les obstacles à la Politique de Réconciliation nationale," *Annuaire de l'Afrique du Nord,* vol. XXXVIII, 1999, p. 125.

had enveloped the country for eight years and caused 100,000 deaths might well lead to 300,000 more deaths and up to three million wounded.[13] In the referendum held on September 16, the official tally indicated 98.6 percent of the 85 percent of voters turning out approved of the law, demonstrating the profound desire of Algerians to bring an end to a decade of horrors and return to normalcy. By January 13, 2000, the final date for compliance, about 5,500 militants had turned themselves in, and subsequently about 5,000 prisoners condemned for "acts of subversion and terrorism" were released.

As President Bouteflika had predicted, the Law of Civil Concord did encounter many bumps along the way. One came from the unbalanced language of the law, which held only Islamists responsible for the eight years of violence. This was quite contrary to the language of the 1997 accord on which Islamist supporters were told the Law of Civil Concord would be based. Many felt they had been deceived and betrayed, especially after the assassination in November of Abdelkader Hachani, which they attributed to security forces. Some former FIS leaders, including Abassi Madani, withdrew their support. Also troubled were the "families of the disappeared" whose loved ones had been arrested and carried off by police or the military, never to be seen again. The number of these disappeared has been reckoned at between 4,000 and 10,000, but the law offered them no recourse. On the other side were families of victims of terrorism. While the law did give them the right to civil suits, thousands were furious at the amnesty granted to murderers and assassins and they formed associations aimed at changing the law.

While some GIA militants did turn themselves in by the deadline, many resented the total amnesty granted to AIS members and the uncertainty of the treatment they would receive if they surrendered. Hundreds decided to fight on, many associated with a prominent group known as the Salafist Group for Preaching and Combat (GSPC). At the same time, elements of the military, disapproving of the law from the outset launched major offensives against the guerrillas immediately after January 13. The result was that the number of violent incidents actually increased during the year 2000, and the number of deaths, rising to about 5,000, was roughly double that of 1999. By 2001, however, the number once again declined except for occasional spikes in mountainous eastern areas and in the Sahara. Nabil Sahraoui, emir of the GSPC, was killed in 2004 after his group had ambushed a military unit.

Debates over national reconciliation and the Law of Civil Concord took place against the background of an ongoing struggle for power within the regime. While this struggle involved a multiplicity of factors, the principal ones concerned the relationship between the presidency and the military and between the presidency and the prime ministry. While both Chief of Staff Lamari and his predecessor Khaled Nezzar were present at his inauguration, Bouteflika, a civilian brought into office via a troubled election, early on showed signs he wanted to prove that he was not the generals' puppet. One sign of this was that, although retired general Larby Belkheir was brought into the presidential cabinet and eventually became its director, Bouteflika

13. Many analysts believe the actual number of deaths to have been as high as 150,000.

himself retained the position of defense minister. Apparently eradicators were opposed early on to the Law of Civil Concord, and after the amnesty decree of January 10, 2000, a military spokesman said the army had not heard of it before the public announcement. In February 2000, Bouteflika personally undertook the reshuffling of many of the operational positions within the army, and throughout the rest of his first term, rumors kept surfacing that the hierarchy was pressuring him to resign.

The fact that Bouteflika did not replace Prime Minister Hamdani or his cabinet until the end of the year—eight months after his election—is said to have been related to the military's attempt to arrange some of the portfolios. It is also true, however, that Bouteflika was having difficulties adjusting to the constitution of 1996 and the division of power created by its definition of the prime ministry. The head of government he finally did choose, economics and finance specialist Ahmed Benbitour, presided over a cabinet composed primarily of technocrats with limited political standing. Benbitour resigned on August 26, complaining about the "minor status" to which he had been relegated. Many other ministers and members of parliament also felt diminished by what they labeled an imperial presidency.

Benbitour was replaced by Ali Benflis, who had managed Bouteflika's presidential campaign and was an FLN member of parliament. After the electoral victory he became Interim Secretary General of the Presidency and then Director of the Cabinet of the Presidency. A lawyer by training, Benflis was appointed minister of justice in 1988 and presided over reform of the judicial system during the period of political liberalization. He also became a member of the FLN Political Bureau and Central Committee of the FLN. With the declaration of the state of emergency, and the incarceration of thousands, Benflis insisted that persons held in detention centers should be accorded their full rights under the law; when the government refused to recognize those rights, he stepped down from his ministry. The ability of Bouteflika to appoint a close confidant as prime minister demonstrated that he was finally taking charge.

FOREIGN POLICY

A major strength Bouteflika brought to his presidency was his concern for and expertise in foreign policy. Conscious of the multi-layered importance of the Franco-Algerian relationship, Bouteflika in June 2000 became the first Algerian president in nearly twenty years to make a state visit to France. There, with major concern about economic relations and security interests, he declared that "Algeria wishes to maintain extraordinary relations with France—not banal, not normal, but exemplary—and exceptional."[14] Although he was reluctant to engage in serious dialogue with Morocco over the Western Sahara, he did participate in the France-Africa summit. On March 2, 2003, President Jacques Chirac landed at Algiers to begin a three-day state visit, the first by a French head of state since the former colony won

14. *Le Monde,* June 17, 2000.

its independence.[15] Traveling along Zirout-Youcef Boulevard (the former Boulevard Carnot) and the length of the waterfront, the motorcade was greeted by more than 500,000 Algerians waving tricolors and the national flag, chanting "Chi-rac! Chi-rac!" and "Vi-sas! Vi-sas!" In a calmer setting, Chirac placed a wreath at a monument to the 800 killed in the November 2001 mudslides and then rode up the steep hills behind the city to pay his respects at the Monument of the Martyrs where Algerian and French flags flapped together in the breeze. That visit was certainly one of powerful historical significance. The next day Chirac delivered a speech before both houses of parliament in which he spoke of the complex, often painful relationship between the two peoples as well as the seven years of "murderous and at times inexpiable" war. He then went on to call for a strengthened political dialogue to lay the foundation for a special economic partnership and the renewal of cultural, technical, and scientific cooperation. In 2003 and 2004 intelligence and military relationships were also strengthening.

During his first term Bouteflika also visited twice with American president George W. Bush and traveled to Texas to meet with executives of oil companies. After the terrorist attacks of September 11, 2001, intelligence cooperation between the two countries strengthened as the United States became increasingly concerned that the Sahara could become a transit zone as well as a staging ground for groups with ties to al-Qa'ida.

CONTINUATION OF THE KABYLE QUESTION

President Bouteflika's diplomatic skills did not invariably translate into effective policies on the home front. On April 26, 2001, he delivered a nationwide speech calling for *national* concord and the need to address critical issues that had generated Algeria's conflict in the first place, so that stronger social cohesion could develop. The Law of Civil Concord was only one element of a much broader program which should address moral, social, political, economic, and civilizational issues. Unfortunately, the president's speech failed to mention ethnic and linguistic problems, just as a wave of protests was exploding across the Kabylia that would soon degenerate into outright insurrection in many places.

On April 18 at Beni Douala, near Tizi Ouzou, gendarmes shot a young high school student inside their headquarters. He died two days later, on the anniversary of Berber Spring, and more than 4,000 people attended his funeral. On April 22, three lycée students at Bejaïa in the Lesser Kabylia were questioned and physically assaulted by police, allegedly for shouting pro-Kabyle slogans. Riots broke out there and then spread, by early May, to sixteen different localities in Kabylia. One organized demonstration assembled between 400,000 and 500,000 protesters and another in Algiers brought out 100,000. But government response was determined. Within a year, more than 100 Kabyles had been killed and as many as 5,000 wounded.

15. There had been many unofficial visits over the years by presidents and premiers.

Reasons for the unrest are complex. The government had made some concessions to Kabyles in recent years, including creation in 1990 of a special institute at Tizi Ouzou to teach Tamazight and the recognition at the end of 1995 that Berber was a dimension of national identity. Nevertheless, the sense of cultural and linguistic exclusion that had developed since independence and exploded during the Berber Spring of 1980 had continued and was clearly exacerbated with the formal completion of the national process of Arabization on July 5, 2000. Rising unemployment and the sense of indignity it entailed for young men across the nation, including Kabyles, also contributed to the protests. Connected to the employment issue was the growing perception of the imperiousness of the regime held responsible for it, most clearly illustrated, in the eyes of many, by the arrogance and lack of accountability of security forces. Ironically, most Kabyles, generally less religiously oriented than other Algerians, had also been highly supportive of the secularism of the regime and its struggle to repress the Islamists.

Bouteflika's insensitive reaction to the killings and protests contributed to their spread. Finally addressing the problem on May 1, 2001, in formal spoken Arabic, which few Kabyles could understand, the president announced he would create a national commission of inquiry to look into the events and the violence surrounding them, which he asserted was not accidental. He went on to assert that "there are forces encouraging these excesses, stoking hatred and sowing subversion and division. Whether they are internal or external we will learn in the future."[16] The suggestion that their protests were the result of an external conspiracy did not sit well with most Kabyles. That same day, Saïd Saadi announced his RCD was pulling out of the government it had joined sixteen months earlier. Bouteflika had never, in fact, been especially popular in the Kabylia. During his presidential campaign in 1999 he had been hooted down during one appearance and pelted with stones at another. Perhaps in response to such unfriendly receptions, he asserted in September 1999 that Tamazight would never become an official language—except by constitutional referendum. What Kabyles retained was the first half of the statement, convinced that the Arabic-speaking majority would certainly reject such a proposal if it were submitted to referendum. Ultimately the national commission of inquiry and a subsequent parliamentary commission rejected the notion that external conspiracy was behind the Kabylia protests and concluded that the gendarmerie had committed the acts either because of individual choices or because the chiefs had lost control of their subordinates.

In response to the violence of the gendarmes and the apparent state sanctioning of it, a Kabyle citizens movement emerged that was based upon tribal (arch) and inter-tribal (arouch) council traditions that had not been visible for generations. Citizens would come together at local and regional levels to share information and discuss responses and soon there emerged a broader organization known as the Coördination Interwilaya des Archs, Daïras et Communes, which coordinated the actions of Kabyles from seven different provinces. On June 11, 2001, this body agreed upon the el

16. Chérif Bennadji, "Chronique Politique 2001," Annuaire de l'Afrique du Nord, vol. XXXIX, 2000–2001, p. 131.

Ksueur platform, further elaborated on in October, which became fundamental to the Kabyle resistance. Its basic demands were that the state should take responsibility for all victims of repression and their families; release all protesters imprisoned or facing trial; withdraw all gendarme brigades and riot police[17] from the Kabylia immediately and place on trial those responsible for the crimes; dissolve all state commissions of inquiry; place under the authority of democratically elected bodies all of the nation's executive and security functions; guarantee the civil and economic rights of all; launch an emergency program of economic renewal for the Kabylia; unconditionally satisfy Amazigh demands of identity, civilization, language, and culture; and establish Tamazight as a national and official language.

By the fall of 2001, as the upheaval continued, the Bouteflika government knew its policies had been wrong. In December, under the leadership of Prime Minister Benflis, rounds of discussions began at Algiers with about 1,000 Kabyles, which then led Bouteflika in March 2002 to make several concessions. While refusing to withdraw the gendarmerie because of the continuing fight against "terrorist barbarism," he asserted that twenty-four gendarmes had been imprisoned for "homicide and abusive use of firearms." He also agreed to compensation for victims of police violence. Most significantly, Bouteflika announced that the constitution would be amended without referendum to include Tamazight as a national language, which the parliament, in fact, did unanimously on April 8. The *Coördination des Archs*, however, claimed the negotiators who had been talking with the government were not truly representative and that the concessions Bouteflika made were insufficient because of his refusal to grant three key demands of the el Ksueur platform: withdrawal of the gendarmerie, creation of jobs, and recognition of Tamazight as an *official* Algerian language. Supported both by the FFS and the RCD, the arch movement called for a boycott of the May 2002 parliamentary elections, a request acceded to by an overwhelming majority of Kabyles.

Protests continued into 2003, when negotiations were resumed under the leadership of Ahmed Ouyahia, who became prime minister again in May. These negotiations broke down in the run-up to the 2004 presidential elections, but by then it was increasingly clear that support for the *Coördination des Archs* and its tactics was beginning to diminish. Saïd Saadi became a candidate for the presidency and, while Kabyle turnout at the polls was still limited, it was significantly higher than for the parliamentaries.

CULTURAL AND OTHER DIVIDES

In the 1990s and early 2000s, most of the attention directed toward Algeria focused on the violence engendered by the questions of religion and ethnicity. There were other issues, however, that continued to raise tensions. A primary one was Arabization, which while closely related to the Kabyle-Tamazight conflict,

---

17. *Compagnies Nationales de Sécurité (CNS)*.

had significantly broader impacts. Arabization, which began rhetorically before independence, proceeded slowly through the educational system beginning in the 1960s and then through governmental institutions in the 1980s. In January 1991, the parliament passed and Bendjedid signed a law requiring that all public institutions, enterprises, and organizations switch to Arabic by Independence Day, 1992, and that all higher education be Arabized two years later. Mohamed Boudiaf suspended the law's implementation before the 1992 deadline, presumably because he was personally uncomfortable with it and also because it seemed untimely to require the military, much of whose leadership was trained in French, to switch while facing a broadening insurrection. In 1996 the National Transitional Council established a new deadline for July 5, 1998, which the High Council of Arabization, citing the need for certain adjustments, subsequently put off until July 5, 2000, when it finally became the law of the land.

The definitive institutionalization of Arabic at all levels of government and education contributed significantly to the tensions in the Kabylia which exploded the next year and it was not by coincidence that signs carried by the thousands of protesters were almost invariably in French, a few in Tamazight, but none in Arabic. For a variety of reasons, however, French would continue to be either a necessary or preferred language for a large number of Algerians. The country remained, as always, an important part of a broader western Mediterranean system, which in many ways had grown even more close-knit in an era of globalization. For an economy based largely on exports and imports and with France the largest trading partner, French was an essential. Furthermore, with more than a million expatriates living in France, interfamily communication in French as well as the transmission of French values were persistent. Language and values were also transmitted by electronic media through radio and especially with the spread of satellite television. At the same time the majority of newspapers in Algeria continued to be published in French and their circulation was far larger than that of the Arabic dailies.

Another difficulty with Arabization was that the formal modern Arabic of the educational system and of government had effectively marginalized native Algerian Arabic, which existed in a range of different forms and which was traditionally a major element of identity from region to region. A large percentage of Algerians were unable to comprehend the public addresses delivered by their political leaders, which was an ironic outcome to an initiative the FLN originally promoted as a vehicle for ushering the masses into the system.

The status of women and their role in Algerian society remained extremely controversial throughout the period covered in this chapter. The Family Code of 1984, promulgated by a regime then seen as the most progressive in the region, was viewed by many as a concession to Islamic fundamentalists who were then becoming politically assertive. The law essentially placed the woman under the tutelage of a male family member or her husband, gave the husband ownership of a couple's home, legalized polygamy, the male right of repudiation, and inequality of inheritance. Many Algerian women, mostly from the better educated and professional strata of society, had protested the law from the beginning. Most politicians, especially from the time of the 1999 elections, agreed while campaigning that the code needed reform, but once elected, neither Bouteflika, Benflis, nor Ouyahia delivered on promises. This dynamic reflects the fact that many Algerian voters retained very conservative views concerning women and family and also that the support of moderate Islamist parties was important in building governing coalitions. It should also be recognized that, while leading politicians expressed a willingness to consider reform of the laws, most female activists contended that change was not enough and pressed for total abrogation of the Family Code. In 2003, six feminist groups came together in a movement named "Vingt Ans, Barakat!" to activate their base and press for abrogation by June 2004, a goal which they failed to achieve.

Numerous observers argue that the status of most women relative to men declined during the 1990s and early 2000s, but in some regards it improved. On the positive side, the average age of marriage for young women had increased considerably, and, with the wider availability of birth control, the total fertility rate per woman had declined to an estimated 2.55 by 2003. With regard to education and literacy, much improvement was needed. By 2003 roughly 79 percent of Algerian males were literate as compared to only 61 percent of females. Literacy rates were reflected by disparities in enrollment in primary, secondary, and tertiary education, where the percentage of females was consistently lower than that of males, although data showed that average achievement levels of girls actually enrolled in schools were markedly higher than those of boys.

Because of the agricultural, artisanal, and *trabendiste* nature of much of the economy, it is difficult to discern with certainly the percentage of women employed outside the home, but it is probable that they accounted for 12 to 15 percent of the active work force in the early 2000s. Women were quite visible in the retail trades and they represented 38 percent of public school personnel. Roughly a quarter of civil servants were female, though few climbed above the lower rungs of the bureaucracy. In the health care sector, however, the situation was markedly different. The number of primary care physicians and medical specialists was roughly equal to that of men, and women actually outnumbered men in dentistry and pharmacy. In the legal profession women were also advancing and 700 of Algeria's 1,700 magistrates in the year 2000 were female. The number of women in various branches of the police force, more than 2,000, was the highest in the Arab world.

Political participation by Algerian women has been quite limited. In 1997 only 38 percent of registered voters were female and in the parliamentary elections female candidates won only 13 of the 380 seats. In 2002 elections, they did only slightly better, taking 25. This time, however, Ali Benflis of the FLN, who had campaigned promising reform of the Family Code, appointed five women to his cabinet, the largest number to sit in Algerian government since independence. In the presidential elections of 2004, Louisa Hanoune, leader of the Trotskyist Workers' Party and an outspoken advocate for abrogation of the Family Code, became the first woman in the Arab world ever to run for the presidency. She won 1.1 percent of the votes cast.

As has been noted in the preceding pages, the generation gap was a major problem for Algeria since the late 1980s. Cultural differences in fashion, style, and popular music—for example, *rai*—certainly contributed to the growing gap, but far more important was the absence of opportunity and the sense among millions that the future held little hope. The enormous unemployment rate among the young was a significant component of the decision by many to join or support violent protest movements or to seek emigration in any way possible. Contributing to this sense of alienation was the dismantling or weakening of government support programs by structural readjustment that diverted income from the working classes and the neediest into pockets of the oligarchs who created and maintained the regime. At the same time, the endless repetition of the national liberation narrative and the gallantry and sacrifice of those who had struggled for Algeria's independence seemed more and more arcane to younger Algerians, who resented the failure of those leaders to deal with problems of the real world in which they were living.

LE POUVOIR

As Algeria progressed into the twenty-first century, it was clear that its political system was more open and vibrant than it had ever been. Yet, the perception of many Algerians was that ultimate authority still remained in the hands of a murky group they called the *pouvoir* (power). While it was presumed that most members of the *pouvoir* were generals, the exact composition of the group at any moment was always a matter of speculation. One of the achievements of the civilian Bouteflika was to shift more and more of that power away from the military and toward his own presidency. But the perception remained widespread that ultimate sovereignty of the Algerian people had yet to be achieved.

Most Algerians knew that their judiciary was far from independent and that the executive branch could intimidate and pressure courts whenever its political interests or those of important personalities were involved. Furthermore, the national state of emergency originally declared in 1991 and renewed on a temporary basis in 1992 was still in force in 2004, in spite of the fact that terrorist and other attacks by insurgents had declined dramatically and that most politically active Algerians and civil rights advocates argued it should be terminated. Special tribunals for those accused of actions against the state continued to operate. The continuing state of siege granted the executive and its security forces greater powers to limit freedom of expression, assembly, and movement than they would ordinarily have exercised.

Another tool in Bouteflika's hands was the ability to restrict freedom of the press. While Algeria's press had become one of the broadest and most vibrant in the Arab world since the liberalization initiated by Bendjedid, the state had always been able to limit it when it saw its interests threatened. A commonly used method was the invocation of its rights as creditor. Algerian newspapers and magazines were dependent upon state-owned presses for the printing of their texts. Periodically the government would cite non-payment or slow payment of bills in order to shut down newspapers or magazines, a process which journalists and others viewed as highly selective, since some indebted publications would be closed, while others with even higher debt would remain open. An even stronger tool was created in 2001 when the ANP passed an amendment to the penal code criminalizing criticism of the president of the Republic that contained injurious, insulting, or defamatory language.

The same law applied to criticism of the parliament, its members, or the military, and those found guilty could be imprisoned for two to twelve months and subjected to fines between 50,000 and 250,000 dinars.

ELECTIONS OF 2002 AND 2004

Under Abdelaziz Bouteflika the office of prime minister was largely marginalized until he named Ali Benflis to the position in August 2000. Benflis, a member of the FLN Central Committee, was very much a populist with a reputation for reaching out to the masses and listening to their concerns. He was deeply admired for his concern for justice and human rights and his attempts to reach out to women and youth. When, in spite of objections from the traditionalist wing of the FLN, the Central Committee named him its Secretary General in September 2001, Benflis now had a powerful apparatus to assist him in communicating and achieving his goals. The Economic Reconstruction Program he launched and his attempts to negotiate with alienated Kabyles were appreciated by many, even though neither turned out to be especially successful.

When the parliamentary elections were held on May 30, 2002, FLN supporters turned out in large numbers, but because of an active, often aggressive boycott by Kabyles, and disillusionment with the RND, which many saw as the generals' party, overall participation fell to 46 percent, the lowest in Algeria's history. The FLN took 199 of the seats, giving it an absolute majority in the ANP, while the seats held by the RND dropped to 47, as compared to 155 in the 1997 parliament. Two Islamist-leaning parties were close to the RND in votes and seats. Abdallah Djaballah's Movement for National Reform (MRN), which spun off from the Nahda in 1998, won 43 seats, and Nahnah's MSP took 38. Louisa Hanoune campaigned intensively for her Workers' Party (PT), the most explicitly secular party in Algeria, and it garnered 21 seats as opposed to its meager 2 in 1997. The number of women in the 2002 parliament rose from 13 to 25, 18 of whom came from the FLN list, and Benflis appointed 5 women to his new cabinet as noted earlier.

In the provincial and local elections that followed on October 10, 2002, the former single party continued its triumph. It won control of 43 of 48 *wilaya* councils and 668 of 1541 communes. It was clear by late 2002 that the political clout and popularity of the prime minister were of growing concern for President Bouteflika, who had never been comfortable with Algeria's bi-cephalic executive system.

In March 2003 the eighth Party Congress of the FLN, whose leadership had been purged of most Benflis opponents, elected him secretary general for a five-year term. During his two-hour opening address, he did not once mention the name of the president, nor were any pictures of Bouteflika to be seen in the auditorium. When Bouteflika asked his former right-hand man in early April whether he was thinking of running for president, Benflis declined to answer. On May 5 Bouteflika fired him and appointed as his replacement Ahmed Ouyahia, who had served as Zéroual's prime minister, in the position of secretary-general of the National Rally for Democracy (RND), and then as justice minister under Benflis. Ouyahia did not enjoy broad popularity, having been responsible for implementation of several unpopular measures required by the plan of economic restructuring. Neither his popularity nor that of the president were enhanced by the results of an earthquake which, on May 21, struck Boumerdès and other towns to the east of Algiers, causing 2,100 deaths and injuring more than 9,000. More than 160,000 Algerians were made homeless, many for weeks and months, due to the collapse of housing, much of which was sloppily constructed by state agencies.

During the summer of 2003 the unofficial race for the presidency began to gather steam. In September Bouteflika fired six FLN ministers and seven more withdrew from the government in protest. Then the contest became a struggle over control of the FLN, which Benflis had transformed into the most powerful political engine in the country. Some fifty FLN traditionalists, supporters of Bouteflika who called themselves "rectifiers," instituted proceedings to invalidate the eighth Party Congress. In a counterattack, Benflis secured approval from the *wali* (governor) of Algiers to convene a special congress of the FLN. Later the same day, the *wali,* on instructions from the minister of the interior, withdrew his approval. On a parallel track, in the night of October 1 to 2, long after closing hours, and without knowledge of the presiding judge, and at least two other judges, the regional prosecutor obtained a ruling from the Administrative Court of Algiers forbidding the special congress. Nevertheless, that congress did convene on October 3 and nominated Ali Benflis its candidate for the presidency. On December 30, the Court of Algiers ordered a freeze on all activities of the FLN, and forbade its secretary general from invoking its name or symbols or using its funds, a ruling confirmed in March 2004 by the Council of State, the body responsible for regulating administrative jurisdictions. Earlier, on January 22, the "rectifiers" convened a congress to reverse the decisions of the eighth Party Congress. When Benflis and his side of the party asked the Court of Algiers to invalidate the rectifiers' meeting, the court claimed it lacked the authority to do so. The overwhelming majority of party leaders and journalists condemned the court's response and concluded that Algeria's constitutionally independent judiciary was being manipulated by the executive branch.

Of the nine individuals who filed for candidacies in the 2004 elections, six were accepted on March 1 by the Constitutional Council. Besides Bouteflika and Benflis, they included Saïd Saadi, who broke ranks with the *Archs* to run; Abdallah Djaballah, of the MRN; the Berber Fawzi Rebaine, head of the small nationalist party called *Ahd 54;* and Louisa Hanoune of the Workers' Party.

The campaign was extremely animated and open. Many predicted that the election would go on to a second round. When the votes were tallied, however, Bouteflika had achieved a landslide victory. Of the 58 percent of registered voters who cast ballots, Bouteflika took 85 percent, Benflis 6.4 percent, Djaballah 5 percent, Saadi 1.9 percent, Hanoune 1.1 percent, and Rebaine 0.6 percent. While Benflis, Saadi, and Djaballah issued a communiqué alleging "fraud at all levels," most outside observers, while astounded at the outcome, saw little specific evidence of fraud. Barracks voting had been eliminated by act of parliament and no one could cite credible instances of false counts at polling places or collection centers. Bouteflika's success in dismantling the FLN certainly tilted matters in his favor, though it is not clear that public opinion, which since the 1999 election had perceived Benflis as a major supporter of the president, could see issues larger than ego and jockeying for power. While a historical pattern of pressure on the press has already been mentioned, there is no evidence that editors were constrained during their coverage of this election. Five major dailies, representing 80 percent of newspaper circulation, had openly opposed Bouteflika. Yet he had enjoyed substantial advantages. As incumbent, he had far greater access to the electronic media than his opponents. Incumbency also favored the sitting president as he toured the country, distributing or promising government favors in ways his challengers could not. At the same time, he proved to be a good listener, hearing the complaints of groups ranging from farmers to women's rights organizations and sufi *zawiyas*. Finally, Bouteflika also enjoyed the support of most civil servants, public institutions, and the extremely influential labor movement, the UGTA. After taking the oath of office on April 19, 2004, Bouteflika stated that the primary goals of his second term would be completing the program of national reconciliation, resolving the Kabyle crisis, and modifying the Family Code. On the same day he re-appointed Ahmed Ouyahia as prime minister. Soon afterward Mohamed Lamari, seen as the most powerful military figure in the country, was forced to resign as chief of staff. Yet there were hints that Abdelaziz Bouteflika might seek revisions of the constitution of 1996 in order to strengthen the presidency even more and to institutionalize a system which some qualified as authoritarian liberalism.

A P P E N D I X

Place Names

Colonial	Independence
Affreville	Khemis Miliana
Alma	Bou Douaou
Aumale	Sour el Ghozlane
Boghari	Ksar Boukhari
Bône	Annaba
Bougie	Bejaïa
Castiglione	Bou Ismail
Chevreul	Ben Aziz
Colomb-Béchar	Béchar
Duperré	Aïn Defla
Fort de l'Eau	Bordj El-Kiffan
Fort Flatters	Zaouiet el-Kahla
Fort National	Larba Nath Iratten
Géryville	El-Bayadth
Inkermann	Oued Riov
LaCalle	El-Kala
Lambèse	Tazoult
Lamoricière	Ouled Mimoun
Legrand	Ben Fereha
Maison Carrée	El-Harrache
Maison Verte	Hassi-Messaoud
Marengo	Hadjoute
Margueritte	Ain Torki
Nemours	Ghazaouet
Orléansville	El-Asnam
Palestro	Lakhdaria
Perrégaux	Mohammedia
Philippeville	Skikda
Reghaia	Ouled Dieb
Relizane	Ighil-Izane
Renan	Hassi Mefessour
St-Arnaud	El-Eulma
St-Cloud	Gdeyel
St-Denis du Sig	Sig
Trézel	Sougheur
Vialar	Tissemsilt

BIBLIOGRAPHICAL
ESSAY

IN GENERAL

The pages that follow offer an overview of scholarly work dealing with the modern history of Algeria. Since an exhaustive study would require at least an additional volume, I have chosen to restrict the discussion to the several hundred books and articles which in my judgment are the most significant. Inevitably, I will have included works others would have omitted and excluded some they find important. It is my hope, however, that the reader wishing to explore further any particular aspect of modern Algerian history will find enough material in this section to start him or her on the way.

Chapters 1 through 5 of this book, dealing with the period before 1954, are mostly based on a scholarly tradition stretching back over a century and a half, a tradition that includes not only history but ethnology, sociology, anthropology, religious studies, and linguistics, in a great variety of schools and styles. It is a body of scholarship dominated by Frenchmen and which Algerians began to penetrate very haltingly only about 1930. One of the best evaluations of that tradition is found in the first chapter of Jean-Claude Vatin's *L'Algérie politique. Histoire et société* (1983). For an overview of the principal scholars and works belonging to it, see the composite work *Histoire et historiens de l'Algérie (1830–1930),* published in connection with the Centenary of French Algeria and, for works between 1931 and 1956, see Xavier Yacono's "L'Algérie depuis 1830," a special issue of the *Revue africaine.*

During the first thirty or forty years of occupation, French soldiers and administrators worked energetically to learn more about the country they were in and the society they were contending with. While the studies they generated came out of a need to control, the best of them are nevertheless characterized by a genuine desire to know and understand, and some reflect considerable scientific rigor. Beginning in the 1860s, and especially after 1871, with Algeria now largely under French control, the focus of scholarship shifted to colonialism itself and to the building of what many settlers at the time saw as a new overseas nation on the model of a United States of America or of an Australia. Algerians were of interest only as adjuncts to that French history, not as its subjects. Those studies of Algerian history and society actually undertaken were aimed at uncovering the factors that made Algeria congenitally incapable of progress and, therefore, an appropriate object of France's *mission civilisatrice.* Whether contemporary, Ottoman, or medieval, that history's function was to explain, rationalize, and justify the colonial adventure. Such work centered on the Faculté des Lettres of the University of Algiers, within which emerged the extremely influential *Algiers school,* whose apogee was reached with the triumphal, self-indulgent celebration of the Centennial in 1930. Among the scores of names closely associated with this school are Eugène Albertini, Emile-Félix Gautier, Georges Marçais, Victor Demontès, and Louis Bertrand.

It was in reaction to such self-congratulation that Algerian scholars like Mubarak al Mili and Ahmad Tawfiq al-Madani began to challenge colonialism's denial of an

Algerian nation. It was also at this time that Charles-André Julien, in his seminal *Histoire de l'Afrique du Nord* (1931), began to question many of the underlying assumptions of the Algiers school. By so doing, he pioneered what is loosely called the liberal school of historiography. This school expanded rapidly in the 1940s and the 1950s, mainly through the growing involvement of metropolitan French scholars in the field who were stimulated in many instances by the escalating Algerian challenge to the colonial status quo. Along with Julien, the most prominent "liberals" are Charles-Robert Ageron, Pierre Boyer, Marcel Emerit, Xavier Yacono, and Hildebert Isnard. These were followed by a group of leftist scholars very loosely labeled Marxists by some observers—André Nouschi, André Prenant, and René Gallissot, for example.

Since independence, leadership in the study of Algerian history, once the virtual monopoly of France, has reverted to the Algerian scholarly community while the field has also opened to scholars of other nationalities. American historians have recently made important contributions to eighteenth- and nineteenth-century Algerian history, especially to the understanding of Islamic movements and institutions. American political scientists are prominent in the study of political dynamics since 1954, and especially since independence. Algerian historians have been most attracted to various phases of Algerian resistance, starting with the War of Independence but also including the Sétif events of 1945, the uprising of 1882, and, of course, the national hero, ᶜAbd al Qadir. In addition, attempts are being made to recast medieval history and, especially, to look anew at the Ottoman period, a period so long denigrated by French scholarship. Not surprisingly, the main thrust of contemporary Algerian historiography is to leap back over the years from 1962 to 1830 in an attempt to establish continuity with precolonial Algeria. Doing so, however, downplays the significance of colonial Algeria in the same way the school of Algiers once downplayed that of medieval and Ottoman Algeria. Colonial Algeria is considered to have only negative influence and even to be a regressive historical force, the same functions assigned by colonialist history to the medieval and Ottoman pasts. As independent Algeria explores its past in search of national myths upon which to build its future, it is inevitable that the Algerian past will be significantly reshaped to produce them. No national history in modern times is free from such manipulation.

Articles dealing with Algerian history and related subjects can be found scattered throughout scholarly journals in many languages. I mention here the most important specialized publications. The most indispensable is the *Annuaire de l'Afrique du Nord,* which has been published annually in Paris since 1962 by the *Centre national de la recherche scientifique.* It contains a comprehensive and well-organized annual bibliography of books and articles on North Africa published in European languages and in Arabic. It also contains useful chronologies, and it publishes key documents of the year as well as a broad range of useful articles.

The same team of scholars at the University of Aix-Marseille responsible for the *Annuaire* produces *Revue de l'Occident musulman et de la Méditerranée,* usually in two issues a year, intended to fill the void left by the disappearance at independence of several French Algerian journals. The most prominent of these was the *Revue africaine,* which began publication in 1856. During much of its history, the *Revue africaine* was the most important forum for members of the Algiers school, but in later years its selection of articles became more heterogeneous. While many of its articles are hopelessly dated, some early ones and many later ones still hold great value for the researcher. Another important collection is found in the *Annales de l'Institut d'Etudes orientales de la Faculté des Lettres d'Alger,* in which a similar mix is apparent. Some of the best history and social-sciences pieces of the colonial period appeared in the *Bulletin de la Société de Géographie et d'Archéologie de la Province d'Oran*. In Algeria since independence, the journals of greatest interest to historians are *Revue algérienne des sciences juridiques, économiques et politiques* and *Majallat al tarikh*. *Tafsut*, published at Tizi-Ouzou and in France, specializes in Berber history and culture. *Maghreb-Machrek*, also published in France, deals primarily in contemporary matters but also accepts historical articles. The *Cahiers de Tunisie* and the *Revue d'histoire maghrebine*, published in Tunis, both have useful articles on Algerian history. The latter publishes pieces in English as well as Arabic and French. The *Maghrib Review*, published in Great Britain, is the only English-language journal in the field.

In order to situate Algeria within the context of the Greater Maghrib, readers will find useful the classic two-volume study of Charles-André Julien, *Histoire de l'Afrique du Nord. Tunisie. Algérie. Maroc* (revised in 1952 and again in 1966). Volume 1, revised with the help of Christian Courtois, deals with the period from prehistory to the Arab conquest. Volume 2, revised and edited by Roger LeTourneau, covers the period from the Arab conquest to the French invasion. In 1970, volume 2 appeared in an English translation by John Petrie under the title *History of North Africa. Tunisia. Algeria. Morocco*. In 1971, Jamil M. Abun-Nasr published a single-volume English *History of the Maghrib*, covering the whole region from antiquity to the present. *A History of the Maghrib in the Islamic Period*, based on the 1971 book but revised and omitting the pre-Islamic period, appeared in 1987. *L'Histoire du Maghreb. Un essai de synthèse*, by the Moroccan scholar Abdallah Laroui, appeared in 1970 and represents a seminal critique of the western historiography of the Maghrib. It was translated in 1977 by Ralph Manheim as *The History of the Maghrib: An Interpretive Essay*.

The most complete overview of Algeria in the colonial period is the *Histoire de l'Algérie contemporaine*. Volume 1, 1827 to 1871, was written by Charles-André Julien. As sympathetic as the author was to Algerians, by following his sources too closely, he weighted it too heavily toward military history, colonial politics, and the experience of the settlers. Volume 2, 1870 to 1954, written by Charles-Robert Ageron, is better balanced. Ageron also wrote the brief but excellent introduction to modern Algeria in the "Que Sais-je" series, *Histoire de l'Algérie contemporaine (1830–1964)*. The most stimulating single-volume history of Algeria in a western language is *L'Algérie. Passé et présent*, by Yves Lacoste, André Nouschi, and André Prenant. Beginning with an excellent geographic survey, it covers Algerian history from prehistory to the end of World War I. Anticolonial and Marxist in perspective, it is thoughtful, provocative, and occasionally flawed. Vatin's *L'Algérie politique. Histoire et société* is an excellent history of Algeria's political development from Ottoman times to 1962, containing invaluable theoretical and bibliographical materials. In Arabic, readers should look at the classic *Kitab al jaza'ir* of Ahmad Tawfiq al-Madani. In English, the reader should consult *The Making of Contemporary Algeria*, by the Algerian sociologist Mahfoud Bennoune, which appeared in 1988. Using a political economy approach, it traces precolonial and colonial economic and social history schematically, and it is especially useful for the period since independence.

CHAPTER 1. INTRODUCTION

The best introduction to Algerian physical geography is found in part 2 of *Géographie de l'Afrique du Nord-Ouest*, by Jean Despois and René Raynal. Despois's *L'Afrique blanche*.

L'Afrique du Nord is good for both physical and human geography of North Africa in general. The first three chapters of *L'Algérie. Passé et présent,* by Yves Lacoste, are also useful.

For people and languages, see Georges-Henri Bousquet, *Les Berbères;* Pierre Bourdieu, *Sociologie de l'Algérie;* A. Basset, *La Langue berbère;* William Marçais, "Comment l'Afrique du Nord s'est arabisée"; and Georges Marçais, *Les Arabes en Berbérie du XIe au XIVe siècle.*

For an introduction to Algerian prehistory and premodern history, see Charles-André Julien, volume 1 of his *Histoire de l'Afrique du Nord;* also, Lacoste, Nouschi, and Prenant, *L'Algérie. Passé et présent.* For prehistory and early Berber history, see Gabriel Camps, *Monuments et rites funéraires protohistoriques. Aux origines de la Berbérie,* and Lionel Balout, *Préhistoire de l'Afrique du Nord. Essai de chronologie.* For the ancient period, the standard works are Stéphane Gsell, *Histoire ancienne de l'Afrique du Nord* (8 vols.), which goes from early Phoenician settlement to the end of the Roman Republic and includes the Berber kingdoms; B. H. Warmington, *Carthage;* Eugene Albertini, *L'Afrique romaine;* Christian Courtois, *Les Vandales et l'Afrique;* and Charles Diehl, *L'Afrique byzantine. Histoire de la domination byzantine en Afrique (533–709)* (2 vols.).

For medieval Algeria, in addition to the general works cited above, see Georges Marçais, *La Berbérie musulmane et l'Orient au Moyen Age* and *Les Arabes en Berbérie du XIe au XIVe siècle;* H. R. Idris, *La Berbérie orientale sous les Zirides, Xe-XII siècle;* L. Golvin, *Le Maghreb central à l'époque des Zirides;* and Robert Brunschwig, *La Berbérie orientale sous les Hafsides des origines à la fin du XVe siècle.* The interested reader should not fail to look at Emile-Félix Gautier, *L'Islamisation de l'Afrique du Nord. Les siècles obscurs du Maghreb.* One of the most controversial books of colonialist historiography, it presses the theses that the Maghrib is a millennial battleground between Oriental and Occidental civilizations (which are essentially incompatible with each other) and that the former is essentially incapable of progress.

Both the premises and methodologies of premodern historiography have been called into question by North African scholars. For examples of the critique, see Abdullah Laroui, *Histoire du Maghreb. Un essai de synthèse;* Mohammed Chérif Sahli, *Décoloniser l'histoire. Introduction à l'histoire du Maghreb;* Mostefa Lacheraf, *L'Algérie: nation et société;* and Mohiedin Djender, *Introduction à l'histoire de l'Algérie.* Specific Algerian attempts to rewrite their medieval history include Attallah Dhina, *Le Royaume abdelwaddide à l'époque d'Abou Hammam Moussa 1er et d'Abou Tachfin 1er* (1985); Rachid Bouriba, *Les Hammadides* (1982); and Mahfoud Kaddache, *L'Algérie médiévale* (1982).

CHAPTER 2. OTTOMAN ALGERIA AND ITS LEGACY

For introductions to the Ottoman period, readers should look at Mouloud Gaid, *L'Algérie sous les Turcs;* chapters 4 and 5 in part 2 of *L'Algérie. Passé et présent,* by André Prenant; chapter 1 of Julien's *Histoire de l'Algérie contemporaine;* and the dated but still fascinating H.-D. de Grammont, *Histoire d'Alger sous la domination turque (1515–1830).*

On political dynamics, see Grammont's interpretation; but especially see the theses of Pierre Boyer, as outlined in "Introduction à une histoire intérieure de la Régence d'Alger," who refutes Grammont's interpretation. Boyer's "Des pachas triennaux à la révolution d'Ali Khodja Dey (1571–1817)" is the best place to start for a view of the central government. One should also consult the short but thoughtful chapter by Vatin in *L'Algérie politique* on the political successes and limitations of the Ottoman period as well as his article "L'Algérie en 1830, essai d'interprétation des recherches historiques sous l'angle de la science politique." Abderrahmane Benachenhou, in *L'Etat algérien en 1830,* presents little new research but some interesting interpretations.

On the controversial question of the population of Ottoman Algeria, begin with William Shaler's *Sketches of Algiers, Political, Historical, and Civil* (1826), and also look at Pelissier de Reynaud's *Annales algériennes.* Lucette Valensi, in her chapter "A Thinly Populated Land" in *On the Eve of Colonialism. North Africa Before the French Conquest,* explains the forces working on population. See also the assessment of Prenant in *Algérie,* pp. 217–18. The most thorough attempt to come to terms with actual numbers is that of Xavier Yacono in "Peut-on évaluer la population de l'Algérie vers 1839?" See also for the Algérois, the well-constructed article of Pierre Boyer, "L'Evolution démographique des populations musulmanes du Département d'Alger (1830/66–1948)." The best Algerian critique of French colonial demographics is found in Mohamed Chérif Sahli, *Décoloniser l'histoire,* who claims the conquest took 2,000,000 Algerian lives between 1830 and 1866.

Urban society in Ottoman Algeria is marginally better known than rural society because of the greater availability of internal documentation and because of the records left by travelers and consuls. For an overview, see chapter 4 of Valensi's *On the Eve of Colonialism.* André Prenant, in *Algérie,* pp. 218–25, paints a sketchy but instructive picture. For Algiers, the reader should consult René Lespès, *Alger. Etude de géographie et d'histoire urbaines* (1930), and Pierre Boyer's 1963 *La Vie quotidienne à Alger à la veille de l'intervention française,* which is indispensable. A thoughtful article by Houari Touati, "Les corporations de métier à Alger à l'époque ottomane," sheds new light on the guilds. For Oran, see Lespès, *Oran. Etude de géographie et d'histoire urbaines* (1938); and for Tlemcen, see Marcel Emerit, *L'Algérie à l'époque d'Abd el-Kader,* pp. 10–14. While a number of articles have appeared on Ottoman Constantine, the best work is by André Nouschi, "Constantine à la veille de la conquête" and *Enquête sur le niveau de vie des populations rurales constantinoises,* which contains introductory material on the city.

For an introduction to rural society, see chapters 2 and 3 of Valensi's *On the Eve of Colonialism;* chapters 1 and 2 of Elbaki Hermassi, *Leadership and National Development in North Africa;* and Prenant, *Algérie,* pp. 173ff. Theoretical materials I have used to understand segmentary tribalism include Emile Durkheim, *De la division du travail social;* Edward Evans-Pritchard, *The Nuer* and *The Sanussi of Cyrenaica;* as well as Ernest Gellner, *Saints of the Atlas.* For great detail on Algerian tribes and their locations, see Louis Rinn, *Le Royaume d'Alger sous le dernier dey.* Specifically on makhzan tribes, consult Marcel Emerit, "Les Tribus privilégiées en Algérie dans la première moitié du XIXe siècle." A remarkable 1887 work, recently republished, is Emile Masqueray's *La Formation des cités chez les populations sédentaires de l'Algérie.* The best ethnographic study of Algeria, which deals with both nomads and sedentaries, is *Sociologie de l'Algérie,* by Pierre Bourdieu, translated in English as *The Algerians.* See also Nouschi. *Enquête,* pp. 17–155, for the Constantinois. For parts of the Algérois, see Hildebert Isnard, 'L'Etat économique de la Mitidja en 1830," "Le Sahel d'Alger en 1830," and *La Réorganisation de la propriété rurale dans la Mitidja.* For land tenure, see the introduction in John Ruedy's *Land Policy in Colonial Algeria;* Louis Milliot, *Démembrements du habous;* and Maurice-Alexandre Pouyanne, *La propriété foncière en Algérie.*

For the best introduction to economic issues, see André Prenant, *L'Algérie.* For the Constantinois, see Nouschi, *Enquête;* and for the Mitidja, see Isnard, "L'Etat économique." Excellent recent work based on new documentation is found in a collection of articles by Nasir al-Din Saʿiyduni, *Dirasat wa abhath fi ta'rikh al jaza'ir. Al ahd al ʿuthmani.* His "Al nizam al mali al jaza'iri fi'l fatra al ʿuthmaniyya, (1800–1830)," as well as Tamimi's "Malamih al wadaᶜ al iqtisadi fi al Maghrib al ᶜarabi qabla al istiᶜmar al gharbi," should also be consulted.

The literature contains much discussion on social formations and mode of production but little meeting of minds. Read Lucette Valensi's *Eve of Colonialism* and her "Le Maghreb pré-colonial: mode de production archaïque ou mode de production féodal?" Read also chapters 4 and 5 in part 2 of Prenant's *L'Algérie;* Ahmed Henni's *Etat, surplus, et société en Algérie avant 1830;* and Abdelkader Djeghloul's article "La formation sociale algérienne à la veille de la colonisation." In addition, René Gallissot's "L'Algérie précoloniale" and "Le système foncier en Algérie au moment de la colonisation française." Abdelhamid Merad Boudia, in *La formation sociale algérienne précoloniale,* presents an excellent overview of the different schools of thought. For Marx's views on Algeria, see Gallissot, *Marxisme et Algérie.*

For an overview of Islam in the region, see volume 1 of Alfred Bel's *La religion musulmane en Berbérie. Esquisse d'histoire et de sociologie religieuses* as well as Georges-Henri Bousquet's *L'Islam maghrebin.* The most thorough cataloguing of brotherhoods is that of Rinn, *Marabouts et Khouan,* but his analysis is dated. Other overall studies are *Les confréries religieuses musulmanes,* by Octave Depont and Xavier Coppolani, and the considerably newer *Le culte des saints dans l'Islam maghrebin,* by Emile Demerghem. To supplement, read Augustin Berque, "Essai d'une bibliographie critique des confréries musulmanes algériennes." Louis Massignon's article "Tarika," in the first edition of the *Encyclopedia of Islam,* is still valuable. With regard to the major individual tariqas, see for the Rahmaniyya, Antoine Giacobetti's *La confrérie des Rahmaniyya* and Julia Clancy-Smith's "The Saharan Rahmaniya: Popular Protest and Desert Society in Southwestern Algerian and the Tunisian Jarid, c. 1750–1881." Jamil M. Abun-Nasr's *The Tijaniyya, a Sufi Order in the Modern World* has become the standard on this wide-spread tariqa. For the Darqawa, consult Roger LeTourneau's article in the second edition *Encyclopedia of Islam.*

CHAPTER 3. INVASION, RESISTANCE, AND COLONIZATION, 1830–1871

The Algiers expedition and the conquest of Algeria generated an enormous correspondence among generals, politicians, and other participants, much of which has been published. It also stimulated the writing of hundreds of books, pamphlets, and articles by participants at many levels. The best place to look for these materials is in volume 1 of Julien's *Algérie contemporaine,* whose ninety-page bibliography of primary and secondary materials published until the early 1960s is the best compilation on the period. With 632 pages of text, his treatment of the age of conquest is the most comprehensive introduction to the period even though critics believe he devotes disproportionate space to the colonizers. Chapters 6, 7, and 8 of part 2 of *Algérie. Passé et présent,* by Prenant and Nouschi, present a briefer but better balanced overview.

The Franco-Algerian crisis that led to the invasion is thoroughly covered in Gabriel Esquer, *Les commencements d'un empire. La prise d'Alger (1830).* See also F. Charles-Roux, *France et Afrique du Nord avant 1830.* For the Muslim side of the crisis, one should read Ottocar de Schlechta's "La prise d'Alger par un Algérien," the translation of an Ottoman language account. The domestic French side of the crisis has been dealt with in many places, including: Pignaud, "Le projet Polignac"; Robin-Harmel, *Polignac;* and Julien, "Question d'Alger devant l'opinion" and "L'opposition et la guerre d'Alger."

For the best first-hand view of the Algiers expedition itself, one should look at the first volume of *Annales algériennes,* by E. Pelissier de Reynaud. The best scholarly studies are Esquer's *Prise d'Alger* and Paul Azan's *L'expédition d'Alger.* A sympathetic, pro-Bourbon view is found in Gustave Gautherot, *La conquête d'Alger,* while the reaction of Algerians as preserved in popular song is registered in J. Desparmet, "L'entrée des Français à Alger par le cheikh Abdelkader," and that of Algiers' Maures in Hamden Ben Othman Khodja, *Aperçu historique et statistique sur la Régence d'Alger.*

For the evolution of French colonial policy, see Christian Schefer, *La politique coloniale de la Monarchie de Juillet. L'Algérie et l'évolution de la colonisation française* and Augustin Bernard, *L'Algérie,* which is also good for the period of the Second Republic and the Second Empire, pp. 267–376. Points of view more sympathetic to the policies of Napoleon III will be found in Emerit, "Les méthodes coloniales de la France sous le Second Empire," and in the short article by Ageron, "L'évolution politique de l'Algérie sous Napoléon III." For the development and institutions of colonial government in the nineteenth century, see André Mallarmé, *L'organisation gouvernementale de l'Algérie;* and for an overview of legislation, see Milliot et al., *L'oeuvre législative de la France en Algérie.* Military history is covered best by Azan in his *Conquête et pacification de l'Algérie* and *L'Armée d'Afrique de 1830 à 1852.*

The resistance of Constantine under Ahmad Bey is covered by Emerit in "Hadj Ahmad Bey et la résistance constantinoise à la conquête française" and by Abdeljelil Temimi, in *Le Beylik de Constantine et Hadj Ahmed Bey (1830–1837).* From the colonial side, see Ernest Mercier, *Les deux sièges de Constantine.* For the crisis in Constantine that followed its capture, see Nouschi, *Enquête sur le niveau de vie,* pp. 160–67.

An enormous amount of material has been published on the resistance of ʿAbd al Qadir and the state he created. The reader of Arabic should begin with the Amir's son, Muhammad ibn ʿAbd al Qadir al Jaza'iri, *Tuhfat al za'ir fi ta'rikh al jaza'ir wa'l amir ʿAbd al Qadir.* The very early and sympathetic work by the Englishman Charles Churchill, *Life of Abdel Kader,* is still of great value. General Azan's book *L'émir Abd el Kader* represents what is today a painful colonialist perspective, but it is factually solid and well researched. Raphael Danziger's more recent *Abdel Qadir and the Algerians* is the major contemporary study in English. It is well researched, matter of fact, and avoids romanticization. An accessible account from a nationalist perspective is Mohamed Chérif Sahli, *Abd el-Kader. Chevalier de la foi* (1953). Examples of the many more recent Algerian studies of the Amir include Muhammad al ʿArabi Zabiri, *Al kifah al mussalah fi ahd al amir ʿAbd al Qadir* (1982), and Ismaʿil al ʿArabi *Al muqawama al jaza'iriyya taht liwa' al amir ʿAbd al Qadir* (1982).

René Gallissot's pair of articles, "Abdel Kader et la nationalité algérienne" and "La guerre d'Abdel Kader ou la ruine de la nationalité algérienne," give an interesting analysis of the movement as an attempt at nation building. One should also look at more general works: for example, André Prenant, *Algérie. Passé et présent,* pp. 272–91; the indispensable Emerit, *L'Algérie à l'époque d'Abd el-Kader;* and Pierre Boyer, *L'évolution de l'Algérie médiane de 1830 à 1956.*

For an overview of the response of the religious brotherhoods to European invasion, see the long article by A. Nadir, "Les ordres religieux et la conquête française (1830–1851)." For millenarian resistances, see the very early *Etude sur l'insurrection du Dahra,* by Charles Richard, and Joseph Bérard's *Les deux villes de Ténès et Bou-Maza.* More recent studies include: Julia Ann Clancy-Smith, "The Saharan Rahmaniyya" and "Saints, Mahdis and Arms: Religion and Resistance in Nineteenth Century North Africa"; Peter Von Sivers, "Alms and Arms," "Realm of Justice: Apocalyptic Revolts in Algeria (1849–1879), and "Insurrection and Accommodation: Indigenous Leadership in Eastern Algeria"; and Fanny Colonna, "Saints furieux et saints studieux ou, dans l'Aurès, comment la religion vient aux tribus."

Hundreds of histories of colonization were written during the colonial period. The soundest overviews are two nineteenth-century studies by Louis de Baudicour, *La colonisation de L'Algérie. Ses éléments* and *Histoire de la colonisation de l'Algérie*. For economic details, one should consult volumes 3, 4, and 6 of *L'Algérie économique*, by Victor Demontès. For land tenure, consult Maurice-Alexandre Pouyanne's *La propriété foncière en Algérie*, the article by Frédéric Godin in *L'oeuvre legislative de la France en Algérie*, and John Ruedy's *Land Policy in Colonial Algeria*.

Although dozens of scholars, administrators and other observers had written about the negative effects of European settlement upon the Algerians, Nouschi's *Enquête sur l'évolution du niveau de vie des populations constantinoises* (1961) was the first serious, large-scale attempt to assess its impact on a whole region. For the Algiers region, in a narrower time frame, one should consult Hildebert Isnard's work: *La réorganisation de la propriété rurale dans la Mitidja,* and "Le cantonnement des indigènes dans le Sahel d'Alger." For the western part of the Algérois, one should consult Xavier Yacono, especially *Les bureaux arabes et l'évolution des genres de vie indigènes dans l'ouest du Tell algérois (Dahra, Chélif, Ouarsenis, Sersou)* and *La colonisation des plaines du Chélif*. More general overviews of the impact of colonialism on the Algerian population are found in chapters 2, 3, and 4, of *The Making of Contemporary Algeria*, by Mahfoud Bennoune; Lahouri Addi, *De l'Algérie pré-coloniale à l'Algérie coloniale. Economie et société;* and Abdellatif Benachenhou, *Formation du sous-développement en Algérie*.

For excellent overviews of the Kabylia insurrection of 1871, read either chapter 9 in volume 1 of Julien's *Algérie contemporaine* or chapter 1 in volume 1 of Ageron's *Les Algériens musulmans et la France*. Two colonialist works unfortunately still remain the standard for extended accounts: Louis Rinn, *Histoire de l'insurrection de 1871 en Algérie* (1891); and N. Robin, *L'insurrection de la Grande Kabylie en 1871* (1901). Rinn sees the insurrection as solely an affair of threatened aristocracies; Robin sees it from a very narrowly military point of view. For some correctives, consult Mouloud Gaïd, *Les Beni Yala et les vérités sur l'insurrection de Mokrani en 1871;* and Yahya Abu ᶜAziz, *Thawra 1871. Dawr ᶜa'ilati al Muqrani wa al Haddad.*

CHAPTER 4. THE COLONIAL SYSTEM AND THE TRANSFORMATION OF ALGERIAN SOCIETY, 1871–1919

The period covered by this chapter is the high-water mark of colonialism in Algeria. A half-century stretch between the victory of the conquerors and the emergence of the Algerian national movement, it is a period when the situation of the native Algerians attracted less attention from scholars than before or since. Yet it was a time when Algerian society was undergoing profound changes. To fill the void left by the self-absorption of colonialist scholarship, Charles-Robert Ageron undertook his massive 1,300-page thesis *Les Algériens musulmans et la France,* which has since become the indispensable foundation for any study of the period. Its most important sections deal with land policy and the dispossession of the natives, the institutions of control, the transformation of native society, the fruitless attempts at reform, and the emergence of new Algerian elites and programs. Much of this material was incorporated into volume

2 of his broader *Histoire de l'Algérie contemporaine*. For the issues discussed below, the reader should consult Ageron in addition to the works cited.

On the high tide of European colonization, see Eugène Robe, *Origine, formation et état actuel de la propriété en Algérie*, dealing essentially with the effects of the Warnier Law; J. de Peyerimhof, *La colonisation officielle de 1871 à 1895*; R. Passeron, *Les grandes sociétés et la colonisation en Afrique du Nord*; and Demontès, *L'Algérie économique*. Consult also Demontès, *Le peuple algérien, essai de démographie algérienne*, which manages its topic with only marginal reference to the native Algerians.

Carefully treated with extensive documentation in Ageron's *Algériens musulmans*, the economic impact of massive colonization on the natives is also dealt with in chapter 4 of Bennoune's *Contemporary Algeria*, in volume 1 of Samir Amin's *L'Economie du Maghreb*, in Benachenhou's *Formation du sous-développement en Algérie*, and in chapters 9 through 11 of Nouschi's *Algérie. Passé et présent*. For regional studies, return, of course, to Nouschi, *Enquête*; Boyer, *Algérie médiane*; Isnard, *Réorganisation*; and Yacono, *Bureaux arabes* and *Colonisation*.

A brief but perceptive analysis of the impact of dispossession on the structure of Algerian society is presented in ten pages of Jean-Claude Vatin's *Algérie politique*, pp. 142–52. One of many studies of the effect on the peasantry is Joost van Vollenhoven, *Etude sur le fellah algérien*; and Abdelghani Megherbi, in *La paysannerie algérienne face à la colonisation*, sees the result as the imperative revolutionizing of the fellah. A remarkable series of early twentieth-century studies by Augustin Berque is collected in *Ecrits sur l'Algérie* (1986). The most instructive are "Décadence des chefs héréditaires," "Dislocation de la tribu," "Esquisse d'une histoire de la seigneurie algérienne," and "Bourgeoisies traditionelles." Marnia Lazreg, in chapter 3 of *The Emergence of Social Classes in Algeria*, sees class differentiation as the most important result of the destruction of the indigenous property system.

For a good introduction to the system of control, see Vincent Confer, *France and Algeria. The Problem of Civil and Political Reform, 1870–1920*. For a contemporary metropolitan statement of the problems in the system, read Jules Ferry, *Le gouvernement de l'Algérie*; but useful in hindsight is P.-E. Viard, *Les droits politiques des indigènes d'Algérie*. For legal status, see F. Marneur, *L'indigénat en Algérie*; for taxes, L. Troussel, *Les impôts arabes en Algérie*. A recent study by Claude Collot, *Les institutions de l'Algérie durant la période coloniale*, is indispensable for the institutional framework and is useful for the whole colonial period.

For glimpses of the cultural history of the period, with emphasis on educational and health questions, see Yvonne Turin, *Affrontements culturels dans l'Algérie coloniale. Ecoles, médecines, religion, 1830–1880*. Also on education, consult H. Andrieu, *Assimilation de l'enseignement des indigènes en Algérie*; E. Fourmestraux, *L'instruction publique en Algérie*; and Fanny Colonna, *Les instituteurs algériens, 1883–1939*. On religion, see Allan Christellow, "Algerian Islam in a Time of Transition, 1890–1930." His *Muslim Law Courts* sheds light not only on culture in transition but upon the evolution of Algerian elites. Jean-Paul Charnay's search of court records produced *La vie musulmane en Algérie d'après la jurisprudence de la première moitié du XXe siècle*, which provides valuable insights into family life and personal property, religious practice, and the conflicts Muslims encountered in adapting to a European system.

On the emergence of the new elites, and their movements, read B. Saadallah, "The Rise of the Algerian Elite 1900–1914"; Mohamed Brahimi, "La formation des intellectuels algériens modernes 1880–1930)"; Rachid Bencheneb, "Le mouvement intellectuel et littéraire algérien à la fin du 19ème et au début du 20ème siècle"; chapters 1 through 3 of Guy Pervillé, *Les étudiants algériens de l'Université française. 1880–1962;* Ali Merad, "Islam et nationalisme arabe en Algérie à la veille de la Première Guerre mondiale." The first chapter of André Nouschi, *La Naissance du nationalisme algérien* is also useful. For Emir Khaled and the Young Algerians, see Gilbert Meynier, *L'Algérie révélée* and Ahmad Koulakssis and Gilbert Meynier, *L'Emir Khaled.*

The question of reform in the first two decades of the twentieth century generated many commentaries and studies. On the side of the Jeunes Algériens, see *Interpellation sur la politique indigène en Algérie,* by Khaled, Benthami, and Bouderba. A range of European views may be found in Ernest Mercier, *La question indigène en Algérie au commencement du vingtième siècle* (1901); Paul Azan, *Recherche d'une solution à la question indigène en Algérie* (1903); Marcel Morand, *Contribution à l'étude des réformes* (1917); and Victor Piquet, *Les réformes en Algérie et le statut des indigènes* (1919).

CHAPTER 5. THE ALGERIAN NATIONALIST MOVEMENT, 1919–1954

The reader interested in the period 1919–54 has a choice of several excellent overviews. The broadest based is volume 2 of Ageron's *Histoire de l'Algérie contemporaine.* The others concentrate more narrowly on the emergence and development of nationalism. The earliest to appear was Charles-André Julien's *L'Afrique du Nord en marche,* which devotes about a third of its pages to Algeria. Written in just a few months in 1952, it is filled with valuable information and contains many insights that have stood the test of time. It is best for the assimilationist, *élus,* moderate nationalist strains of the movement. Julien, the tireless liberal who hoped that one day his compatriots would demand reform of colonial systems gone wrong, wrote this book with special passion. The bibliography in the third edition (1972) is extensive and useful. Roger LeTourneau, in *L'évolution politique de l'Afrique du Nord musulmane, 1920–1961,* gives a systematic and evenhanded treatment marginally more sympathetic to the French establishments. André Nouschi, in *Naissance du nationalisme algérien,* devotes more space to movements of the left. Mahfoud Kaddache's very extensive two-volume treatment, *Histoire du nationalisme algérien,* focuses on the PPA-MTLD strain, as does the narrower monograph of Abul Qasim Saᶜdalla, *Al haraka al wataniyya fi'l jaza'ir, 1930–1945.* In 1978, Claude Collot and Jean-Robert Henry edited *Le mouvement national algérien,* a useful collection of nationalist documents.

Ageron is excellent for economic issues and social change in this period, and volume 1 of Samir Amin's *L'Économie du Maghreb* is invaluable. For the latter part of the period, *Economie algérienne,* by Joseph St.-Germès, is also useful. Continuing where Nouschi's thesis left off, Johan H. Meuleman published in 1985 *Le Constantinois entre les deux guerres mondiales; l'évolution économique et sociale de la population rurale.* For a scathing, Marxist exposition of the position of the peasantry, read *La question algérienne* (1936), by N. d'Orient and M. Loew. The first sixty pages of Rachid Tlemcani's *State and Revolution in Algeria* present the period emphatically in class terms. For urbanization, see the concluding chapter of Bourdieu's *Sociologie de l'Algérie.* Jacques Berque's *Le Maghreb entre deux guerres* is a work *sui generis* of which several chapters deal with the mind and society of Algeria between the wars. Algerian women, their status, and its transformation are dealt with by Germaine Tillion in her seminal *Le harem et les cousins;* by David C. Gordon in his short but excellent *Women of Algeria,* who takes up some of Tillon's theses; and by Fadéla M'Rabet in *La femme algérienne.*

To begin a study of political development in the 1920s see (in addition to Kaddache, Nouschi, and Ageron) E.-E. Azoulay, *De la condition politique des indigènes musulmans d'Algérie*. See also Meynier, *L'Algérie révélée,* and Koulakssis and Meynier, *L'Emir Khaled.* For development on the political left, consult Béchir Tlili, *Nationalismes, socialisme et syndicalisme dans le Maghrib des années 1919–1934;* the early chapters of Emmanuel Sivan, *Communisme et nationalisme en Algérie;* and Koulakssis and Meynier, "Sur le mouvement ouvrier et les communistes algériens d'Algérie au lendemain de la première guerre mondiale." For an overview emphasizing the *Etoile nord-africaine* tradition, read Benjamin Stora's *Les sources du nationalisme algérien.*

The assmilationist tradition and the Fédération des élus are best covered in Julien, *En marche,* and in Nouschi, *Naissance.* See also Habiba Zerkine's "La Fédération des élus musulmans de Constantine." Of four books written by Ferhat Abbas, two cover the period before 1954: *Le jeune Algérien* and *La nuit coloniale.* On the *Islah* movement, consult first Ali Merad, *Le réformisme musulman en Algérie de 1925 à 1940,* and then, in Arabic, Ammar al Talibi's biography and collected works, *Ibn Badis. Hayatuhu wa atharuhu.* Kaddache's *Nationalisme* is also useful on reformism.

For the PPA-MTLD tradition, consult Mahfoud Kaddache again; P. Rossignol, "Les partis politiques musulmans"; Ahmed Mahsas, *Le mouvement révolutionnaire en Algérie;* and Mohamed Harbi, *Aux origines du F.L.N.: les scissions du PPA-MTLD.* See also *Les mémoires de Messali Hadj* and Benjamin Stora's biography, *Messali Hadj, pionnier du nationalisme algérien.*

The post–World War II crisis in Algeria opened with the Sétif movement and massacres, which receive much attention in each of the overviews cited. For more concentrated treatment, see Manfred Halpern, "The Algerian Uprising of 1945," and Charles-Robert Ageron, "Les troubles du nord-constantinois en mai 1945 une tentative insurrectionelle?" Especially see the thesis of Radouane Ainad Tabet, *Le mouvement du 8 mai 1945 en Algérie.* For the best surveys of deteriorating Franco-Algerian relations after World War II, consult *Les origines de la guerre d'Algérie,* edited by Raymond Aron, and Paul-Emile Sarrasin's *La crise algérienne.* Guy Pervillé has written about the Muslim Reform Commission of 1944 in "La commission des réformes musulmanes de 1944" and Tayeb Chentouf on the fate of the reforms mandated by the Organic Law of September 1947 in "L'Assemblée algérienne et l'application des réformes." For internal developments in the nationalist movement, read Mohamed Harbi, *Aux origines du F.L.N.;* Benjamin Stora, "Continuité et ruptures dans la direction nationaliste algérienne à la veille du 1er novembre 1954"; Rachid Bencheneb, "L'Algérie à la veille du soulèvement de 1954." William B. Quandt, in chapters 1 through 5 of his *Revolution and Political Leadership,* explains the fissures in the nationalist movement as a function of the differing political socializations of succeeding elite cohorts.

CHAPTER 6. THE WAR OF INDEPENDENCE, 1954–1962

Beginning with the War of Independence, this book is no longer primarily a synthesis of historical studies. Instead, it relies mostly on the work of social scientists analyzing phenomena that when written were more or less contemporary and whose focus is by definition restricted. It also relies on the work of journalists, some of which is of very high quality, and some of which tends to the superficial and descriptive. Finally, it attempts to make its way through various writings of participants in the events themselves.

The Algerian War of Independence has generated an enormous literature, only a fraction of which attempts to follow scholarly standards. The bulk of it is by participants in or direct observers of that war and therefore constitutes documentation historians call "primary." The participants can be loosely divided into *winners* and *losers*. Of these two categories, the losers have written more than anyone else. These include colonial and other French officials, generals and middle-level officers, OAS militants and other members of the colon community—explaining, rationalizing, reminiscing, deploring the trauma that was *la guerre d'Algérie*. They include names like Soustelle, Challe, Jouhaud, Sérigny, Massu, Ortiz, Tricot, Tripier, and scores of others, only a few of which are of direct interest to a history of the Algerian nation itself. The category of losers also includes a smaller number of Algerian losers, by which is meant members of the Algerian elite who lost out in the struggles for power that followed independence. Among these are Abbas, Ait Ahmed, Boudiaf, Farès, and a number of liberal and leftist intellectuals whom the sweep of postwar history left behind. Because of their inside perspectives, these works, when used with care, are very useful to the researcher.

The winners, interestingly, have written far less than the losers. Memoirs from men who managed to hold on to power are almost nonexistent. For the first two decades after independence, work on the Algerian revolution by Algerians was limited to widely scattered testimony by people like Saadi Yacef, Mohamed Lebjaoui, Zohra, and others. During the 1980s, publication accelerated, including for the most part reflections on personal experience, collections of reminiscences, accounts of action in different wilayas, and works tending to glorify or edify. One suspects that in addition to the problems posed by limitations on archival access, the political and cultural ambiguities of the independence period have acted as a brake. Because it was a time of great internal conflict, physically and ideologically, systematic exploration of the revolutionary period threatens to project past pain and division into the present and so is avoided.

The person seeking an introduction to the bibliography of the Algerian War of Independence should first consult the *Annuaire de l'Afrique de Nord,* where Guy Pervillé offered in 1976 a to-date survey of works on the war, which he has updated annually ever since. Document collections are unfortunately still sparse, but see André Mandouze's *La révolution algérienne par les textes* and *Textes fondamentaux du Front de Libération Nationale,* published by the Algerian Ministry of Information and Culture. For texts dealing with some of the divergent threads of the FLN experience, see Harbi's *Archives de la Révolution algérienne.*

The history of the Algerian revolution that successfully integrates the social, economic, political, ideological, military, and diplomatic, while at the same time providing appropriate linkages to the nation's earlier experiences, has yet to be written. An early attempt, which is well written and particularly good for questions of culture and identity, is David Gordon's *The Passing of French Algeria* (1966). More narrowly focused on political and military questions is Edgar O'Ballance's *The Algerian Insurrection* (1967). Yves Courrière's four-volume account, *La guerre d'Algérie,* published between 1968 and 1971, is epic in scope and colorful. Based upon scores of personal interviews on both sides, it is filled with fascinating detail. Unfortunately, the personalistic, anecdotal aspects that make the book excellent reading limit its value for the scholar. Alistair Horne's *A Savage War of Peace* is the best account in English and has been translated into French as well as Arabic. It is an excellent, well-written narrative presented by a writer with considerable knowledge of contemporary France, far less of Algeria, and in which the personal, the diplomatic, and the military are the main variables. The serious student would look for deeper analysis and greater understanding of the social, economic, and cultural realities underlying the Algerian struggle than he can offer. The three-volume *Guerre d'Algérie,* edited by Henri Alleg, features the best documentary base, but it is remarkable for its approbation of the role of the French Communist Party. The best balanced account may be the 1982 *Histoire de la guerre de l'Algérie* of Bernard Droz and Evelyne Lever, though it is more critical of French excesses than of Algerian. One should also look at Abbas's view of the war in *La Nuit coloniale* and *Autopsie d'une guerre* as well as the eloquent little book of Hocine Ait Ahmed, *La guerre et l'après-guerre.*

For the outbreak of the war, look at volume 1 of Courrière and chapters 3 and 4 of Horne; and examine the incisive account by Mohamed Boudiaf, *La préparation du 1er novembre.* See also Raymond Aron, *Origines,* and Mohamed Harbi, *La guerre commence en Algérie.*

For a brief overview of the FLN and its development, see Henry Jackson, *The FLN in Algeria.* An excellent analysis of the revolution and the relationships between FLN and society from a class viewpoint is *L'Algérie en armes, ou le temps des certitudes,* by Slimane Chikh. Mohamed Harbi's *Le FLN, mirage et réalité* demystifies the building of the FLN and its internal relationships. Jacques Duchemin's *Histoire du FLN,* from a press usually associated with right-wing tendencies, is remarkably incisive. In chapters 3 through 9 of *Revolution and Political Leadership,* William Quandt explains elite conflict in the FLN as a function of differing conditions of political socialization and the perception that the preceding cohorts have failed in their tasks.

For the long and tortured path toward negotiations between the FLN and France, see Horne, chapters 14 through 20, and Droz, chapters 7 and 8. Read also Robert Buron, *Carnets politiques de la guerre d'Algérie;* Bernard Tricot, *Les sentiers de la paix;* and Jean Lacouture, *La Guerre est fini.* Pierre Viansson-Ponté in volume 1 of *Histoire de la république gaulienne,* provides excellent context from the metropolitan side.

The impact of war and revolution on Algerian society is dealt with in many ways. At the economic level, see volume 1 of Samir Amin, *Economie du Maghreb,* and chapter 4 of Bennoune, *The Making of Contemporary Algeria.* On resettlement of Algerian populations, see Alf Heggoy, *Insurgency and Counterinsurgency in Algeria,* and Michel Cornation, *Les regroupements de la décolonisation en Algérie.* On the aftermath of *regroupement,* see also Pierre Bourdieu and Abdelmalek Sayad, *Le déracinement;* Bourdieu et al., *Travail et travailleurs;* and Michel Launay, *Paysans algériens.* On the question of war deaths, consult Xavier Yacono, "Les pertes algériennes de 1954 à 1962," and Guy Pervillé, "Combien de morts pendant la guerre d'Algérie?"

CHAPTER 7. THE CHALLENGES OF INDEPENDENCE, 1962–1978

The most satisfactory overview of independent Algeria is John P. Entelis, *Algeria. The Revolution Institutionalized.* Strongest on political development and especially for its treatment of political culture, it also offers useful sections on economics, cultural issues, and foreign policy. For a more narrowly political overview ending in the Boumediene period, see Jean Leca and Jean-Claude Vatin, *L'Algérie politique. Institutions et régime.*

The article by Hugh Roberts, "The Politics of Algerian Socialism," gives an incisive shorter overview of political development from independence to the early Bendjedid years. Bennoune's political economy approach, clearly favorable to the *industrie industrialisante* strategy of the Boumediene era and critical of what followed, is rich in data on society and particularly on the economy from independence until the middle 1980s. A less ambitious but still serious political economy approach is that of Mohamed Dahmani, *Algérie. Légitimité historique et continuité politique.*

The crisis of independence, the Ben Bella years, and the 1965 coup are dealt with in detail by many writers including Hervé Bourgès, *L'Algérie à l'épreuve du pouvoir,* and David and Marina Ottaway, *Algeria: The Politics of a Socialist Revolution,* which is one of the most detailed treatments. Quandt covers the period from an elitist perspective in *Revolution and Political Leadership.* Arslan Humbaraci, in *Algeria: A Revolution That Failed,* offers a left/liberal critique. Conventional Marxist critiques are found in many places, including Gérard Chaliand, *L'Algérie est-elle socialiste?* and Chaliand and Minces, *Bilan d'une révolution.* Critiques by leaders who lost out in the early struggles are given by Abbas in *Autopsie d'une guerre* and *L'indépendance confisquée* and by Ait Ahmed in *Guerre et après-guerre.* A biography of Ben Bella written by Robert Merle in 1965 displays all the hallmarks and therefore the shortcomings of an "official" biography. On the Algíers Charter, see LeTourneau's "Le Congrès du F.L.N. et la Charte d'Alger." For the specific evolution of the party under Ben Bella and into the Boumediene years, consult Jackson, *The FLN in Algeria;* Leca and Vatin, *L'Algérie politique: institutions et régime;* and Harbi, "The Party and the State."

Most political analyses are strongest for the Boumediene years. In addition to Entelis, *Revolution Institutionalized,* see Hugh Roberts, "The Politics of Algerian Socialism," which is an incisive short analysis. Juliette Minces, in *L'Algérie de Boumediene,* as well as Balta and Rulleau all provide more or less leftist perspectives. For studies of the elites in the Boumediene era, see Entelis, "Elite Political Culture and Socialization in Algeria," and I. William Zartman, "Algeria: A Post-Revolutionary Elite." Both have also addressed the political role of the military in, respectively, "Algeria: Technocratic Rule, Military Power" and "The Algerian Army in Politics." The only biography of Houari Boumediene, which is by Ania Francos and Jean-Pierre Sereni, is far from scholarly. For the evolution of the FLN in the 1970s see Jackson, *The FLN in Algeria;* Harbi "The Party and the State"; and William Lewis, "The Decline of Algeria's FLN." See John Nellis, *The Algerian Charter of 1976* for a good study that in many ways summarizes the political achievements of the Boumediene era.

For introductions to economic development, see the excellent chapter by Entelis in *Revolution Institutionalized;* Karen Farsoun's "State Capitalism in Algeria"; and the thoughtful overview by Richard Lawless, "The Contradictions of Rapid Industrialization." More detailed economic studies were written by Tahar Benhouria, *L'économie de l'Algérie,* and by M. E. Benissad, *L'économie algérienne contemporaine.* Bennoune's *Contemporary Algeria* is critical in detail of economic performance but approving in concept. Benachenhou, in *Planification,* and John Nellis, in "Socialist Management," deal with management questions. For the contribution of the agriculture sector, consult George Mutin's "Agriculture et dépendance alimentaire."

Every general study of Algeria in the 1960s addresses the experience of autogestion, but there are also several specialized studies. For industrial self-management, one should look at Damien Heile's "Industrial Self-Management in Algeria" and Ian Clegg's *Workers' Self-Management in Algeria.* For agricultural self-management, see Thomas L. Blair's *The Land to Those Who Work It* and Gérard Duprat's *Révolution et autogestion rurale en Algérie.*

For a view of agriculture in the 1970s, one could start with Keith B. Griffin's "Algerian Agriculture in Transition" or Tony Smith's "The Political and Economic Ambitions of Algerian Land Reform, 1962–1974." For an overview of the agrarian reform, see Peter Knauss, "Algeria's 'Agrarian Revolution.' " The two most ambitious works on agrarian reform are Karen Pfeifer, *Agrarian Reform Under State Capitalism in Algeria,* and François Burgat and Nancy Michel, *Les villages socialistes de la révolution agraire algérienne.*

For the course and problems of rapid urbanization, consult Pierre Bourdieu, *Les déracinés,* and Bourdieu et al., *Travail et travailleurs.* See also M. Cornation on the new society in *Les regroupements de la décolonisation en Algérie.* For an overview with more perspective of the same process, see Keith Sutton, "Population resettlement— Traumatic Upheavals and the Algerian Experience." The most cogent class analyses of Algeria in the period 1962–78 are those of Marnia Lazreg and Rachid Tlemcani, whose books have already been introduced.

David Gordon's 1968 short study *Women of Algeria: An Essay on Change* continues to stand out as a major contribution in women's history. From the period of the 1960s as well, one should also look at Minces and Fernissi, *Algerian Women Speak.* Other contributions are by Susan Marshall and Randall Stokes, "Tradition and the Veil"; Alf Heggoy, "The Evolution of Algerian Women"; and Nadia Ainad-Tabet, "Participation des algériennes à la vie du pays." The book by Peter Knauss, *Persistence of Patriarchy,* situates the position of women and men's attitudes toward them in a long cultural tradition.

John Entelis's well-balanced chapter on worldview in *Revolution Institutionalized* is an excellent place to begin the study of Algeria's foreign policy. The most thorough study of the subject, however, is Nicole Grimaud's *La politique extérieure de l'Algérie.* Abbassi Lassassi's *Non-alignment and Algerian Foreign Policy* seems to ascribe more than it should to ideological factors, a tendency that is also evident but not as emphatic in Korany's "Third Worldism and Pragmatic Rationalism."

CHAPTER 8. THE BENDJEDID YEARS— READJUSTMENT AND CRISIS

Many of the studies used for the Boumediene years extend into the Bendjedid period as well. For political evolution, see Hugh Roberts, "Politics of Algerian Socialism" and John P. Entelis, *The Revolution Institutionalized.* See, too, Redjala Ramdane, *L'opposition en Algérie depuis 1962.* Except for Robert Mortimer's "Algeria After the Explosion" and his "Islam and Multiparty Politics in Algeria," little scholarly work was available when this chapter was written on the political restructuring of 1989–91.

For economic development, see Mahfoud Bennoune, *Contemporary Algeria,* chapter 13, "The New Economic Policy and Its Implications." Other useful studies include Marc Ollivier, "L'économie algérienne vingt ans après 1966: l'indépendance nationale en question" and Rabah Abdoun, "Algeria: The Problem of Nation-building." I was especially aided by the latter's "Crise, politique économique et transnationalisation en Algérie," an excellent analysis of the economic crisis and the initiatives of the late 1980s.

Both Bennoune and Entelis offer good material on cultural issues in the 1980s. The short article of Abderrahim Taleb-Bendiab, "La politique de la culture en Algérie," provides a good compass. For women's status and the new family code, consult Knauss, *The Persistence of Patriarchy.* For basic elements of the Islamic resurgence, one should consult Jean-Claude Vatin's "Revival in the Maghreb: Islam as an Alternative Political Language," pp. 232–38, and especially Ahmed Rouadjia's *Les frères et la mosquée. Enquête sur le mouvement islamiste en Algérie.* On Berber issues, one should read Salem Chaker, "L'émergence du fait Berber" and "L'affirmation identitaire berbère"; Hugh Roberts, "Towards an Understanding of the Kabyle Question in Contemporary Algeria"; and Mohamed Harbi, "Nationalisme algérien et identité berbère."

For information on the most recent events in Algeria, the author conducted a series of interviews and relied heavily upon the daily and weekly press. Periodicals of most value were *Le Monde, El Moudjahid, Révolution africaine, Maghreb-Machreq,* and *Jeune Afrique.*

CHAPTER 9. INSURGENCY AND THE PURSUIT OF DEMOCRACY

For basic documentation on this period, the *Annuaire de l'Afrique du Nord* is very helpful through 1996. It contains chronologies, documents, and exhaustive bibliographical listings of relevant works in Arabic, French, and other languages published each year. After 1996 the format was changed, eliminating detailed chronologies and bibliographies, but retaining selective documents and some excellent scholarly analyses of contemporary issues. As a substitution for the eliminated chronologies, one may consult the less complete, though still helpful ones, published each quarter in *The Middle East Journal.* An important vehicle for accessing legislative and other government documents is the website of the *Journal Officiel de la République Algérienne,* which has a helpful index available. Algeria now has a wide selection of newspapers available for researching contemporary issues, though hard copies are usually required, because internet access to archives is limited. The most useful dailies are the highly respected *El Watan, Le Matin, Le Jeune Indépendant, La Quotidienne d'Oran, Le Soir d'Algérie,* and the military's *El Djeich,* all of which are in French. The most widely read Arabic daily is *al-Khabar.* For research purposes, the Parisian *Le Monde,* which covers Algeria extensively, provides internet access to all issues since 1987.

The best scholarly overviews of Algeria from the early to the mid-1990s include Martin Stone's *The Agony of Algeria,* Lahouari Addi's *L'Algérie et la démocratie: pouvoir et crise politique dans l'Algérie contemporaine,* and that of William B. Quandt, who situates the issues within a range of theoretical perspectives in his *Between Ballots and Bullets. Algeria's Transition from Authoritarianism.* Hugh Roberts has published an insightful collection of his essays in *The Battlefield Algeria. 1988–2002.* The edited collection by Ahmed Mahiou and Jean-Robert Henry, *Où va l'Algérie?* offers a range of perspectives from the political, to the social, cultural, and economic.

With regard to the dynamics of the Islamic insurgency, excellent backgrounding may be found in Ahmed Rouadjia, *Les Frères et la mosquée: enquête sur le mouvement islamiste en Algérie,* and in chapter 4 of Emad Shahin's *Political Ascent. Contemporary Islamic Movements in North Africa.* Chapters by John Ruedy, Séverine Labat, John Entelis, and Hugh Roberts in Ruedy's *Islamism and Secularism in North Africa* deal with the early stages of the insurgency. The book of Séverine Labat, *Les Islamistes algériens entre les urnes et le maquis,* by defining branches of Islamism and their interconnections as the insurgency develops, has become an essential. The work of Camille al-Tawil, *Al-haraka al-islamiyya al musalaha fi al-jaza'ir* is an excellent analysis of the transition from politics to insurgency, while the most detailed analysis of the dynamics of the insurgency itself is provided by Luis Martinez in *The Algerian Civil War, 1990–1998.* Quantitative progression of types of violence is provided by Mohammed M. Hafez in his article "Armed Islamist Movements and Political Violence in Algeria" in *The Middle East Journal*. Studies focusing upon abuses by the military include Habib Souaïda's *La Sale Guerre* and Hichem Aboud's *La Mafia des Généraux*.

For a broad overview of economic development, readers should consult Ahmed Dahmani's *L'Algérie à l'épreuve. Economie politique des Réformes (1980–1997)*. Detailed studies on the economy are included in Part Two of Mahiou and Henry in chapters by Abdelkader Sid Ahmed, Larbi Talha, Ahmed Bouyacoub, Slimane Bedrani, and Amor Khelif. Bradford L. Dillman's *State and Private Sector in Algeria: the Politics of Rent-Seeking and Failed Development*, is the best overview in English.

Political developments and elections are well covered in articles by Slaheddine Bariki in the 1996 and 1997 editions of the *Annuaire de l'Afrique du Nord* and by those of Chérif Bennadji in those of 1999 and 2000. Bennadji also includes detailed coverage of the Black Spring crisis in his 2001 article. The overview presented by Rachid Tlemçani in *Elections et élites en Algérie* is the best analysis of political processes during the 2000s. Important foreign policy issues are in *France and the Algeria Conflict. Issues in Democracy and Political Stability, 1988–1995* by Camille Bonora-Waisman and in *France and Algeria. A History of Decolonization and Transformation* by Phillip C. Naylor. Khaoula Taleb Ibrahimi's *Les Algériens et leurs langues* is a comprehensive study of language issues. For the status of women, consult Mounira M. Charrad, *States and Women's Rights. The Making of Postcolonial Tunisia, Algeria, and Morocco*. Rachid Tlemçani also includes useful insights and data.

BIBLIOGRAPHY

Abbas, Ferhat. *Autopsie d'une guerre*. Paris: Garnier, 1980.

——. *De la colonie vers la province. Le jeune Algérien*. 2nd ed. Paris: Garnier, 1981.

——. *Guerre et révolution d'Algérie. La nuit coloniale*. Paris: Julliard, 1962.

——. *L'indépendance confisquée*. Paris: Flammarion, 1984.

Abdoun, Rabah. "Algeria: The Problem of Nation-building." In A. Mahjoub, ed., *Adjustment or Delinking? The African Experience*. London: Zed, 1990.

——. "Crise, politique économique et transnationalisation en Algérie." Unpublished paper in author's collection, Nov. 1990.

Aboud, Hichem. *La Mafia des Généraux*. Paris: J.C. Lattès, 2002.

Abu ʿAziz, Yahya. *Thawra 1871. Dawr ʿa'ilati al Muqrani wa'l Haddad*. Algiers: SNED, 1982.

Abun-Nasr, Jamil M. *A History of the Maghrib*. Cambridge: Cambridge University Press, 1971.

——. *A History of the Maghrib in the Islamic Period*. Cambridge: Cambridge University Press, 1987.

——. *The Tijaniyya. A Sufi Order in the Modern World*. Oxford: Oxford University Press, 1965.

Addi, Lahraoui. *L'Algérie et la démocratie: pouvoir et crise politique dans l'Algérie contemporaine*. Paris: La Découverte, 1994.

——. *De l'Algérie pré-coloniale à l'Algérie coloniale. Economie et société*. Algiers: ENAL, 1985.

Ageron, Charles-Robert. *L'Algérie algérienne de Napoléon III à de Gaulle*. Paris: Sinbad, 1980.

——. *Les Algériens musulmans et la France (1871–1919)*. 2 vols. Paris: Presses universitaires de France, 1968.

——. "L'évolution politique de l'Algérie sous Napoléon III." *L'Information historique* (Sept.–Oct. 1969).

——. *Histoire de l'Algérie contemporaine (1830–1964)*. Paris: Presses universitaires de France, 1964.

——. *Histoire de l'Algérie contemporaine*. Vol. II, *De l'insurrection de 1871 au déclenchement de la guerre de libération (1954)*. Paris: Presses universitaires de France, 1979.

——. "Les troubles du nord-constantinois en mai 1945 une tentative insurrectionelle?" *Vingtième siècle. Revue d'histoire*, IV (Oct. 1984): 23–38.

Ainad-Tabet, Nadia. "Participation des algériennes à la vie du pays." In Ainad-Tabet et al., *Femmes et politique autour de la Méditerranée*, pp. 235–250. Paris: L'Harmattan, 1980.

Ainad-Tabet, Radouane. *Le mouvement du 8 mai 1945 en Algérie*. Algiers: Office des publications universitaires, 1985.

Aït Ahmed, Hocine. *La guerre et l'après guerre*. Paris: Minuit, 1964.

Albertini, Eugène. *L'Afrique romaine*. Algiers: Imprimerie officielle, 1955. (1st ed., 1922.)

Alleg, Henri, ed. *La guerre d'Algérie*. Paris: Temps actuels, 1981. 3 vols.

Amin, Samir. *L'Economie du Maghreb. La colonisation et la décolonisation*. Paris: Minuit, 1966. 2 vols.

Andrieu, H. *Assimilation de l'enseignement des indigènes en Algérie*. Algiers: 1897.

al ʿArabi, Ismaʿil. *Al muqawama al jaza'iriyya taht liwa' al amir ʿAbd al Qadir*. Algiers: Société nationale d'édition, 1982.

Aron, Raymond, ed. *Les origines de la guerre d'Algérie*. Paris: Fayard, 1952.

Azan, Paul. *L'Armée d'Afrique de 1830 à 1852*. Paris: Plon, 1936.

——. *Conquête et pacification de l'Algérie*. Paris: Librairie de France, 1931.

——. *L'émir Abd el-Kader (1808–1883). Du fanatisme musulman au patriotisme français*. Paris: Hachette, 1925.

——. *L'expédition d'Alger*. Paris: Plon, 1930.

————. *Recherche d'une solution à la question indigène en Algérie.* Paris: 1903.

Azoulay, E.-E. *De la condition politique des indigènes musulmans d'Algérie. Essai critique sur la loi du 4 février 1919.* Algiers: Crescenz, n.d. [1921].

Balout, Lionel. *Préhistoire de l'Afrique du Nord. Essai de chronologie.* Paris: Arts et métiers graphiques, 1955.

Balta, Paul, and Claudine Rulleau. *L'Algérie des Algériens, vingt ans après. . . .* Paris: Editions Ouvrières, 1981.

Bariki, Slaheddine. "Algérie. Chronique intérieur." *Annuaire de l'Afrique du Nord* XXXV (1996), pp. 119–141 and XXXVI (1997), pp. 407–440.

Basset, André. *La langue berbère.* Oxford: Oxford University Press, 1952.

Baudicour, Louis de. *La colonisation de l'Algérie. Ses éléments.* Paris: Lecoffre, 1846.

————. *Histoire de la colonisation de l'Algérie.* Paris: Challamel, 1860.

Bel, Alfred. *La religion musulmane en Berbérie. Esquisse d'une histoire et de sociologie religieuses.* Paris: Geunther, 1938.

Benachenhou, Abellatif. *Formation du sous-développement en Algérie. Essai sur les limites du développement du capitalisme.* Algiers: Imprimerie commerciale, 1978.

————. *Planification et développement en Algérie, 1962–1980.* Algiers: Presses de l'E.N. Imprimerie commerciale, 1980.

Bencheneb, Rachid. "L'Algérie à la veille du soulèvement de 1954." In *Les chemins de la décolonisation de l'empire français, 1936–1956,* pp. 415–30. Paris: CNRS, 1986.

————. *L'état algérien en 1830.* Algiers: Société nationale de diffusion, n.d. [1972].

————. "Le mouvement intellectuel et littéraire algérien à la fin du 19ème et au début du 20ème siècle." *Revue française d'outre-mer,* LXX (Jan.–May 1983): 11–24.

Benhouria, Tahar. *L'économie de l'Algérie.* Paris: Maspéro, 1980.

Benissad, M. E. *L'économie algérienne contemporaine.* Paris: Presses universitaires de France, 1980.

Bennadji, Chérif. "Chronique politique." *Annuaire de l'Afrique du Nord,* XXXIX (2000–2001): 127–145.

Bennoune, Mahfoud. "Algerian Peasants and National Politics." *MERIP Reports,* no. 48 (June 1976): 3–24.

————. "Industrialization of Algeria: An Overview." In Halim Barakat, ed., *Contemporary North Africa: Issues of Development and Integration,* pp. 178–213. Washington: Center for Contemporary Arab Studies, 1985.

————. *The Making of Contemporary Algeria, 1830–1987. Colonial Upheavals and Post-Independence Development.* Cambridge: Cambridge University Press, 1988.

Bérard, Joseph. *Les deux ville de Ténès et Bou-Maza.* Algiers: Bastide, 1864.

Bernard, Augustin. *L'Algérie.* Paris: Plon, 1930.

Berque, Augustin. *Ecrits sur l'Algérie.* Collected and edited by Jacques Berque. Aix-en-Provence: Edisud, 1986.

————. "Essai d'une bibliographie critique des confréries musulmanes algériennes." *Bulletin trimestriel de la Société de Géographie et d'Archéologie d'Oran* (1919): 135–74, 193–233.

Berque, Jacques. *Le Maghreb entre deux guerres.* 2nd ed. Paris: Seuil, 1970.

Blair, Thomas L. *"The Land to Those Who Work It": Algeria's Experiment in Workers' Management.* Garden City, N.Y.: Anchor Books, 1970.

Bonora-Waisman. *France and the Algerian Conflict. Issues in Democracy and Political Stability, 1988–1995.* Aldershot, U.K.: Ashgate, 2003.

Boudiaf, Mohamed. *Où va l'Algérie?* Paris: Librairie de l'Etoile, 1964.

————. *La préparation du 1er novembre. Suivi de lettre ouverte aux Algériens.* Paris: Collection El Jarida, 1976.

Bourdieu, Pierre. *Sociologie de l'Algérie.* Paris: Presses universitaires de France, 1958. (English trans., *The Algerians.* Boston: Beacon Press, 1962.)

Bourdieu, Pierre, et al. *Travail et travailleurs en Algérie.* Paris: Mouton, 1963.

Bourdieu, Pierre, and Abdelmalek Sayad. *Le déracinement: la crise de l'agriculture traditionelle en Algérie.* Paris: Editions de Minuit, 1964.

Bourgès, Hervé. *L'Algérie à l'épreuve du pouvoir.* Paris: B. Grasset, 1967.

Bouriba, Rachid. *Les Hammadides.* Algiers: PUB, 1982.

Bousquet, Georges-Henri. *Les Berbères. Histoire et institutions.* Paris: Presses universitaires de France, 1961.

―――. *L'Islam magrebin. Introduction à l'étude générale de l'Islam.* 4th ed. Algiers: Maison des Livres, 1955.

Boyer, Pierre. "Des pachas triennaux à la révolution d'Ali Khodja Dey, 1571–1817)." *Revue historique* (juillet–septembre 1970).

―――. *L'évolution de l'Algérie médiane (ancien département d'Alger) de 1830 à 1956.* Paris: Maisonneuve, 1960.

―――. "Introduction à une histoire intérieure de la Régence d'Alger." *Revue historique* CCXXXV, no. 2 (avril–juin 1966): 297–316.

―――. "Le problème kouloughli dans la Régence d'Alger." *Revue de l'Occident musulman et de la Méditerranée* V, no. 1 (1966).

―――. *La vie quotidienne à Alger à la veille de l'intervention française.* Paris: Hachette, 1963.

Brahimi, Mohamed. "La formation des intellectuels algériens modernes 1880–1930)." *Revue algérien des sciences juridiques, économiques et politiques,* 22 (Oct.–Dec. 1985): 639–64.

Brunschvig, Robert. *La Berbérie orientale sous les Hafsides. Des origines à la fin du XVe siècle.* Paris: Librairie d'Amérique et d'Orient, 1940–1947. 2 vols.

Burgat, François, and Nancy Michel. *Les Villages socialistes de la révolution agraire algérienne.* Paris: Editions du CNRS, 1984.

Buron, Robert. *Carnets politiques de la guerre d'Algérie.* Paris: Plon, 1965.

Camps, Gabriel. *Monuments et rites funéraires protohistoriques (aux origines de la Berbérie).* Paris: Douin, 1974.

Chaker, Salem. "L'affirmation identitaire berbère à partir de 1900. Constantes et mutations (Kabylie)." *Revue de l'Occident musulman et de la Méditerranée,* 44 (1987): 14–33.

―――. "L'émergence du fait berbère. Le cas de l'Algérie." *Annuaire de l'Afrique du Nord,* XIX (1980): 473–83.

Chaliand, Gérard. *L'Algérie est-elle socialiste?* Paris: Maspéro, 1965.

Chaliand, Gérard, and Juliette Minces. *L'Algérie indépendante: Bilan d'une révolution nationale.* Paris: Maspéro, 1972.

Charles-Roux, F. *France et Afrique du Nord avant 1830. Les précurseurs de la conquête.* Paris: Alcan, 1932.

Charnay, Jean-Paul. *La vie musulmane en Algérie d'après la jurisprudence de la première moitié du XXe siècle.* Paris: Presses universitaires de France, 1965.

Charrad, Mounira M. *States and Women's Rights. The Making of Postcolonial Tunisia, Algeria, and Morocco.* Berkeley: University of California Press, 2001.

Chentouf, Tayeb. "L'Assemblée algérienne et l'application des réformes prévues par le statut du 20 septembre 1947." In *Les chemins de la décolonisation de l'empire français, 1936–1956,* pp. 367–75. Paris: CNRS, 1986.

Chikh, Slimane. *L'Algérie en armes ou le temps des certitudes.* Paris: Economica, 1981.Christellow, Allan. "Algerian Islam in a Time of Transition: c. 1890–c. 1930." *The Maghrib Review* VIII, no. 4 (1983): 124–30.

―――. *Muslim Law Courts and the French Colonial State in Algeria.* Princeton: Princeton University Press, 1985.

Churchill, Charles. *The Life of Abdel Kader, Ex-Sultan of the Arabs of Algeria.* London: Chapman and Hall, 1867.

Clancy-Smith, Julia Ann. "The Saharan Rahmaniya: Popular Protest and Desert Society in Southeastern Algeria and the Tunisian Jarid, c. 1750–1881." Unpublished doctoral dissertation, University of California, Los Angeles, 1988.

―――. "Saints, Mahdis and Arms: Religion and Resistance in Nineteenth Century North Africa." In Edmund Burke II and Ira M. Lapidus, eds., *Islam, Politics, and Social Movements.* Berkeley: University of California Press, 1988.

Clegg, Ian. *Workers' Self-Management in Algeria.* New York: Monthly Review Press, 1972.

Collot, Claude. *Les institutions de l'Algérie durant la période coloniale (1830–1962)*. Paris: CNRS, 1987.

Collot, Claude, and Jean-Robert Henry. *Le mouvement national algérien. Textes 1912–1954*. Paris: L'Harmattan, 1978.

Colonna, Fanny. *Les instituteurs algériens, 1883–1939*. Algiers: OPU, 1975.

———. "Saints furieux et saints studieux ou, dans l'Aurès, comment la religion vient aux tribus." *Annales* 35 (1980).

Confer, Vincent. *France and Algeria. The Problem of Civil and Political Reform, 1870–1920*. Syracuse, N.Y.: Syracuse University Press, 1966.

Cornation, M. *Les regroupements de la décolonisation en Algérie*. Paris: Les Editions Ouvrières, 1967.

Courrière, Yves. *La Guerre d'Algérie*. Vol. I, *Les Fils de la Toussaint;* Vol. II, *Le temps des léopards;* Vol. III, *L'heure des colonels;* Vol. IV, *Les feux du désespoir (la fin d'un empire)*. Paris: Fayard, 1968–1971.

Courtois, Christian. *Les Vandales et l'Afrique*. Paris: Arts et métiers graphiques, 1955.

Dahmani, Mohamed. *L'Algérie: Légitimité historique et continuité politique*. Paris: Editions Le Sycomore, 1980.

———. *Economie politique des réformes (1980–1997)*. Algiers: Casbah Editions, 1999.

Danziger, Raphael. *Abdel Qadir and the Algerians. Resistance to the French and Internal Consolidation*. New York: Holmes and Meier, 1977.

Demerghem, Emile. *Les cultes des saints dans l'Islam maghrebin*. Paris: Gallimard, 1954.

Demontès, Victor. *L'Algérie économique*. Algiers: Imprimerie algérienne, 1922–1930. 5 vols.

———. *Le peuple algérien, essai de démographie algérienne*. Algiers: Imprimerie algérienne, 1906.

Depont, Octave, and Xavier Coppolani. *Les confréries religieuses musulmanes*. Algiers: Jourdan, 1847.

Descloitres, R., C. Descloitres, and J. C. Reverdy. "Urban Organization and Social Structure in Algeria." In I. William Zartman, ed., *Man, State, and Society in the Contemporary Maghrib*, pp. 424–38. New York: Praeger, 1973.

Desparmet, J. "L'entrée des Français à Alger par le cheikh Abdelkader." *Revue africaine*, 3–4 (1930): 225–56.

Despois, Jean. *L'Afrique Blanche*. Vol. I, *Afrique du Nord*. Paris: Presses universitaires de France, 1964.

Despois, Jean, and René Raynal. *Géographie de l'Afrique du Nord-Ouest*. Paris: Payot, 1967.

Dhina, Attallah. *Le Royaume abdelwaddide à l'époque d'Abdou Hammam Moussa 1er et d'Abou Tachfin 1er*. Algiers: OPU, 1985.

Diehl, Charles. *L'Afrique byzantine. Histoire de la domination byzantine en Afrique (533–709)*. New York: Franklin, Burt, 1959. (Reprint of 1896 ed.)

Dillman, Bradford L. *State and Private Sector in Algeria: The Politics of Rent-Seeking and Failed Development*. Boulder, Colo.: Westview Press, 2000.

Djeghloul, Abdelkader. "La formation des intellectuels modernes (1880–1830)." In *Aspects de la culture algérienne. Problèmes et perspectives*, pp. 53–82. Paris: CCA, 1986.

———. "La formation sociale algérienne à la veille de la colonisation." *Pensée*, 185 (1976): 61–66.

Djender, Mohiedin. *Introduction à l'histoire de l'Algérie*. Algiers: Société nationale de diffusion, 1968.

Droz, Bernard, and Evelyne Lever. *Histoire de la guerre d'Algérie, 1954–1962*. Paris: Le Seuil, 1982.

Duchemin, Jacques C. *Histoire du F.L.N.* Paris: La Table Ronde, 1962.

Dufour, Dany. "L'enseignement en Algérie." *Maghreb-Machrek* 80, no. 3: 33–53.

Dunand, Fabien. *L'indépendance de l'Algérie. Décision politique sous la Ve République, 1958–1962*. Berne: Lang, 1977.

Duprat, Gérard. *Révolution et autogestion rurale en Algérie*. Paris: A. Colin, 1973.

Durkheim, Emile. *De la division du travail social. Etude sur l'organisation des sociétés supérieures.* Paris: Alcan, 1893.

Emerit, Marcel. *L'Algérie à l'époque d'Abd el-Kader.* Paris: Larose, 1951.

————. "Les méthodes coloniales de la France sous le Second Empire." *Revue africaine* 87, no. 3–4 (1983): 184–218.

————. "Les tribus privilégiées en Algérie dans la première moitié du XIXe siècle," *Annales,* XXI (janvier–février 1966): 44–58.

Entelis, John P. "Algeria: Technocratic Rule, Military Power." In I. William Zartman et al., *Political Elites in Arab North Africa,* pp. 92–143. New York: Longman, 1982.

————. *Algeria: The Revolution Institutionalized.* Boulder, Colo.: Westview Press, 1986.

————. "Algeria in World Politics: Foreign Policy Orientation and the New International Economic Order." *American-Arab Affairs,* no. 6 (Fall 1983): 70–78.

————. "Elite Political Culture and Socialization in Algeria: Tensions and Discontinuities." *The Middle East Journal* 35, no. 2 (Spring 1981): 191–208.

————. "Islam, Democracy, and the State: The Reemergence of Authoritarian Politics in Algeria." In John Ruedy, *Islam and Secularism in North Africa.* New York: St. Martin's Press, 1994, pp. 219–251.

Esquer, Gabriel. *Les commencements d'un empire. La prise d'Alger (1830).* 2nd ed. Paris: Larose, 1929.

Evans-Pritchard, Edward. *The Nuer.* Oxford: Oxford University Press, 1940.

————. *The Sanussi of Cyrenaica.* Oxford: Oxford University Press, 1954.

Farsoun, Karen. "State Capitalism in Algeria." *MERIP Reports,* no. 35 (Feb. 1975): 3–30.

Ferry, Jules. *Le gouvernement de l'Algérie.* Paris: Colin, 1892.

Francos, Ania, and Jean-Pierre Sereni. *Un Algérien nommé Boumediene.* Paris: Stock, 1976.

Gaid, Mouloud. *L'Algérie sous les Turcs.* Tunis: Maison tunisienne de l'édition, 1976.

————. *Les Beni Yala et les vérités sur l'insurrection de Mokrani en 1871.* Algiers: Imprimerie générale [1952].

Gallissot, René. "Abdel Kader et la nationalité algérienne; interprétation de la chute de la Régence d'Alger et des premières résistances à la conquête française (1830–1839)." *Revue historique* 2 (1965): 339–68.

————. "L'Algérie précoloniale." In *Sur le féodalisme.* Paris: CREM, 1974.

————. *L'économie de l'Afrique du Nord.* Paris: Presses universitaires de France, 1969.

————. "La guerre d'Abdel Kader ou la ruine de la nationalité algérienne." *Hespéris-Tamuda* (1964): 119–41.

————. *Marxisme et Algérie.* Paris: 1976.

————. "Le système foncier en Algérie au moment de la colonisation française." In *Sur le féodalisme.* Paris: CREM, 1974.

Gautherot, Gustave. *La conquête d'Alger, 1830, d'après les papiers inédits du maréchal de Bourmont.* Paris: Payot, 1929.

Gautier, Emile-Félix. *Le passé de l'Afrique du Nord. Les siècles obscurs.* Paris: Payot, 1952.

Gellner, Ernest. *Saints of the Atlas.* Chicago: University of Chicago Press, 1969.

Giacobetti, Antoine. *La Confrérie des Rahmaniyya.* Algiers: Maison Carrée, 1946.

Godin, Frédéric. "Le régime foncier de l'Algérie." In Louis Milliot et al., *L'oeuvre législative de la France en Algérie.* Paris: Alcan, 1930.

Golvin, Lucien. *Le Maghrib central à l'époque des Zirides. Recherches d'archéologie et d'histoire.* Paris: Arts et métiers graphiques, 1957.

Gordon, David. *The Passing of French Algeria.* London: Oxford University Press, 1986.

————. *Women of Algeria: An Essay on Change.* Cambridge, Mass.: Harvard University Press, 1968.

Grammont, Henri-Delmas de. *Histoire d'Alger sous la domination turque 1515–1830.* Paris: Leroux, 1887.

Griffin, Keith B. "Algerian Agriculture in Transition." In I. William Zartman, ed., *Man, State and Society in the Contemporary Maghrib,* pp. 395–414. New York: Praeger, 1973.

Grimaud, Nicole. *La politique extérieure de l'Algérie.* Paris: Karthala, 1984.

Gsell, Stéphane. *Histoire ancienne de l'Afrique du Nord.* 8 volumes. Paris: Hachette, 1914–1928.

Hadj, Messali. *Les mémoires de Messali Hadj, 1898–1938.* Edited by Renaud de Rochebrune. Paris: Lattès, 1982.

Hafez, Mohammed M. "Armed Islamist Movements and Political Violence in Algeria." *Middle East Journal* 54 (Autumn 2000): 572–91.

Halpern, Manfred. "The Algerian Uprising of 1945." *Middle East Journal* (1948): 191–202.

Hamdan Ben Othman Khodja. *Aperçu historique et statistique sur la Régence d'Alger, intitulé en arabe le Miroir.* Paris: Dezauche, 1834.

Harbi, Mohamed. *Les archives de la Révolution algérienne.* Paris: Editions Jeune Afrique, 1981.

———. *Aux origines du F.L.N.: la scission du PPA-MTLD.* Paris: Christian Bourgeois, 1975.

———. *Le FLN, mirage et réalité, des origines à la prise du pouvoir (1945–1962).* Paris: Editions Jeune Afrique, 1980.

———. "Nationalisme algérien et identité berbère." *Peuples méditerranéens,* 11: 59–68.

———. *1954. La guerre commence en Algérie.* Brussels: Editions complexe, 1984.

———. "The Party and the State." In I. William Zartman, ed., *Man, State, and Society in the Contemporary Maghrib,* pp. 159–67. New York: Praeger, 1973.

Hardoun, Ali. *La 7e wilaya, la guerre du FLN en France (1954–1962).* Paris: Le Seuil, 1986.

Heggoy, Alf. "The Evolution of Algerian Women." *African Studies Review* XVII, no. 2 (Sept. 1974): 449–56.

———. *Insurgency and Counterinsurgency in Algeria.* Bloomington: Indiana University Press, 1972.

Heile, Damien. "Industrial Self-Management in Algeria." In I. William Zartman, ed., *Man, State, and Society in the Contemporary Maghrib,* pp. 465–74. New York: Praeger, 1973.

Henni, Ahmed. *Etat, surplus, et société en Algérie avant 1830.* Algiers: ENAL, 1986.

Hermassi, Elbaki. *Leadership and National Development in North Africa: A Comparative Study.* Berkeley: University of California Press, 1972.

Histoire et historiens de l'Algérie (1830–1930). Intro. by Stéphane Gsell. Paris: Librairie Alcan, 1931.

Horne, Alistair. *A Savage War of Peace. Algeria 1954–1962.* London: Penguin, 1985. (1st ed., Macmillan, 1977.)

Humbaraci, Arslan. *Algeria: A Revolution That Failed—A Political History since 1954.* New York: Praeger, 1966.

Hutchinson, Martha Crenshaw. *Revolutionary Terrorism: The FLN in Algeria 1954–1962.* Stanford, Calif.: Hoover Institution Press, 1978.

Idris, Hady Roger. *La Berbérie orientale sous les Zirides. Xe–XIIe siècles.* 2 vols. Paris: Adrien-Maisonneuve, 1962.

Isnard, Hildebert. "Le cantonnement des indigènes dans le Sahel d'Alger (1852–1864)." In *Mélanges de géographie et d'orientalisme offerts à E.-F. Gautier,* pp. 245–55. Tours: 1937.

———. "L'état économique et social de la Mitidja en 1830." *Revue africaine,* extra number (1938): 717–25.

———. *La réorganisation de la propriété rurale dans la Mitidja (Ordonnance royale du 21 juillet 1846 et Commission des Transactions et Partages, 1851–67) Ses conséquences sur la vie indigène.* Algiers: A. Joyeux, 1947.

———. "Le Sahel d'Alger en 1830." *Revue africaine* (1937): 587–96.

Jackson, Henry. *The FLN in Algeria. Party and Development in a Revolutionary Society.* Westport, Conn.: Greenwood, 1977.

al Jaza'iri, Muhammad ibn ʿAbd al Qadir. *Tuhfat al zaʾir fi taʾrikh al jazaʾir waʾl amir ʿAbd al Qadir.* Beirut: Dar al yaqiz al ʿarabiyya lil taʾalif wal tarjama wal nashr, 1964.

Julien, Charles-André. *L'Afrique du Nord en marche. Nationalismes musulmans et souveraineté française.* 3rd ed. Paris: Julliard, 1972.

———. *Histoire de l'Afrique du Nord. Tunisie. Algérie. Maroc.* 2nd ed. Vol. I, *Des origines à la conquête arabe (647 ap. J.-C.)*, rev. and ed. by Christian Courtois. Paris: Payot, 1966; 2nd ed. Vol. II, *De la conquête arabe à 1830*, rev. and ed. by Roger LeTourneau. Paris: Payot. English trans. by John Petrie, *History of North Africa. Tunisia. Algeria. Morocco. From the Arab Conquest to 1830.* New York: Praeger, 1970.

———. *Histoire de l'Algérie contemporaine.* Vol. I, *La conquête et les débuts de la colonisation (1827–1871).* Paris: Presses universitaires de France, 1964.

———. "L'opposition et la guerre d'Alger à la veille de la conquête." *Bulletin de la Société de Géographie et d'Archéologie de la Province d'Oran,* 1 (1921): 21–44.

———. "La question d'Alger devant l'opinion de 1827 à 1830." *Bulletin de la Société de Géographie et d'Archéologie de la Province d'Oran,* 3–4 (1922): 225–58.

Kaddache, Mahfoud. *L'Algérie médiévale.* Algiers: SNED, 1982.

———. *Histoire du nationalisme algérien. Question nationale et politique algérienne. 1919–1951.* 2nd ed. Algiers: Société nationale de l'édition, 1981.

Khalid ibn Hashimi, Benthami ould Hamida, Omar Bouderbah. *Interpellation sur la politique indigène en Algérie.* Algiers: 1914.Knauss, Peter R. "Algeria Under Boumedienne: The Mythical Revolution 1965 to 1978." In Isaac J. Mowoe, ed., *The Performance of Soldiers as Governors: African Politics and the African Military,* pp. 27–100. Washington: University Press of America, 1980.

———. "Algeria's 'Agrarian Revolution': Peasant Control or Control of Peasants?" *African Studies Review* 20, no. 3 (Dec. 1977): 65–78.

———. *The Persistence of Patriarchy. Class, Gender, and Ideology in Twentieth Century Algeria.* New York: Praeger, 1987.

Korany, Bahgat. "Third Worldism and Pragmatic Radicalism: The Foreign Policy of Algeria." In Bahgat Korany and Ali E. Hillal Dessouki, eds., *The Foreign Policies of Arab States,* pp. 79–118. Boulder, Colo.: Westview Press, 1984.

Koulakssis, Ahmed, and Gilbert Meynier. *L'Emir Khaled, premier zaʿim? Identité algérienne et colonialisme français.* Paris: Editions l'Harmattan, 1987.

———. "Sur le mouvement ouvrier et les communistes algériens d'Algérie au lendemain de la première guerre mondiale." *Le mouvement social* 1 (1985): 3–32.

Labat, Séverine. "Islamism and Islamists: The Emergence of New Types of Politic-Religious Militants." In John Ruedy, ed., *Islamism and Secularism in North Africa,* pp. 103–121. New York: St. Martin's Press, 1994.

———. *Les Islamistes algériens: entre les urnes et le maquis.* Paris: Editions du Seuil, 1995.

Lacheraf, Mostefa. *L'Algérie: nation et société.* Paris: Maspéro, 1965.

Lacoste, Yves, André Nouschi, and André Prenant. *L'Algérie. Passé et présent Le cadre et les étapes de la constitution de l'Algérie actuelle.* Paris: Editions sociales, 1960.

Lacouture, Jean. *La guerre est finie.* Brussels: Editions complexe, 1985.

Laroui, Abdallah. *L'Histoire du maghreb. Un essai de synthèse.* Paris: François Maspéro, 1970. English trans., *The History of the Maghrib: An Interpretive Essay.* Princeton: Princeton University Press, 1977.

Lassassi, Abbassi. *Non-Alignment and Algerian Foreign Policy.* Aldershot, U.K.: Avebury, 1988.

Launay, Michel. *Paysans algériens.* Paris: Editions du Seuil, 1963.

Lawless, Richard I. "Algeria: The Contradictions of Rapid Industrialization." In Richard Lawless and Allan Findlay, eds., *North Africa: Contemporary Politics and Economic Development,* pp. 153–90. London: Croom Helms, 1984.

Lazreg, Marnia. *The Emergence of Social Classes in Algeria. A Study of Colonialism and Socio-Political Change.* Boulder, Colo.: Westview Press, 1976.

Leca, Jean. "Algerian Socialism: Nationalism, Industrialization, and State-Building." In Helen Desfosses and Jacques Levesque, eds., *Socialism in the Third World,* pp. 121–60. New York: Praeger, 1975.

Leca, Jean, et al. *Développements politiques au Maghreb. Aménagements institutionels et processus électoraux.* Paris: CNRS, 1979.

314   *Bibliography*

Leca, Jean, and Jean-Claude Vatin. *L'Algérie politique: institutions et régime.* Paris: Colin, 1975.

Lepès, René. *Alger. Etude de géographie et d'histoire urbaines.* Paris: Alcan, 1930.

———. *Oran. Etude de géographie et d'histoire urbaines.* Paris: Alcan, 1938.

LeTourneau, Roger. "Le Congrès du F.L.N. (Alger, 16–21 avril 1965[4]) et la Charte d'Alger." In *Annuaire de l'Afrique du Nord,* vol. III, 1964, pp. 9–26. Paris: CNRS, 1965.

———. "Darkawa." Vol. 2, *Encyclopedia of Islam.* 2nd ed. Leiden: Brill, 1965.

———. *L'évolution politique de l'Afrique du Nord musulman, 1920–1961.* Paris: Colin, 1962.

Lewis, William H. "The Decline of Algeria's FLN." In I. William Zartman, *Man, State, and Society in the Contemporary Maghrib,* pp. 330–39. New York: Praeger, 1973.

al Madani, Ahmad Tawfiq. *Kitab al jaza'ir.* Algiers: al mutba‘a ‘arabiyya fil jaza'ir, 1350h.

Mahiou, Ahmed, and Jean-Paul Henri, eds. *Où va l'Algérie?* Paris: Karthala, 2001.

Mahsas, Ahmed. *Le mouvement révolutionnaire en Algérie: essai sur la formation du mouvement national de la 1re guerre mondiale à 1954.* Paris: L'Harmattan, 1979.

Mallarmé, André. *L'organisation gouvernementale de l'Algérie. Etude sur son évolution historique, son état actuel et les projets de réforme.* Paris: Chevalier-Marescq, 1900.

Mandouze, André. *La révolution algérienne par les textes.* Paris: Maspéro, 1961.

Marçais, Georges. *Les Arabes en Berbérie du XIe au XIVe siècle.* Paris: 1913.

———. *La Berbérie musulmane et l'Orient au Moyen Age.* Paris: Montaigne, 1946.

Marçais, William. "Comment l'Afrique du Nord s'est arabisée." *Annales de l'Institut d'Etudes orientales de la Faculté des Lettres d'Alger* 4 (1938): 1–22.

Marneur, F. *L'indigénat en Algérie.* Paris: 1914.

Marshall, Susan E., and Randall G. Stokes. "Tradition and the Veil: Female Status in Tunisia and Algeria." *Journal of Modern African Studies* 19, no. 4 (Dec. 1981): 625–46.

Martinez, Luis. *The Algerian Civil War. 1990–1998.* New York: Columbia University Press, 2000.

———. "Les obstacles à la Politique de Réconciliation nationale." *Annuaire de l'Afrique du Nord* XXXVIII (1999): 119–136.

Masqueray, Emile. *La formation des cités chez les populations sédentaires de l'Algérie.* Aix-en-Provence: Edisud, 1983.

Massignon, Louis. "Tarika." In *First Encyclopedia of Islam. 1913–1936,* pp. 667–72. Leiden: E.J. Brill, 1987.

Megherbi, Abdelghani. *La paysannerie algérienne face à la colonisation: pour comprendre l'impératif de la révolution agraire.* Algiers: ENAP, 1973.

Merad, Ali. *Le réformisme musulman en Algérie de 1925 à 1940.* Paris: Mouton, 1967.

Merad Boudia, Abdelhamid. *La formation sociale algérienne précoloniale.* Algiers: Office nationale des publications universitaires, 1981.

Mercier, Ernest. *Les deux sièges de Constantine.* Constantine: Poulet, 1896.

Merle, Robert. *Ahmed Ben Bella.* Paris: Gallimard, 1965.

Meuleman, Johan H. *Le Constantinois entre les deux guerres mondiales: l'évolution économique et sociale de la population rurale.* Assen, Netherlands: Van Gorcum, 1985.

Meynier, Gilbert. *L'Algérie révélée. La guerre de 1914–1918 et le premier quart du XXe siècle.* Geneva: Librairie Droz, 1981.

Milliot, Louis. *Démembrement du habous.* Paris: E. Leroux, 1918.

Milliot, Louis, Marcel Morand, and Frédéric Godin. *L'oeuvre législative de la France en Algérie.* Paris: Librairie Félix Alcan, 1930.

Minces, Juliette. *L'Algérie de Boumediene.* Paris: Presses de la Cité, 1979.

Morand, Marcel. *Contribution à l'étude des réformes concernant la situation politique et économique des indigènes algériens.* Algiers: 1917.

Mortimer, Robert. "Algeria after the Explosion." *Current History* 89 (Apr. 1990): 161–64.

———. "Islam and Multiparty Politics in Algeria." *Middle East Journal* 45, no. 4 (Autumn 1991): 575–93.

M'Rabet, Fadéla. *La femme algérienne.* Paris: Maspéro, 1969.

Mutin, Georges. "Agriculture et dépendance alimentaire en Algérie." *Maghreb-Machrek* 4, no. 90: 40–64.

Naylor, Phillip C. *France and Algeria: A History of Decolonization and Transformation.* Gainesville: University of Florida Press, 2000.

Nellis, John. *The Algerian National Charter of 1976: Content, Public Reaction and Significance.* Washington: Center for Contemporary Arab Studies, 1980.

———. "Socialist Management in Algeria." *Journal of Modern African Studies* 15, no. 4 (Dec. 1977): 529–54.

Nouschi, André. "Constantine à la veille de la conquête." *Cahiers de Tunisie,* 3 (1955): 370–87.

———. *Enquête sur le niveau de vie des populations rurales constantinoises.* Paris: Presses universitaires de France, 1961.

———. *La naissance du nationalisme algérien.* Paris: Minuit, 1979.

O'Ballance, Edgar. *The Algerian Insurrection, 1954–1962.* London: Archon Books, 1967.

Ollivier, Marc. "L'économie algérienne vingt ans après 1966: l'indépendance nationale en question." *Annuaire de l'Afrique du Nord* 24 (1985): 417–57.

d'Orient, N., and M. Loew. *La question algérienne.* Paris: Bureau d'édition, 1936.

Ottaway, David, and Marina Ottaway. *Algeria: The Politics of a Socialist Revolution.* Berkeley and Los Angeles: University of California Press, 1970.

Palmer, Monte. *The Dilemmas of Political Development; an Introduction to the Politics of Developing Areas.* Itasca, Ill.: F. E. Peacock, 1973.

Passeron, R. *Les grandes sociétés et la colonisation en Afrique du Nord.* Algiers: 1926.

Pelissier de Reynaud, E. *Annales algériennes.* Paris: Anselin et Taultier-Laguionie, 1836–1839. 3 vols.

Perkins, Kenneth J. *Qaids, Captains, and Colons. French Military Administration in the Colonial Maghrib, 1844–1934.* New York: Africana Publishing Co., 1981.

Pervillé, Guy. "Combien de morts pendant la guerre d'Algérie?" *L'Histoire* 53 (Feb. 1983): 89–92.

———. "La commission des réformes musulmanes de 1944 et l'élaboration d'une nouvelle politique algérienne de la France." In *Les chemins de la décolonisation de l'empire français, 1936–1956,* pp. 357–65. Paris: CNRS, 1986.

———. *Les étudiants algériens de l'Université française. 1880–1962.* Paris: CNRS/CRESM, 1984.

Peyerimhof, J. de. *La colonisation officielle en Algérie de 1871 à 1895.* Tunis: Imprimerie rapide, 1928.

Pfeifer, Karen. *Agrarian Reform Under State Capitalism in Algeria.* Boulder, Colo.: Westview Press, 1985.

Pignaud, A. "Le projet Polignac." *Revue d'histoire diplomatique* (1900): 402–409.

Piquet, Victor. *Les réformes en Algérie et le statut des indigènes.* Paris: Armand, Colin, 1919.

Pouyanne, Maurice-Alexandre. *La propriété foncière en Algérie.* Paris: Edouard Duchemin, 1895.

Quandt, William B. "The Berbers in the Algerian Political Elite." In Ernest Gellner and Charles Micaud, eds., *Arabs and Berbers: From Tribe to Nation in North Africa,* pp. 285–303. Lexington, Mass.: Lexington Books, 1972.

———. *Between Ballots and Bullets: Algeria's Transition from Authoritarianism.* Washington, D.C.: Brookings Institution Press, 1998.

———. *Revolution and Political Leadership: Algeria, 1954–1968.* Cambridge, Mass.: M.I.T. Press, 1969.

Ramdane, Redjala. *L'opposition en Algérie depuis 1962.* Paris: L'Harmattan, 1988.

Richard, Charles. *Etude sur l'insurrection du Dahra (1845–1846).* Algiers: 1846.

Rinn, Louis. *Histoire de l'insurrection de 1871 en Algérie.* Algiers: Jourdan, 1891.

———. *Marabouts et Khouan. Etude sur l'Islam en Algérie, avec une carte indiquant la marche, la situation et l'importance des ordres religieux musulmans.* Algiers: Jourdan, 1884.

————. *Le Royaume d'Alger sous le dernier dey.* Algiers: Jourdan, 1900. Also available in *Revue africaine* (1897): 121–52, 331–35; (1898): 5–21, 1133–39, 289–309; (1899): 105–41, 297–320.

Robe, Eugène. *Essai sur l'histoire de la propriété en Algérie.* Bône: Imprimerie de Dagand, 1848.

Roberts, Hugh. *The Battlefield Algieria 1988–2002. Studies in a Broken Polity.* London: Verso, 2003.

————. "The Politics of Algerian Socialism." In Richard Lawless and Allan Findlay, eds., *North Africa: Contemporary Politics and Economic Development,* pp. 4–49. New York: St. Martin's Press, 1984.

————. "Towards an Understanding of the Kabyle Question in Contemporary Algeria." *The Maghrib Review* 5 (May–June 1980): 115–24.

Robin, N. *L'insurrection de la Grande Kabylie en 1871.* Paris: Lavauzelle, 1901.

Robin-Harmel, Pierre. *Le prince Jules de Polignac, ministre de Charles X (1780–1847).* Avignon: Aubanel, 1950.

Rossignol, P. *"Les partis politiques musulmans en Algérie de leur origine au 1er novembre 1954."* Unpublished law thesis, University of Paris, 1962.

Rouadjia, Ahmed. *Les frères et la mosquée. Enquête sur le mouvement islamiste en Algérie.* Paris: Karthala, 1990.

Ruedy, John. "Continuities and Discontinuities in the Algerian Confrontation with Europe." In John Ruedy, *Islamism and Secularism in North Africa.* New York: St. Martin's Press, 1994.

————. *Land Policy in Colonial Algeria: The Origins of the Rural Public Domain.* Berkeley and Los Angeles: University of California Press, 1967.

————, ed. *Islamism and Secularism in North Africa.* New York: St. Martin's Press, 1994.

Saadalla, Boulkassim. *Al haraka al wataniyya fi'l jaza'ir, 1930–1945.* Cairo: Jamiᶜat al duwwal al ᶜarabiyya; mahad al buhuth wa'l dirasat, 1975.

————. "The Rise of the Algerian Elite 1900–1914." *Journal of Modern African Studies* 1 (1967): 1–11.

Sahli, Mohamed Chérif. *Abd el-Kader, chevalier de la foi.* Algiers: En-Nahda, 1953.

————. *Décoloniser l'histoire. Introduction à l'histoire du Maghreb.* Paris: Maspéro, 1965.

St.-Germès, Joseph. *Economie algérienne.* Algiers: Maison des Livres, 1957.

Saᶜiyduni, Nasir al Din. *Dirasat wa abhath fi ta'rikh al jaza'ir. Al ahd al ᶜuthmani.* Algiers: al Mu'asasa al wataniyya li'l kitab, 1984.

————. *Al-nizam al mali al jaza'iriyya fi 'l fatra al ᶜuthmaniyya.* Algiers: 1979.

Sarrasin, Paul-Emile. *La crise algérienne.* Paris: Editions du Cerf, 1949.

Schefer, Christian. *La politique coloniale de la Monarchie de Juillet. L'Algérie et l'évolution de la colonisation française.* Paris: Champion, 1928.

Schlechta, Ottoçar de. "La prise d'Alger par un Algérien." *Journal asiatique* XI (Sept.–Oct. 1862): 319–40.

Shahin, Emad Eldin. *Political Ascent. Contemporary Islamic Movements in North Africa.* Boulder, Colo.: Westview Press, 1997.

Shaler, William. *Sketches of Algiers: Political, Historical, and Civil.* Boston: Cummings, Hilliand, and Co., 1826.

Sivan, Emmanuel. *Communisme et nationalisme en Algérie, 1920–1962.* Paris: Presses de la Fondation nationale des sciences politiques, 1976.

Smith, Tony. "The Political and Economic Ambitions of Algerian Land Reform, 1962–1974." *The Middle East Journal,* no. 3 (Summer 1975): 259–78.

Souaïda, Habib. *La sale guerre. Le témoignage d'un ancien officier des forces spéciales de l'armée algérienne.* Paris: La Découverte, 2001.

Stone, Martin. *The Agony of Algeria.* New York: Columbia University Press, 1997.

Stora, Benjamin. "Continuité et ruptures dans la direction nationalise algérienne à la veille du 1er novembre 1954." In *Les chemins de la décolonisation de l'empire français, 1936–1956,* pp. 401–14. Paris: CNRS, 1986.

————. *Messali Hadj, pionnier du nationalisme algérien (1898–1974)*. Paris: Le Sycamore, 1982.

————. *Les sources du nationalisme algérien. Parcours idéologique. Origines des acteurs*. Paris: L'Harmattan, 1989.

Sutton, Keith. "Population Resettlement—Traumatic Upheavals and the Algerian Experience." *The Journal of Modern African Studies* 15, no. 2 (June 1977): 279–300.

Taleb Ibrahimi, Khaoula. *Les algériens et leur(s) langue(s). Eléments pour une approche sociolinguistique de la société algérienne*. Algiers: El Hikma, 1997.

Talibi, Ammar. *Ibn Badis. Hayatuhu wa atharuhu*. Algiers: Dar wa maktabat al sharika al jaza'iriyya, 1968. 4 vols.

Tamimi, ʿAbd al Malik Khalaf. "Malamih al wadᶜ al iqtisadi fi al Maghrib al ᶜArabi qabla al istiᶜmar al gharbi." *Revue d'histoire maghrebine* VII (1983): 109–24.

al Tawil, Camille. *Al-haraka al-islamiyya al musalaha fi al-jaza'ir*. Beirut: Dar al-Nahar, 1998.

Temimi, Abdeljelil. *Le Beylik de Constantine et hadj Ahmed Bey (1830–1837).* Tunis: Publications de la Revue d'Histoire maghrebine, 1978.

Textes fondamentaux du Front de Libération Nationale. Algiers: Ministry of Information and Culture, 1976.

Tillion, Germaine. *Le harem et les cousins*. Paris: Editions du Seuil, 1966.

Tlemçani, Rachid. *Elections et élites en Algérie. Paroles de candidats*. Algiers: Chihab Editions, 2003.

————. *State and Revolution in Algeria*. London: Zed Press, 1986.

Tlili, Béchir. *Nationalismes, socialisme et syndicalisme dans le Maghreb des années 1919–1934*. Tunis: Publications de l'Université, 1984.

Tocqueville, Alexis de. *Oeuvres complètes*. Vol. III, *Ecrits et discours politiques*, Part I. Paris: Gallimard, 1962.

Touati, Houari. "Les corporations de métier à Alger à l'époque ottomane," Mélanges Robert Mantran. *Revue d'histoire maghrebine* VII, nos. 47–48 (Dec. 1987): 109–24.

Tricot, Bernard. *Les sentiers de la paix*. Paris: Plon, 1972.

Troussel, L. *Les impôts arabes en Algérie*. Algiers: 1922.

Turin, Yvonne. *Affrontements culturels dans l'Algérie coloniale. Ecoles, médecines, religion, 1830–1880*. Paris: Maspéro, 1971.

Valensi, Lucette. *Le Maghreb avant la prise d'Alger, 1770–1830*. Paris: Flammarion, 1969. English trans. by Kenneth Perkins, *On the Eve of Colonialism: North Africa Before the French Conquest*. New York: Africana, 1977.

————. "Le Maghreb précolonial: mode de production archaïque ou mode de production féodal?" *Pensée* 142 (1968): 57–93.

Vatin, Jean-Claude. *L'Algérie politique. Histoire et société*. Paris: Presses de la Fondation nationale des sciences politiques, 1983.

————. "Revival in the Maghreb: Islam as an Alternative Political Language." In Ali E. Hillal Dessouki, ed., *Islamic Resurgence in the Arab World*, pp. 221–50. New York: Praeger, 1982.

Viansson-Ponté. *Histoire de la République gaulienne*. Vol. I, 1958–1962. *La fin d'une époque*. Paris: Fayard, 1970.

Viard, P.-E. *Les droits politiques des indigènes en Algérie*. Paris: Librairie du Recueil Sirey, 1937.

Vitatelle, Gérard. *L'Algérie algérienne*. Paris: Editions economie et humanisme, 1973.

Von Sivers, Peter. "Arms and Alms: The Combative Saintliness of the Awlad Sidi Shaykh in the Algerian Sahara, 16th to 19th Centuries." *The Maghreb Review* VIII, no. 4 (1983): 113–23.

————. "Realm of Justice: Apocalyptic Revolts in Algeria (1849–1879)." *Humaniora Islamica* I (1973).

Warmington, Brian Herbert. *Carthage*. London: Hale, 1960.

Yacono, Xavier. "L'Algérie depuis 1830." *Revue africaine*, 1956. Special number.

————. *Les bureaux arabes et l'évolution des genres de vie dans l'ouest du Tell algérois (Dahra, Chélif, Ouarsensis, Sersou)*. Paris: Larose, 1953.

————. *La colonisation des plaines du Chélif.* Algiers: Imprimerie Imbert, 1955–1956. 2 vols.

————. "Les pertes algériennes de 1954 à 1962." *Revue de l'occident musulman et de la Méditer-ranée* 34, no. 2 (1982): 119–34.

————. "Peut-on évaluer la population de l'Algérie vers 1830?" *Revue africaine* XCVIII, nos. 3–4 (1954): 227–307.

Zabiri, Muhammad al ʿArabi. *Al kifah al mussalah fi ahd al amir ʿAbd al Qadir.* Algiers: Société nationale d'édition, 1982.

Zartman, I. William. "Algeria: A Post-Revolutionary Elite." In Frank Tachau, ed., *Political Elites and Political Development in the Middle East,* pp. 255–92. New York: Schenkman Publishing Co., 1975.

————. "The Algerian Army in Politics." In Zartman, ed., *Man, State, and Society in the Contemporary Maghrib,* pp. 211–27. New York: Praeger, 1973.

Zerkine, Habiba. "The Federation of Elected Muslims of the Department of Constantine." Unpublished Ph.D. dissertation, Georgetown University, Washington, D.C., 1983.

INDEX

JOHN RUEDY is Emeritus Professor of History at Georgetown University. He is author of *Land Policy in Colonial Algeria* and *Islamism and Secularism in North Africa* and has served most recently as the North Africa editor for the *Encyclopedia of the Modern Middle East and North Africa*.